MASTERING GAMMA KNIFE RADIOSURGERY

INSIGHTS FROM CASE-BASED LEARNINGS

Dr SS Kale

Dr Deepak Agrawal

BookLeaf Publishing

www.bookleafpub.com

Presentation by *BookLeaf Publishing*

Web: www.bookleafpub.com
E-mail: info@bookleafpub.com

ISBN: 9789369542796

First edition 2025

DEDICATION

To our parents, whose guidance and support have been the foundation of our academic pursuits.

To our patients, whose experiences continue to inspire our commitment to research and discovery.

Contents

Contributors | xi

Preface | xiii

Foreword | xv

Acknowledgments | xvii

Abbreviation List | xix

SECTION 1 — BASICS OF GAMMA KNIFE RADIOSURGERY

1 Evolution of Gamma Knife Radiosurgery at AIIMS Delhi | 3
Deepak Agrawal | SS Kale | Chirag Bansal

2 Physics of Gamma Knife | 13
Gopishankar Natanasabapathi

3 Frameless Gamma Knife Radiosurgery | 20
R Shiva Krishna | Deepak Agrawal

SECTION 2 — TUMOURS

4 Gamma Knife Radiosurgery in Koos Grade 2 Vestibular Schwannoma | 27
Ashwin Bharadwaj R | Shweta Kedia

5 Pseudoprogression in Vestibular Schwannoma Following Gamma-Knife Radiosurgery | 34
Kanwaljeet Garg | Abhilash Reddy | Deepak Agrawal

6 Repeat Gamma Knife Radiosurgery for Progressive Vestibular Schwannoma | 41
Kanwaljeet Garg | Sandeep Mishra

7 Gamma Knife Radiosurgery for Vestibular Schwannomas in NF2 | 48
Dattaraj Parmanand Sawarkar | Abhishek Kumar

8 Gamma-Knife Stereotactic Radiosurgery for Large Vestibular Schwannoma | 52
Satish Verma | Deepak Agrawal

9 Role of Gamma-Knife in Treating Multiple Meningiomas in NF2 Patients | 59
Kushagra Pandey | Shweta Kedia

vi CONTENTS

10 Gamma Knife Radiosurgery for Parasagittal/Parafalcine Meningiomas 66
Sandeep Mishra | Kanwaljeet Garg

11 Gamma Knife Radiosurgery for Atypical Meningioma 72
Sarvesh Goyal | Manoj Phalak

12 Gamma Knife Radiosurgery for Non-Functioning Pituitary Tumours 77
Dattaraj Parmanand Sawarkar | Abhishek Kumar

13 Gamma Knife Radiosurgery in Functional Pituitary Tumours 81
Hanoksrithej Rayappa | Shweta Kedia

14 Primary Gamma Knife Radiosurgery in Pituitary Adenomas 87
Chandra Kiran A | Deepak Agarwal

15 Gamma Knife Radiosurgery In Low-Grade Gliomas 94
Deepak Agrawal | Chirag Bansal

16 Gamma Knife Radiosurgery in High-Grade Gliomas 99
Deepak Agrawal | Chirag Bansal

17 Role of Gamma Knife in Glioblastoma 103
Deepak Agrawal | Rakshay Kaul

18 Gamma Knife in Multiple Metastasis 110
Rakshay Kaul | Deepak Agrawal

19 Gamma Knife High Cervical Lesions 116
Deepak Agrawal | Chirag Bansal | Kushagra Pandey

20 Gamma Knife in Craniopharyngiomas: Current Gold Standard? 121
Prachi Singh | Deepak Agrawal

21 Primary Gamma Knife Radiosurgery for Craniopharyngioma 127
Satish Verma | Deepak Agrawal

22 Gamma Knife Radiosurgery in Hypothalamic Hamartomas 134
Deepak Agrawal | Chirag Bansal

23 Gamma Knife in Cavernous Hemangioma 140
Sarvesh Goyal | Manoj Phalak

24 Gamma Knife for Uveal Melanoma 144
Abhishek Kumar | Manoj Phalak | Neiwete Lomi

25 Stitchless Eye Fixation for Gamma Knife in Uveal Melanoma 151
Deepak Agrawal | Aruja Gangwani | Bhavna Chawla

26 Gamma Knife Radiosurgery In Juvenile Nasopharyngeal Angiofibroma 155
R Siva Krishna | Deepak Agrawal

27 Gamma Knife Radiosurgery for Glomus Jugular 161
Dattaraj P Sawarkar | Abhishek Kumar

28 Gamma Knife in Pineal Region Tumors 167
Prachi Singh | Deepak Agrawal

29 Gamma Knife Radiosurgery in Intracranial Angiosarcoma   172
Mahnaaz Sultana Azeem | Deepak Agrawal | Sarvesh Goyal

SECTION 3 VASCULAR

30 Gamma Knife Radiosurgery for Spetzler-Martin Grade III Cerebral Arterio-Venous Malformations   179
Satish Verma | Deepak Agrawal

31 Gamma Knife Radiosurgery for Basal Ganglia & Thalamic Arteriovenous Malformations   187
Abhishek Kumar | Manoj Phalak

32 Draining Vein Shielding During Gamma Knife Radiosurgery in Intracranial Arteriovenous Malformations   195
Deepak Agrawal | Mahnaaz Sultana Azeem

33 Fractionated Gamma Knife Radiosurgery for Large Arteriovenous Malformations   200
Kanwaljeet Garg | Sandeep Mishra | Manmohan Singh

34 Adverse Radiation Effects of Gamma Knife Radiosurgery   209
Sarvesh Goyal | Shweta Kedia | Mahnaaz Sultana Azeem

35 Gamma Knife Radiosurgery for Intracranial Cavernomas   216
Dattaraj Parmanand Sawarkar | Abhishek Kumar

36 Gamma Knife Surgery in Intracranial Dural Arteriovenous Fistulas 221
Prachi Singh | Deepak Agrawal

SECTION 4 FUNCTIONAL

37 Gamma Knife Radiosurgery for Trigeminal Neuralgia   229
Sarvesh Goyal | Manoj Phalak

38 Management of Intractable Cancer Pain Using Gamma Knife Radiosurgery   233
Deepak Agrawal | R Shiva Krishna

39 Gamma Knife Radiosurgery in Obsessive-Compulsive Disorder (OCD)   237
Deepak Agrawal | Mahnaaz Sultana Azeem

Publications From Gamma Knife Centre, AIIMS Delhi   242

Gamma Knife Legacy   245

Gamma Knife Image Collage   246

Faculty
Gamma Knife Radiosurgery,
AIIMS, New Delhi

SS Kale
Professor and Head

Dr. Rajinder Kumar
Professor

Dr. Deepak Agrawal,
Professor

Dr. Shweta Kedia,
Additional Professor

Dr Dattaraj Sawarkar,
Additional Professor

Dr. Kanwaljeet Garg,
Associate Professor

Dr. Manoj Phalak,
Associate Professor

Dr Satish Kumar Verma,
Associate Professor

Contributors

Dr. Deepak Agrawal, MBBS, MS, MCh
Professor,
Department of Neurosurgery & Gamma Knife, AIIMS, New Delhi

Dr. Mahnaaz Sultana Azeem, MBBS, MS
Senior Resident,
Department of Neurosurgery & Gamma Knife, AIIMS, New Delhi

Dr. Chirag Bansal, MBBS
Junior Resident,
Department of Neurosurgery & Gamma Knife, AIIMS,
New Delhi

Dr. Ashwin Bharadwaj R, MBBS
Junior Resident,
Department of Neurosurgery & Gamma Knife, AIIMS, New Delhi

Dr. Bhavna Chawla, MBBS, MS
Professor,
Department of Ophthalmology, AIIMS, New Delhi

Dr. Aruja Gangwani, MBBS, MS
Junior Resident,
Department of Ophthalmology,
AIIMS, New Delhi

Dr. Kanwaljeet Garg, MBBS, MCh
Associate Professor,
Department of Neurosurgery & Gamma Knife, AIIMS, New Delhi

Dr. Sarvesh Goyal, MBBS, MS
Senior Resident,
Department of Neurosurgery & Gamma Knife, AIIMS, New Delhi

Dr. SS Kale, MBBS, MS, MCh
Professor & Head,
Department of Neurosurgery & Gamma Knife, AIIMS, New Delhi

Dr. Rakshay Kaul, MBBS, MS
Senior Resident,
Department of Neurosurgery & Gamma Knife, AIIMS, New Delhi

Dr. Shweta Kedia, MBBS, MS, MCh
Additional Professor,
Department of Neurosurgery & Gamma Knife, AIIMS, New Delhi

Dr. Chandra Kiran, MBBS
Junior Resident,
Department of Neurosurgery & Gamma Knife, AIIMS, New Delhi

Dr. R Siva Krishna, MBBS
Junior Resident,
Department of Neurosurgery & Gamma Knife, AIIMS, New Delhi

Dr. Abhishek Kumar, MBBS, MS
Senior Resident,
Department of Neurosurgery & Gamma Knife, AIIMS, New Delhi

Dr. Sandeep Mishra, MBBS, MS
Senior Resident,
Department of Neurosurgery & Gamma
Knife, AIIMS, New Delhi

Dr. Gopishankar Natanasabapathi, PhD
Associate Professor,
Department of Radiation Oncology
(Medical Physics), IRCH, AIIMS,
New Delhi

Dr. Neiwete Lomi, MBBS, MS
Associate Professor,
Department of Ophthalmology,
AIIMS, New Delhi

Dr. Kushagra Pandey, MBBS
Junior Resident,
Department of Neurosurgery &
Gamma Knife, AIIMS, New Delhi

Dr. Manoj Phalak, MBBS, MCh
Associate Professor,
Department of Neurosurgery & Gamma
Knife, AIIMS, New Delhi

Dr. Hanoksrithej Rayappa, MBBS
Junior Resident,
Department of Neurosurgery &
Gamma Knife, AIIMS, New Delhi

Dr. Abhilash Reddy, MBBS, MS, MCh
Senior Resident,
Department of Neurosurgery &
Gamma Knife, AIIMS, New Delhi

Dr. Dattaraj Sawarkar, MBBS, MS, MCh
Associate Professor,
Department of Neurosurgery & Gamma
Knife, AIIMS, New Delhi

Dr. Manmohan Singh, MBBS, MS, MCh
Professor,
Department of Neurosurgery & Gamma
Knife, AIIMS, New Delhi

Dr. Prachi Singh, MBBS
Junior Resident,
Department of Neurosurgery & Gamma
Knife, AIIMS, New Delhi

Dr. Satish Verma, MBBS, MCh
Associate Professor,
Department of Neurosurgery & Gamma
Knife, AIIMS, New Delhi

Preface

Gamma Knife radiosurgery has revolutionised the field of neurosurgery, offering a groundbreaking approach to treating a wide array of neurosurgical conditions. This advanced technology is now used in nearly 50% of all neurosurgical cases, its adoption continues to grow with advances, in a proportion that continues to rise annually with the advent of more accurate diagnostic techniques. Known for its safety, precision, and durability, Gamma Knife is among the few radiotherapy delivery systems specifically designed and operated by neurosurgeons. Given its immense potential, every neurosurgeon must understand its utility and incorporate it into their clinical workflows.

This book has been meticulously crafted to serve as an indispensable guide for both novice and experienced practitioners of Gamma Knife radiosurgery, as well as those who may not practice it directly. It provides comprehensive insights into the use of this technology, empowering readers with the knowledge required to better manage their patients, make well-informed decisions, and achieve. By understanding its capabilities and applications, neurosurgeons can enhance the care they provide to their patients, ensuring that the best possible outcomes are achieved.

Foreword

Gamma Knife Radiosurgery has transformed the landscape of neurosurgery and radiation oncology, offering a precise, minimally invasive approach to treating a variety of intracranial disorders. Over the past few decades, this revolutionary technique has not only evolved in its technological sophistication but has also expanded its indications, providing hope and healing to patients worldwide.

The Department of Neurosurgery at All India Institute of Medical Sciences, New Delhi has a long history of collaborating with Scandinavian neurosurgeons. Professor PN Tandon and Professor Ravi Bhatia were trained in Norway and Sweden and brought to AIIMS, stereotactic neurosurgery, functional neurosurgery and the use of A mode ultrasound in head trauma. The arrival of the Gamma Knife completed that cycle of its inventor Professor Lars Leksell's influence on the department and was a game changer for the development of radiosurgery in India.

This book serves as a comprehensive resource, bringing together the collective expertise of distinguished AIIMS specialists in the field. The Gamma Knife Unit at AIIMS has the largest experience in India and the greatest variety of pathology treated in Asia. The uniquely Indian context will enrich the literature in this field and provide a reference to others practicing in India and Asia and contrasting data to experts in other parts of the world.

With contributions from senior neurosurgeons, radiation oncologists, and medical physicists, it offers an in-depth exploration of the principles, applications, and advancements of Gamma Knife technology. From its historical evolution at AIIMS Delhi to the latest developments in frameless radiosurgery, tumor management, vascular malformations, and functional disorders, this work stands as a testament to the remarkable progress made in this domain.

Each chapter provides evidence-based insights, practical clinical experience, and discussions on challenging cases, ensuring that readers—whether experienced practitioners or those new to the field—gain a deeper understanding of Gamma Knife Radiosurgery's potential. The inclusion of cutting-edge topics, such as fractionated radiosurgery, repeat treatments, and novel fixation techniques, underscores the dynamic and evolving nature of this discipline.

As Gamma Knife technology continues to push the boundaries of precision medicine, this book will undoubtedly serve as an invaluable guide for clinicians, researchers, and students seeking to refine their knowledge and enhance patient outcomes. I commend Professor Kale and Professor Deepak Agrawal and all authors for their dedication in compiling this authoritative volume and for their unwavering commitment to advancing the science and practice of stereotactic radiosurgery.

Dheerendra Prasad MD, MCh (Neurosurgery), FASTRO
Chief, Gamma Knife Radiosurgery
Medical Director, Department of Radiation Medicine,
Professor of Neurosurgery, Radiation Medicine and Oncology
Director, CNS and Pediatric Radiation Medicine
Past Chairman Leksell Gamma Knife Society
Roswell Park Comprehensive Cancer Center
Elm and Carlton Streets, Buffalo, NY USA

February 9, 2025

Acknowledgments

We extend our deepest gratitude to everyone who contributed to the development of this book.

A special thanks to **Dr. Venencia Albert** for her invaluable support in editorial refinement, content structuring, and overall project management. Her meticulous attention to detail, coordination, and commitment to excellence have shaped this work.

We are also immensely grateful to the **AIIMS, New Delhi Gamma Knife team**, whose expertise, dedication, and clinical excellence have continuously advanced radiosurgery. Their contributions have enriched this book with real-world insights and evidence-based knowledge.

We would like to acknowledge the leadership and guidance of the previous Heads of the Department of Neurosurgery at AIIMS, whose vision and commitment have laid the foundation for the continued success of Gamma Knife Radiosurgery at AIIMS, New Delhi. Their pioneering efforts in neurosurgery and Gamma Knife treatment have significantly contributed to advancements in the field.

Lastly, we sincerely appreciate all the patients whose experiences and trust in Gamma Knife radiosurgery have provided invaluable learning opportunities. Their journeys inspire continuous research, innovation, and improvement in patient care.

SS Kale
Deepak Agrawal

AAPM	American Association of Physicists in Medicine
AIIMS	All India Institute of Medical Sciences
AREs	Adverse Radiation Effects
AVMs	Arterio-Venous Malformations
CECT	Contrast-Enhanced CT
CEH	Chronic Encapsulated Hematoma
CEMR	Contrast-Enhanced MRI
CF	Cyst Formation
CH	Cavernous Hemangiomas
CNS	Congress of Neurosurgeons
CPA	Cerebellopontine Angle
CPS	Complex Partial Seizures
CSF	Cerebrospinal Fluid
CSHs	Cavernous Sinus Hemangiomas
CSOM	Chronic Suppurative Otitis Media
CV	Craniovertebral
CVD	Cortical Venous Drainage
dAVFs	dural Arteriovenous Fistulas
DF-SRS	Dose-Fractionated Stereotactic Radiosurgery
DSA	Digital Subtraction Angiography
DWI	Diffusion-Weighted Imaging
EBRT	External Beam Radiation Therapy
FRT	Fractionated Radiotherapy
GBM	Glioblastoma Multiforme
GKRS	Gamma Knife Radiosurgery
GKT	Gamma Knife Treatment
GSR	Gamma Stereotactic Radiosurgery
GTCS	Generalized Tonic-Clonic Seizures
GTR	Gross Total Resection
HGGs	High-Grade Gliomas
HH	Hypothalamic Hamartomas
IAEA	International Atomic Energy Agency
ICP	Increased Intracranial Pressure
ICH	Intracranial Haemorrhage
IGF	Insulin-Like Growth Factor
IOF	Inferior Orbital Fissure
ITF	Infratemporal Fossa

JNA	Juvenile Nasopharyngeal Angiofibroma
LC	Local Control
LCPE	Lateral Charged Particle Equilibrium
LMOS	Last Man Out Switch
LGGs	Low-Grade Gliomas
LGP	Low-Grade Gliomas
MPRAGE	Magnetization-Prepared 180 Degrees Radio-Frequency Pulses and Rapid-Gradient-Echo
MRI	Magnetic Resonance Imaging
MRV	Magnetic Resonance Venography
NF	Neurofibromatosis
OA	Orbital Apex
OARs	Organ at Risk
PFS	Progression-Free Survival
PPF	Pterygopalatine Fossa
PTA	Pure Tone Average
QA	Quality Assurance
RCT	Randomized Controlled Trial
RFP	Radiation Focal Point
RICs	Radiation-Induced Changes
RO	Radiation Oncologists
RTOG	Radiation Therapy Oncology Group
RTT	Radiotherapy Technologists
SFD	Small Field Dosimetry
SM	Spetzler-Martin
SSA	Somatostatin Analog
SRS	Stereotactic Radiosurgery
SRT	Stereotactic Radiotherapy
TG	Task Group
TMR	Tissue-Maximum-Ratio
TPS	Treatment Planning System
TRS	Technical Report Series
UCP	Unit Centre Point
VEGF	Vascular Endothelial Growth Factor
VF-SRS	Volume-Fractionated Stereotactic Radiosurgery
VS	Vestibular Schwannomas
WBRT	Whole Brain Radiotherapy

SECTION 1

BASICS OF GAMMA KNIFE RADIOSURGERY

Evolution of Gamma Knife Radiosurgery at AIIMS Delhi

1

Deepak Agrawal | SS Kale | Chirag Bansal

KEY LEARNING POINTS

1. The use of Gamma knife radiosurgery has increased dramatically over the years at AIIMS, Delhi
2. This increase is disproportionate to the increase in patient load and is multifactorial in nature.
3. Although Vestibular schwanomas, Meningiomas and Arteriovenous Malformations constitute the bulk of the cases, there have been significant changes in the types of lesions treated over the years.
4. Gamma knife has the potential to treat upto 50% of all Neurosurgical lesions and we are currently utilising a fraction of this potential.

HISTORY

AIIMS, New Delhi is the biggest institute in India providing Gamma Knife radio-therapy to patients for many years. The first Gamma-knife machine (Model B) was installed in 1997 and later upgraded to the 4C model. In 2011, AIIMS installed Perfexion and upgraded to frameless stereotaxy with Icon in 2022. The Gamma Knife Center also has an in-house 1.5-T wide-bore magnetic resonance imaging (MRI) for imaging and follow-up of Gamma-knife patients.

GKRS PROCEDURE PRICE

The price for undergoing a Gamma Knife procedure at AIIMS was fixed at Rs 75,000 and has remained the same since 1997. If one were to account for inflation, the actual price would have been Rs 4 lakhs today. However, by keeping the price constant, we believe that we have been able to serve a larger proportion of patients in India.

INITIATIVES

One of the major concerns was the lack of follow-up for patients undergoing GKRS. Upon investigation, it was found that the primary reason was the high cost of contrast MRI brain scans which required follow-up at least every 2 years for life. A proposal was floated, and in 2016, it was decided that all follow-up MRIs would be free for GKRS patients for life. This initiative revolutionised follow-up care, now available to more than 90% of patients.

Also, patients who needed repeat GKRS had to pay again for the procedure, which was a significant limitation as most patients came from poor socio-economic backgrounds. In 2017, administrative approval was obtained to provide repeat GKRS free of cost to all patients. This initiative unlocked the full potential of GKRS and benefited hundreds of patients since coming into force.

These two initiatives, collectively called '**Gamma-knife for Life,**' show the holistic view the department has taken to improve access and follow-up to GKRS at AIIMS, Delhi. They also set the stage for other publicly funded institutes to emulate them.

ROLE OF GKRS TO IMPROVE NEUROSURGICAL ACCESS IN OUR COUNTRY

Due to the heterogeneous quality of Neurosurgical training across different hospitals, there is a lack of surgical consistency and patient outcomes across centres. Follow-up is also lacking due to poor socio-economic status of most of the treated population. Additionally, as only a few centres handle complex Neurosurgical cases, the waiting period for surgery can be extremely long. Most tumours and vascular pathologies, however, are amenable to radiosurgery, and preferentially providing GK to these patients significantly decreases the surgical load on the Neurosurgeons. Importantly, as both GK and surgery are performed by Neurosurgeons, treatment decisions tend to be more balanced and 'patient-centric,' potentially resulting in better outcomes. Prior to this program, patients who could not afford GK were put on the waiting list for surgery, which already exceeds 2 years at our institute!

The current paucity of personnel and infrastructure to build and operate GK centres calls for new policies that could help deliver GK neurosurgical care in LMICs with limited resources. A paradigm policy shift with an increase in Gamma-knife installations, along with telemedicine, remote planning, and treatment delivery may transform Neurosurgical healthcare delivery for India's 1.4 billion population. We have previously shown that GKRS may help bridge the gap between demand and availability of Neurosurgical care in our institute, even during the pandemic.[1]

FIGURE 1.1 Trends in the number of total Neurosurgical procedures and Gamma knife procedures carried out at AIIMS, Delhi in the last decade.

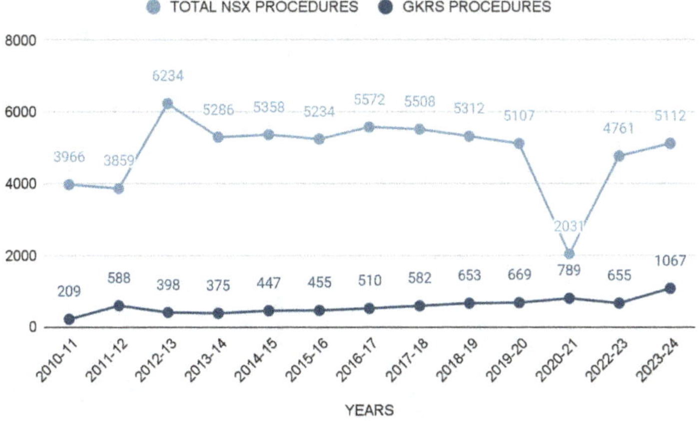

LIFE CYCLE COSTING OF SETTING UP A GAMMA-KNIFE CENTRE IN INDIA

A Gamma knife ICON® machine costs around 3 million USD in India (including a 10-year maintenance contract). Source reloading costs another million USD and is normally done every 5 years. Despite these costs, we have shown that if more than 1000 cases are performed per year, setting up a Gamma Knife unit is viable, even with a charge of Rs 75,000/ procedure![1]

AIIMS DELHI DATA

The evolution of Gamma Knife radiosurgery at AIIMS, New Delhi is represented via the following figures.

FIGURE 1.2 Chart representing various Neurosurgical disease cases treated by Gamma Knife Radiosurgery, AIIMS, New Delhi, from 1997 till 2024.

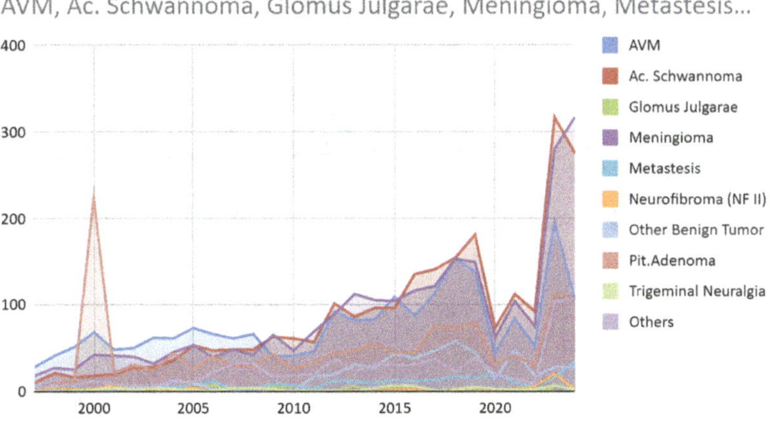

Following charts represent the evolution of Individual Neurosurgical disorder cases being treated by GKRS at AIIMS, New Delhi over the years:

AVM vs. YEAR

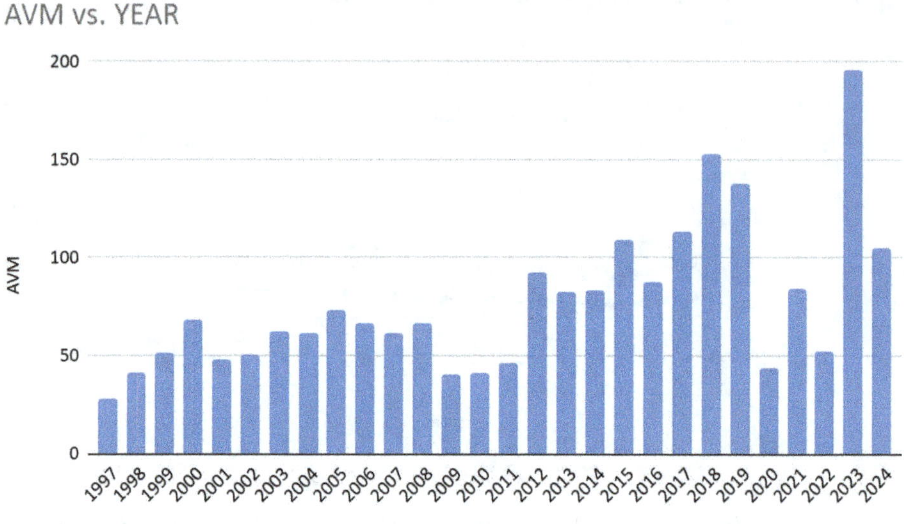

Ac. Schwannoma vs. YEAR

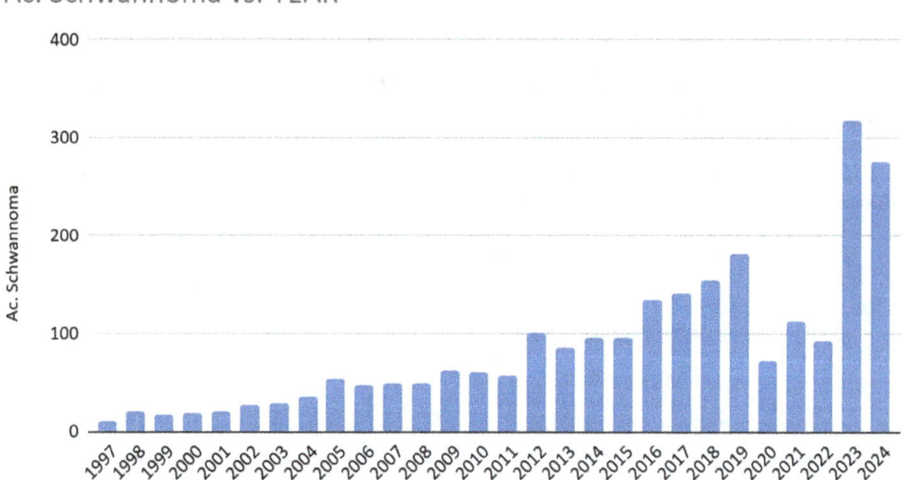

Glomus Julgarae vs. YEAR

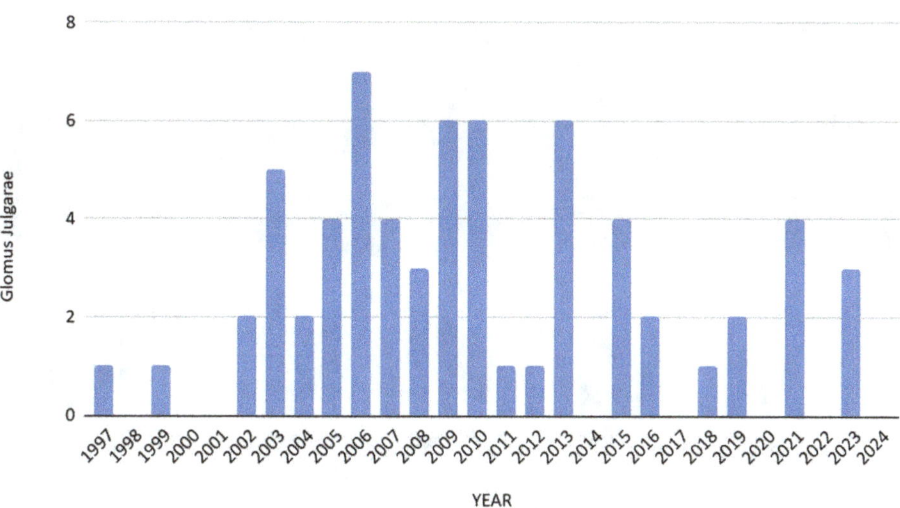

Meningioma vs. YEAR

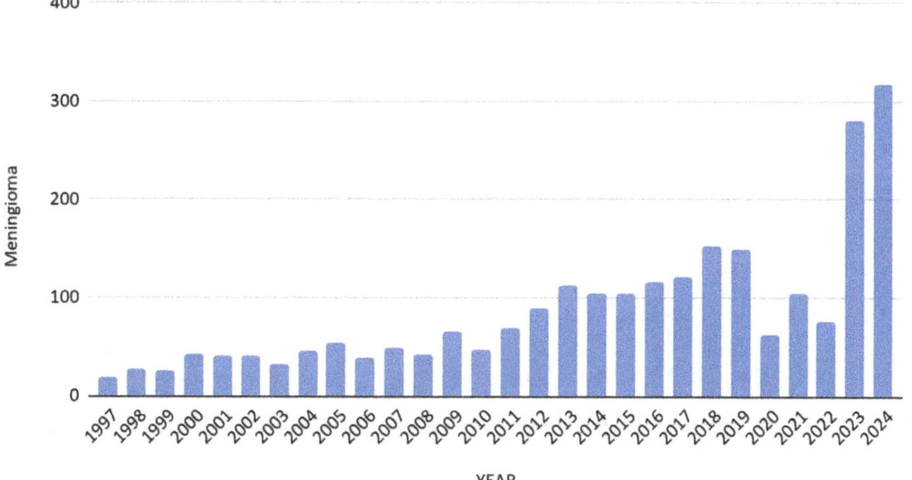

Metastesis vs. YEAR

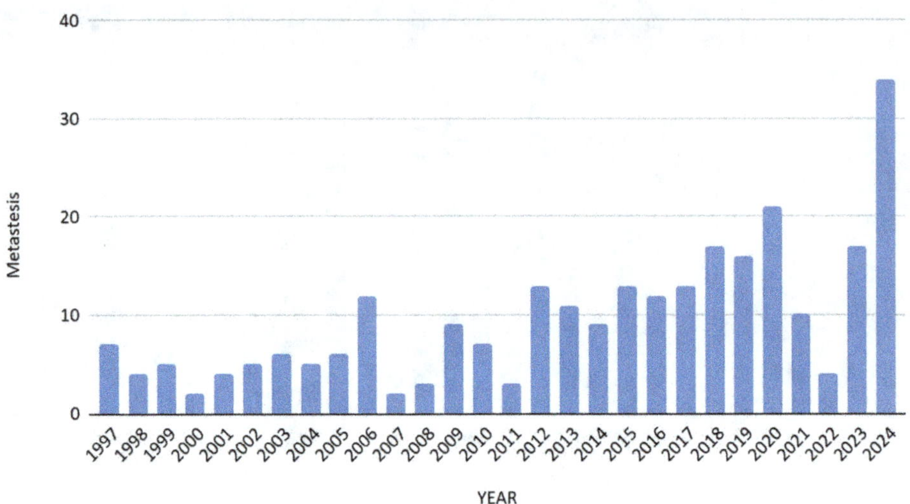

Neurofibroma (NF II) vs. YEAR

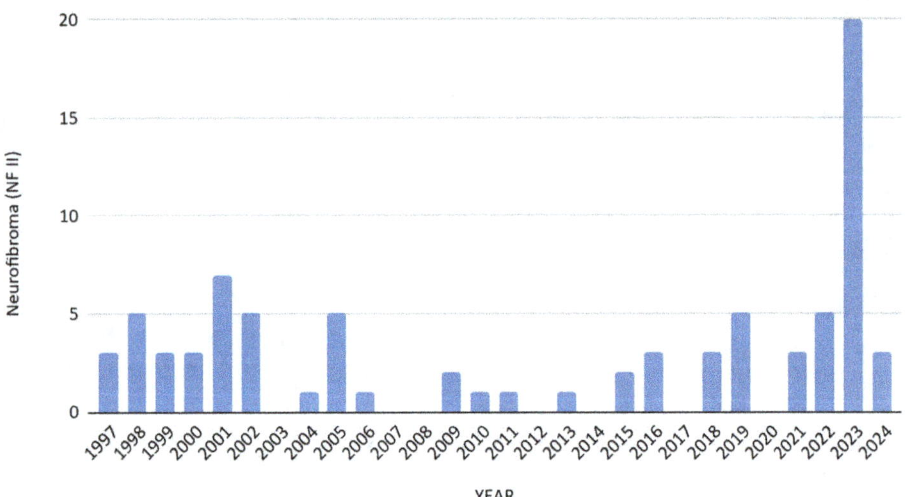

Other Benign Tumor vs. YEAR

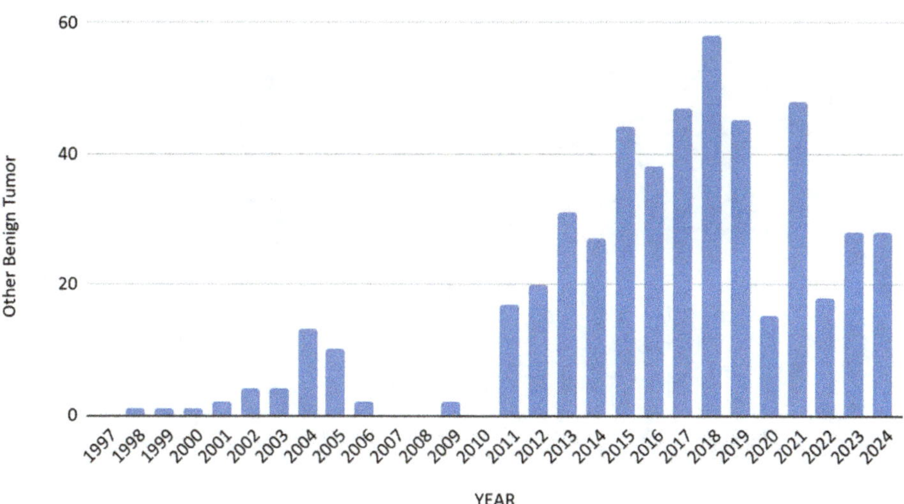

Pit.Adenoma vs. YEAR

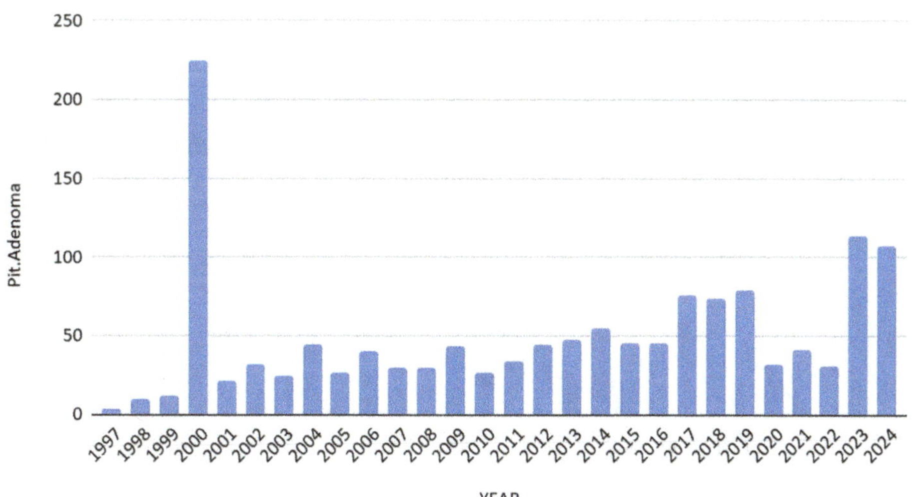

Trigeminal Neuralgia vs. YEAR

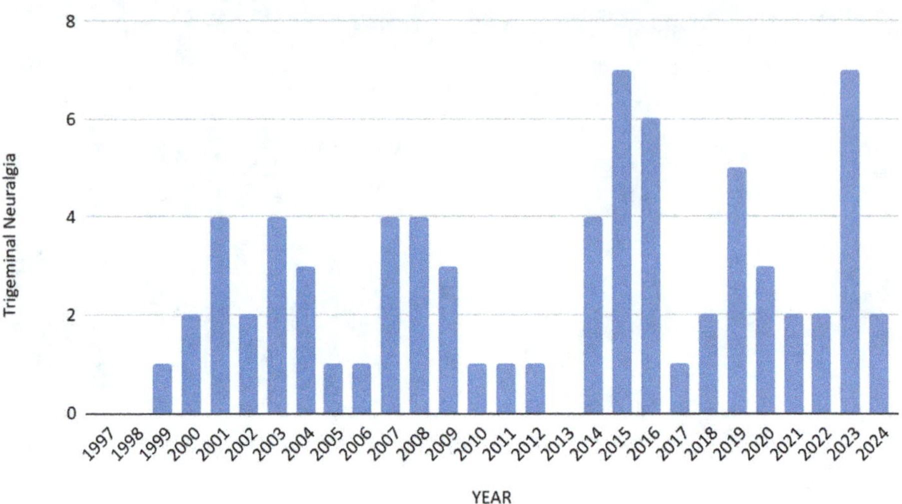

Other Diseases vs. YEAR

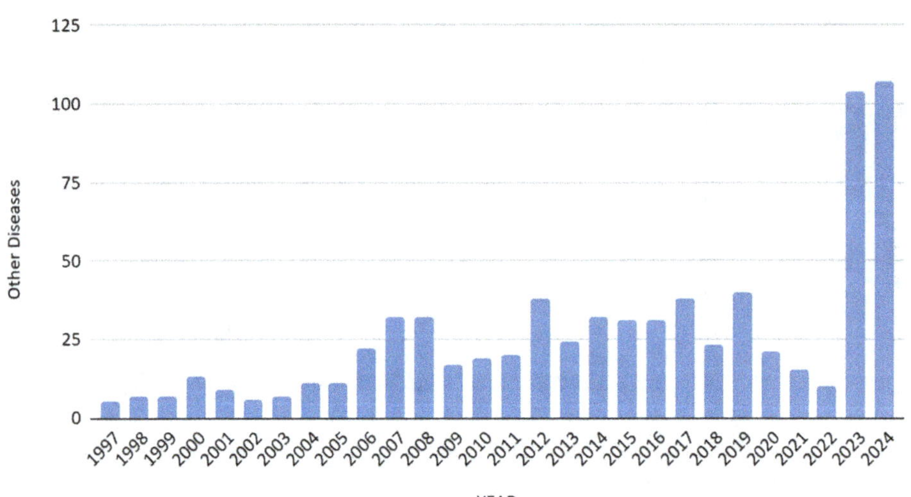

Total GKRS done per year vs. YEAR

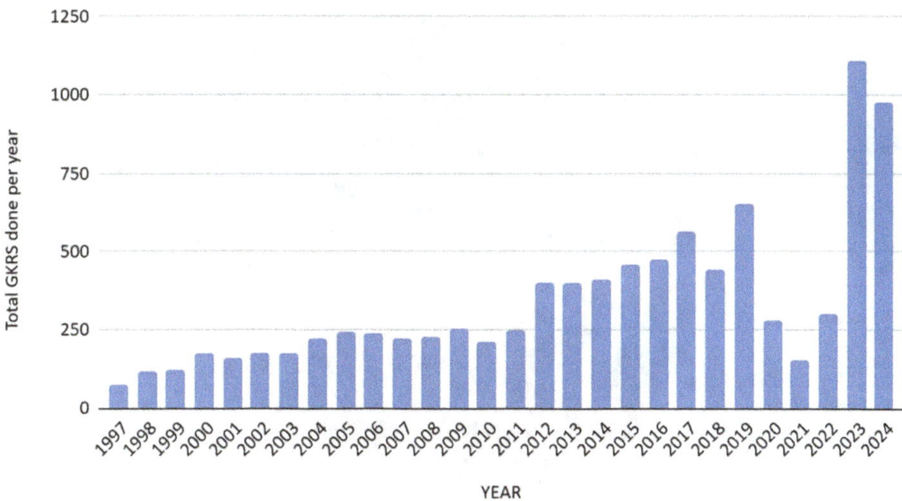

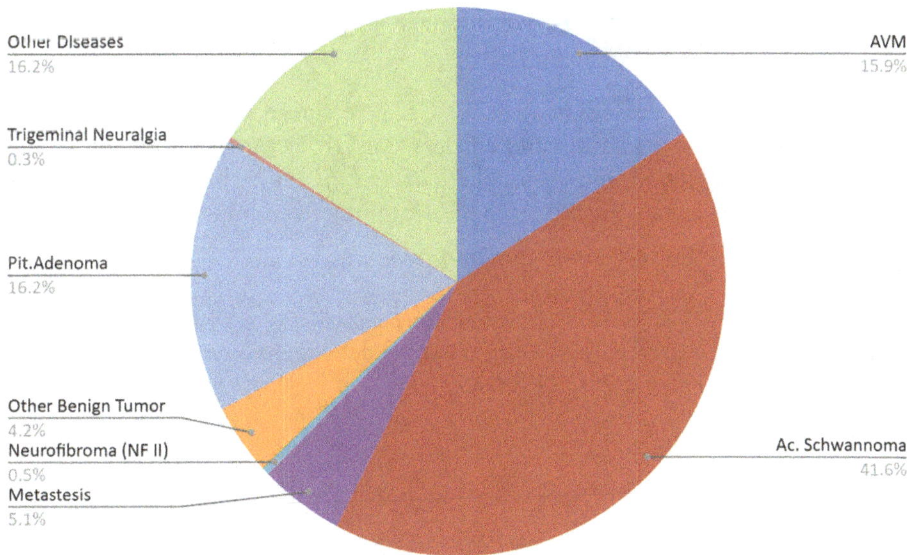

PIE CHART representing Various neurosurgical diseases treated by GKRS in year 2024

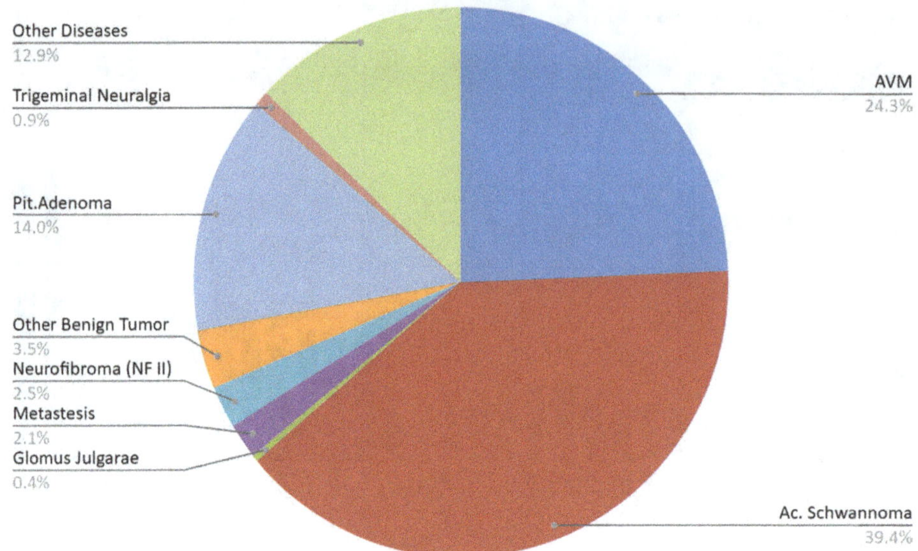

PIE CHART representing Various neurosurgical diseases treated by GKRS in year 2023

TAKE HOME MESSAGE

Foremost measure in expanding access of GK is to spread awareness amongst the masses regarding the utilisation and efficiency of GK in the management of neurosurgical pathologies. More policies like *"GK for Life"* can be implemented around the globe, thereby enhancing the reach of GK to otherwise impossible areas.

REFERENCES

1. Pahwa B, Agrawal D. Role of novel policy implementation for Gamma Knife (GK) procedures in improving access to neurosurgical care in lower middle income countries (LMICs) GK in LMICs. *World Neurosurg X.* 2023;18:100166.

Physics of Gamma Knife

Gopishankar Natanasabapathi

KEY LEARNING POINTS

1. Principles of Stereotactic Radiosurgery
2. Radiation interactions
3. Co-60 source
4. Treatment planning algorithm(s)
5. Quality Assurance

INTRODUCTION

The Gamma Knife (GK) has been the gold standard among all the stereotactic radiosurgery (SRS) tools existing to date. The concept of targeting a brain tumour from multiple angles using multiple Co-60 sources was an innovative idea developed by Prof. Lars Leksell and his colleague Prof. Bjore Larsson in the 1950s. The Co-60 source emits gamma rays, an electromagnetic radiation that undergoes various radiation interactions along its beam path. In the latest GK Esprit model there are 192 Co-60 sources. All Co-60 source beams converge at a unit centre point (UCP). This chapter discusses the intricacies of physics principles that underpin GK SRS.

HISTORY

Over the years, there has been significant improvisation in Gamma Knife technology. The advancement in GK has undergone a paradigm shift, yet the basic cross-section, internal design and physics principle of the GK unit have been maintained the same. During the installation and commissioning of a new GK unit for clinical use, various acceptance tests are performed by the physics team in coordination with vendors to meet the basic clinical requirements. The most important radiation measurement procedure during GK commissioning is the quantification of the dose rate at the UCP. The dose rate value is fed into the physics data of the treatment planning system (TPS) and the related radiation source decay correction factor is applied in the TPS automatically on a daily basis.[1] The gamma rays emitted by Co-60 sources undergo exponential decay as time progresses.

GAMMA KNIFE SOURCE

The number of Co60 sources varies from 179 to 201 in various GK models till date. The present GK models "ICON" and "Esprit" consist of 192 Co60 sources. Each of the sources contains 12 to 20 cylindrical pellets of Co60 with a pellet measuring 1 mm in length with a diameter of 1 mm. The pellets are axially stacked in a cylindrical source capsule made of stainless steel. The loaded capsule is hermetically closed by welding it. This source capsule is then enclosed in a second stainless steel capsule and finally placed in a small aluminum container. This whole assembly is called the 'source'. The number of Co60 pellets used in each source depends on the specific activity of the Co60 when it is delivered. The total activity of the GK is specified to be 6000 Ci $\pm$ 10 % (2.22×10^{14} Bq). The radiation beam goes through various collimator arrangements before hitting the target at UCP (Fig. 2.1).

RADIATION PHYSICS APPLICATION IN TREATMENT PLANNING

In the current GK technology, the role of the Treatment Planning System (TPS) is indispensable for executing radiosurgical procedures. The TPS is built with a computer algorithm that generates a radiation pattern on the patient's skull based on the various radiation interactions that occur when Gamma ray photons enter the skull surface. The TPS in GK, offers the user two dose calculation algorithms: a tissue-maximum-ratio-based algorithm, TMR10, and convolution. TMR10 models the head entirely as water, whereas convolution uses electron density values derived from CT data to account for heterogeneities, most significantly bone and air.[2] Fig. 2.2 shows the TMR10 algorithm with various physical factors that quantify the radiation dose given to the tumour region in the skull.

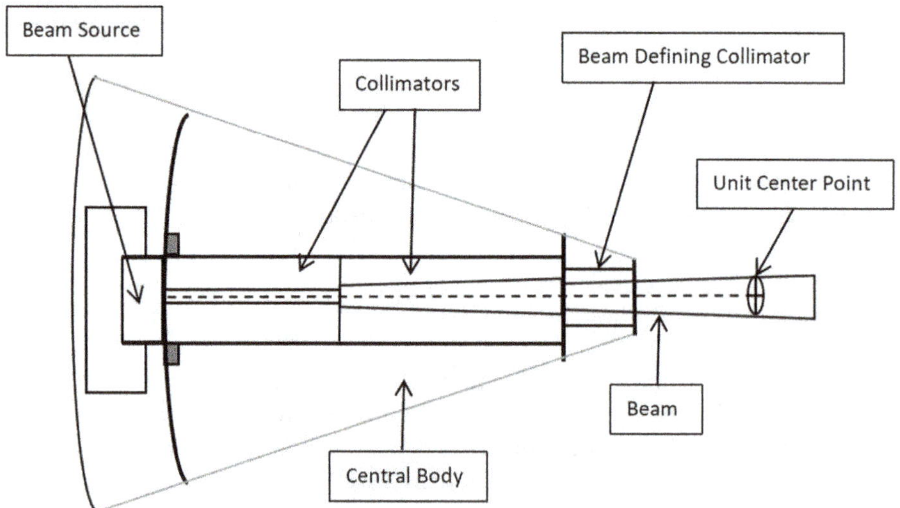

FIGURE 2.1   Cross section of a single source beam channel.

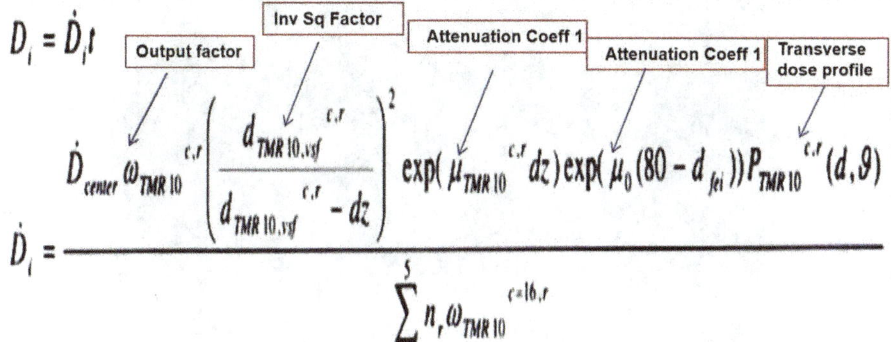

FIGURE 2.2   The physical parameters TMR10 algorithm are used for determining the dose at a point.

The Gamma Knife delivers a high radiation dose to the target volume through 192 Cobalt-60 sources positioned and collimated so that the beams from these sources intersect at the isocenter. The resulting volume of high dose around the isocenter is called a "shot". A GK treatment consists of single or several shots, each specified by its position in stereotactic space, its collimator setting (4mm, 8mm, or 16mm) and its weighting. The planner sets the position, collimation, and weighting of each shot, and based upon this information, along with the prescription, the decay-corrected calibration dose rate of the machine, and the radiation attenuation between the patient surface and shot centre, LGP calculates the beam-on-time (BOT) required for each shot.[2] We have shown how to perform radiation treatment planning in a few GK cases through our studies in past.[3,4]

The latest GK TPS, Leksell Gamma Plan, v 11.3 is a software package for complete dose calculation for plan optimization which uses an inverse planning optimizer. It is also known as Lightning Software. It performs automatic multiple isocenter placements within the target, optimizes collimator sizes, and changes sector configurations concerning specified constraints.[5] The key role of the software is to provide optimal dose to the target, minimise OAR dose and reduce Beam on time (BOT).

IMAGING

The heart of the GK planning relies on MR imaging for localising the target for radiation placement at the region of interest. The major advantage of MR imaging for GK is its superior soft tissue contrast which makes it easier to delineate the intracranial tumours. The MPRAGE sequence is a three-dimensional MR sequence an abbreviation of Magnetization-prepared 180 degrees radio-frequency pulses and rapid-gradient-echo (MP RAGE) sampling. The image quality and contrast between grey and white matter were superior with the MP RAGE sequence compared to the T1-weighted sequence (Fig. 2.3). For intracranial stereotactic radiosurgery (SRS), MRI can also be used for dosimetry planning as the brain is considered

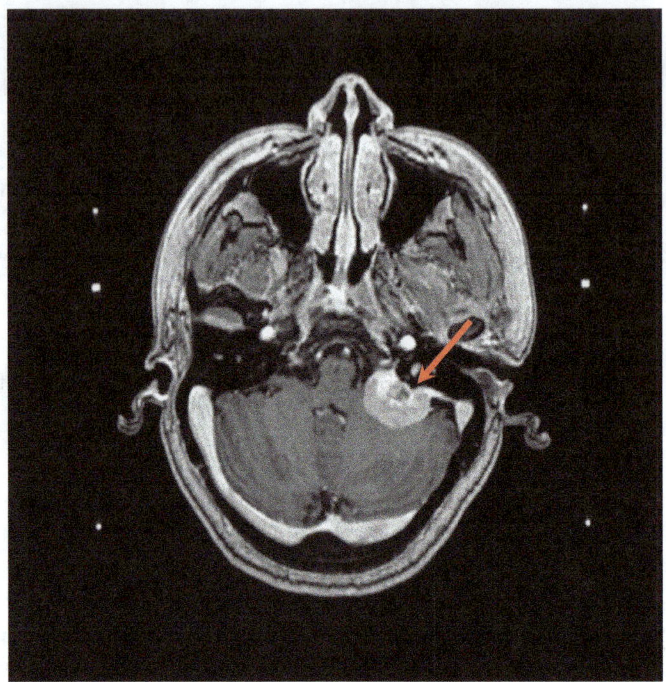

FIGURE 2.3   MR image of a patient having left-sided acoustic tumour (white region). The tumour is well distinguished from the normal brain by MPRAGE sequence.

homogeneous. The advantages of using MRI alone in intracranial SRS include avoiding systematic errors that may occur due to CT-MRI registration, and the risks associated with ionizing radiation exposure from CT scans.

GK PROTOCOL

The American Association of Physicists in Medicine (AAPM) Report 54 on "Stereotactic Radiosurgery" was published in 1995. This report provided critical direction to the newly emerging field of radiosurgery and was divided into sections that introduced the field and the techniques then in use (Leksell Gamma Knife®, linear accelerator-based radiosurgery, and charged particle therapy). The field has developed rapidly and expanded greatly since 1995 with the advent of new gamma stereotactic radiosurgery (GSR) devices, dedicated radiosurgery linear accelerators, and robotic linear accelerators. (TG-51) and International Atomic Energy Agency (IAEA) Technical Report Series Report 398 (TRS-398), have specified doses in liquid water measurement, which is challenging for GSR units.

The AAPM formed Task Group 178 (TG-178) to implement the following tasks: review in-phantom and in-air calibration protocols for GK SRS, suggestions for dose rate calibration protocol that can be successfully utilised with all GK models, and update quality assurance (QA) protocols in TG-42 (AAPM Report 54,

TABLE 2.1 ▪ **The table highlights some of the necessary QA protocols followed for GK**

Frequency of QA	QA procedure
Daily	• Machine Switch On & OFF • Dry Run of equipment • Emergency Alarm working • Last Man Out Switch (LMOS) functioning
Weekly	• CBCT QA. • Collision tool check. • QA tool plus test to check the spatial accuracy of the CBCT. • MRI Distortion Study • Radiation Survey • MRI Distortion checks
Monthly	• Radiation Output Measurement • Mechanical Tests • Dosimetric Tests • Battery checks on Survey meter • Validity of calibration periods of various instruments
Annual	• Area Survey • Preventive Maintenance Service (PMS) by Vendor • Radiation Output Measurement

1995) for static GK devices. The report describes routine mechanical, dosimetric, and safety checks for GSR devices, and provides treatment process quality assurance recommendations.[6]

During the installation of a Leksell Gamma Knife Perfexion or Icon unit, and subsequently, during preventive maintenance procedures, the UCP and Radiation Focal Point (RFP) coincidence is checked by the manufacturer using the "installation-diode tool". This tool attaches directly to the PPS and can accommodate up to three diodes. The dose rate consistency of the GK unit is measured monthly through an ionisation chamber (IC), a 1D radiation detector inserted into a 160 mm diameter spherical phantom further mounted on the GK couch. The IC centre point is positioned at UCP which has x, y and z coordinate values of 100,100,100. In addition to the recommended QA procedures, our institute developed our own QA procedures for validation of the treatment delivery accuracy (Table 2.1). Through our published work we have shown methodology to perform 2D and 3D dosimetry in GK.[7,8,9,10,11]

DISCUSSION

The gamma radiation emitted by the Co60 source interacts with the atoms of tissues almost exclusively by the Compton effect. In other words, a gamma photon scatters from an atomic electron, producing a lower energy photon and an energetic electron. The Compton photon further may undergo new Compton processes, interact with other processes, or leave the tissue. At each Compton process, the created photon and electron are scattered in relation to the incoming photon. Most of the beam energy absorbed by the molecules of the tissue is transferred by the Compton electrons.[1]

Therefore, the energy, or range in tissue, of these electrons determines the smallest theoretical size of the penumbra of the beam, i.e., how "sharp" the edge of the beam is. In Co60 beams penumbra size in tissue cannot be smaller than approximately 1.5 mm.

The high steep dose gradients at the edges of the radiation fields can only be correctly determined with detectors that have good spatial resolution. The GK is a classic case of small field dosimetry (SFD). The SFD has three physical conditions. [1] There is a loss of lateral charged particle equilibrium (LCPE) on the beam axis. [2] There is partial occlusion of the primary photon source by the collimating devices on the beam axis. [3] The size of the detector is similar or large compared to beam dimensions. [12] The FWHM of the resulting field $\neq$ geometrical definition of the field. The irradiation field size is specified at 50% relative dose level > geometrical field size defined by the projected collimator settings. An effect called the apparent widening of the field. In small fields, owing to partial occlusion of the finite primary photon source and loss of LCPE results in a drastic reduction of beam output, and congruence between GF and IF breaks down.

The GK treatment delivery procedure is a team effort. All GK team members, including neurosurgeons (NS), radiation oncologists (RO), medical physicists (MP), radiotherapy technologists (RTT) and nurses, are responsible for some aspects of treatment QA. The MP is generally responsible for the integrity of the image acquisition process and data entry. A physician is responsible for ensuring that the correct imaging studies have been ordered. Ideally, both a physician and a physicist should review all image co-registrations. This includes the co-registration of planning images to the reference CT and, before the start of each treatment, the co-registration of the setup CBCT to the reference CBCT. The procedural checklists are implemented to confirm adherence to GSR policies and promote the safe and effective delivery of GSR treatments. [6]

In our institute, we were fortunate to work with three GK models. In the year 1997 when GK Model B was used for clinical purposes, the treatment technique was entirely manual mode based. Each treatment shot was manually set for x, y and z coordinates. In 2011 we installed the GK Perfexion Model which performed robotic treatment delivery. Following this in the year 2021 we upgraded our equipment to the ICON model. This upgrade in technology advancement has fastened our treatment and QA procedures. The capacity to handle patient load has become five-fold than it was in the year 1997. The necessary QA and maintenance of the unit has become more demanding and require high standards. To meet global standards at our institute, we have periodically tuned our QA procedures based on the demands of that time. [10,11]

TAKE HOME MESSAGE

To summarise the role of physics in gamma knife, it can be generally divided into three aspects:

1. Equipment design: Radiation physics principles are applied to focus the radiation at the isocenter which is also known as UCP.

2. Treatment planning: Various radiation interactions are modelled through calculation algorithms to deliver the desired radiation dose to the target.

3. Radiation safety: This encompasses the design of the radiation bunker to deliver radiation in a controlled manner, quantifying radiation received by GK staff, general public and establishing dose limits.

REFERENCES

1. M. H. Phillips. Physical Aspects of Stereotactic Radiosurgery.Plenum Press, New York, NY; 1993

2. Fallows P, Wright G, Harrold N, Bownes P. A comparison of the convolution and TMR10 treatment planning algorithms for Gamma Knife® radiosurgery. *J Radiosurg SBRT*. 2018;5(2):157-167.

3. Bose R, Agrawal D, Singh M, et al. Draining vein shielding in intracranial arteriovenous malformations during gamma-knife: a new way of preventing post gamma-knife edema and hemorrhage. *Neurosurgery*. 2015;76(5):623-632.

4. Agarwal P, Natanasabapathi G, Bisht RK, Malhotra RK, Kale SS. Investigation of optimal planning strategy in gamma knife perfexion for vestibular schwannoma tumour using hybrid plan technique. *Biomed Phys Eng Express*. 2022;8(6):10.1088/2057-1976/ac9abb. Published 2022 Nov 18.

5. Pokhrel D, Bernard ME, Knight J 2nd, St Clair W, Fraser JF. Clinical validation of novel lightning dose optimizer for gamma knife radiosurgery of irregular-shaped arteriovenous malformations and pituitary adenomas. *J Appl Clin Med Phys*. 2022;23(8):e13669.

6. Petti PL, Rivard MJ, Alvarez PE, et al. Recommendations on the practice of calibration, dosimetry, and quality assurance for gamma stereotactic radiosurgery: Report of AAPM Task Group 178. *Med Phys*. 2021;48(7):e733-e770.

7. Gopishankar N, Vivekanandhan S, Kale S, *et al.* MAGAT gel dosimetry for its application in small field treatment techniques. *J Phys. Conf. Ser*;2010;250: 012061

8. Gopishankar N, Watanabe Y, Subbiah V. MRI-based polymer gel dosimetry for validating plans with multiple matrices in Gamma Knife stereotactic radiosurgery. *J Appl Clin Med Phys*. 2011;12(2):3333. Published 2011 Jan 31.

9. Natanasabapathi G, Subbiah V, Kale SS, et al. MAGAT gel and EBT2 film-based dosimetry for evaluating source plugging-based treatment plan in Gamma Knife stereotactic radiosurgery. *J Appl Clin Med Phys*. 2012;13(6):3877. Published 2012 Nov 8.

10. Natanasabapathi G, Bisht RK. Verification of Gamma Knife extend system based fractionated treatment planning using EBT2 film. *Med Phys*. 2013;40(12):122104.

11. Bisht RK, Kale SS, Natanasabapathi G, et al. Verification of Gamma Knife based fractionated radiosurgery with newly developed head-thorax phantom. Radiat Measur. 2016;91:65-74.

12. International Atomic Energy Agency. Dosimetry of small static fields used in external beam radiotherapy. IAEA technical reports series, 2017; vol 483

Frameless Gamma Knife Radiosurgery

R Shiva Krishna | Deepak Agrawal

KEY LEARNING POINTS

1. Frameless Gamma Knife radiosurgery (GKRS) is a precise and patient-friendly alternative to conventional frame-based fixation.
2. The integration of cone-beam computed tomography (CBCT) and high-definition motion management (HDMM) ensures accurate image registration and real-time patient monitoring.
3. Studies confirm that frameless GKRS achieves submillimeter accuracy, making it a viable treatment option.
4. Augmented reality (AR)-based navigation aids in patient repositioning and minimises the need for repeated CBCT scans.
5. Recent research highlights the effectiveness of frameless fractionated GKRS in treating large brain metastases with improved local control rates.
6. Further research is required to refine treatment protocols, optimise dose-volume relationships, and establish comprehensive patient selection criteria.

INTRODUCTION

Gamma Knife radiosurgery (GKRS) is an established method for delivering highly focused radiation to intracranial lesions. Traditional GKRS requires rigid frame-based fixation to maintain accuracy. However, recent advancements in imaging and motion tracking have facilitated the adoption of frameless GKRS, which relies on non-invasive fixation techniques.

Patients with large tumours who undergo single-fraction radiosurgery are at higher risk of radiation necrosis.[1] Radiation doses are generally reduced for this reason which can decrease tumour control. GKRS in multiple smaller doses leverages the radiobiological benefit of fractionation, with increased DNA repair in normal tissues compared to tumour cells.

Frameless GKRS is particularly beneficial for patients requiring fractionated therapy or those unable to tolerate invasive fixation. Research has demonstrated its ability to achieve comparable precision to frame-based methods while enhancing patient comfort and procedural flexibility.[1-4]

CORE PRINCIPLES OF FRAMELESS GKRS

Frameless GKRS employs a combination of imaging, immobilisation, and motion-tracking technologies:

1. Image Registration: CBCT aligns the patient's anatomy with preoperative MRI or CT scans to ensure precise targeting.
2. Non-invasive Immobilisation: A customised thermoplastic mask secures the patient's head to the treatment couch.
3. Real-time Motion Monitoring: HDMM continuously tracks patient movement, pausing treatment if deviations exceed a set threshold.
4. Targeted Radiation Delivery: Highly focused gamma rays converge on the lesion, minimising exposure to surrounding healthy tissue.

REPRESENTATIVE CASE STUDY

PATIENT BACKGROUND

A 35-year-old male patient presented with a history of multiple episodes of generalised tonic-clonic seizures. Neurological examination revealed no focal deficits. Imaging showed a $6.3 \times 4.2 \times 5.7$ cm right frontoparietal AVM with feeders from Right MCA distal segments and draining into the anterior aspect of superior sagittal sinus. The patient was planned for multifraction GKRS, as a traditional frame-based GKRS was unsuitable for this case.

DIAGNOSTIC IMAGING

CBCT was performed for stereotactic alignment. MRI with contrast revealed a large right frontoparietal AVM (Fig. 3.1).

GK PROTOCOL

The patient underwent frameless GKRS using the Gamma Knife Icon system. A thermoplastic mask was used for fixation, which was made by heating the mask in a water bath and then applying it to the patient's face. The thermoplastic hardens and takes the contours of the face. CBCT and preoperative MRI were coregistered for accurate target localisation. A marginal dose of 21 Gy was used and the patient was planned for multifraction GKRS. HDMM monitored patient movement throughout the procedure.

DISCUSSION

ACCURACY AND STABILITY OF FRAMELESS GKRS

Research has validated the accuracy of frameless GKRS. Chung et al. demonstrated that the mean 3D deviation in frameless GKRS is approximately 0.5 mm, ensuring

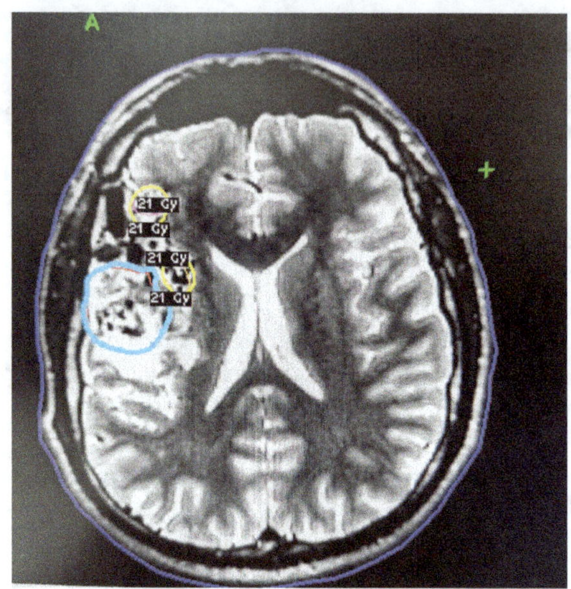

FIGURE 3.1   Shows the volume outline of the 1st fraction of GKRS (in blue) along with the volume outline for the 2nd fraction of GKRS (in yellow).

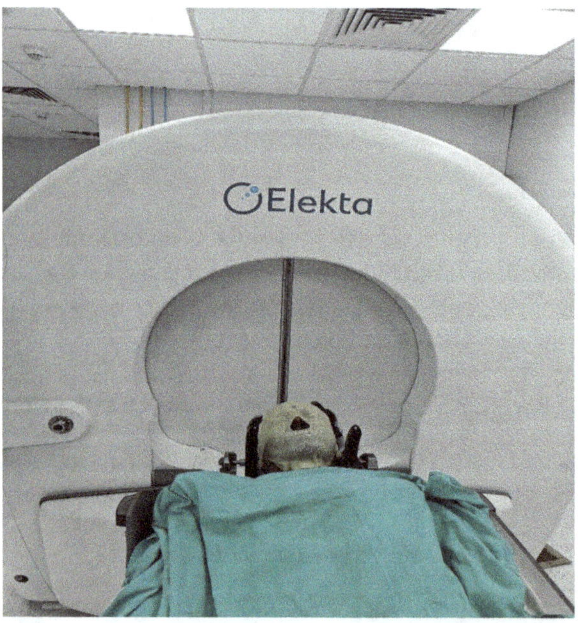

FIGURE 3.2   Patient with thermoplastic mask applied for Frameless GKRS.

high precision.[2] Moon et al. explored AR-assisted navigation for frameless GKRS, highlighting its role in reducing unnecessary CBCT scans.[3] A study of 100 patients undergoing frameless GKRS showed improved workflow efficiency and increased patient eligibility due to the ability to fractionate treatments.[4] Also, a study on large brain metastases found that fractionated frameless GKRS yielded a 100% local control rate with minimal toxicity.[5]

ADVANTAGES AND CHALLENGES

Being a non-invasive approach, it enhances patient comfort and compliance. Also with mask, **fractionation feasibility** is not a concern and treatment of larger tumours over multiple sessions can be done. **Real-time tracking** ensures accurate treatment by pausing radiation if movement exceeds safe limits. Also, **AR-assisted navigation** streamlines repositioning and minimises redundant imaging. Use of inbuilt CBCT imaging enhances precision in target localisation.

However, there is extended setup time as initial mask fitting and image registration require additional time **and the potential for movement** remains, even with HDMM. MRI and CBCT distortions may also impact target localisation, **with** some studies reporting motion-related errors requiring repeated image acquisition.

FUTURE DIRECTIONS

To optimise frameless GKRS, future efforts should focus on:
- Establishing standardised dose guidelines tailored to tumour volume and location.
- Enhancing AR-based navigation tools for improved efficiency.
- Conducting large-scale clinical trials to validate long-term outcomes and safety profiles
- Further refining motion management techniques to reduce intra-fraction errors.

TAKE HOME MESSAGE

Frameless GKRS represents a significant advancement in radiosurgical technology, offering a non-invasive, precise, and patient-friendly alternative to traditional frame-based techniques. As imaging, motion tracking, and AR-assisted navigation continue to evolve, frameless GKRS is expected to become a mainstay in the treatment of intracranial lesions.

REFERENCE

1. Sneed PK, Mendez J, Vemer-van den Hoek JG, et al. Adverse radiation effect after stereotactic radiosurgery for brain metastases: incidence, time course, and risk factors. J Neurosurg. 2015;123(2):373-386.
2. Chung HT, Park WY, Kim TH, Kim YK, Chun KJ. Assessment of the accuracy and stability of frameless gamma knife radiosurgery. J Appl Clin Med Phys. 2018;19(4):148-154.

3. Moon HC, Park SJ, Kim YD, et al. Navigation of frameless fixation for gamma knife radiosurgery using fixed augmented reality. Sci Rep. 2022;12(1):4486. Published 2022 Mar 16.
4. Vulpe H, Save AV, Xu Y, et al. Frameless Stereotactic Radiosurgery on the Gamma Knife Icon: Early Experience From 100 Patients. Neurosurgery. 2020;86(4):509-516.
5. Park HR, Park KW, Lee JM, et al. Frameless Fractionated Gamma Knife Radiosurgery with ICON™ for Large Metastatic Brain Tumors. J Korean Med Sci. 2019;34(8):e57. Published 2019 Feb 12.

SECTION 2

TUMOURS

Gamma Knife Radiosurgery in Koos Grade 2 Vestibular Schwannoma

4

Ashwin Bharadwaj R | Shweta Kedia

INTRODUCTION

Vestibular Schwannomas are one of the most frequently treated benign tumours in radiosurgery. The choice of treatment modality is usually guided by the size and consistency of the tumour. The rough guide to the size of the tumour is based on Koos classification. This classification system categorises vestibular schwannomas based on their size and extent of impact on surrounding neurological structures. This system is particularly useful in clinical practice, as it helps clinicians make informed decisions about management strategies. Koos Grade 2 vestibular schwannomas are moderate in size and are significant enough to cause local effects, such as hearing loss and balance disturbances, but without direct contact with the brainstem. By definition, the tumour size is less than 2 cm and is apt for radio-surgical management.

REPRESENTATIVE CASE

HISTORY & EXAMINATION

The index case is a 53-year-old gentleman, who presented with tinnitus in the right ear with minimal hearing loss. The patient was troubled with tinnitus but the hearing was not very bothersome. These symptoms had been present for 2 years, during which he had been seeing an ENT specialist. Upon detailed history, this tinnitus was described as persistent, high-pitched, and associated with hearing loss in the right ear. There was no history of any ear discharge or earache. On leading questions, he confirmed that he had stopped using his mobile phone on the affected side. There was also a history suggesting difficulty with speech discrimination. However, there were no signs suggestive of involvement of the right-sided fifth, seventh and lower cranial nerves involvement. There was no history of such illness in the family. On examination, there was the presence of right-sided retro-cochlear sensorineural hearing loss but nothing to suggest pyramidal tracts, brainstem compression or cerebellar features. Pure tone audiometry was done which was suggestive of right side mild sensorineural hearing loss (Fig. 4.1).

IMAGING

This patient was referred with a contrast-enhanced MRI (CEMR), which revealed a 2 cm lesion in the Right cerebellopontine angle just abutting the brainstem and going into the internal auditory canal. As per the classification, the tumour was Koos grade 2 Vestibular schwannoma. Routinely we do the T2 weighted imaging and CISS Sequences for the extra-axial lesions located in the cerebello pontine angle region.

Considering the lesion size, both the option for surgery and Gamma Knife Radiosurgery (GKRS) were offered to him. There is no role for observation in this scenario and this was thoroughly discussed with the patient. The patient opted for Gamma Knife Radiosurgery due to its safety profile and good tumour control rate.

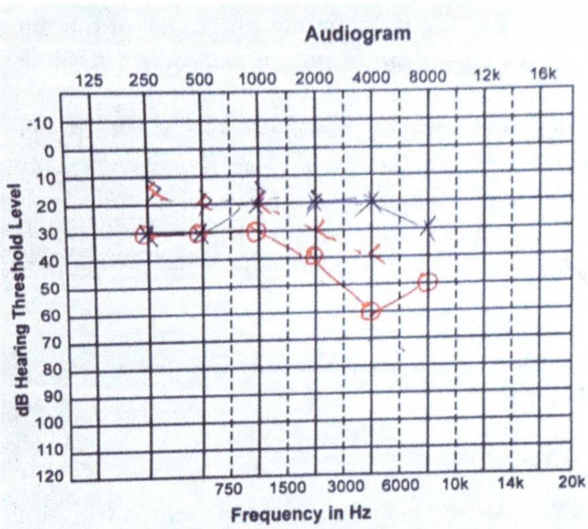

FIGURE 4.1   Pure tone audiometry of the patient showing a dip to 60dB at the 4000Hz. Suggestive of mild sensory neural hearing loss.

GK PROTOCOL

The patient was planned for the marginal dose of 12 Gy at 50% isodose line primary GKRS. Single fraction Gamma knife radiosurgery was executed as a day-care procedure. The lesion, along with the brainstem and cochlea were marked as organs at risk on the contrast sequence and FIESTA sequence to ensure appropriate dose constraints. The total time of the treatment was 33 minutes with coverage of 92%. Forward planning followed by inverse planning was used to achieve the best possible plan. The selectivity was 0.89 and the Gradient index of 2.89. After the procedure, the frame was removed, and the patient was observed for a few hours before being discharged (Fig. 4.2).

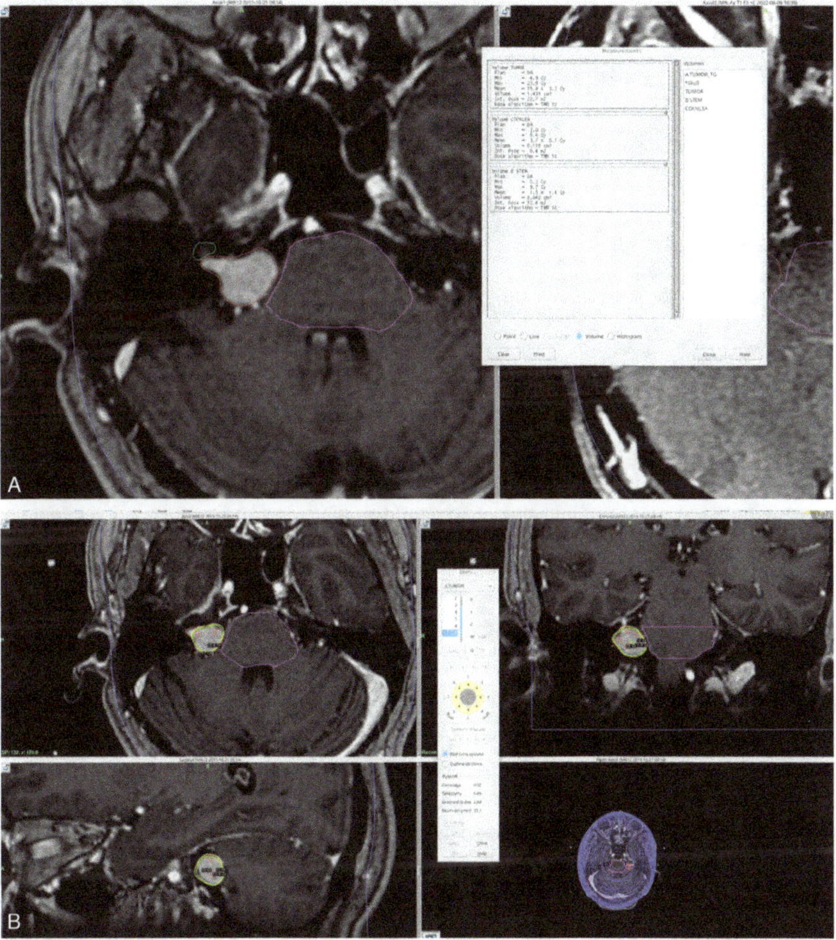

FIGURE 4.2   (A) Imaging shows the marking of the lesion along with organs at risk. (B) The shot distribution along with the isodose line.

Continued

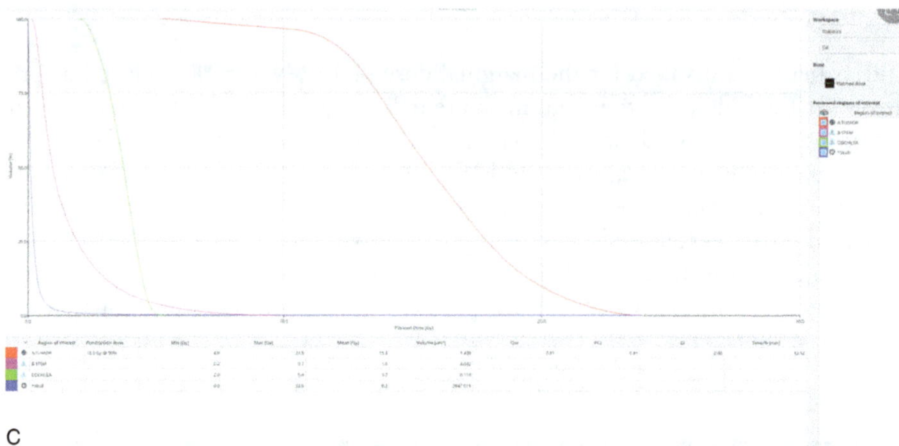

C

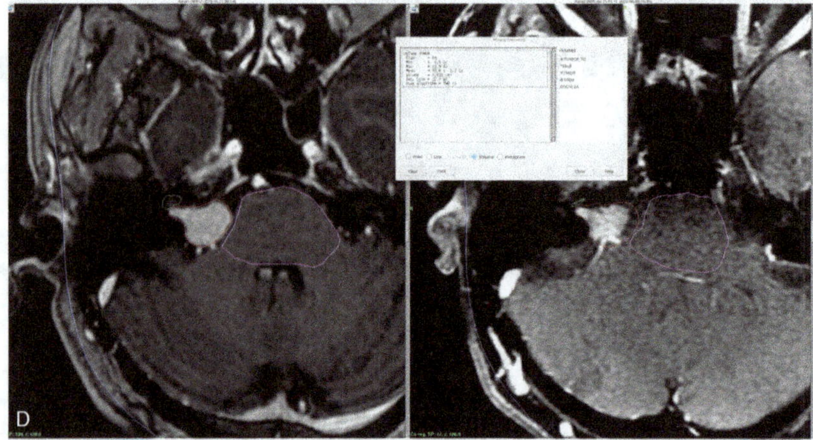

D

FIGURE 4.2 (Con't)   (C) The statistics chart with dose-volume histogram shows the margin and the mean dose to target organs and organs at risk. (D) The follow-up scan after 8 years of follow-up showed volume reduction. The new volume is 0.73 cc, reduced in size by 50%.

FOLLOW-UP

This patient did well post-GKRS, with the follow-up scan at the end of 1 year and subsequent follow-up showing a reduction in the size of the tumour. The latest follow-up was conducted 8 years post-GKRS. Tinnitus, however, persisted and there was mild deterioration in hearing compared to the pre-GKRS status. The patient also underwent a repeat audiometry test to assess the hearing objectively. There was a mild reduction in the decibels with moderate worsening in hearing over time (Fig. 4.3).

DISCUSSION

A large number of patients are now being detected with small-sized vestibular schwannomas due to the wide availability of imaging modalities. Vestibular schwan-

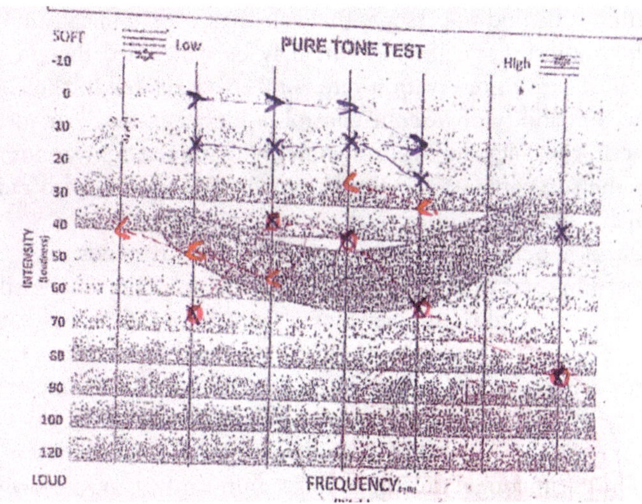

FIGURE 4.3   Follow-up Pure tone audiometry after 8 years of radiosurgery showing deterioration in hearing and moderate sensory neural hearing loss.

noma is a benign disease that was historically primarily treated with surgery. Multiple studies have shown that patients with unilateral vestibular schwannoma, with no personal or family history of NF2 and lesion size corresponding to Koos grade 1 or 2, are increasingly being treated with upfront Gamma Knife Radiosurgery (GKRS).[1]

The treatment options available for Koos grade 2 vestibular schwannomas are microsurgery and radiosurgery. Wait-and-watch policies have not been proven to be a good alternative. The randomised controlled trial (V-REX RCT) suggested the superiority of upfront GKRS over observation in small to medium-sized lesions, with a significant reduction in tumour volume at the end of 4 years, with one of the patients requiring repeat radiosurgery and two of 48 patients needing salvage microsurgery. In contrast, 42% of patients in the observation group required radiosurgery due to documented tumour growth during the study period.[1]

The goal of radiosurgery in Koos grade 2 tumours is to achieve good tumour control along with functional preservation. Long-term follow-up results comparing the outcome of microsurgery versus radiosurgery in these patients have also been published. Preservation of baseline hearing is defined as a change in the pure tone average (PTA) of not more than 20 dB. The serviceable hearing preservation rate in patients treated with microsurgery and radiosurgery is around 55-60% and statistically not very different from each other. Long-term tumour control is around 92% overall versus 98% in the microsurgery group of patients, and this difference is significant. However, 0.5-5% of the patients treated with microsurgery may have tumour recurrence. The facial nerve deficit is more common in patients treated microsurgically, with around 10% of them getting affected, compared to only 2% in the radio-surgical group.[2]

The improvement in intra-operative monitoring has led to better facial nerve preservation post-microsurgery. Yet, it is observed that most surgeons would leave the residual tumour behind to preserve the facial nerve anatomically and then refer the patients for radiosurgery. Therefore, it may be concluded that in the present scenario, the facial nerve preservation rate is inversely related to the completeness of surgery. The probability of tumour control is higher in small or medium-sized tumours. Overall, the microsurgical outcome of vestibular schwannoma is highly dependent on the surgeon and is inconsistent when compared with radio-surgical outcomes, which have a smaller learning curve.[2,3]

The radio-surgical outcome for Koos grade 2 tumours depends on several factors, one of the most important being the size of the tumour. The smaller the size, the higher the likelihood of good tumour control with fewer adverse radiation effects. The preoperative functional status of the patients largely determines the outcomes for hearing preservation and facial nerve function. Radiologically, one of the favourable prognostic indicators for good preservation of baseline hearing is the presence of a fundal cap on the pre-GKRS MRI in the vestibular schwannomas.

Deterioration in functional outcomes was significantly associated with the dose of Gamma Knife used for irradiation, which is why a dose of 12 Gy is used at the margin of the tumour for a safe outcome.[3] Cochlear dose constraints have been used with the aim of preserving functional hearing, although the literature on this remains inconclusive. The mean dose of less than 4 Gy is the standard protocol followed in patients with good hearing pre-GKRS. The hearing preservation rate post-radiosurgery declines with an increase in the duration of follow-up, especially when we look at follow-ups greater than 10 years. According to the Congress on Neurological Surgeons, 50% of patients are likely to lose their serviceable hearing by the end of 5 years, irrespective of the treatment modality.[3,4]

The planning strategy includes marking the tumour and identifying the cochlea and brainstem. The single fraction of the lesion is planned using a hybrid planning methodology to obtain coverage of more than 95% with the highest selectivity possible.

The expected adverse radiation effects in these tumours may include tumour progression requiring micro-neurosurgical intervention and hydrocephalus. The initial response of the tumour to radiosurgery is increased central necrosis with enlargement of the tumour size. This typically occurs within 18 months post-radiosurgery in almost 75% of cases. The tumour eventually stabilises in size or regresses with sequential follow-ups over the years. Patients are followed up annually for the first two years and then every two years for at least 10-15 years. Other possible complications could be cystic changes in the tumour requiring intervention, which is more commonly seen with GKRS given in residual tumours post-microsurgery. Few patients present with features of raised intracranial pressure secondary to hydrocephalus requiring cerebrospinal fluid (CSF) diversion procedures.[1,4]

The first follow-up of the patient is routinely done at the end of one year, with subsequent follow-ups every 2-3 years. Patients are followed up for life to rule out any new growth and to check for new radiation-induced changes. The follow-up scan includes contrast MRI and T2 sequences to assess tumour response and brainstem changes. PTA is also done yearly in patients with serviceable hearing, though it may not be required for other patients.

TAKE HOME MESSAGE

The current standard of treatment for Koos grade 2 tumours is upfront Gamma Knife Radiosurgery. The standard prescribed dose is 12-13 Gy at the tumour margin in a single fraction. The mean dose to the cochlea is targeted to be kept less than 4 Gy in patients with serviceable hearing pre-GKRS.

REFERENCES

1. Dhayalan D, Tveiten ØV, Finnkirk M, et al. Upfront Radiosurgery vs a Wait-and-Scan Approach for Small- or Medium-Sized Vestibular Schwannoma: The V-REX Randomized Clinical Trial. *JAMA*. 2023;330(5):421-431.

2. Savardekar AR, Terrell D, Lele SJ, et al. Primary Treatment of Small to Medium (<3 cm) Sporadic Vestibular Schwannomas: A Systematic Review and Meta-Analysis on Hearing Preservation and Tumor Control Rates for Microsurgery versus Radiosurgery. *World Neurosurg*. 2022;160:102-113.e12.

3. Govindaraj R, Khong J, Byrne A, Zacest A, Roos D. The Effect of Cochlear Dose on Hearing Preservation After Low-Dose Stereotactic Radiosurgery for Vestibular Schwannomas: A Systematic Review. *Adv Radiat Oncol*. 2022;7(6):101059. Published 2022 Aug 28.

4. Agarwal P, Natanasabapathi G, Bisht RK, Malhotra RK, Kale SS. Investigation of optimal planning strategy in gamma knife perfexion for vestibular schwannoma tumor using hybrid plan technique. *Biomed Phys Eng Express*. 2022;8(6):10.1088/2057-1976/ac9abb. Published 2022 Nov 18.

5 Pseudoprogression in Vestibular Schwannoma Following Gamma-Knife Radiosurgery

Kanwaljeet Garg | Abhilash Reddy | Deepak Agrawal

KEY LEARNING POINTS

1. Pseudoprogression is a commonly encountered phenomenon following GKRS for VS.
2. Pseudoprogression can be symptomatic or asymptomatic.
3. Observation is preferred over immediate surgical intervention in asymptomatic patients.

INTRODUCTION

Vestibular schwannomas (VS) are histologically benign tumours that usually arise from the Schwann cells of the vestibular nerve. It is one of the most common intracranial tumours, representing approximately 6-8% of all intracranial tumours with a reported annual incidence of 1 in every 100,000 people.[1] SRS is a commonly used treatment modality for VS. Pseudoprogression, characterised by a significant volume increase following treatment, which later resolves/stabilises on subsequent imaging, may be observed after radiotherapy/radiosurgery for VS.[5] Although tumour growth with increasing symptoms or neurological deficit may herald treatment failure, pseudoprogression, or a transient increase in size followed by stability or regression, has been increasingly recognised after radio surgical treatment of VS.[6] The reported incidence of pseudoprogression following radiosurgery for VS has varied widely from 6-74%, using different methods of measurement. We will present a patient who experienced pseudoprogression following GKRS for VS.

REPRESENTATIVE CASES

CASE 1

History & Examination

A 39-year-old female was operated on for left vestibular schwannoma in February 2015 at another hospital. On examination, the patient had left-sided profound SNHL, grade 4 facial palsy, with no cerebellar signs.

Imaging

Post-operative MRI showed a residual lesion for which the patient was planned for secondary GKRS. Contrast-enhanced MRI brain showed a tumour in the left-right cerebellopontine angle with extension into the internal acoustic meatus and abutting the brainstem without significant brain stem compression. There was no evidence of hydrocephalus.

GK Protocol

The patient opted for GKRS after being explained all the possible options, including watchful waiting with serial MRI scans, surgery and GKRS. MRI brain was done following fixation of stereotactic frame (Leksell Model G) MRI brain included T1-weighted high-resolution magnetization-prepared 180 degrees radio-frequency pulses and rapid gradient-echo (MPRAGE) sequences with 192 slices with a slice-thickness of 1 mm without intersectional gaps were acquired. These images were imported to the treatment planning station, and GKRS planning was done using GammaPlan® v11.3 (Elekta AB, Sweden) software. Tumour volume (by volumetric method) was found to be 3.408cc. The treatment plan was made, and GKRS was administered using Leksell Gamma Knife Perfexion™. A dose of 12 Gy to the 50% isodose line was administered. The procedure was uneventful, and the patient was discharged in stable condition.

Follow Up

A follow-up MRI of the brain done 13 months post-procedure showed an interval increase in the tumour size from 3.408 cc to 4.715 cc. Differentials included a non-response to GKRS or pseudoprogression. Treatment options considered were observation, surgery, and repeat radiation. The patient was clinically stable, with no signs of brainstem compression, and had no radiation-related adverse effects. After a discussion with the patient, it was decided that the patient should be followed up with interval imaging. Further MRI of the brain done at 30 months post-procedure showed an interval reduction in tumour volume from 4.71 cc to 3.654 cc, and at 56 months post-procedure, a further reduction to 2.6 cc (Fig. 5.1 and 5.2). The patient is under regular follow-up and remains clinically stable with new symptoms, no signs of brainstem compression, and no new radiation-induced adverse effects.

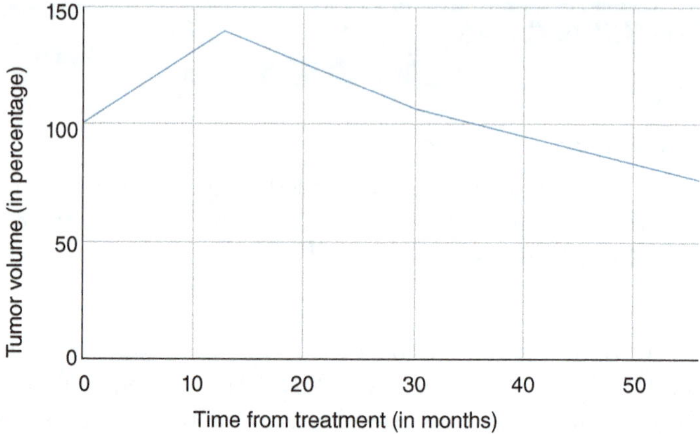

FIGURE 5.1   Line graph showing the change in the size of the lesion over time following GKRS.

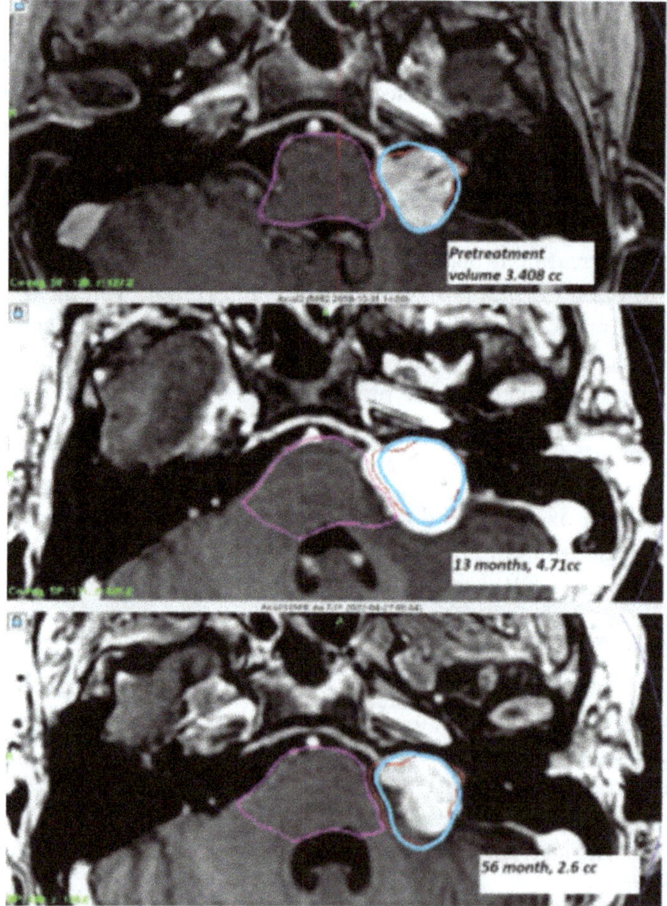

FIGURE 5.2   Serial MRIs of representative case 1 showing pseudoprogression with transient increase followed by regression.

CASE 2

History & Examination

A 34-year-old female presented with complaints of vertigo and tinnitus. On evaluation, the patient had no facial sensory loss, facial palsy, no cerebellar signs, and no signs of raised ICP. She has mild right-sided SNHL.

Imaging

MRI of the brain was suggestive of a contrast-enhancing lesion in the right cerebellopontine angle extending to the internal acoustic meatus.

GK Protocol

Treatment options, including GKRS, surgery and observation, were discussed with the patient, and the patient opted for primary GKRS. An MRI brain was done at the Gamma Knife MRI centre using the Gamma Knife protocol. Tumour volume, measured using the volumetric method, was found to be 0.378 cc. These images were imported to the treatment planning station, and planning was done using GammaPlan® v11.3 (Elekta AB, Sweden) software.

Treatment plan was made and GKRS was administered using Leksell GammaKnife Perfexion™. Dose of 12 Gy to the 50% isodose line was administered. The procedure was uneventful, and the patient was discharged the same day in stable condition.

Follow Up

A follow-up MRI done at an interval of 15 months revealed an increase in tumour size to 0.563 ccs. The patient was clinically stable and had no radiation-related adverse effects. Treatment options considered were observation, surgery, and repeat radiation. After a discussion with the patient, it was decided that the patient should be followed up with interval imaging. Further imaging revealed an increase in tumour volume to 1.41 cc at an interval of 28 months post-procedure. The patient was clinically stable and opted for follow-up with imaging. A follow-up MRI done at 52 months post-procedure showed regression in tumour volume to 1.164 cc (Fig. 5.3 and 5.4).

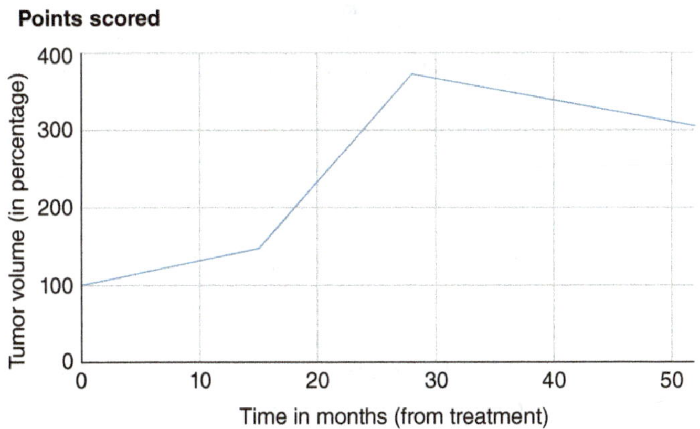

FIGURE 5.3   Line graph showing the change in the size of the lesion over time following GKRS.

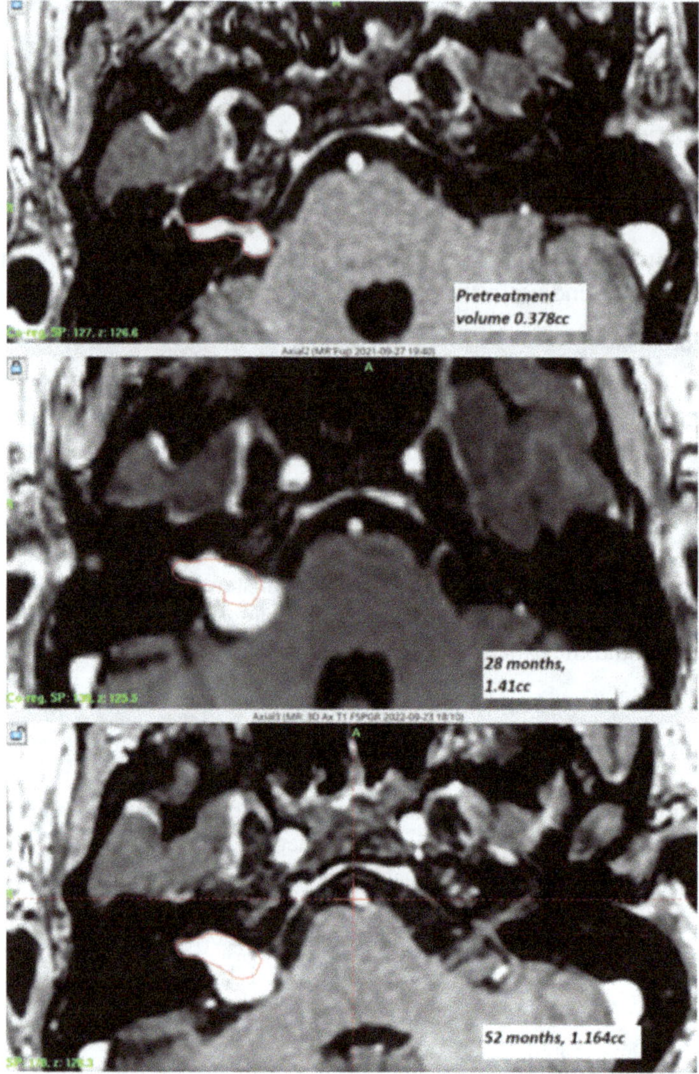

FIGURE 5.4   Serial MRIs of representative case 2 showing pseudoprogression with a transient increase followed by regression.

DISCUSSION

GKRS has become the primary treatment choice for small and medium-sized tumours in view of improved facial nerve outcomes, hearing preservation rates, and lower overall morbidity. Post-radiosurgery surveillance of the patients is done using regular imaging, with MRI being the most used modality. Pseudoprogression, defined as a significant volume increase at any time following treatment, which resolves on subsequent imaging, may be observed after radiotherapy for VS.

The reported incidence of pseudoprogression following radiosurgery ranges from 6% to 74%, depending on the methods of measurement.[1-8] Here, we presented two cases of pseudoprogression in vestibular schwannoma to understand the temporal dynamics of tumour response post-GKRS. One case was upfront treated with GKRS, while another was treated with adjuvant GKRS for residual tumour post-subtotal resection.

The published literature on pseudoprogression reports the incidence, time to onset, time to peak volume, maximum volume change, and the percentage of volume change per year as aids for diagnosis and subsequent decision-making. The timing of tumour regression is highly variable. The onset of pseudoprogression can occur from 3 to 69 months following treatment, and resolution can occur from 6 months to 110 months.[1,9,10] Few studies show that about 1/3rd of the tumours regress between the 4th and 6th years after treatment.[1]

In our cases, an increase in tumour size was noted at 13 months and 15 months, and regression was noted at 30 months and 52 months, respectively. Previous studies have reported a 20 to 88% increase in tumour volume, with one study reporting a 167% increase from a pretreatment volume of 8 cc to 20 cc before the onset of regression. Our cases show an increase in volume up to 40% and 248% before the onset of regression. Our cases demonstrate how observation remains an option even with the percentage increase in the tumour volume, as long as the patient remains asymptomatic, regardless of alarming radiological findings. The tumour removal remains associated with difficulty in preserving cranial nerve function with a risk of hearing loss, facial palsy, facial numbness, and other surgical morbidity. In the absence of new symptoms, patients with this finding can be observed with serial MRI and clinical examination, without undergoing unnecessary and potentially morbidity-producing surgery.

TAKE HOME MESSAGE

- Pseudoprogression is a possible entity following the radiosurgical treatment of VS.
- It may be challenging to differentiate it from the true progression of the tumour.
- One may continue to observe the patient if there are no compression symptoms due to the enlargement in the tumour size.

REFERENCES

1. Breshears JD, Chang J, Molinaro AM, et al. Temporal Dynamics of Pseudoprogression After Gamma Knife Radiosurgery for Vestibular Schwannomas-A Retrospective Volumetric Study. *Neurosurgery*. 2019;84(1):123-131.
2. Hayhurst C, Zadeh G. Tumor pseudoprogression following radiosurgery for vestibular schwannoma. *Neuro Oncol*. 2012;14(1):87-92.
3. Nagano O, Serizawa T, Higuchi Y, et al. Tumor shrinkage of vestibular schwannomas after Gamma Knife surgery: results after more than 5 years of follow-up. *J Neurosurg*. 2010;113 Suppl:122-127.

4. Nakamura H, Jokura H, Takahashi K, Boku N, Akabane A, Yoshimoto T. Serial follow-up MR imaging after gamma knife radiosurgery for vestibular schwannoma. *AJNR Am J Neuroradiol*. 2000;21(8):1540-1546.

5. Hasegawa T, Kida Y, Yoshimoto M, Koike J, Goto K. Evaluation of tumor expansion after stereotactic radiosurgery in patients harboring vestibular schwannomas. *Neurosurgery*. 2006;58(6):1119-1128.

6. Gaviolli E, Zheng J, Sinclair J, Szanto J, Alkherayf F, Malone J, et al. 32 Long Term Results of 120 Cases of Vestibular Schwannoma Treated with Cyberknifetm Robotic Stereotactic Radiosurgery at the Ottawa Hospital Cancer Centre. *Radiother Oncol*. 2019;1(139): S16–7.

7. Kim JH, Jung HH, Chang JH, Chang JW, Park YG, Chang WS. Predictive Factors of Unfavorable Events After Gamma Knife Radiosurgery for Vestibular Schwannoma. *World Neurosurg*. 2017;107:175-184.

8. Delsanti C, Roche PH, Thomassin JM, Régis J. Morphological changes of vestibular schwannomas after radiosurgical treatment: pitfalls and diagnosis of failure. *Prog Neurol Surg*. 2008;21:93-97.

9. Hayhurst C, Zadeh G. Tumor pseudoprogression following radiosurgery for vestibular schwannoma. *Neuro Oncol*. 2012;14(1):87-92.

10. Hasegawa T, Kida Y, Yoshimoto M, Koike J, Goto K. Evaluation of tumor expansion after stereotactic radiosurgery in patients harboring vestibular schwannomas. *Neurosurgery*. 2006;58(6):1119-1128.

Repeat Gamma Knife Radiosurgery for Progressive Vestibular Schwannoma

6

Kanwaljeet Garg | Sandeep Mishra

KEY LEARNING POINTS

1. VS are benign CPA tumours causing hearing loss and ataxia; MRI is key for diagnosis.
2. GKRS is effective for small-to-medium VS; repeat GKRS works for progressive cases with precise dosing.
3. Optimise dosing and imaging to minimise complications like TTE, facial and trigeminal neuropathies, and hearing loss.
4. Use serial MRIs to differentiate true progression from TTE.
5. Marginal dose ≥11 Gy ensures efficacy while protecting critical structures.
6. Regular follow-ups ensure tumour control and address delayed radiation effects.

INTRODUCTION

Vestibular schwannomas (VSs) are benign, intracranial extra-axial slow-growing tumours arising from Schwann cells of the vestibular nerve. Although histologically benign, these tumours have the potential to cause significant morbidity due to their potential growth within the confined space of the cerebellopontine angle (CPA), where they can compress critical structures such as the brainstem and cerebellum, and impair vestibulocochlear functionality. For newly diagnosed VS, treatment options include observation with regular monitoring, conventional radiotherapy, stereotactic radiosurgery (SRS), or microsurgical resection.[1] For recurrent VS where there is progressive tumour enlargement, SRS or microsurgical resection may be considered, depending on the tumour volume and individual patient factors, such as age and medical comorbidities.[2,3]

SRS has established itself as an effective treatment for small to medium-sized VS, offering good tumour control rates with minimal risk of complications. SRS alone typically achieves excellent outcomes for most small tumours.[4] In cases of failure of SRS therapy, microsurgical resection is typically recommended. Recent evidence increasingly supports the use of repeat SRS for vestibular schwannomas that show continued growth after a failed SRS treatment.[2,5] Repeat SRS therapy can be either a standalone or combined with microsurgery, as an alternative to immediate resection when feasible.[6]

REPRESENTATIVE CASE

HISTORY AND EXAMINATION

A 42-year-old female, previously operated case of left VS treated with a secondary Gamma Knife radiosurgery (GKRS) for a residual lesion in 2018, presented with gait ataxia, left-sided facial sensory loss, facial palsy, and hearing impairment. Neurological examination revealed intact higher mental functions but noted gait ataxia, a 20% sensory loss on the left side of the face, a grade V left facial palsy, and left-sided sensorineural hearing loss. Examination of the remaining cranial nerves was normal, and motor strength was preserved bilaterally. Positive cerebellar signs were observed.

IMAGING

Magnetic resonance imaging (MRI) axial T1-weighted contrast-enhanced images reveal an non-homogeneous contrast-enhancing extra-axial in the left cerebellopontine angle (CPA) with intracanalicular extension, accompanied by post-craniotomy changes, consistent with a residual vestibular schwannoma (Fig. 6.1A). Coronal contrast-enhanced MRI shows the lesion in the left CPA exerting mass effect on the brainstem (Fig. 6.1B). Sagittal contrast-enhanced MRI confirms the non-homogeneous contrast-enhancing lesion in the left CPA (Fig. 6.1C). A dose-volume histogram illustrates the prescribed radiation dose coverage for the tumour, ensuring minimal exposure to the brainstem (Fig. 6.1D).

Follow-up imaging indicated an increase in lesion size, and she was subsequently scheduled for an additional GKRS treatment.

GK PROTOCOL

MRI was used to define the lesion boundaries, and a stereotactic head frame ensured precise targeting. The dose was carefully planned to achieve effective tumour control while minimising radiation to surrounding critical structures. In January 2018, the patient's lesion received a prescription isodose of 12 Gy at 50 % to the margin (maximum dose - 24.1 Gy). A total of 11 isocenters were used, with a beam-on time of 37 minutes, achieving 99% coverage and 80% selectivity Maximum point dose spillage to brainstem was 11.6 Gy which was within the safe limits.

FOLLOW UP

The lesion initially remained stable but the started gradually increasing in size by the end of third-year follow-up. The lesion was followed for two years and was planned

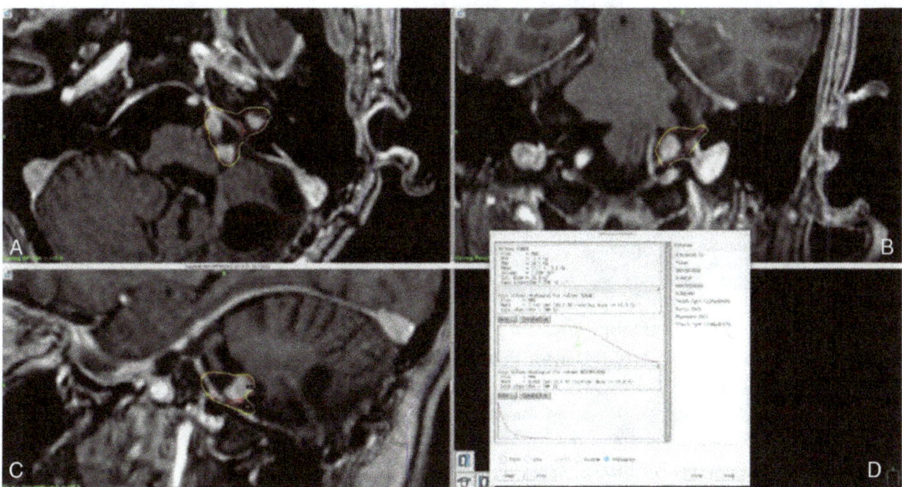

FIGURE 6.1 Magnetic resonance imaging (MRI) axial T1-weighted contrast-enhanced images reveal an ill-defined non-homogeneous contrast-enhancing extra-axial lesion in the left cerebellopontine angle (CPA) with intracanalicular extension, accompanied by post-craniotomy changes, consistent with a residual vestibular schwannoma (A). Coronal contrast-enhanced MRI shows the lesion in the left CPA exerting mass effect on the brainstem (B). Sagittal contrast-enhanced MRI confirms the non-homogeneous contrast-enhancing lesion in the left CPA (C). A dose-volume histogram illustrates the prescribed radiation dose coverage for the tumour, ensuring minimal exposure to the brainstem (D).

for redo GKRS in 2023 as the tumour has demonstrated significant continued growth (Fig. 6.2). Subsequently, the patient's lesion received a repeat maximum dose of 20.2 Gy with a prescription isodose of 12 Gy at 50 % to the margin. A total of 11 isocenters were used, with a beam-on time of 95 minutes, achieving 95% coverage and 67% selectivity. The patient showed no adverse effects or cranial neuropathies at the 6-year follow-up. An MRI at the 6-year mark revealed a significant tumour control of the VS (Fig. 6.3).

DISCUSSION

The most common initial presentation of VS is unilateral hearing loss, typically presenting as a subtle reduction in clarity but occasionally as sudden hearing loss, though this is rare. Tinnitus, often unilateral, frequently manifests as a high-pitched ringing or buzzing sound that can be continuous or intermittent. Vertigo is unexpectedly uncommon due to the tumour's slow growth, but many patients report sensation of unsteadiness or disequilibrium. Facial nerve involvement is rare in smaller tumours but may occur in larger VSs, where nerve compression can lead to facial weakness. Headaches are more commonly associated with larger tumours that obstruct cerebrospinal fluid (CSF) flow. Larger VSs may also compress the cerebellar hemisphere, causing cerebellar symptoms such as ataxia, dysmetria, or intention tremor.

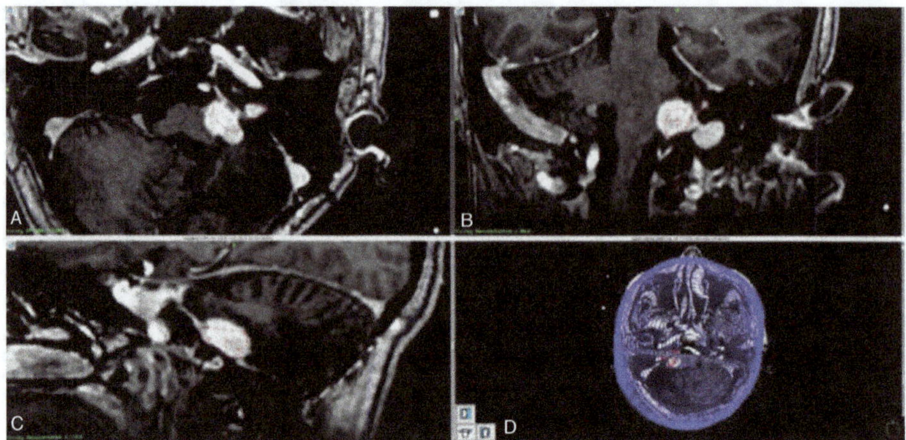

FIGURE 6.2   Follow-up MRI axial, coronal, and sagittal T1-weighted contrast-enhanced images show a well-defined, homogeneous contrast-enhancing extra-axial lesion in the left cerebellopontine angle (CPA) with intracanalicular extension. The imaging findings indicate an increase in the size of the vestibular schwannoma (A–D).

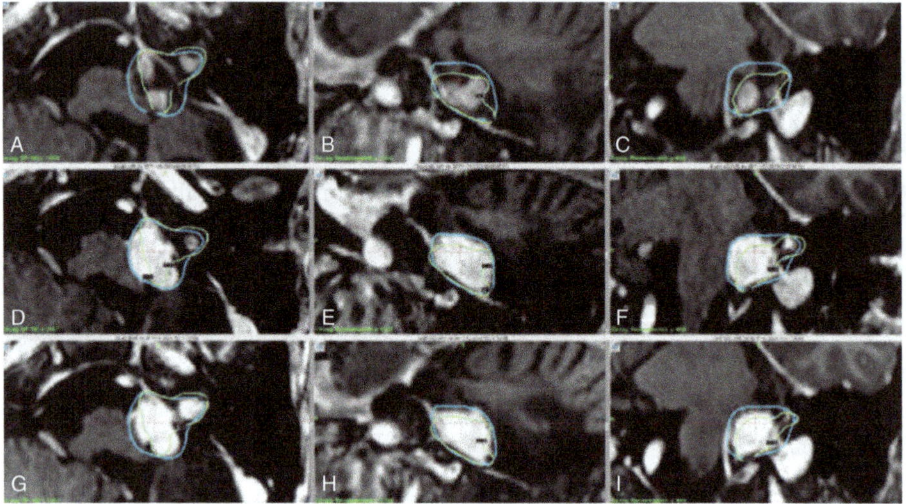

FIGURE 6.3   MRI axial sagittal and coronal section T1-weighted contrast-enhanced images illustrate a comparative analysis of a left vestibular schwannoma across three stages: the initial Gamma Knife radiosurgery (GKRS) treatment (A–C), the second GKRS session (D–F), and the follow-up at one year post-second treatment (G–I).

Hearing loss in VS is typically sensorineural due to cochlear nerve compression or reduced blood flow to the inner ear, often leading to gradual, high-frequency hearing loss, though sudden loss may occur with acute ischemia. Tinnitus may result from abnormal nerve activity due to compression, while the brain's compensatory changes can further amplify this effect. Vertigo in VS is uncommon as the brain adapts to slow vestibular nerve involvement, often resulting in a general sense of unsteadiness rather than true vertigo. As the tumour expands within the internal auditory canal (IAC) and CPA, it may compress the facial nerve, causing numbness or weakness, or obstruct CSF flow, leading to hydrocephalus and increased intracranial pressure (ICP), which can present with headaches, nausea, and cognitive changes. Large VS tumours can also compress the cerebellum, disrupting coordination and balance and impairing motor control and gait.

The present case presents with left-sided sensorineural hearing loss, left facial numbness and weakness, accompanied by gait ataxia. Magnetic resonance imaging (MRI) axial T1-weighted contrast-enhanced images reveal an ill-defined non-homogeneous contrast-enhancing extra-axial in the left cerebellopontine angle (CPA) with intracanalicular extension exerting mass effect on the brainstem, accompanied by post-craniotomy changes, consistent with a residual vestibular schwannoma. This radiological finding depicting significant mass lesion originating from the IAC and compressing the brainstem explains the left-sided hearing loss along with gait ataxia. Due to the lesion's location and expected favourable outcome with Gamma knife radiosurgery, the patient was taken up for repeat gamma knife radiosurgery.

The responses to Gamma Knife treatment can be categorised as follows: regression (<10% reduction in tumour volume), stabilisation (volume change within 10%), enlargement (>10% increase in volume not requiring further treatment), and failure (uncontrolled tumour growth necessitating additional treatment and/or the development of serious radiation-related side effects).[7] Tumour control rates following repeat SRS for VS have been reported as high as 92–100%, though the risk of mild facial and trigeminal nerve dysfunction is higher compared to the first SRS.[2,8] The volumetric response of the tumour after the second SRS procedure did not correlate with its response to the first treatment. Therefore, the authors suggest that repeat SRS may be warranted even for tumours that showed no volumetric reduction and continued to grow after the initial treatment. An essential factor for effective tumour control is the prescribed marginal dose, with recommended doses generally above 11 Gy for initial or repeat Gamma Knife treatments. Lower doses, such as those under 10 Gy, have been associated with higher rates of treatment failure.[9]

The definition of treatment failure and the timing of retreatment after initial SRS failure in VS remain controversial. Key factors to consider before concluding failure include: a follow-up duration of at least 2 years (ideally 3–4 years unless symptomatic mass effect is present) and consistent growth across at least three MRI time points. Retreatment should be delayed if no symptomatic mass effect is observed. Indications for retreatment with either microsurgery or repeat SRS depend on tumour-specific factors like volume and edema, and patient-specific factors such as age, symptoms, comorbidities. TTE, occurring in 17–45% of cases typically within 3–9 months post-treatment, should not be mistaken for true progressions. [10-12] TTE is often accompanied by temporary loss of central contrast enhancement, making subsequent volumetric assessment essential.[13] At least two years of follow-up is recommended to distinguish transient swelling from actual growth. Retreatment considerations also include symptoms like trigeminal neuropathy, facial neuropathy, and major vestibular imbalance.

For retreatment, it's essential to confirm that the initial SRS was unsuccessful. Typically, retreatment is indicated for small- to medium-sized VS (under 3 cm) with documented growth. SRS remains the preferred retreatment option as it avoids risks associated with invasive surgery, including meningitis, hydrocephalus, and CSF leakage. Trigeminal neuropathy occurs in up to 10% of cases after repeat SRS, particularly when the tumour is near or contacting the trigeminal nerve.[14] Key considerations include the tumour's proximity to the trigeminal REZ, which should ideally be outside the prescription isodose line, and ensuring a steep dose gradient at the brainstem interface. Facial neuropathy is uncommon after repeated SRS, with an incidence of up to 5%, similar to rates observed following the first SRS.[14] Preserving hearing is often the most difficult aspect after a second Gamma Knife procedure, with cochlear dosing well-documented for initial SRS but less so for repeat treatments.[15]

TAKE HOME MESSAGE

Repeat radiosurgery is a viable treatment option for large-volume recurrent or progressive VS, although associated with risk of facial neuropathy and hearing loss, highlighting the importance for meticulous planning and patient selection.

REFERENCES

1. Lees KA, Tombers NM, Link MJ, et al. Natural History of Sporadic Vestibular Schwannoma: A Volumetric Study of Tumor Growth. *Otolaryngol Head Neck Surg.* 2018;159(3):535-542.

2. Iorio-Morin C, Liscak R, Vladyka V, et al. Repeat Stereotactic Radiosurgery for Progressive or Recurrent Vestibular Schwannomas. *Neurosurgery.* 2019;85(4):535-542.

3. Perry A, Graffeo CS, Copeland WR 3rd, et al. Microsurgery for Recurrent Vestibular Schwannoma After Previous Gross Total Resection. *Otol Neurotol.* 2017;38(6):882-888.

4. Ogino A, Lunsford LD, Long H, et al. Stereotactic radiosurgery as the first-line treatment for intracanalicular vestibular schwannomas. *J Neurosurg.* 2021;135(4):1051-1057. Published 2021 Feb 5.

5. Hafez RFA, Morgan MS, Fahmy OM, Hassan HT. Outcomes of Gamma Knife Surgery retreatment for growing vestibular schwannoma and review of the literature. *Clin Neurol Neurosurg.* 2020;198:106171.

6. van de Langenberg R, Hanssens PE, van Overbeeke JJ, et al. Management of large vestibular schwannoma. Part I. Planned subtotal resection followed by Gamma Knife surgery: radiological and clinical aspects. *J Neurosurg.* 2011;115(5):875-884.

7. Yomo S, Arkha Y, Delsanti C, Roche PH, Thomassin JM, Régis J. Repeat gamma knife surgery for regrowth of vestibular schwannomas. *Neurosurgery.* 2009;64(1):48-55.

8. Fu VX, Verheul JB, Beute GN, et al. Retreatment of vestibular schwannoma with Gamma Knife radiosurgery: clinical outcome, tumor control, and review of literature. *J Neurosurg.* 2018;129(1):137-145.

9. Kondziolka D, Lunsford LD, McLaughlin MR, Flickinger JC. Long-term outcomes after radiosurgery for acoustic neuromas. *N Engl J Med.* 1998;339(20):1426-1433.

10. Nagano O, Higuchi Y, Serizawa T, et al. Transient expansion of vestibular schwannoma following stereotactic radiosurgery. *J Neurosurg.* 2008;109(5):811-816.

11. Yu CP, Cheung JY, Leung S, Ho R. Sequential volume mapping for confirmation of negative growth in vestibular schwannomas treated by gamma knife radiosurgery. *J Neurosurg.* 2000;93 Suppl 3:82-89.

12. Hasegawa T, Kida Y, Yoshimoto M, Koike J, Goto K. Evaluation of tumor expansion after stereotactic radiosurgery in patients harboring vestibular schwannomas. *Neurosurgery.* 2006;58(6):1119-1128.

13. Nakamura H, Jokura H, Takahashi K, Boku N, Akabane A, Yoshimoto T. Serial follow-up MR imaging after gamma knife radiosurgery for vestibular schwannoma. *AJNR Am J Neuroradiol.* 2000;21(8):1540-1546.

14. Balossier A, Régis J, Reyns N, et al. Repeat stereotactic radiosurgery for progressive vestibular schwannomas after previous radiosurgery: a systematic review and meta-analysis. *Neurosurg Rev.* 2021;44(6):3177-3188.

15. Massager N, Nissim O, Delbrouck C, et al. Irradiation of cochlear structures during vestibular schwannoma radiosurgery and associated hearing outcome. *J Neurosurg.* 2007;107(4):733-739.

7 Gamma Knife Radiosurgery for Vestibular Schwannomas in NF2

Dattaraj Parmanand Sawarkar | Abhishek Kumar

KEY LEARNING POINTS

1. Vestibular Schwannomas (VS) in NF2 carry worse prognosis than solitary VS.
2. Hearing preservation takes precedence over tumour control, with even larger tumours with serviceable hearing being managed conservatively.
3. In case of progressive tumours, Bivacizumab may play a role in tumour control.

INTRODUCTION

Vestibular schwannomas are benign tumours arising from the inferior division of the vestibular nerve in cerebello-pontine angle, internal acoustic meatus, or both.[1] Bilateral vestibular schwannomas are seen in patients with NF-2, caused by mutations in the gene encoding Merlin protein located on chromosome 22.[2] Though benign and slow-growing, these tumours can cause a multitude of symptoms such as hearing loss, tinnitus, facial nerve dysfunction, impairment of lower cranial nerves, cerebellar dysfunction, etc. The management of vestibular schwannomas has evolved significantly since Hirsh, and colleagues first described radiosurgery for such patients.[3] Evidence-based practice supports the use of GKRS in patients with vestibular schwannoma having a cisternal diameter of less than 30 mm.[4] GKRS also carries the best prognosis in terms of facial nerve outcome and hearing preservation.[4] However, GKRS is not without risks and complications. In a series presented by Kedia et al., 11% of the patients required salvage therapy for the treatment of adverse radiation effects.[5]

REPRESENTATIVE CASE

HISTORY & EXAMINATION

A 37-year-old gentleman presented to our OPD with complaints of bilateral hearing loss, Left > Right for 3 years, imbalance in walking for 1 year, and recent onset facial asymmetry. On neurological examination, he had B/L SNHL, grade 2 facial palsy on the left side with intact lower cranial nerves bilaterally and positive cerebellar signs. Pure tone audiometry revealed moderate hearing loss on the right side and complete hearing loss on the left side.

IMAGING

On MR imaging, the patient was found to have bilateral vestibular schwannomas, signifying NF-2, with a larger tumour on the left side, measuring $8 \times 9 \times 8$ mm and $14 \times 12 \times 12$ mm respectively.

DECISION MAKING

Given the small size of both tumours, no brainstem compression, and no edema or hydrocephalus, the patient was planned for Primary GKRS.

DOSE PLANNING

We planned a 12 Gy dose at 50% isodense for both tumours, with the constraints of a maximum of 12 Gy for the brainstem and 4.5 Gy for cochlea on both sides. As per the plan, 98% of right acoustic schwannoma receives >= 12 Gy, and 96% of left acoustic schwannoma receives >=12 Gy dose safeguarding brainstem and cochlea.

FOLLOW-UP

At the 4-year follow-up, the patient is doing well, with a reduction in the size of both tumours and no fresh complaints.

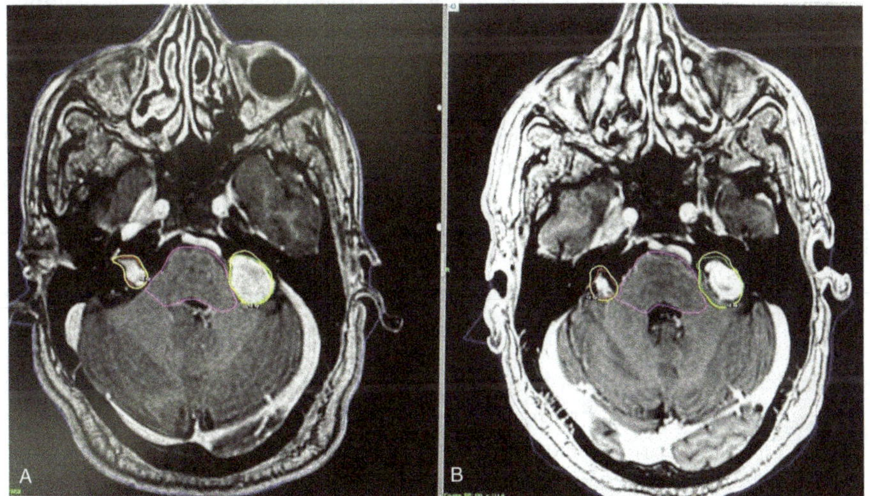

FIGURE 7.1   (A) Shows MR image of the patient at the time of planning GKRS. (B) shows post-GKRS MR image of the same patient at 4 years follow-up with excellent disease control.

DISCUSSION

Management of vestibular schwannomas depends on several factors such as the age of the patient, presence or absence of comorbidities, size of the lesion, associated hydrocephalus/brainstem compression, cisternal or intra-canalicular location of the tumour, etc. The primary goal in the treatment of vestibular schwannoma is tumour control without the need for additional interventions, while secondary outcomes focus on facial nerve function and hearing preservation. Elderly patients with smaller tumours and predominant hearing loss are candidates for conservative management.[6]

Micro-surgical excision of tumours with advanced operating microscopes, improved radiological sequences, intra-operative neuromonitoring and surgical skills have heralded an era of excellent outcomes with significantly reduced mortality and morbidity.[7] However, the risks associated with intracranial surgery, such as mortality, CSF leak, facial nerve damage, and meningitis, remain a concern.[7]

GKRS is a non-invasive alternative therapy for patients with smaller tumours and offers control rates similar to microsurgical excision.[1,7] With improvements in radiological techniques, planning software and navigation techniques, the brainstem, cochlea and other neural structures can be effectively shielded from radiation, offering better facial and hearing outcomes.[8] Also, the effective dose of radiation required for optimum results has reduced significantly over the last two decades, with a marginal dose of 12 Gy and a maximum dose of 20-25 Gy.[7] Sharma et al., in their study on NF-2 patients with bilateral vestibular schwannomas treated with GKRS, reported 66.7% hearing preservation in patients with prior useful hearing, along with tumour control in 87.5% of patients at 27 months of follow-up.[9] Pollock et al. found better outcomes for GKRS patients than for surgery patients using a health status questionnaire, though most of the positive effects were seen within 3 months post-treatment.[10]

When compared to Microsurgery, GKRS carries minimal risks and complications. During a 10-year follow-up, Kedia et al. reported adverse radiation effects in just 11% of the patients, who required either redo GKRS or surgical management.[5] Other studies have noted new-onset hearing loss after GKRS owing to the overlapping of dose margins with cochlea or cochlear nuclei in brainstem.[11] Fractionated stereotactic radiotherapy (SRT) has emerged as another non-invasive tool for managing vestibular schwannoma.[12] Available evidence suggests better hearing preservation and lower cranial neuropathy with fractionated SRT than with GKRS.[12]

TAKE HOME MESSAGE

- Management options for VS include a wait-and-watch policy, gamma knife radio-surgery, fractionated radiotherapy or microsurgery.
- GKRS is the best treatment modality for NF2-related vestibular schwannomas with a cisternal diameter less than 30 mm.
- GKRS carries a small risk of adverse radiation effects that include worsening facial weakness, facial numbness, facial pain, and hydrocephalus.

REFERENCES

1. Karpinos M, Teh BS, Zeck O, et al. Treatment of acoustic neuroma: stereotactic radiosurgery vs. microsurgery. *Int J Radiat Oncol Biol Phys*. 2002;54(5):1410-1421.

2. Evans DG, Baser ME, O'Reilly B, et al. Management of the patient and family with neurofibromatosis 2: a consensus conference statement. *Br J Neurosurg*. 2005;19(1):5-12.

3. Hirsch A, Norén G, Anderson H. Audiologic findings after stereotactic radiosurgery in nine cases of acoustic neurinomas. *Acta Otolaryngol*. 1979;88(3-4):155-160.

4. Wolbers JG, Dallenga AH, Mendez Romero A, van Linge A. What intervention is best practice for vestibular schwannomas? A systematic review of controlled studies. *BMJ Open*. 2013;3(2):e001345. Published 2013 Feb 22.

5. Kedia S, Santhoor H, Singh M. Adverse Radiation Effects Following Gamma Knife Radiosurgery. *Neurol India*. 2023;71(Supplement):S59-S67.

6. Smouha EE, Yoo M, Mohr K, Davis RP. Conservative management of acoustic neuroma: a meta-analysis and proposed treatment algorithm. *Laryngoscope*. 2005;115(3):450-454.

7. Myrseth E, Pedersen PH, Møller P, Lund-Johansen M. Treatment of vestibular schwannomas. Why, when and how?. *Acta Neurochir (Wien)*. 2007;149(7):647-660.

8. Linskey ME. Hearing preservation in vestibular schwannoma stereotactic radiosurgery: what really matters?. *J Neurosurg*. 2008;109 Suppl:129-136.

9. Sharma MS, Singh R, Kale SS, Agrawal D, Sharma BS, Mahapatra AK. Tumor control and hearing preservation after Gamma Knife radiosurgery for vestibular schwannomas in neurofibromatosis type 2. *J Neurooncol*. 2010;98(2):265-270.

10. Pollock BE, Driscoll CL, Foote RL, et al. Patient outcomes after vestibular schwannoma management: a prospective comparison of microsurgical resection and stereotactic radiosurgery. *Neurosurgery*. 2006;59(1):77-85.

11. Kim KM, Park CK, Chung HT, Paek SH, Jung HW, Kim DG. Long-term Outcomes of Gamma Knife Stereotactic Radiosurgery of Vestibular Schwannomas. *J Korean Neurosurg Soc*. 2007;42(4):286-292.

12. Abram S, Rosenblatt P, Holcomb S. Stereotactic radiation techniques in the treatment of acoustic schwannomas. 2007. *Neurosurg Clin N Am*. 2008;19(2):367-viii.

8 Gamma-Knife Stereotactic Radiosurgery for Large Vestibular Schwannoma

Satish Verma | Deepak Agrawal

KEY LEARNING POINTS

1. Large VS (>8 cc) can be effectively managed with GKRS in carefully selected cases.
2. Large VS presenting without disabling symptoms may be offered upfront GKRS. Less than 10% of cases require a surgical intervention later on.
3. Elderly patients with multiple co-morbidities and high anaesthesia risk may be suitable for GKRS.
4. GKRS provides better cranial nerve function preservation.
5. Serviceable hearing at treatment is likely to be preserved longer than microsurgical controls.

INTRODUCTION

Management of large vestibular schwannoma remains a significant challenge. The standard treatment is microsurgical maximal safe resection, with preservation of the facial nerve. However, many patients, even with large vestibular schwannomas (VS) are not symptomatic for the mass effect on the brainstem and few of them still retain serviceable hearing. Many of them present at an advanced age may have poor functional status, whether on mandatory anticoagulation or other co-morbidities. There are rare cases in which a large residual lesion remains after a failed micro-surgical resection due to various reasons, and the patient refuses any further surgery. Because of these practical concerns, many authors have evaluated the role of GKRS in large vestibular schwannoma. There is no clear definition of 'large' vestibular schwannomas, with almost all studies defining large tumours with volumes >8-10 cc. Conventionally, tumours greater than 2.5 cm in diameter (equivalent to a volume of about 8 cubic centimetres (cc) were not considered suitable for stereotactic radiosurgery (SRS) because of poor tumour control and significant long-term radiation-induced toxicity.[1-3] Recent studies suggest that GKRS for lesions more than 3 cm or volume ≥14 cc is a feasible option, with acceptable tumour control and adverse radiation effects.[4-7] Hypo-fractionated GKRS has shown similar results for large vestibular schwannoma.

REPRESENTATIVE CASE

HISTORY & EXAMINATION

A 55-year-old male, an engineer by profession, presented with progressive hearing loss on the right side for 9 months, which was later associated with tinnitus and vertigo for 3 months. The symptoms were not accompanied by facial sensory loss, paresthesia or neuralgia, facial deviation, gait ataxia, headache, or vomiting. On examination, the patient had reduced hearing on the right side. Rinne's test was positive bilaterally and Weber's test lateralised towards the right side. Audiometric evaluation with pure tone audiometry (PTA) was consistent with profound sensory-neural hearing loss on the right side of >70 decibel at 2 kiloHertz (kHz) frequency. The rest of the neurological examination was within normal limits.

IMAGING

Contrast-enhanced MRI of the brain demonstrated a large heterogeneously enhancing lesion in the right cerebello-pontine angle, extending into the internal auditory meatus and causing mass effect on cerebellar peduncle and brainstem without obliterating the fourth ventricle. Hydrocephalus was absent. He was offered GKRS as there were no disabling symptoms attributable to brainstem compression. The hearing was non-serviceable, and the prognosis was explained to the patient.

GK PROTOCOL

Gamma knife was performed on a Leksell Gamma Knife Perfexion unit (Elekta AB, Stockholm, Sweden) with Leksell GammaPlan. Manual AVM segmentation was done for the tumour and Organ-at-risk (OAR) (brainstem and cochlea/modiolus). The total tumour volume was 21.59 cubic centimetres (cc). Inverse planning with optimisation of 19 iso-centres (combinations of 4-, 8- and 16-mm collimators) was performed with a prescription dose of 12 Gy at 50% isodose line to the tumour margin (Fig. 8.1). Further optimisation was done manually to exclude OARs out of the prescribed dose constraints, achieving the following parameters: coverage -90%, selectivity - 98%, and Gradient Index – 2.80. Beam-on time (BOT) was 57.2 minutes with a treatment dose rate of 2.196 Gy/min. The maximum dose to the segmented volumes was as follows: tumour – 24.3 Gy, brainstem – 11.7 Gy and Cochlea – 6.5 Gy (Fig. 8.2). The tumour coverage was intentionally kept at 90% to limit the dose to the brainstem. Still, the marginal dose to >94% of tumour volume was >11.5 Gy. This strategy ensured that not more than 0.1 cc of brainstem received >10 Gy.

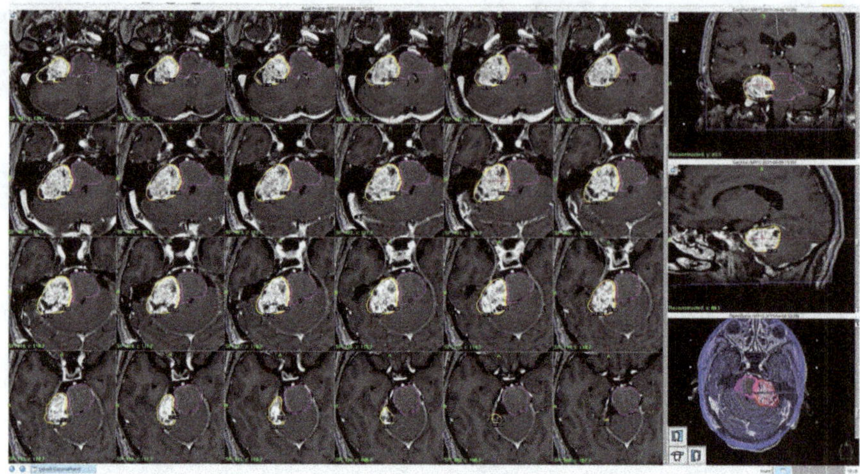

FIGURE 8.1   Gamma Knife planning for the index case. Tumour margin (red), 12 Gy (prescription dose) isodose line (yellow).

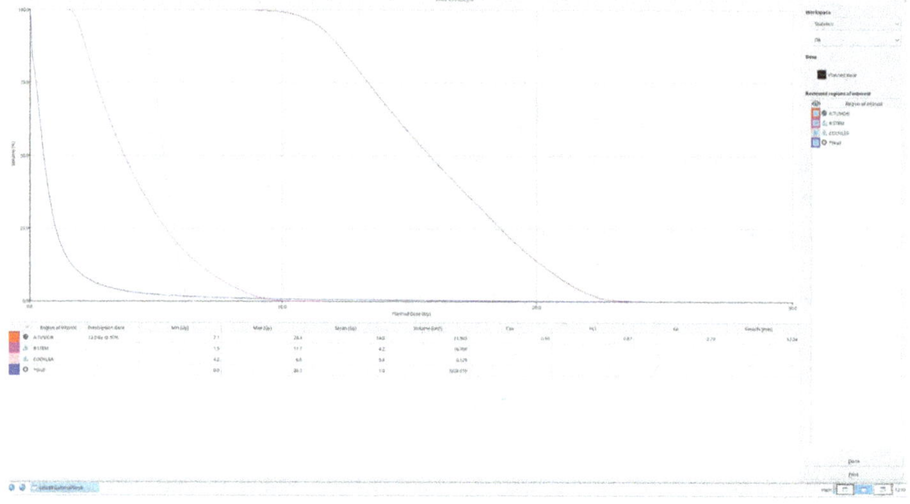

FIGURE 8.2   Dose volume histogram (DVH) for the tumour, brainstem and cochlea.

FOLLOW-UP

The patient tolerated the procedure well. Follow-up clinical visit after 3 months was done and no features of gait ataxia or raised intracranial pressure were observed. Follow-up CEMRI was done annually for the first three years and then after 2 years, which showed a gradual reduction in tumour volume. At the last follow-up available, at 75 months, the residual tumour volume was 7.8 cc (Fig. 8.2). Tinnitus persisted for 6 months post-operatively. Post-GKRS PTA was done after 1 year which showed further impairment to >80 dB loss. This worsening was expected and explained to the patient as the hearing was not serviceable and no attempt was made to preserve hearing.

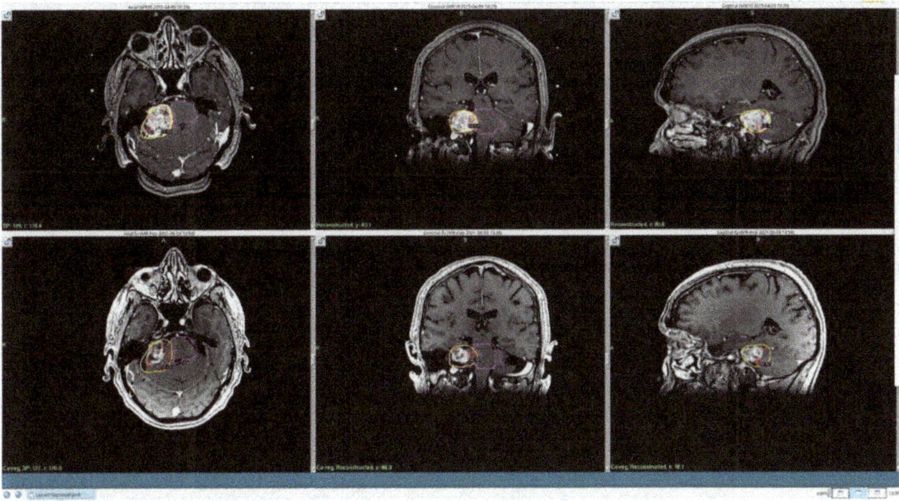

FIGURE 8.3 Follow-up MRI done after 75 months (lower panel) compared to the baseline MRI at the time of GKRS (upper panel) showing marked reduction in tumour size.

DISCUSSION

For large vestibular schwannoma, microsurgery is generally considered the treatment of choice, primarily to reduce the mass effect on the brainstem. However, for various reasons, surgery may not be feasible or refused by the patient. In such cases, GKRS provides an effective, non-invasive modality for good long-term tumour control. Primary GKRS is a standard treatment modality for small vestibular schwannoma presenting without any mass effect on the brainstem or cerebellar peduncles.[6-11] Conventionally, GKRS has been reserved for tumours with volume <8-10 cc or diameter ≤2.5 cc due to concerns regarding poor tumour control rates, acute or subacute tumour swelling leading to an increase in brainstem compression and risk of radiation-induced brain stem injury.[12-14] Microsurgery has its own limitations. The reported rates of serviceable hearing preservation are extremely low with microsurgery. Post-operative facial nerve outcomes are mostly sub-optimal.

Over the last three decades, the role of radiosurgery for large vestibular schwannoma has been assessed by many centres with encouraging results.[15,16] For large VS, the need for microsurgical decompression should be considered depending upon pre-treatment symptom burden, specifically attributable to brainstem compression rather than the tumour size. Recommended ideal candidates are those without symptomatic mass effect and disabling symptoms like ataxia or hemiparesis, with serviceable hearing and with comorbidities that increase the peri-operative procedure and anaesthesia-related risks. The patient's wish to avoid microsurgical resection may be evaluated on an individual basis considering the above-mentioned recommendations. Most of the studies are based on single-fraction GKRS. Hypofractionation

(2-5 fractions) regimens have recently been proposed by many centres due to their potential for treating relatively larger tumour volumes while reducing adverse radiation effects. However, no well-controlled studies are yet available to compare these two methods of GKRS.

Tumour control rates of 57%-100% are reported at follow-up periods spanning from 21-156 months.[17] A recent study reported a tumour control rate of 91% at a mean follow-up of 78.5 months.[18] Cranial nerve preservation rates are high. Reported rates of preservation of serviceable hearing are up to 56.5% at 2-year follow-up, ranging from 37%-75.1%. Similarly, excellent facial nerve preservation rates are reported, reaching nearly 100% (range 99.9%-100%). Complications related to trigeminal nerves remain very low, <6% (range 2.9% – 9.2%). However, new-onset vestibular symptoms (tinnitus and vertigo) are reported up to 9%.[18] Radiosurgery offers an acceptable tumour control rate of 89% at 6-year and 84.5% at 10-year follow-up.

A marginal dose of 12-13 Gy is recommended for good tumour control. To avoid adverse radiation effects on the brainstem, a maximum point dose of <12 Gy and a maximum dose of <10 Gy to a volume of 0.1 cc is practised. A maximum point dose of up to 15 Gy is accepted at many centres. Marginal dose <13 Gy and early pseudo-progression predicts deterioration of facial nerve function. Tumour volume less than 10 cc and non-cystic schwannoma predict good facial nerve function. For hearing preservation, the recommended mean dose or point dose to the cochlea and modiolus is <4 Gy. Patients with better hearing (Gardner-Robertson grade 1) at the time of GKRS and less than 60 years of age predict better hearing preservation. Salvage resection may still be required in cases who fail to respond to GKRS and this possibility must be clearly conveyed to the patient. Few cases required further surgical intervention in the form of either ventriculoperitoneal shunt (VP shunt) to manage hydrocephalus or microsurgical resection to salvage symptomatic brainstem compression. Shunting may be needed in up to 5% of cases, and salvage resection may be required in up to 8% in most of the series.

Cystic VS are a particular entity where the role of GKRS is unclear, especially in large cystic VS. Due to their unique characteristics like unpredictable biological behaviour—marked by rapid cyst expansion, haemorrhage and adherence to brainstem and cranial nerves—complete microsurgical resection is difficult and associated with poor facial nerve function and hearing preservation rates, as compared to solid VS. Initially considered as poorly responsive to radiosurgery, recent studies have conclusively shown that cystic VS do respond well to radiosurgery, with tumour shrinkage rates up to 92%.[19]

Upfront GKRS for large VS is effective for elderly patients. The incidence of co-morbidities and frailty increases with age. Many of the patients in this age group are on mandatory anticoagulation or antiplatelet medications for various reasons. A recent study assessed the role of GKRS in large VS in elderly patients >65 years. Tumour control rates were 96% at 5 years and 86.2% at 10 years. Additionally, the actuarial serviceable hearing preservation rate was 51% while the rate for facial nerve function preservation or improvement reached 91% in 10 years.

TAKE HOME MESSAGE

Gamma Knife radiosurgery for large VS–either upfront or post-resection–is an effective treatment option in carefully selected cases without any disabling symptoms due to brainstem compression. Patient-related factors like advanced age, co-morbidities and patient refusal may be important in decision-making. Serviceable hearing rates are much better with GKRS even for large VS. Facial nerve and trigeminal nerve outcomes are better with GKRS. Presentations with trigeminal neuralgia or hemifacial spasm are ideally managed with microsurgical decompression. Patients should be properly conveyed that GKRS may aggravate symptoms and may require a surgical intervention.

REFERENCES

1. Kondziolka D, Lunsford LD. Radiosurgery of meningiomas. *Neurosurg Clin N Am.* 1992;3(1):219-230.
2. Lunsford LD KD, Flickinger JC. Stereotactic radiosurgery of meningioma. Gamma Knife Brain Surgery. Karger; 1998.
3. Kondziolka D LL, Linskey ME, Flickinger JC. Skull base radiosurgery. McGraw Hill; 1993.
4. Haselsberger K, Maier T, Dominikus K, et al. Staged gamma knife radiosurgery for large critically located benign meningiomas: evaluation of a series comprising 20 patients. *J Neurol Neurosurg Psychiatry.* 2009;80(10):1172-1175.
5. Pendl G, Unger F, Papaefthymiou G, Eustacchio S. Staged radiosurgical treatment for large benign cerebral lesions. *J Neurosurg.* 2000;93 Suppl 3:107-112.
6. Rashid A, Memon MA, Ahmed U, et al. Multisession stereotactic radiosurgery for large benign brain tumors of >3cm- early clinical outcomes. *J Radiosurg SBRT.* 2012;2(1):29-40.
7. Tuniz F, Soltys SG, Choi CY, et al. Multisession cyberknife stereotactic radiosurgery of large, benign cranial base tumors: preliminary study. *Neurosurgery.* 2009;65(5):898-907.
8. Davidson L, Fishback D, Russin JJ, et al. Postoperative Gamma Knife surgery for benign meningiomas of the cranial base. *Neurosurg Focus.* 2007;23(4):E6.
9. Iwai Y, Yamanaka K, Nakajima H. The treatment of skull base meningiomas--combining surgery and radiosurgery. *J Clin Neurosci.* 2001;8(6):528-533.
10. Ganz JC, Reda WA, Abdelkarim K. Gamma Knife surgery of large meningiomas: early response to treatment. *Acta Neurochir (Wien).* 2009;151(1):1-8.
11. Metellus P, Regis J, Muracciole X, et al. Evaluation of fractionated radiotherapy and gamma knife radiosurgery in cavernous sinus meningiomas: treatment strategy. *Neurosurgery.* 2005;57(5):873-886.
12. Bledsoe JM, Link MJ, Stafford SL, Park PJ, Pollock BE. Radiosurgery for large-volume (> 10 cm3) benign meningiomas. *J Neurosurg.* 2010;112(5):951-956.
13. Flannery TJ, Kano H, Lunsford LD, et al. Long-term control of petroclival meningiomas through radiosurgery. *J Neurosurg.* 2010;112(5):957-964.
14. Nam TK, Lee JI, Jung YJ, et al. Gamma knife surgery for brain metastases in patients harboring four or more lesions: survival and prognostic factors. *J Neurosurg.* 2005;102 Suppl:147-150.
15. Yang HC, Kano H, Awan NR, et al. Gamma Knife radiosurgery for larger-volume vestibular schwannomas. Clinical article. *J Neurosurg.* 2011;114(3):801-807.

16. Inoue HK. Low-dose radiosurgery for large vestibular schwannomas: long-term results of functional preservation. *J Neurosurg.* 2005;102 Suppl:111-113.
17. van de Langenberg R, Hanssens PE, Verheul JB, et al. Management of large vestibular schwannoma. Part II. Primary Gamma Knife surgery: radiological and clinical aspects. *J Neurosurg.* 2011;115(5):885-893.
18. Szymoniuk M, Kochański M, Wilk K, et al. Stereotactic radiosurgery for Koos grade IV vestibular schwannoma: a systematic review and meta-analysis. *Acta Neurochir (Wien).* 2024;166(1):101. Published 2024 Feb 23.
19. Peker S, Samanci Y, Ozdemir IE, Kunst HPM, Eekers DBP, Temel Y. Long-term results of upfront, single-session Gamma Knife radiosurgery for large cystic vestibular schwannomas. *Neurosurg Rev.* 2022;46(1):2. Published 2022 Dec 6.

Role of Gamma-Knife in Treating Multiple Meningiomas in NF2 Patients

Kushagra Pandey | Shweta Kedia

KEY LEARNING POINTS

1. Meningiomas associated with NF2 are dynamic and require close follow-up.
2. Despite Meningiomas associated with NF2 being usually Gr 1, these patients carry a worse prognosis.
3. GKRS is an excellent modality to treat Meningiomas associated with NF2.

INTRODUCTION

Neurofibromatosis Type 2 (NF2) is a rare genetic disorder characterised by the development of multiple tumours within the nervous system. The hallmark of NF2 is the formation of bilateral vestibular schwannomas, which lead to a variety of symptoms such as hearing loss, balance issues, and tinnitus. However, individuals with NF2 are also predisposed to the development of other types of tumours, including meningiomas, which can significantly impact both quality of life and neurological function. It occurs due to the loss of copy number of chromosome 22. Mortality in NF2 patients with meningiomas is around 2.5 times higher than in those without. The management of NF2-associated meningiomas presents unique challenges, particularly when multiple tumours are present, and traditional treatment options, such as surgery and radiation therapy, may not always be viable or effective. Gamma Knife Radiosurgery (GKRS) provides a suitable treatment option. In this chapter, we aim to comprehensively explore the efficacy of GKRS in these patients.

REPRESENTATIVE CASE

HISTORY & EXAMINATION

A 55-year-old male presented with hearing loss in the right ear associated with tinnitus for 10 years and now had complaints of seizures. On eliciting the history, the seizures were focal and involved the left lower limb. On clinical examination, there was no higher mental function abnormality noticed. The hearing loss in the right ear was sensorineural with no other cranial nerve involvement, and no motor and sensory deficit present on the neurological exam. Pure tone audiometry was done for the patient revealed right-sided moderate hearing loss and mild hearing loss in the left ear. The patient had been referred to our centre with the contrast-enhanced MRI for treatment of right-sided Koos grade 2 acoustic schwannoma with gamma knife radiosurgery.

IMAGING

CMRI brain, however, revealed multiple lesions as described in the imaging. The lesions spanned across the supra and infratentorial region and also from the anterior skull base to the posterior tent area. The left CP angle was however clear (Fig. 9.1).

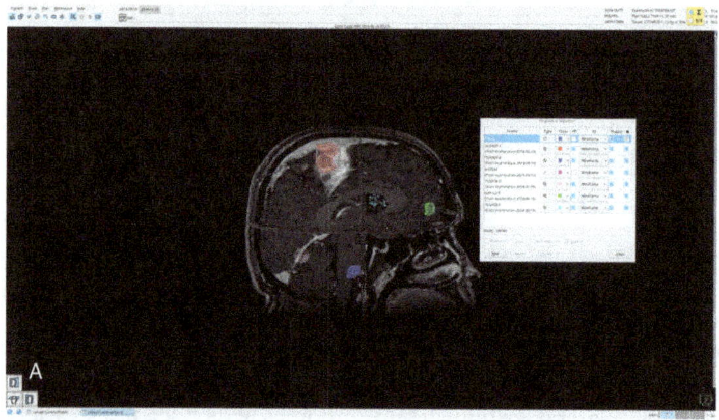

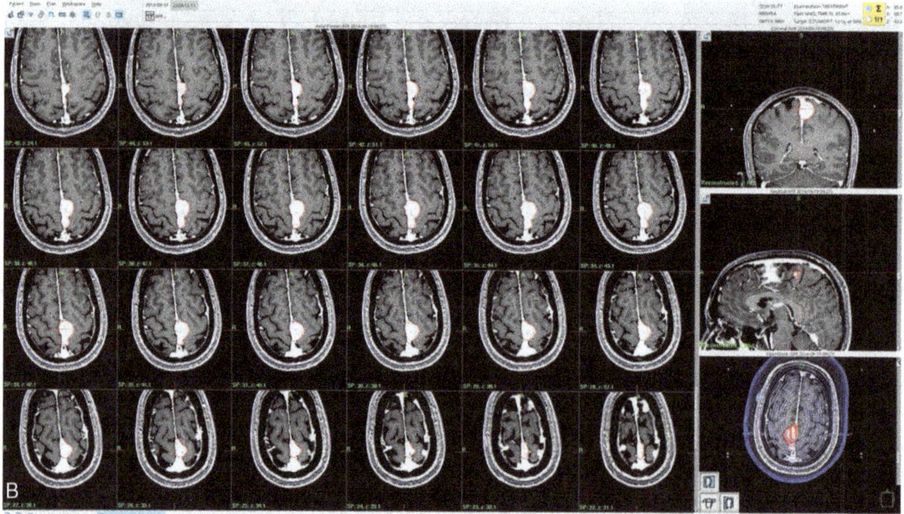

FIGURE 9.1   (A) CEMR brain at the time of first presentation to the centre revealed five lesions located both supra and infratentorial. The lesion was seen in the left middle third para sagittal region, the anterior skull base, left lateral sphenoid wing, tentorial and right cerebello pontine area. (B) The convexity dura in the uppercuts did show pathological changes, not significant enough to be targeted.

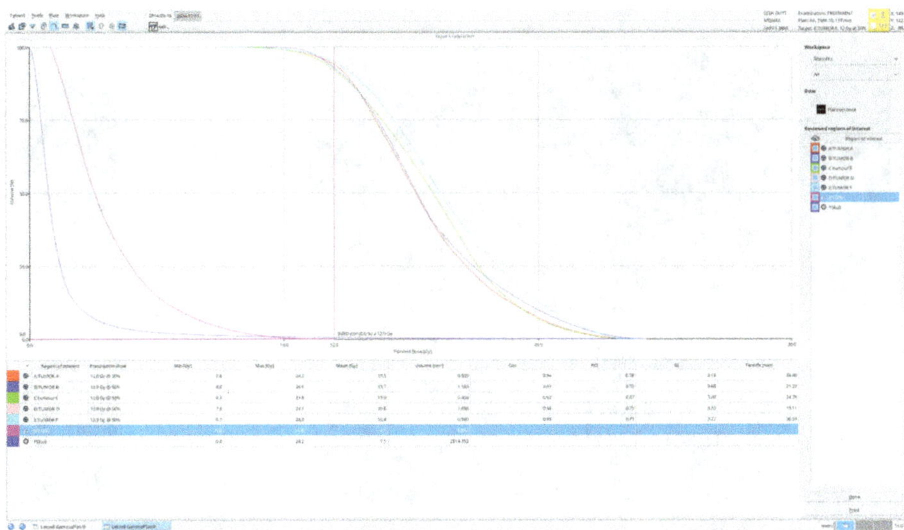

FIGURE 9.2   The figure reveals the dose histogram curve of all the five lesions targeted. The primary GKRS was given to all the lesions with marginal dose of 12 Gy at 50 % isodose line.

GK PROTOCOL

The patient was planned for primary GKRS for all of these lesions. The total tumour volume was 12.732 cc. The Leksell G frame was fixed to get most of the lesions towards the centre of the arc. The contrast MRI was done with a frame in situ to get the stereotactic reference. The planning was then carried out using the Leksell Gamma plan (Fig. 9.2). The lesions and the organs at risk were marked in this case which included the brainstem, optic apparatus and the cochlea. 12 Gy at 50 % isodose line at the margin was prescribed in the standard format. The planning was carried out in a hybrid manner, using both the forward and inverse planning techniques. The goal was to achieve more than 95% coverage with selectivity of more than 0.80. Because of the ageing source of cobalt, the total duration of the treatment was around 137 minutes.

FOLLOW-UP

The patient initially showed a good tumour response on follow-up. However, seven years later, a scan revealed the presence of new lesions. This time there was the presence of left-sided Vestibular schwannoma, and multiple other small meningiomas again distributed, both supra and infra-tentorial. The lesions treated earlier had responded well to GKRS with all of them showing significant reduction in the tumour volume in the follow-up. In view of the small size of all the lesions and the good response to GKRS, the plan was to treat new lesions as well with GKRS. The standard dosing protocol with good coverage and sensitivity was followed (Fig. 9.3).

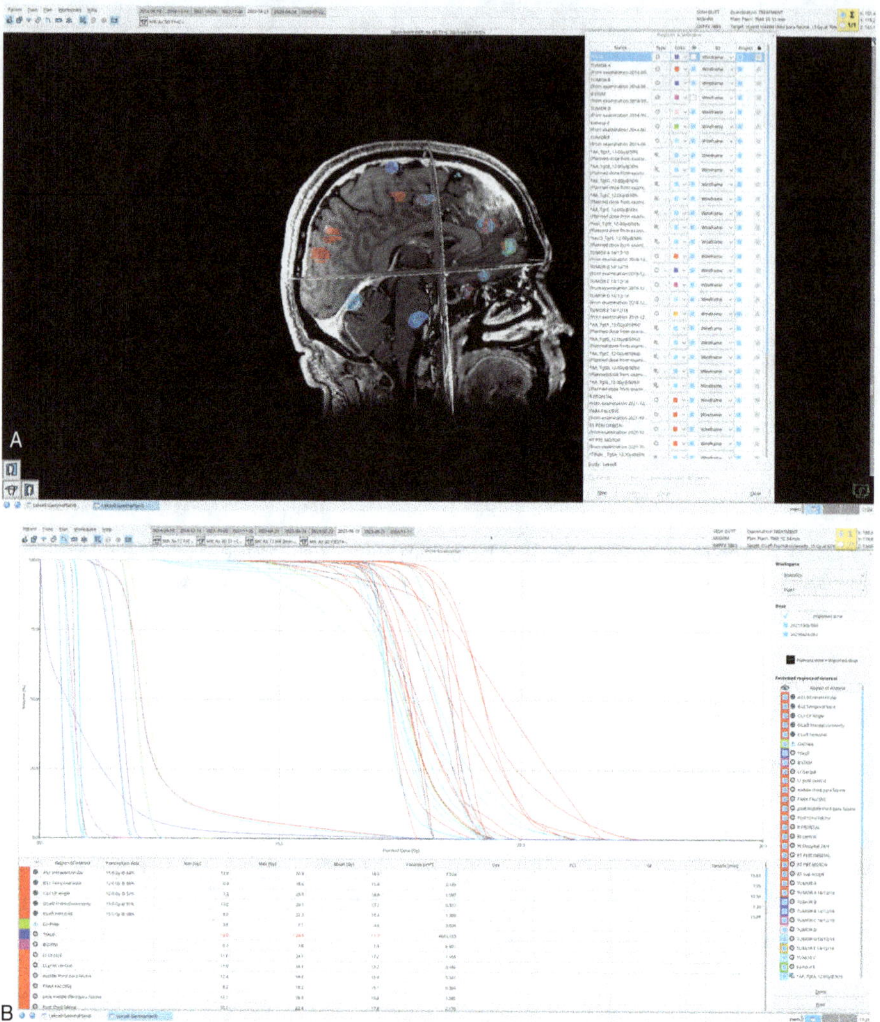

FIGURE 9.3 (A) CEMR brain showing the new lesions that were picked up in the follow-up scan 9 years later and (B) the treatment delivery to each lesion with dose volume histogram curves.

This patient continues to develop newer lesions which are planned for treatment with primary GKRS (Fig. 9.4).

DISCUSSION

Loss-of-function mutations in the NF2 gene result in the development of various CNS tumours, the most common being bilateral vestibular schwannomas. In addition, almost 50% of individuals with NF2 commonly develop meningiomas,[1] often

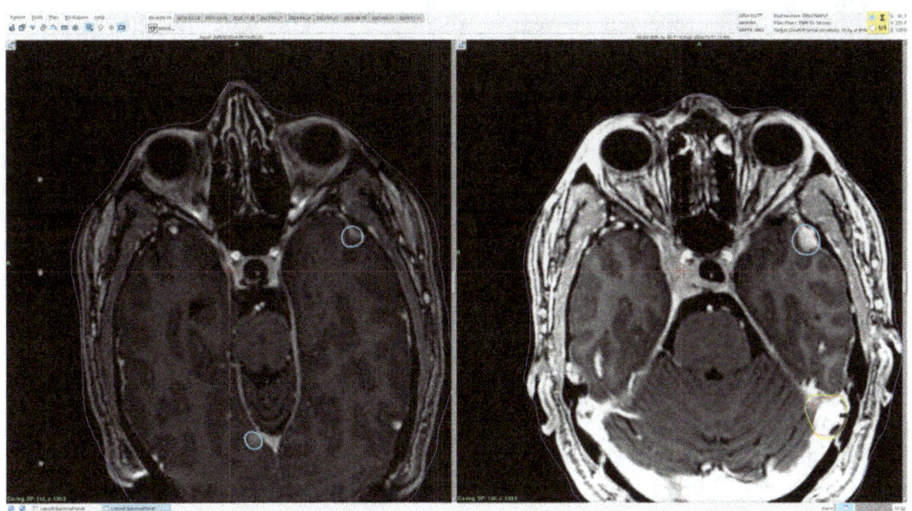

FIGURE 9.4 New lesion at the right cavernous sinus region seen at the 10-year follow-up from initial treatment.

multiple, and occurring throughout the cranial and spinal regions. Histologically, they are usually benign and stable. The more aggressive and symptomatic meningiomas constitute only 4.5% of the total lesions and are classified as grade II or III meningiomas, with a higher rate of recurrence.[1,2] These tumours may arise from various locations, including the parasagittal, falcine, and convexity areas of the brain or the spinal cord. They can cause significant morbidity due to their location, size, and tendency to compress adjacent brain structures, leading to symptoms such as seizures, headaches, and neurological deficits. The presence of meningiomas in patients with NF2 increases the mortality risk by 2.5 times.[1,2]

It is unclear how to treat NF2-associated meningiomas that exhibit symptoms or growth. For small, asymptomatic meningiomas that show little growth over time, observation is a suitable option. Although surgical resection remains the gold standard for treating accessible meningiomas, the presence of multiple tumours, risk of neurological damage, or inoperable tumour locations may complicate the surgery in NF2 patients. While surgery offers the potential for complete tumour removal, Gamma Knife therapy has the advantage of being non-invasive and suitable for multiple tumours, particularly in cases where surgical intervention carries significant risk. To reduce the number of invasive procedures, a non-surgical approach is frequently preferred by both the patient and the surgeon for patients who are anticipated to need therapy over several years. Due to its ability to treat multiple tumours over time and space, GKRS has emerged as a promising treatment option, though limited studies exist on its role for NF2 patients with multiple meningiomatosis.[2,3]

Previous studies report that patients treated with GKRS range from 27 to 54 years. The number of lesions in an individual can vary anywhere between 2 and multiple. Usually, only the growing and symptomatic tumours are considered for treatment. Studies reported 10-year local control rates of more than 96% with no radiation-associated malignancies. Overall survival at 5 and 10 years is 100% and 44%, respectively. Increasing the maximal dose and lower number of meningiomas at presentation predicted better outcomes. Increasing the maximal dose is especially needed for grade 1 tumours. The cumulative 10-year progression-free survival was 94.8%. Radiation-induced adverse effects were seen in 10% of patients. The maximum radiation dosage delivered as suggested by various studies ranges from 20-50 Gy, while the marginal dose ranges from 10-25 Gy. In our practice, we prescribe 12 Gy to the margin of the tumour.[1,3]

Various reports suggest that NF2-linked meningiomas are more prevalent in parasagittal, convexity, and falcine areas than in the skull base. These sites are also associated with increased radiological complications and more peritumoral edema on follow-up imaging. The rates reported for peritumoral edema have been 10-20%, and usually, a short course of steroid therapy is needed for symptomatic management, with significant edematous changes requiring surgical decompression.[2]

Patients with NF2 are usually subjected to radiation-related treatments at a younger age, either post-surgery or upfront. This usually leads to radiation-associated malignancies on longer follow-up. The median follow-up for patients with NF2 is also usually long, ranging from 1-25 years. The radiation therapy in GKRS leads to the second hit of the NF2 gene, which may lead to secondary malignancies, as explained by Knudson's two-hit hypothesis. In our experience of more than 25 years, we have yet to see this complication in NF2 patients. However, longer follow-up periods are needed. Only two new high-grade lesions were found in the 116 NF2 patients treated with GKRS for vestibular schwannomas and meningiomas, which was the biggest series of NF2 patients to date, by Rowe et al. The median follow-up period in their study was 7.7 years. Hence, there does not appear to be an appreciable increase in malignancy (new or transformed) in the post-GKRS NF2 patients.[3]

Familial history is of great significance in NF2 cases. The early age of onset, with hearing loss and an increasing number of meningiomas, are more severe with increased risk of morbidity and mortality. There have been studies on the use of Bevacizumab and mTOR inhibitors in these patients, but they do not have a long-lasting effect. These patients require a multidisciplinary approach for holistic treatment.[1,2]

TAKE HOME MESSAGE

NF2 patients with multiple meningiomas carry a worse prognosis. The meningiomas that are symptomatic and show growth on serial scans need therapeutic intervention. Larger lesions accessible by surgery should be excised. The current advances in radiology have triggered controversy by picking up these lesions at an early stage. GKRS is a good treatment choice in these cases. Most of these meningiomas are grade 1, and therefore, GKRS is delivered following the recommendations for grade I meningiomas. These patients require close follow-up to detect newer lesions.

REFERENCES

1. Liu A, Kuhn EN, Lucas JT Jr, Laxton AW, Tatter SB, Chan MD. Gamma Knife radiosurgery for meningiomas in patients with neurofibromatosis Type 2. *J Neurosurg*. 2015;122(3):536-542.

2. Mohammed N, Hung YC, Xu Z, et al. Neurofibromatosis type 2-associated meningiomas: an international multicenter study of outcomes after Gamma Knife stereotactic radiosurgery. *J Neurosurg*. 2021;136(1):109-114. Published 2021 Jun 18.

3. Ruiz-Garcia H, Trifiletti DM, Mohammed N, et al. Skull Base Meningiomas in Patients with Neurofibromatosis Type 2: An International Multicenter Study Evaluating Stereotactic Radiosurgery. *J Neurol Surg B Skull Base*. 2021;83(Suppl 2):e173-e180. Published 2021 Jan 19.

Gamma Knife Radiosurgery for Parasagittal/Parafalcine Meningiomas

Sandeep Mishra | Kanwaljeet Garg

KEY LEARNING POINTS

1. Meningiomas are common intracranial tumours, with parasagittal and parafalcine locations posing unique challenges due to proximity to critical structures.
2. Contrast-enhanced MRI is the gold standard, with MR venography assessing sinus involvement.
3. GKRS is a safe, minimally invasive alternative to surgery, offering tumour control comparable to Simpson grade I resection.
4. Doses of 12–14 Gy (benign) and 12–20 Gy (high-grade) are used.
5. Post-radiosurgical edema occurs in 7–38% of cases, often managed with corticosteroids.

INTRODUCTION

Meningiomas are most common intracranial extra-axial tumours, arising from arachnoid cap cells of the dura mater, accounting for 13–26% of primary intracranial tumours in adults.[1] Meningiomas are generally benign encapsulated tumours. Common locations include the convexity, parasagittal region, frontobasal area, sphenoid ridge and posterior fossa. Parasagittal and parafalcine meningiomas are particularly significant because of their site and potential to cause neurological deficits by compressing adjacent structures. Current treatment options for meningiomas include observation, microsurgical excision, external beam radiotherapy (EBRT), and stereotactic radiosurgery (SRS).

Observation may be considered for patients with incidentally discovered meningiomas, elderly individuals who are unfit for surgery or have a limited life expectancy, or in cases where the patient opts against surgical intervention. Surgical excision is considered an optimal treatment option when gross total excision is feasible, particularly in convexity or falx meningiomas. However, in parasagittal meningiomas, complete excision is often challenging due to involvement of dural venous sinuses and bridging cortical veins. Subtotal resection carries a high rate of recurrence, with repeated surgeries increasing morbidity due to scarring and further local infiltration. SRS has emerged as a widely established treatment option for these intracranial meningiomas. It offers a relatively safe, minimally invasive option that preserves the patient's functional status, offering an alternative to the binary choice between craniotomy and observation. Progression-free survival (PFS) rates following SRS are equivalent to Simpson Grade 1 resection.[2]

REPRESENTATIVE CASE

HISTORY AND EXAMINATION

A 40-year-old female presented with a dull aching headache, occasional left-sided paraesthesia and numbness, and a single episode of seizure. Her medical history was notable for bilateral chronic suppurative otitis media (CSOM), for which she underwent surgery 10 years ago, resulting in persistent hearing loss. Neurological examination revealed intact higher mental functions but a left-sided conductive hearing loss. Examination of the remaining cranial nerves was normal, and motor strength was preserved bilaterally.

PREOPERATIVE IMAGING

MRI of the brain revealed a 26x23x28 mm right parietal region extra-axial with dural tail and a broad attachment to the falx consistent with a parafalcine meningioma (Fig. 10.1A). Coronal contrast-enhanced MRI shows the lesion in the right parietal region exerting mass effect on the adjacent cortex (Fig. 10.1B). Sagittal contrast-enhanced MRI confirms the homogeneous contrast-enhancing lesion in the right parietal region attached to the falx (Fig. 10.1C).

GK PROTOCOL

She was subsequently scheduled for a primary GKRS treatment. MRI was used to meticulously define the lesion boundaries, and a stereotactic head frame ensured precise targeting. The dose was carefully planned to achieve effective tumour control while minimising radiation to surrounding critical structures. In May 2019, the patient's lesion received a prescription isodose of 12 Gy at 50% to the margin. The lesion was followed for three years through serial imaging and the tumor demonstrated a 50% regression in 39 months (Fig. 10.2).

DISCUSSION

Current evidence does not support including hyperostotic bone within the radiation treatment fields.[3] The dural tail, which may contain tumour cells or represent a reactive process caused by vascular congestion and oedema, poses a dilemma. Includ-

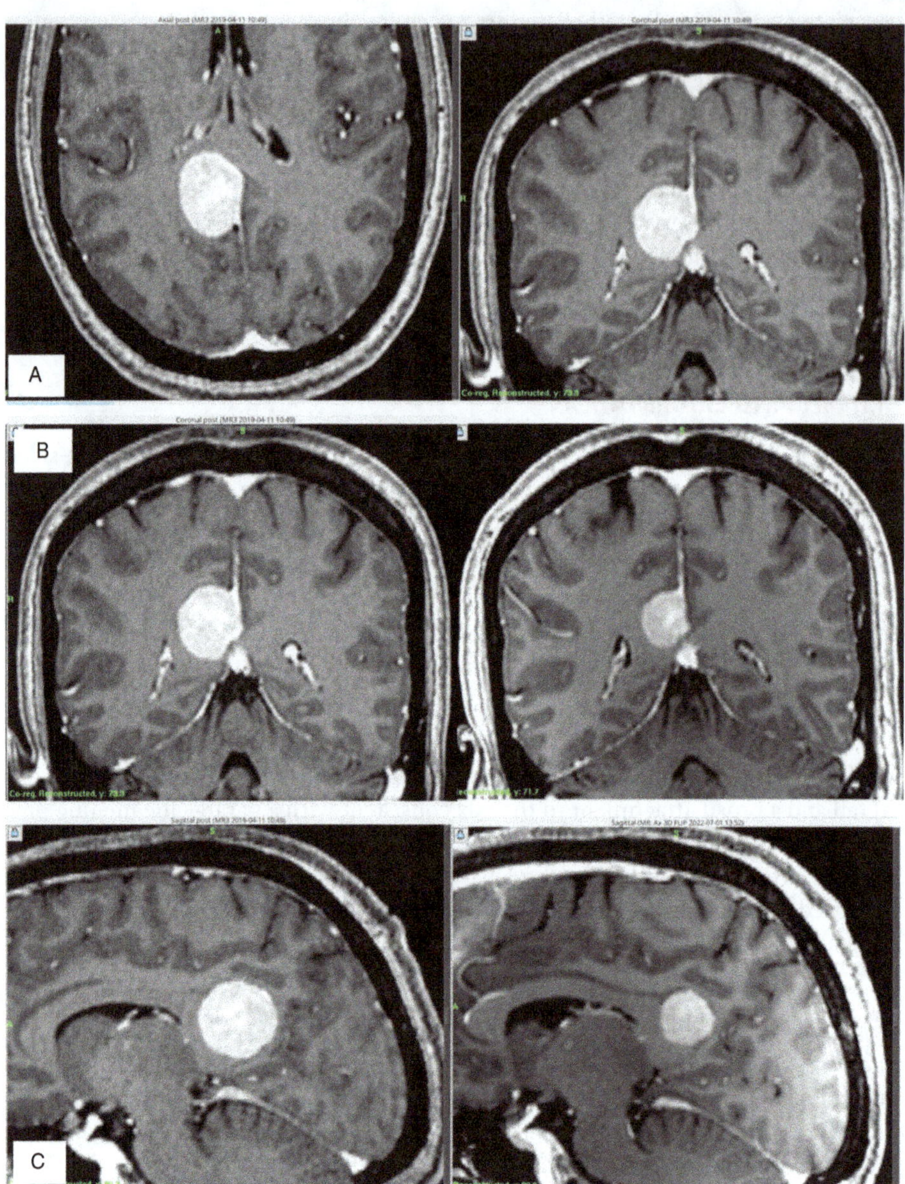

FIGURE 10.1 (A) Shows Axial and coronal images of contrast MRI of the parafalcine meningioma demonstrating the dural tail. (B) Showing coronal images of T1 Weighted MRI with contrast revealing the homogeneously contrast enhancing meningioma arising from the midline falx. (C) Showing the sagittal images revealing the homogeneously contrast-enhancing meningioma located in the parietal region involving the splenium of corpus callosum.

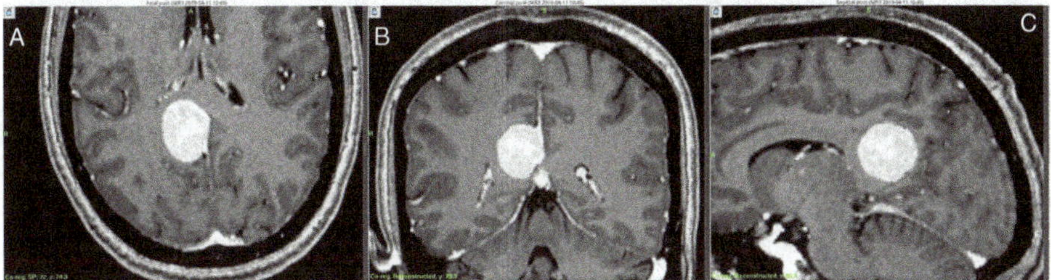

FIGURE 10.2   Magnetic resonance imaging (MRI) axial T1-weighted contrast-enhanced images reveal a well-defined homogeneous contrast-enhancing extra-axial in the right parietal region, with dural tail and a broad attachment to the falx, consistent with a parafalcine meningioma (A). Coronal contrast-enhanced MRI shows the lesion in the right parietal region exerting mass effect on the adjacent cortex (B). Sagittal contrast-enhanced MRI confirms the homogeneous contrast-enhancing lesion in the right parietal region attached to the falx (C).

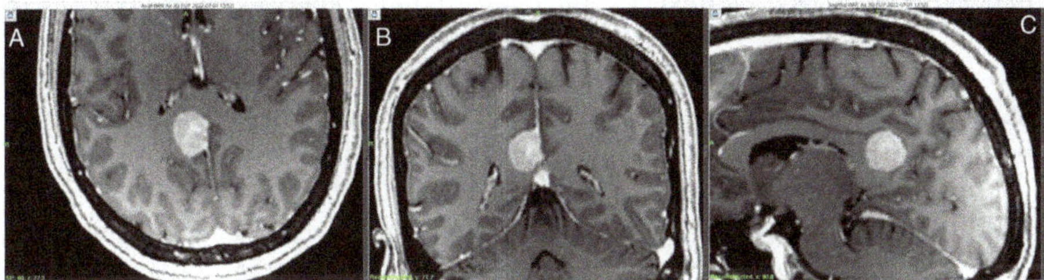

FIGURE 10.3   Follow-up MRI axial T1-weighted contrast-enhanced images reveal a parafalcine meningioma with almost a 50% reduction in size at the end of 39 months (A). Coronal contrast-enhanced MRI further illustrates the lesion in the right parietal region, parafalcine meningioma, consistent with decreased tumour size (B). Sagittal contrast-enhanced MRI confirms the excellent tumour control of the right parietal parafalcine meningioma (C).

ing the dural tail can increase radiation spill and prolong treatment time. However, the consensus is to include nodular dural enhancement adjacent to the primary tumour within the treatment volume.[4]

SRS is regarded as a safe treatment option for meningiomas, with a reported morbidity rate of less than 10%, majority of which are transient.[5] Parasagittal meningiomas carry higher risks due to their proximity to the sagittal sinus. Delayed effects, including edema or radionecrosis, may lead to headaches, seizures, or neurological deficits, while long-term complications can include cysts or vascular malformations.

Acute complications from GKRS treatment are rare and may include mild headaches and occasional episodes of vomiting. Peritumoral edema is common in parasagittal and parafalcine meningiomas and may be temporary or persistent.[6] New or worsening peritumoral edema occurs in 7% to 38% of cases and typically develops in a delayed manner.[7] The onset is most commonly observed between 4–8 months after treatment (range 1–23 months). The edema is usually a combination of vasogenic and cytotoxic in nature. Brain edema is caused by the impairment of the blood-brain barrier, with vascular endothelial growth factor (VEGF) playing a key role in increasing vascular permeability.[5] Additionally, occlusion of the superior sagittal sinus or bridging veins can lead to impaired venous drainage, further contributing to edema. This condition is strongly associated with the pial blood supply.[8] The risk factors include age over 60 years, parasagittal location, the presence of perilesional edema before radiosurgery, sagittal sinus occlusion, and the use of a fractionation scheme in treatment planning.[9] Temporary edema typically resolves within a few months and is managed with corticosteroids. Persistent edema, however, can be challenging to treat due to the risks associated with prolonged steroid use and may occasionally require surgical tumour resection.

Vascular complications following radiosurgical treatment of meningiomas are rare and are primarily attributed to radiation-induced venous thrombosis and vessel occlusion. Vessel occlusion occurs in approximately 1–2% of cases, typically presenting in a delayed period between 14 and 60 months after Gamma Knife radiosurgery.[10]

The use of SRS as primary or adjuvant treatment depends on the clinical context. Standalone SRS shows outcomes comparable to Simpson grade I resections, with a 97% 4-year tumour control rate for small tumours.[11] Studies report higher 5-year PFS rates for primary SRS (93%) compared to post-surgical SRS (70%).[12] Primary SRS is particularly advantageous due to better tumour control and cranial nerve preservation,[13] with its efficacy highlighted in ISRS guidelines for cases where surgery poses challenges or subtotal resection is required.[14]

SRS demonstrates excellent tumour control, with 5-year PFS rates exceeding 90% for smaller meningiomas. A study comparing surgical resection and Gamma Knife radiosurgery (GKRS) showed lower tumour progression in the GKRS group (2% vs. 12%) and fewer complications (10% vs. 22%). GKRS also performed better than Simpson grade II–IV resections and required fewer subsequent treatments.[15] For small-to-moderate tumours without significant mass effect, GKRS offers superior control with minimal morbidity.

SRS achieves excellent long-term control for benign meningiomas, with 5-year PFS rates over 90%. For higher-grade lesions, PFS rates are lower due to increased recurrence risks.[16] Studies report 5-year control rates of 70% for parafalcine tumours treated with SRS. Symptomatic peritumoral edema is rare, occurring in 8% of cases, mostly transient.[12] GKRS is a reliable option for small-to-medium tumours in non-surgical cases, offering durable control with minimal toxicity.

TAKE HOME MESSAGE

Radiosurgery is a viable treatment option for parasagittal meningiomas, although associated with risk of post-radiosurgical edema, highlighting the importance for meticulous planning and patient selection.

REFERENCES

1. Louis DN, Perry A, Reifenberger G, et al. The 2016 World Health Organization Classification of Tumors of the Central Nervous System: a summary. *Acta Neuropathol.* 2016;131(6):803-820.

2. Pollock BE, Stafford SL, Utter A, Giannini C, Schreiner SA. Stereotactic radiosurgery provides equivalent tumor control to Simpson Grade 1 resection for patients with small- to medium-size meningiomas. *Int J Radiat Oncol Biol Phys*. 2003;55(4):1000-1005.

3. Maclean J, Fersht N, Short S. Controversies in radiotherapy for meningioma. *Clin Oncol (R Coll Radiol)*. 2014;26(1):51-64.

4. Kondziolka D, Flickinger JC, Perez B. Judicious resection and/or radiosurgery for parasagittal meningiomas: outcomes from a multicenter review. Gamma Knife Meningioma Study Group. *Neurosurgery*. 1998;43(3):405-414.

5. Kollová A, Liscák R, Novotný J Jr, Vladyka V, Simonová G, Janousková L. Gamma Knife surgery for benign meningioma. *J Neurosurg*. 2007;107(2):325-336.

6. Sheehan JP, Cohen-Inbar O, Ruangkanchanasetr R, et al. Post-radiosurgical edema associated with parasagittal and parafalcine meningiomas: a multicenter study. *J Neurooncol*. 2015;125(2):317-324.

7. Cai R, Barnett GH, Novak E, Chao ST, Suh JH. Principal risk of peritumoral edema after stereotactic radiosurgery for intracranial meningioma is tumor-brain contact interface area. *Neurosurgery*. 2010;66(3):513-522.

8. Bitzer M, Wöckel L, Luft AR, et al. The importance of pial blood supply to the development of peritumoral brain edema in meningiomas. *J Neurosurg*. 1997;87(3):368-373.

9. Kalapurakal JA, Silverman CL, Akhtar N, et al. Intracranial meningiomas: factors that influence the development of cerebral edema after stereotactic radiosurgery and radiation therapy. *Radiology*. 1997;204(2):461-465.

10. Barami K, Grow A, Brem S, Dagnew E, Sloan AE. Vascular complications after radiosurgery for meningiomas. *Neurosurg Focus*. 2007;22(3):E9. Published 2007 Mar 15.

11. Kondziolka D, Mathieu D, Lunsford LD, et al. Radiosurgery as definitive management of intracranial meningiomas. *Neurosurgery*. 2008;62(1):53-60.

12. Ding D, Xu Z, McNeill IT, Yen CP, Sheehan JP. Radiosurgery for parasagittal and parafalcine meningiomas. *J Neurosurg*. 2013;119(4):871-877.

13. Park KJ, Kano H, Iyer A, et al. Gamma Knife stereotactic radiosurgery for cavernous sinus meningioma: long-term follow-up in 200 patients. *J Neurosurg*. 2018;130(6):1799-1808. Published 2018 Jul 20.

14. Lee CC, Trifiletti DM, Sahgal A, et al. Stereotactic Radiosurgery for Benign (World Health Organization Grade I) Cavernous Sinus Meningiomas-International Stereotactic Radiosurgery Society (ISRS) Practice Guideline: A Systematic Review. *Neurosurgery*. 2018;83(6):1128-1142.

15. Pollock BE, Stafford SL, Utter A, Giannini C, Schreiner SA. Stereotactic radiosurgery provides equivalent tumor control to Simpson Grade 1 resection for patients with small- to medium-size meningiomas. *Int J Radiat Oncol Biol Phys*. 2003;55(4):1000-1005.

16. Kondziolka D, Madhok R, Lunsford LD, et al. Stereotactic radiosurgery for convexity meningiomas. *J Neurosurg*. 2009;111(3):458-463.

11

Gamma Knife Radiosurgery for Atypical Meningioma

Sarvesh Goyal | Manoj Phalak

KEY LEARNING POINTS

1. GKRS offers good tumour control rates with improved functional outcomes in Atypical Meningiomas.
2. Advances in imaging, including the use of 68Ga-DOTATOC PET/CT, have further enhanced GKRS's efficacy by improving tumour delineation and reducing recurrence risk.

INTRODUCTION

Atypical meningiomas (WHO Grade II) represent 15–20% of all meningiomas and are distinguished by increased mitotic activity ($\geq$4 mitoses per 10 high-power fields), along with other features of aggressive biological behaviour, including brain invasion and necrosis. They exhibit recurrence rates as high as 40% even after gross total resection (GTR), necessitating multimodal treatment approaches. While surgical resection remains the cornerstone of management, the role of Gamma Knife Radiosurgery (GKRS) has expanded for residual and recurrent atypical meningiomas, owing to its precision and minimal invasiveness.

CASE REPORT

CLINICAL HISTORY AND PRESENTATION

A 31-year-old female presented with a six-month history of progressively worsening headaches and loss of vision in her left eye. Neurological examination revealed no motor or sensory deficits, with the primary concern being visual loss. Preoperative imaging suggested a left frontal lesion with features consistent with meningioma. The lesion exhibited intense contrast enhancement with minimal surrounding edema, measuring 6.2×6.2 cm. The patient had no prior history of systemic conditions such as diabetes, hypertension, or bleeding disorders. She was deemed a suitable candidate for surgical intervention based on her clinical presentation and imaging findings.

The patient underwent left frontal craniotomy with Simpson Grade 2 tumour excision. Intraoperative findings included a grayish-pink, firm, and moderately vascular lesion. Hemostasis was achieved using standard techniques, and the dura was reconstructed and closed in a watertight fashion. Postoperative imaging confirmed no residual tumour in the surgical cavity.

Histopathology reported the lesion as an atypical meningioma (WHO Grade 2) with a high proliferative index (Ki-67: 15%), indicating a higher likelihood of recurrence. This warranted further evaluation for adjuvant therapy.

IMAGING

Follow-up imaging was performed three months post-surgery. Contrast-enhanced MRI (CEMRI) showed no gross residual tumour or evidence of recurrence in the left frontal region, although subtle post-surgical changes were observed.

A Ga-68 DOTANOC PET-CT was performed to assess the metabolic activity of the lesion. This imaging modality provided functional data, revealing mild peripheral tracer uptake in the left frontal lobe, suggestive of residual disease. DOTANOC PET-CT, which targets somatostatin receptor expression in meningiomas, was instrumental in detecting metabolically active residual tumour tissue that was not overtly visible on structural imaging.

GK PROTOCOL (FIG 11.1D–H)

Given the WHO Grade 2 histology, elevated Ki-67 index, and evidence of residual metabolic activity on PET-CT, the patient was referred for Gamma Knife Radiosurgery (GKR) as an adjuvant therapy.

PLANNING AND PARAMETERS

Using fusion imaging of CEMRI and Ga-68 DOTANOC PET, the residual lesion was accurately delineated, ensuring precise targeting of metabolically active tumour tissue while sparing adjacent healthy brain structures. A marginal dose of 15 Gy was prescribed to the 50% isodose line. The dose plan aimed to minimise exposure to critical structures, including the optic nerves and chiasm, given the tumour's frontal location. The procedure was performed as a single-session radiosurgery. Immobilisation was achieved using a stereotactic frame, and the patient tolerated the procedure without complications.

FOLLOW-UP (FIG. 11.1I)

Follow-up MRI Findings: At the two-year mark, MRI revealed a significant reduction in the size of the residual lesion.

Clinically, the patient remained stable, with no recurrence of headaches or worsening of visual symptoms. She continues to be monitored annually with imaging and clinical evaluations to ensure sustained tumour control and to detect any signs of recurrence at the earliest.

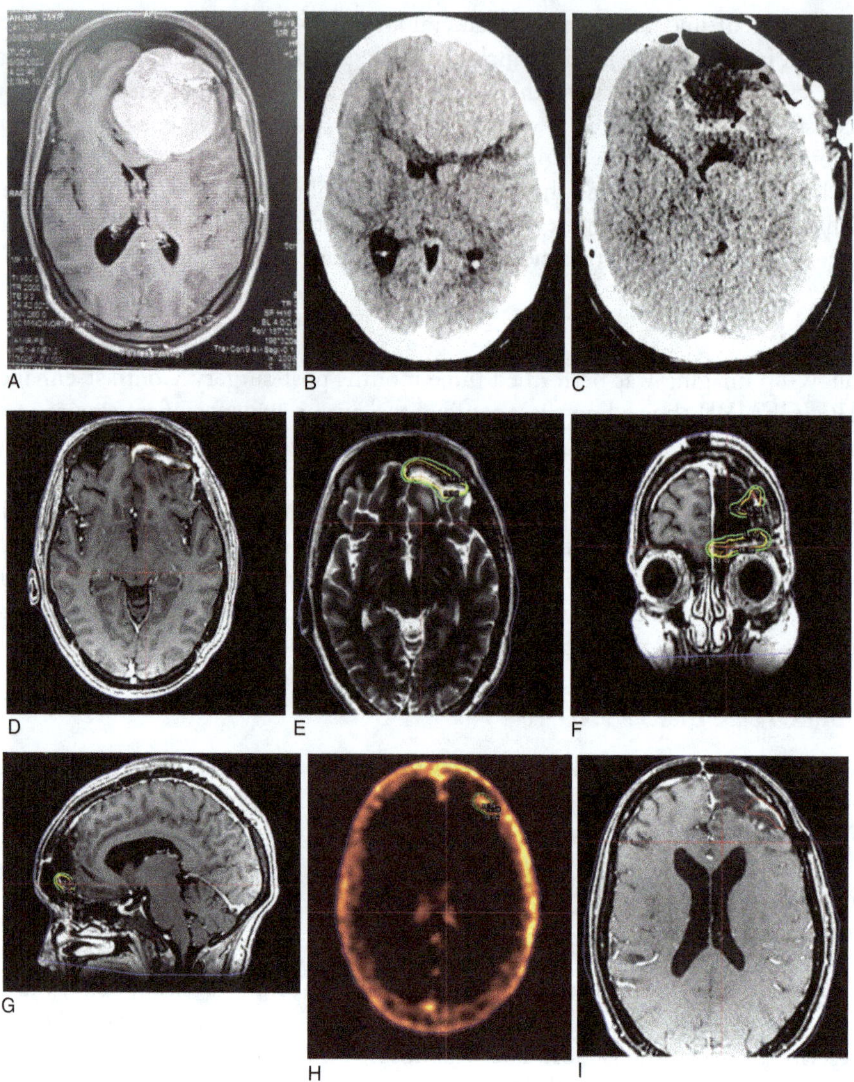

FIGURE 11.1 Comprehensive imaging of the atypical meningioma case. (A) Preoperative MRI T1-weighted axial contrast-enhanced image showing a left frontal lesion with intense contrast enhancement and minimal surrounding edema, measuring 6.2 x 6.2 cm. (B) Preoperative contrast-enhanced CT (CECT) of the head demonstrating a hyperdense left frontal mass with well-defined borders and no significant calcifications or haemorrhage. (C) Postoperative CT scan highlighting the surgical cavity after Simpson Grade 2 tumour excision, with no gross residual tumour visible. (D) Pre-Gamma Knife Radiosurgery (GKR) MRI T1-weighted axial image showing subtle residual enhancement in the left frontal region. (E) Pre-GKR MRI T2-weighted image indicating mild hyper-intensity adjacent to the surgical site, consistent with postoperative changes. (F) Pre-GKR MRI T1-weighted coronal image illustrating the extent and location of the residual lesion. (G) Pre-GKR MRI T1-weighted sagittal image showing the residual tumour and its proximity to adjacent structures. (H) Ga-68 DOTANOC PET-CT image demonstrating mild peripheral tracer uptake in the residual lesion, indicative of metabolically active tumour tissue. (I) Post-treatment MRI scan at the two-year follow-up, T1-weighted axial image showing significant tumour regression with reduced dimensions and no abnormal contrast enhancement, consistent with effective disease control.

DISCUSSION

Atypical meningiomas represent a complex subset of meningiomas due to their aggressive biological behaviour and high recurrence rates. They account for 15–20% of all meningiomas and have a recurrence rate of 30–40% even after gross total resection (GTR). Key histological features include brain invasion, increased mitotic figures, necrosis, and atypical cellular architecture. Gamma Knife Radiosurgery (GKRS) has emerged as a critical adjunct in the treatment algorithm, particularly for residual or recurrent tumours and those in surgically challenging locations.[1] Atypical meningiomas' aggressive nature warrants multimodal treatment. Studies (e.g., Hanakita et al., 2013) have demonstrated that GKRS achieves local control (LC) rates of 74%, 39%, and 16% at 1, 2, and 5 years, respectively, for atypical meningiomas. Critical factors influencing outcomes include tumour volume <6 cc, marginal doses >18 Gy and Karnofsky Performance Scale (KPS) ≥90.

Compared to surgery, GKRS offers lower morbidity for residual or recurrent disease, especially for deep-seated or skull-base tumours. It complements fractionated radiotherapy (FRT) as a boost in cases of larger or infiltrative tumours.[2]

High-resolution contrast-enhanced MRI is the gold standard for planning. However, the addition of 68Ga-DOTATOC PET/CT has significantly improved tumour visualisation. These imaging techniques enhance tumour delineation by highlighting somatostatin receptor expression, which is overexpressed in meningiomas. Barone et al. demonstrated that 68Ga-DOTATOC PET/CT is particularly valuable in differentiating viable tumour tissue from post-treatment changes like radiation necrosis or scar tissue.[1]

Tumour size plays a critical role in GKRS planning. Smaller tumours (<6 cc) are associated with better outcomes, as highlighted in Hanakita et al. Larger tumours (>20 cc) may require hypofractionated treatment or staged approaches. The median marginal dose for atypical meningiomas ranges from 14 to 20 Gy, with higher doses (>18 Gy) significantly improving local control (LC). The median number of isocenters varies based on tumour complexity and location, optimising dose conformity and reducing exposure to surrounding critical structures.[3]

Hanakita et al. reported LC rates of 74%, 39%, and 16% at 1, 2, and 5 years, respectively, for atypical meningiomas treated with GKRS. Higher marginal doses (>18 Gy), smaller tumour volumes (<6 cc), and better KPS scores were significantly associated with longer LC durations. Similarly, Barone et al. observed biological responses to treatment in most patients, with SUV reductions on 68Ga-DOTATOC PET/CT correlating with tumour control.[1] Studies demonstrate neurological improvement in 16.7% of patients following GKRS. Reduction in tumour size and associated mass effect alleviates symptoms such as headache, cranial neuropathies, and hemiparesis. Symptom relief is typically observed within 6–12 months post-treatment and correlates with radiological tumour shrinkage.

Overall survival (OS) rates at 1, 2, and 5 years were reported as 91%, 68%, and 68%, respectively, by Hanakita et al. However, atypical meningiomas recurrence tendency necessitates vigilant long-term follow-up with MRI or PET imaging to detect early recurrence or marginal progression.[4]

Perilesional edema is the most common adverse event, affecting 10-20% of patients. This typically occurs within the first few months post-treatment and is managed effectively with corticosteroids. Edema is more likely in larger tumours or those located near critical structures like the brainstem. Permanent complications are rare (<5%) but may include cranial nerve palsies or radiation-induced neuropathy, especially for tumours in the skull base. Hanakita et al. reported one case of trigeminal neuropathy following repeat GKRS for a temporal base tumour.[2] While uncommon, radiation necrosis may occur in larger tumours or with higher doses. Advanced imaging modalities like 68Ga-DOTATOC PET/CT are instrumental in distinguishing necrosis from recurrence, facilitating timely intervention.[4]

CONCLUSIONS

Gamma Knife Radiosurgery has established itself as a cornerstone in the management of atypical meningiomas, offering durable tumour control with minimal morbidity. Advances in imaging, particularly with 68Ga-DOTATOC PET, have further enhanced its efficacy, ensuring precise targeting and better long-term outcomes for patients with this challenging pathology.

TAKE HOME MESSAGE

GKRS is pivotal in managing recurrent or residual atypical meningiomas. Marginal doses of 14–20 Gy, tailored to tumour size and location, achieve optimal outcomes. Regular MRI and PET follow-ups are essential for detecting recurrence or treatment-related changes.

REFERENCES:

1. Barone F, Inserra F, Scalia G, et al. 68Ga-DOTATOC PET/CT Follow Up after Single or Hypofractionated Gamma Knife ICON Radiosurgery for Meningioma Patients. *Brain Sci.* 2021;11(3):375. Published 2021 Mar 15.
2. Hanakita S, Koga T, Igaki H, et al. Role of gamma knife surgery for intracranial atypical (WHO grade II) meningiomas. *J Neurosurg.* 2013;119(6):1410-1414.
3. Vagnoni L, Aburas S, Giraffa M, et al. Radiation therapy for atypical and anaplastic meningiomas: an overview of current results and controversial issues. *Neurosurg Rev.* 2022;45(5):3019-3033.
4. Linskey ME, Davis SA, Ratanatharathorn V. Relative roles of microsurgery and stereotactic radiosurgery for the treatment of patients with cranial meningiomas: a single-surgeon 4-year integrated experience with both modalities. *J Neurosurg.* 2005;102 Suppl:59-70.
5. Huffmann BC, Reinacher PC, Gilsbach JM. Gamma knife surgery for atypical meningiomas. *J Neurosurg.* 2005;102 Suppl:283-286.

Gamma Knife Radiosurgery for Non-Functioning Pituitary Tumours

12

Dattaraj Parmanand Sawarkar | Abhishek Kumar

KEY LEARNING POINTS

1. Primary GKRS may be a viable option for small NFPTs, especially those at least 2 mm away from the optic apparatus.
2. Tumor control rates exceed 80% at 10 years.
3. The Incidence of Pituitary dysfunction is <10% at 10 years.
4. NFPTs whose immunohistochemistry is positive for prolactin or Growth Hormone should be treated as functional tumours.

INTRODUCTION

Pituitary adenomas can be classified as microadenomas or macroadenomas based on size (smaller or larger than 10 mm) and as functioning or non-functioning adenomas based on whether they secrete a particular hormone type, causing patients to exhibit specific clinical manifestations. Non-functional adenomas account for 30% of all pituitary tumours and usually present as macroadenomas causing visual loss, headache, and hypopituitarism due to mass effect.[1] GKRS is a proven therapeutic management option for recurrent/residual and even primary adenomas.[2] GKRS is believed to work by directly inducing DNA damage through radiation and indirectly by generating free radicals, as well as causing progressive vascular damage.[1] The objectives of Gamma Knife radiosurgery are twofold: (1) to halt the tumour's further growth, which reduces compression over the optic pathways and other neural or vascular structures, and (2) to reduce the excessive production of pituitary hormones without impairing normal pituitary function.[3]

REPRESENTATIVE CASE

A 23-year-old lady presented to our outpatient department with complaints of insidious onset, gradually progressive, mild-to-moderate intensity, holocranial headache that required medications to settle. She had no history of symptoms related to hormonal excess, visual loss, nausea, or vomiting. On neurological examination, her visual acuity was 6/6 bilaterally with no field cuts on confrontation. Her hormone profile was within normal limits for her age and sex. Her contrast MRI brain showed a 39 x 27 x 35 mm sellar-suprasellar lesion displacing the pituitary posteriorly with encasement of cavernous ICA on the right side. She was diagnosed with non-functioning pituitary macroadenoma and underwent Endoscopic Trans-nasal-trans-sphenoidal surgery at our centre. Postoperatively, the patient was relieved of her headache but developed panhypopituitarism, for which she was managed medically. Her biopsy came out to be gonadotroph adenoma. Her follow-up MRI showed a small residual lesion in the right cavernous sinus for which she was planned for GKRS at our centre.

On GK planning, 97.6% of her tumor volume came out to be 5.808 cc which received a dose of 15 Gy at 60% prescribed isodose. The GK Protocol details are as follows:

- Dose volume Histogram for volume: Tumour: 5.808 cc (97.6%) receives dose >=15 Gy

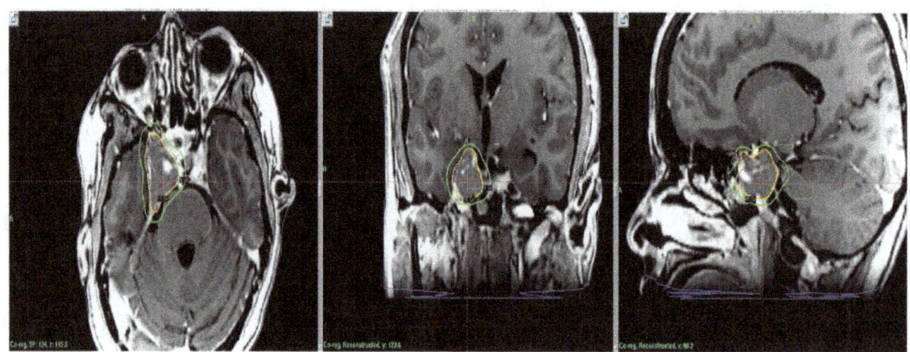

FIGURE 12.1A   Shows pre-GK MRI of the patient showing residual pituitary adenoma with right cavernous sinus lesion.

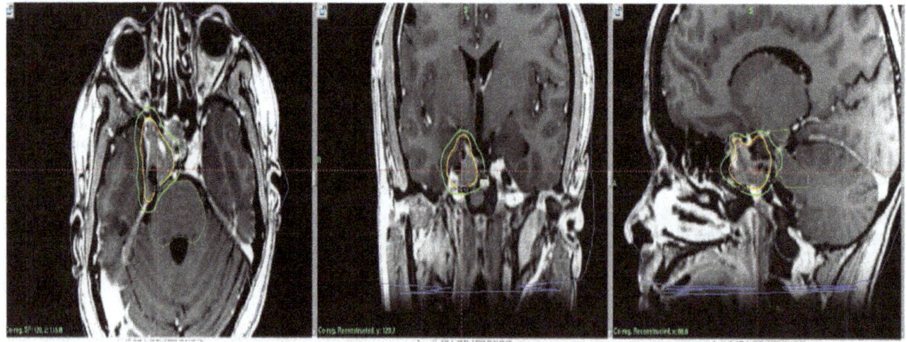

FIGURE 12.1B   Shows post-GK MRI, done 1.5 years later with a significant reduction in the size of the lesion.

- Dose volume Histogram for volume: Right optic pathway:0.00 cc (0%) receives dose >=10 Gy
- Dose volume Histogram for volume: Brainstem: 0.00 cc (0%) receives dose >=12 Gy

The patient tolerated the procedure well and required only a short course of analgesics. She did not develop any post-GK complications. Her post-GK MRI, done after an interval of 1.5 years, showed a 40% reduction in tumour volume. However, the patient continues to have panhypopituitarism and is currently on Levo-thyroxine, prednisolone and desmopressin.

DISCUSSION

Trans-nasal trans-sphenoidal surgery is the treatment of choice for non-functioning pituitary macroadenomas, but supra and parasellar extensions of the tumour often preclude gross total resection.[4] In the cases of giant pituitary macroadenomas with cavernous sinus extension, part of the tumour extending into cavernous sinuses is usually left behind and later subjected to GKRS.[5] Hence, GKRS is reserved for patients with recurrent or residual lesions or small primary lesions.[2] It can also be used as a primary treatment modality in patients with poor performance status or those wanting to delay the surgery owing to complication risks.[3]

GKRS aims to preserve the normal pituitary gland and optic apparatus while delivering an effective radiation dose to the tumour tissue.[5] Studies have reported tumour control rates between 94-100% and 76-87% at 5 years and 10 years of follow-up, respectively, with a minimum marginal dose ranging from 14-16.6 Gy.[5] In their study, Sheehan et al. noted that a margin dose of 13–14 Gy was effective[6] while Mingione et al. reported that a minimum dose of 12 Gy was needed for tumour shrinkage.[7] Therefore, 12 Gy is the minimum effective single-session dose necessary for tumour control, while a dose below 10 Gy is deemed ineffective and is associated with treatment failure.[5] Also, Mingione et al. noted that peripheral doses of >20 Gy do not provide additional benefits.[7] Anterior optic apparatus is the most radiosensitive intracranial structure, and a dose of less than 10 Gy or less directed at a small volume is generally considered safe.[8] Contrary to that, cranial nerves passing through the cavernous sinus have a greater tolerance and usually tolerate dosing up to 40 Gy well.[8] SRS is associated with low rates of permanent neurological deficits, however, transient deficits do occur and this needs to be counseled to patients.[9] A recent meta-analysis by Kotecha et al. found that post-SRS hypopituitarism was the most prevalent side effect, affecting about 21.0% of patients (95% CI: 15.0-27.0%).[9] In contrast, visual dysfunction and other cranial nerve injuries were rare, occurring in a range of 0-7%.[9]

In conclusion, SRS is an effective treatment, with 10-year outcome data for patients receiving doses of 14-16 Gy, and promising 5-year results for radio-biologically equivalent HSRT schedules. The long-term risks include the development of new hypopituitarism, rare cranial nerve or vascular injuries, and an extremely low risk of radiation-induced malignancy.[9]

TAKE HOME MESSAGE

- GKRS is a safe and effective treatment modality for recurrent/residual or primary pituitary macroadenomas.
- Anterior optic apparatus is the most radiosensitive intracranial structure, with a dose of up to 10 Gy or less is considered safe (a standard protocol to restrict dose at 8 Gy) while nerves traversing through cavernous sinus tolerate radiation doses up to 40 Gy.
- Long-term risks associated with GKRS include the development of hypopituitarism, rare cranial nerve or vascular injuries, and an extremely low risk of radiation-induced malignancy.

REFERENCES

1. Jagannathan J, Yen CP, Pouratian N, Laws ER, Sheehan JP. Stereotactic radiosurgery for pituitary adenomas: a comprehensive review of indications, techniques and long-term results using the Gamma Knife. *J Neurooncol.* 2009;92(3):345-356.
2. Iwai Y, Yamanaka K, Yoshioka K. Radiosurgery for nonfunctioning pituitary adenomas. *Neurosurgery.* 2005;56(4):699-705; discussion 699-705.
3. Jackson IM, Norén G. Role of gamma knife therapy in the management of pituitary tumors. *Endocrinol Metab Clin North Am.* 1999;28(1):133-142.
4. Mortini P, Losa M, Barzaghi R, Boari N, Giovanelli M. Results of transsphenoidal surgery in a large series of patients with pituitary adenoma. *Neurosurgery.* 2005;56(6):1222-1233; discussion 1233.
5. Garg K, Singh M. Role of Stereotactic Radiosurgery in Pituitary Adenomas. *Neurol India.* 2020;68(Supplement):S123-S128.
6. Sheehan JP, Kondziolka D, Flickinger J, Lunsford LD. Radiosurgery for residual or recurrent nonfunctioning pituitary adenoma. *J Neurosurg.* 2002;97(5 Suppl):408-414.
7. Mingione V, Yen CP, Vance ML, et al. Gamma surgery in the treatment of nonsecretory pituitary macroadenoma. *J Neurosurg.* 2006;104(6):876-883.
8. Leber KA, Berglöff J, Pendl G. Dose-response tolerance of the visual pathways and cranial nerves of the cavernous sinus to stereotactic radiosurgery. *J Neurosurg.* 1998;88(1):43-50.
9. Kotecha R, Sahgal A, Rubens M, et al. Stereotactic radiosurgery for non-functioning pituitary adenomas: meta-analysis and International Stereotactic Radiosurgery Society practice opinion. *Neuro Oncol.* 2020;22(3):318-332.

Gamma Knife Radiosurgery in Functional Pituitary Tumours

13

Hanoksrithej Rayappa | Shweta Kedia

KEY LEARNING POINTS

1. Surgery is the modality of choice for functional pituitary tumours, except for Prolactinomas, which are primarily managed medically.
2. GKRS is used as adjuvant therapy in Acromegaly. However, primary Gamma-knife can be considered in Cushing's disease.
3. A marginal dose of 20-25 Gy is prescribed to the tumour.
4. The dose may be hypofractionated when the optic apparatus is extremely close to the tumour.
5. Reported remission rates post-GKRS range between 50% and 65%.

INTRODUCTION

Surgery is the primary modality of treatment for functional pituitary tumors, except for Prolactinomas which respond well to medication. The second line of treatment in Acromegaly, Cushing, TSHomas, and Prolactinomas after the primary modality has failed to achieve the target hormone remission is either medical or radiosurgery. The drugs are required for a lifetime, and the cost of the medical treatment is huge and may not always yield the desired outcome. Gamma Knife Radiosurgery forms an alternative to medical therapy in these tumours, with its role serving to stop tumour growth and excess hormone secretion, i.e., both biochemical and radiological, after the surgical and medical options have been exhausted. In this case-based discussion, we shall elaborate on the control rate following GKRS in functional pituitary tumours and its long-term impact on hormone status.

REPRESENTATIVE CASE OF ACROMEGALY

HISTORY & EXAMINATION

This is a case of a 48-year-old female with Growth hormone-secreting pituitary macroadenoma. The patient underwent Endoscopic TNTS and tumour excision and was found to have tumour residual. Post-surgery, her growth hormone values reduced but remained on the higher side. GH: 9.30 ng/dl (0.06-5ng/dl); IGF1: 567. Her visual acuity and visual fields were normal.

IMAGING

The patient underwent a contrast MRI of the brain which revealed a residual lesion in the left parasellar area. The distance between the tumour and the optic apparatus was sufficient to plan the radiosurgery in a single fraction.

GK PROTOCOL

The tumour volume of 1.52 cc received a dose of 24 Gy at a 50 % isodose line in the margin. The dose constraints to the optic apparatus were kept at 8 Gy (Fig. 13.1).

FOLLOW-UP

The response at the 1-year follow-up showed near complete resolution of the tumour (Fig. 13.2). At the latest follow-up, 9 years post-GKRS, there was both biochemical and radiological remission, with the latest Serum-GH being 0.68 (0-18ng/ml).

REPRESENTATIVE CASE OF CUSHING'S DISEASE

HISTORY & EXAMINATION

This is a case of a 25-year-old female operated for ACTH-secreting pituitary macroadenoma via endoscopic transsphenoidal route but achieved only partial remis-

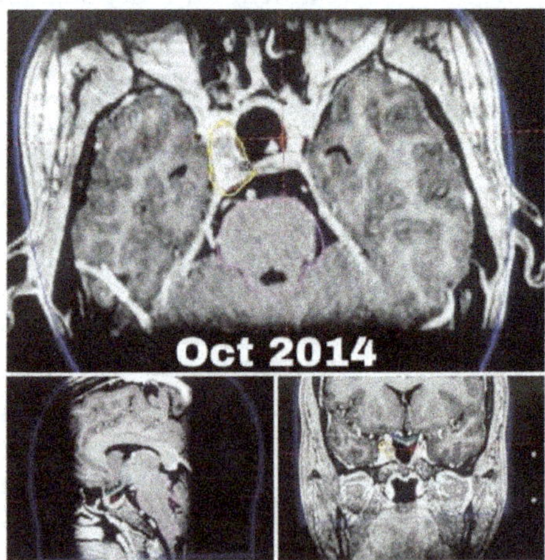

FIGURE 13.1 Tumour volume: 1.52cm3. Min dose: 17.7Gy, Max dose: 48.6Gy, Mean dose: 32.8+/– 5.6Gy 1.44cm3 of tumour (95%) received 24gy; 108.1mm3 of brainstem (1%) received 6.4Gy; 2.8mm3 of right optic nerve (1%) received 5.8Gy; 1.4mm3 of right optic nerve (1%) received 3.4Gy; 9.0mm3 of chiasm (1%) received 6.35Gy.

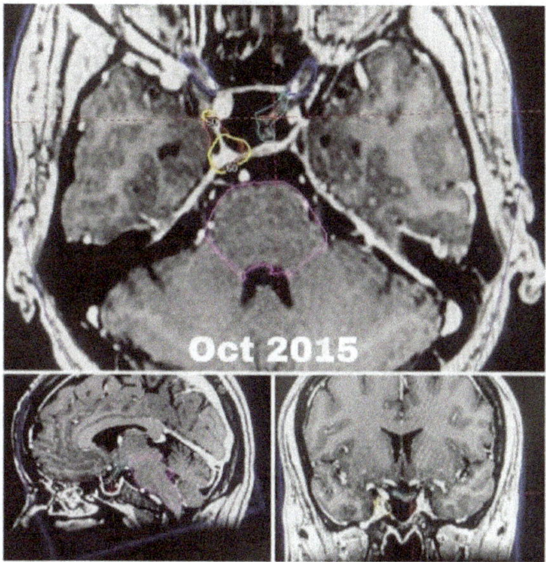

FIGURE 13.2   Reduced tumor volume at 1 year follow up.

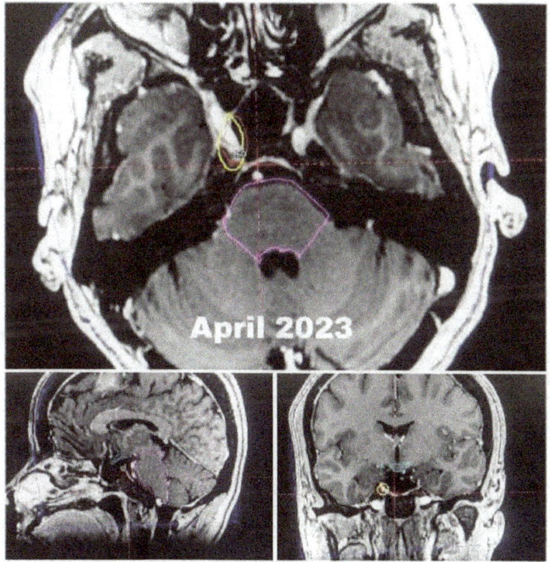

FIGURE 13.3   Long-term follow-up of the same patient, shows no recurrence.

sion and residual lesion. Therefore, she underwent repeat transnasal surgery and gross total excision a year later. The patient had a history of diplopia with right lateral gaze palsy. The vision was intact. The hormone values post-surgery were still on the higher side with S-ACTH being 403 pg/mL.

GK PROTOCOL

She received Secondary GKRS with a dose of 20 Gy at 50% isodose line given.

FOLLOW-UP

The lesion reduced in size but hormone remission still could not be achieved (Fig. 13.4). The patient was then taken up for laparoscopic bilateral adrenalectomy. Following this, the ACTH values dropped to 100.2 pg/mL.

DISCUSSION

Adequate control in a timely manner is essential for optimal outcome of functional pituitary tumours. GKRS is the second line of treatment for functional pituitary tumours, either those that are recurrent, residual or invasive and therefore not amenable to surgery or medicine. The criteria for cure in patients treated by GK are mainly based on the normalisation of hormones in functional pituitary tumours. Thus, monitoring of insulin-like growth factor 1 (IGF1) and/or GH levels (typically <1 mcg/L) and ACTH becomes crucial to decide on remission.[1]

GKRS is usually given as a single fraction, however lesions which are in close proximity or invasive may require fractionation. When given as a single dose, 20-25 Gy at the margin is sufficient to get the desired outcome. Routinely the optic apparatus is marked separately as both optic nerves and chiasm as organs at risk and the dose constraint of 10 Gy as the max dose is adhered to.[1] The factors that affect the remission rates post-GKRS include age, invasive nature and functional nature. Each of the functional tumours responds differently to GKRS. The age-appropriate normalisation of hormones after GKRS is taken as the criterion for cure post-GKRS.

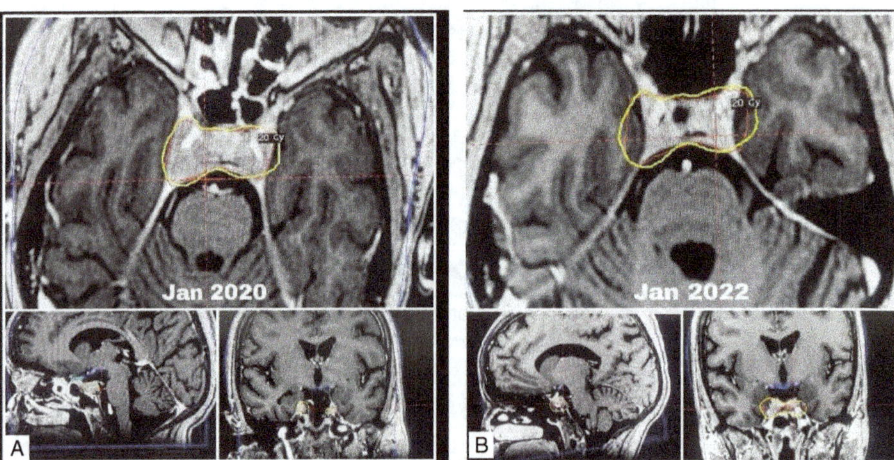

FIGURE 13.4.   (A) C/o Cushing disease with tumour invading both the cavernous sinus region. (B) Follow-up scan at the end of 2.5 years showing significant reduction in tumour size.

While there is variability in the criteria for hormonal remission, the majority of studies on GK for acromegaly reported remission rates ranging between 50% and 65%.[2,3] The five-year-recurrence-free survival in acromegaly post-GKRS is around 50%. New onset hypopituitarism involving single hormones ranged around 40% and optic neuropathy was seen in 0-5% of patients as seen after a meta-analysis. Remission of hypercortisolism occurs in more than 50% of cases treated by GK. In contrast to GH-secreting adenomas, most of the remissions occur within three to four years from GK. A difference in radiosensitivity between the two types of secreting pituitary adenoma is, therefore, suggested. The recurrence-free survival in Hypercortisolic patients is 73%. New onset hypopituitarism affects around 36%, and optic neuropathy is seen in around 2% of the patients.[4]

The patients are referred post-surgery and therefore the tumour volume is usually small. Some of the tumours may be left behind very close to the optic apparatus. Patients of prolactinomas have a larger tumour volume when compared to these two and in close proximity to visual apparatus. The remission in prolactinomas is seen in 15-50% of the patients.[5] New onset hormone disturbances and optic neuropathy occur similarly to other functional tumours.

In ACTH-secreting adenomas, the use of cortisol-lowering medications, especially ketoconazole, has been associated with an unfavourable GK outcome or with a slower time of hormone normalisation. Since ketoconazole is prescribed to reduce the adrenal manufacturing of cortisol, several authors suggest quitting antisecretory medications before GK. In patients with GH-secreting adenoma, some studies found a negative association between somatostatin analogue (SSA) use at the time of GK and the effects of radiosurgery, whereas others failed to find a significant relationship. However, almost all studies found a trend towards worse results in patients taking SSA than in untreated patients, or in those who had quit medical treatment while waiting for GK. In this context, the largest series published to date by Ding et al. confirmed a negative impact of concomitant use of growth hormone production agents such as sandostatin.

Almost 40-50% of the patients with Cushing's disease may not have the visible tumour on MRI at the time of GKRS. These patients are then subjected to whole sella irradiation by GK. The possibility of remission remains the same in these patients as in others, however, the risk of hypopituitarism increases.[5]

As with other benign lesions, the response is appreciated only in 2-3 years. Hypopituitarism is more common in functional adenomas post-radiosurgery occurring in the range of 20-30%, compared to radiosurgery outcomes in non-functioning pituitary tumors.[4] This is attributed to the higher prescription dose that is used in functional tumours. Thyroid functions most commonly get affected, however, panhypopituitarism is also not uncommon, necessitating regular assessment and hormone replacement in symptomatic patients. The suprasellar extension of the tumour with a higher dose received by the infundibulum is the most important factor affecting hormone dysfunction. The risk of optic neuropathy is <1% when the point max dose to optic apparatus is kept at <10Gy. Therefore in patients with lesions in close proximity to optic apparatus, it is best advised to hypo-fractionate. There are case reports of radiation-induced injury to the oculomotor nerve and intracavernous carotids following GKRS to functional pituitary tumours.

The treatment of functional adenomas is always a team effort, with the close involvement of an endocrinologist along with other team members of radiosurgery to help in decision-making in these cases.

TAKE HOME MESSAGE

Gamma knife enables one to deliver a very high radiation dose to the target in a single fraction and therefore, it is a suitable option for functional pituitary tumours as an adjuvant treatment modality. Due to steep radiation falling out of the Gamma Knife, the adjacent visual apparatus gets minimal radiation. It is a treatment option in the definitive, adjuvant, and salvage settings as it is associated with tumour control rates of 80%-90% and clinically acceptable rates of toxicity. Additionally, GKRS is a well-tolerated treatment in the definitive setting in patients who are unable or choose not to undergo surgical resection. Patients who are poor candidates for single-fraction SRS may be treated with conventional radiotherapy or hypofractionated SRS.

REFERENCES

1. Garg K, Singh M. Role of Stereotactic Radiosurgery in Pituitary Adenomas. *Neurol India*. 2020;68(Supplement):S123-S128.
2. Lehrer EJ, Kowalchuk RO, Trifiletti DM, Sheehan JP. The Role of Stereotactic Radiosurgery for Functioning and Nonfunctioning Pituitary Adenomas. *Neurol India*. 2023;71 (Supplement):S133-S139.
3. Hemaidia RM, Cebula H, Goichot B, Noel G. Radiation therapy in functioning and no functioning pituitary neuroendocrine tumor: systematic review of the recent literature after 2011. *Front Endocrinol (Lausanne)*. 2024;15:1468724. Published 2024 Nov 12.
4. Albano L, Losa M, Barzaghi LR, et al. Gamma Knife Radiosurgery for Pituitary Tumors: A Systematic Review and Meta-Analysis. *Cancers (Basel)*. 2021;13(19):4998. Published 2021 Oct 5.
5. Kowalchuk RO, Trifiletti DM, Brown PD, Sheehan JP. Contemporary radiotherapy and radiosurgery techniques for refractory pituitary adenomas. *Pituitary*. 2023;26(3):298-302.

Primary Gamma Knife Radiosurgery in Pituitary Adenomas

Chandra Kiran A | Deepak Agarwal

KEY LEARNING POINTS

1. Primary Gamma Knife radiosurgery has proven to be an effective and safe treatment modality for patients with giant pituitary adenomas.
2. It is particularly valuable in cases where surgical intervention is not feasible or where tumour involvement of critical structures poses a significant risk to the patient.
3. Continued follow-up and careful monitoring of both tumour growth and endocrine function are essential to optimise patient outcomes in whom primary GKRS is given.

INTRODUCTION

Pituitary adenomas represent a heterogeneous group of tumours that arise from the pituitary gland.[1,2] These tumours often cause significant neuroendocrine dysfunction, neuro-ophthalmic dysfunction or compression of adjacent structures and may present with neurologic deficits. Gamma Knife radiosurgery (GKRS) has emerged as an effective non-invasive modality for treating pituitary adenomas, offering both tumour control and symptom relief, particularly in patients with residual tumours following surgery, or in whom surgical resection is not feasible or carries substantial risk. Preliminary data suggest that the resolution of pituitary hypersecretion is faster with high durable rates of tumour control in gamma knife therapy. We present here a case report of successful single fraction Gamma Knife radiosurgery in a case of GPA (Giant Pituitary Adenoma) and the noteworthy functional recovery of the patient.

CASE PRESENTATION

A 55-year-old male patient presented with a 6-month history of progressive visual disturbance in the right eye, and a 3-day acute onset headache, dizziness, diplopia, and fatigue. His past medical history was significant for hypothyroidism and type 2 diabetes mellitus both being treated adequately. On examination, he was vitally stable and had a corrected visual acuity of FC @ 6 feet in the right eye and 6/18 in the left eye. He was found to have a bilateral temporal visual field defect consistent with bitemporal hemianopia. He also had a right eye lateral rectus palsy. Hormonal evaluation revealed subnormal levels of serum Prolactin (0.3mcg/L, reference-2.1-17.7), and elevated serum cortisol levels (49mcg/dl, reference range 5-23). The patient was asked to get a visual field charting done which confirmed the presence of bitemporal homonymous hemianopia (Fig. 14.1A, B).

IMAGING

Magnetic resonance imaging (MRI) revealed a pituitary adenoma measuring 31 × 34 × 25 mm (approx. 27 cc in volume), with non-visualisation of the anterior pituitary and causing significant compression and splaying of the optic chiasm (Fig. 14.2). Due to the tumour's size and its intimate involvement with critical neurovascular structures, surgery was offered. However, on the patient's insistence to not want surgical intervention, the decision was made to proceed with Gamma Knife radiosurgery after detailed informed written consent was taken from the patient and proper risks and benefits were explained.

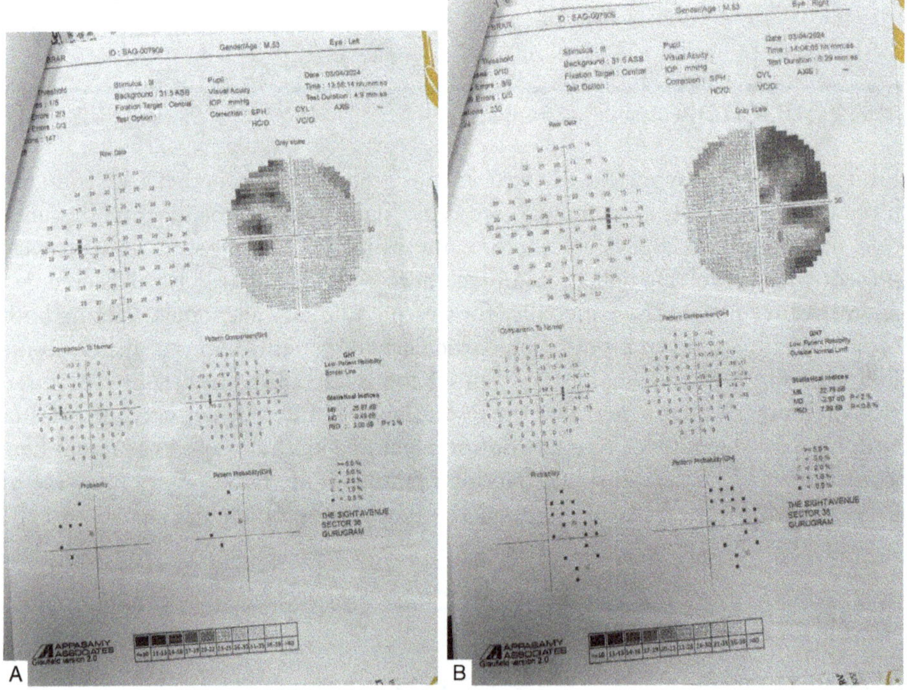

FIGURE 14.1   (A, B) correspond to Visual field charting of left eye and right eye respectively prior to GKRS suggesting of a BITEMPORAL HETERONYMOUS HEMIANOPIA indicating a lesion at the optic chiasm of the visual pathway).

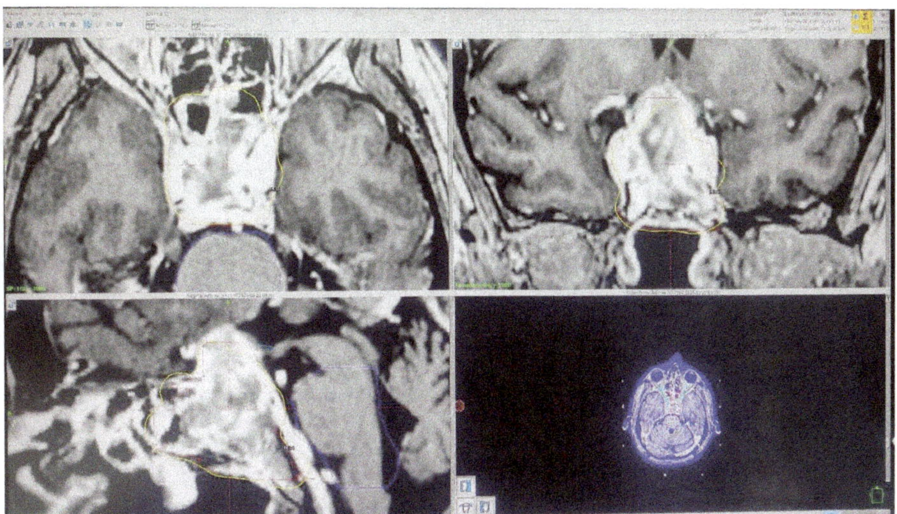

FIGURE 14.2   Corresponds to the pre GKRS CE-T1 weighted MRI imaging of the subject showing the lesion as described earlier measuring 31 x 34 x 25 mm (approx. 27 cc in volume).

GK PROTOCOL

Given the size and location of the tumour, a treatment plan was carefully designed to minimise radiation exposure to surrounding healthy tissues, particularly the optic pathways and hypothalamus. The patient underwent a high-precision stereotactic MRI scan, followed by the placement of a stereotactic frame under local anaesthesia. The tumour was delineated with high accuracy on the imaging, and a total dose of 14 Gy was prescribed to the tumour with a volume of 28.195 cc and a coverage of 92.6%, delivered in a single fraction. The superior most portion of tumour in proximity to the optic apparatus was left untreated. Left and right optic nerve, along with optic chiasma were strategically spared effectively receiving almost nil radiation. The patient was discharged on the same day of irradiation with a set of supportive medications.

FOLLOW UP

Post-treatment immediate 2-week and 1-month follow-up showed no evidence of acute complications such as radiation-induced oedema or haemorrhage. The patient was followed up with clinical evaluation and serial imaging. At 12 months, MRI demonstrated a significant shrinkage of tumour size (Fig. 14.3A, B), and the patient reported significant improvement in visual acuity, with near normalisation of his visual field (Fig. 14.4A, B).

Endocrine follow-up at 12 months showed adequate control of hormonal values under medication, though not entirely within the normal reference range. More significantly, the patient's symptoms of fatigue and headache had improved dramatically, and his quality of life was markedly better.

FIGURE 14.3   (A, B) Corresponds to the CE-T1 weighted MRI imaging of the subject 1 year post PRIMARY GKRS suggestive of a significant shrinkage of tumour volume compared to pre-GKRS.

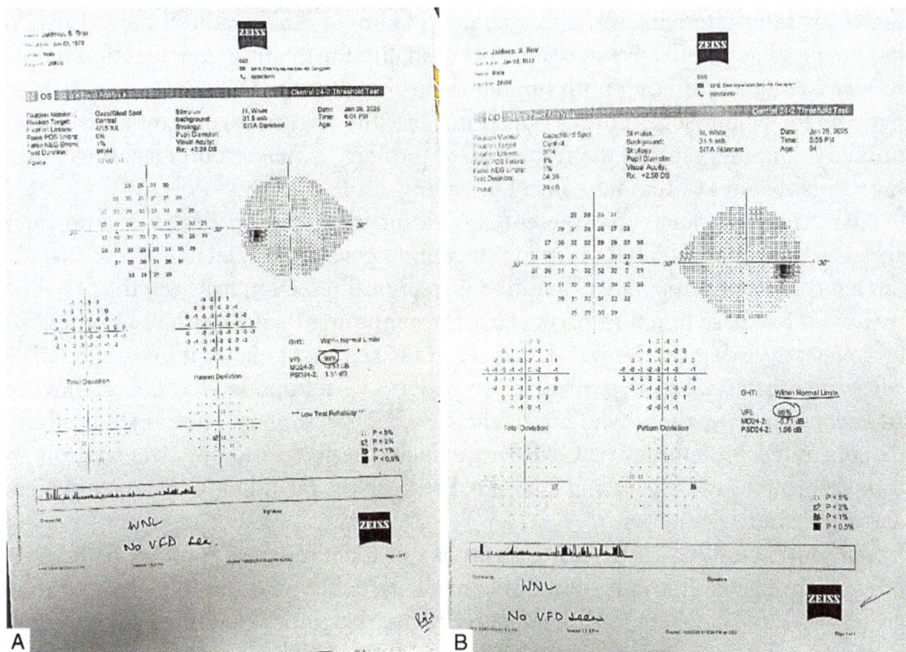

FIGURE 14.4 (A, B) Corresponds to the visual acuity charting of the left eye and right eye of the subject at 1 year post PRIMARY GKRS suggesting near normalisation of the visual field as compared to pre-GKRS).

DISCUSSION

Pituitary adenomas represent a heterogeneous group of tumours that arise from the pituitary gland. While most pituitary adenomas are microadenomas (size <1cm) or macroadenomas (size >1cm), giant pituitary adenomas defined as tumours with a maximum diameter greater than 4 cm or tumour volume more than 10 cc[1] present unique challenges in diagnosis, management, and treatment. These tumours account for a very small fraction (8%) of pituitary adenomas.[2] These tumours often cause significant neuroendocrine dysfunction, neuro-ophthalmic dysfunction or compression of adjacent structures and may present with neurologic deficits. This proximity to vital structures makes safe gross resection of GPA a nightmare for most neurosurgeons. Even after gross total removal, additional therapies may be necessary to achieve long-term control of tumour growth. This multimodal approach with surgery as its keystone, is being used as a way of bringing about tumour control in giant pituitary adenomas.[3] However studies suggest that tumour volume >19 cc, transverse measurement >25mm and ap distance >35mm are significant thresholds for predicting reduced GTE (gross total excision) rates in pituitary tumours. [4] In addition, the need for multiple surgeries, extended endoscopic, or transcranial approaches along with a higher rate of postoperative complications, pushes us in search of safer alternatives. In this context, Gamma Knife radiosurgery (GKRS) has emerged as an effective non-invasive modality for treating non-functioning pituitary adenomas, offering both tumour control and symptom relief, particularly in patients for whom surgical resection is not feasible or carries substantial risk. Preliminary data suggest that the resolution of pituitary hypersecretion is faster[5] with high durable rates of tumour control in gamma knife therapy.[6]

Giant pituitary adenomas present significant treatment challenges due to their size, location, and potential to invade surrounding structures, including the cavernous sinus and optic apparatus. Traditionally, surgical resection has been the first-line treatment for these tumours, particularly for symptomatic cases with visual or endocrinologic disturbances. However, surgery in the setting of giant pituitary adenomas can carry substantial risks, particularly in patients with tumours that extend into the cavernous sinus or those who are medically unfit for surgery. Several studies have demonstrated the efficacy of GKRS in reducing residual tumour size, controlling tumour growth, and alleviating associated symptoms, including visual disturbances and endocrine dysfunction.[7]

Although Gamma Knife radiosurgery is not a definitive cure for all patients, it offers a promising option for tumour control, particularly for tumours located near critical structures, where traditional surgery may be too risky. Moreover, radiosurgery's non-invasive nature and its ability to deliver high doses of radiation with precision make it an attractive choice in cases where maximal tumour reduction is desired without the need for craniotomy or transsphenoidal surgery.

The success of Gamma Knife radiosurgery in the current case mirrors findings in the literature, where similar outcomes have been reported in patients with giant pituitary adenomas (Sathish et al., 2023)[8] and other studies using fractionated dosing.[9,10] Importantly, the preservation of surrounding structures, such as the optic nerves and pituitary gland, is a key advantage of this technique, especially in light of the tumour's proximity to the optic chiasm and the hypothalamus.[8]

However, one must note that the response to radiosurgery can be slow, often requiring several months to years for optimal results. Endocrine normalisation is also not guaranteed, and patients may continue to require medical therapy for hormone control. As such, Gamma Knife radiosurgery should be considered a complementary treatment, often as an adjunct to medical therapy or as part of a multimodal approach to managing giant pituitary adenomas.

TAKE HOME MESSAGE

Primary Gamma Knife radiosurgery has proven to be an effective and safe treatment modality for patients with pituitary adenomas, offering significant tumour control and symptomatic relief with minimal invasiveness. It is particularly valuable in cases where surgical intervention is not feasible or where tumour involvement of critical structures poses a significant risk to the patient. Continued follow-up and careful monitoring of both tumour growth and endocrine function are essential to optimise patient outcomes. As our understanding of radiosurgery evolves, it is likely that Gamma Knife will evolve to play the primary role in the management of challenging pituitary adenomas.

REFERENCES

1. Hofstetter CP, Nanaszko MJ, Mubita LL, Tsiouris J, Anand VK, Schwartz TH. Volumetric classification of pituitary macroadenomas predicts outcome and morbidity following endoscopic endonasal transsphenoidal surgery. Pituitary. 2012;15(3):450-463.

2. Gaillard S, Adeniran S, Villa C, et al. Outcome of giant pituitary tumors requiring surgery. Front Endocrinol (Lausanne). 2022;13:975560. Published 2022 Aug 29.

3. Sharma, Ravi; Suri, Ashish. Giant pituitary adenomas: Operative strategies. International *Journal of Neurooncology* 4(Suppl 1):p S94-S110, November 2021.

4. Chohan MO, Levin AM, Singh R, et al. Three-dimensional volumetric measurements in defining endoscope-guided giant adenoma surgery outcomes. Pituitary. 2016;19(3):311-321.

5. Jackson IM, Norén G. Role of gamma knife therapy in the management of pituitary tumors. Endocrinol Metab Clin North Am. 1999;28(1):133-142.

6. Long-term outcomes after Gamma Knife radiosurgery for patients with a nonfunctioning pituitary adenoma.

7. Garg K, Singh M. Role of Stereotactic Radiosurgery in Pituitary Adenomas. Neurol India. 2020;68(Supplement):S123-S128.

8. Verma SK, Agrawal D, Santhoor HA, Singh M, Kale SS. Gamma Knife Stereotactic Radiosurgery for Giant Intracranial Tumors - A Series of 70 Patients. Neurol India. 2023;71(Supplement):S123-S132.

9. Rak VA, Evdokimova OL, Stepanov VN, Godkov IM, Tokarev AS. Bilateral extracranial extension of giant somatotropic pituitary adenoma after combined treatment. Two-stage gamma knife radiosurgery as a solution. Clin Neurol Neurosurg. 2020;198:106245.

10. Zhao K, Liu X, Liu D, et al. Fractionated Gamma Knife surgery for giant pituitary adenomas. Clin Neurol Neurosurg. 2016;150:139-142.

15 Gamma Knife Radiosurgery In Low-Grade Gliomas

Deepak Agrawal | Chirag Bansal

KEY LEARNING POINTS

1. GKRS is preferred for gliomas located near critical areas like motor cortex, language centres, and brainstem, where conventional surgery poses significant risks. Tumours deep in the brain, such as in the thalamus or hypothalamus, are ideal candidates due to the non-invasive nature of radiosurgery.

2. Most studies recommend a maximum tumour size of ≤3 cm in diameter for optimal control. Larger tumours may require staged treatments or combined therapies.

3. Residual or recurrent tumours after partial resection are suitable for GKRS to manage growth.

4. These slow-growing LGGs respond favourably to GKRS, showing stabilisation or shrinkage without functional compromise.

5. Selected cases show improved local control with radiosurgery after confirming sensitivity to radiation.[3]

6. Patients with a Karnofsky Performance Scale score >70 typically benefit most.

7. Older patients or those unfit for open surgery due to comorbidities are excellent candidates.[4]

8. GKRS is effective as an adjunct to chemotherapy or traditional radiotherapy in cases of tumour progression or recurrence.

9. Careful consideration of cumulative radiation exposure is essential before opting for GKRS.

INTRODUCTION

Gamma Knife Radiosurgery (GKRS), a highly precise, non-invasive treatment, has emerged as a complementary or alternative option for managing low-grade gliomas (LGGs). While traditionally used for malignant or high-grade gliomas, recent evidence suggests its efficacy in managing specific cases of LGGs, especially in inoperable tumours, eloquent brain regions, or after conventional treatments like surgery and chemotherapy. Benefits include its ability to target the tumour with minimal damage to surrounding healthy tissue, leading to improved functional outcomes and quality of life.[1] This chapter highlights the role of GKRS in managing low-grade gliomas with favourable outcomes and reduced risks as compared to invasive surgeries. We also review the patient selection criteria, including tumour size, proximity to critical regions, and prior treatments, in this chapter.[2]

REPRESENTATIVE CASE

HISTORY & EXAMINATION

A 21-year-old female patient presented with h/o Headache and seizures (GTCS) for 6 months (Frequency: 1– per month). Imaging findings were suggestive of right medial temporal glioma. The patient underwent surgery for the same in 2019, with a biopsy suggestive of Pilocytic astrocytoma. The examination showed no motor, sensory, or cranial nerve deficits. Cerebellar signs were absent and higher mental functions were within normal limits. The patient is followed up over 4 years.

IMAGING (FIG. 15.1)

CEMRI brain suggestive of T1 isointense, T2 hyperintense rounded mass in the region of the hypothalamus, projecting inferiorly behind the infundibulum of pituitary gland mildly enhancing on post-contrast images.

GK PROTOCOL

Primary GKRS therapy was performed in 2019 on a gamma knife model B machine. Leksell Coordinate Frame G was used for fixation Configuration and planning was done on Gamma plan version 11.3.2. 15 Gy at 50% isodose line was planned with

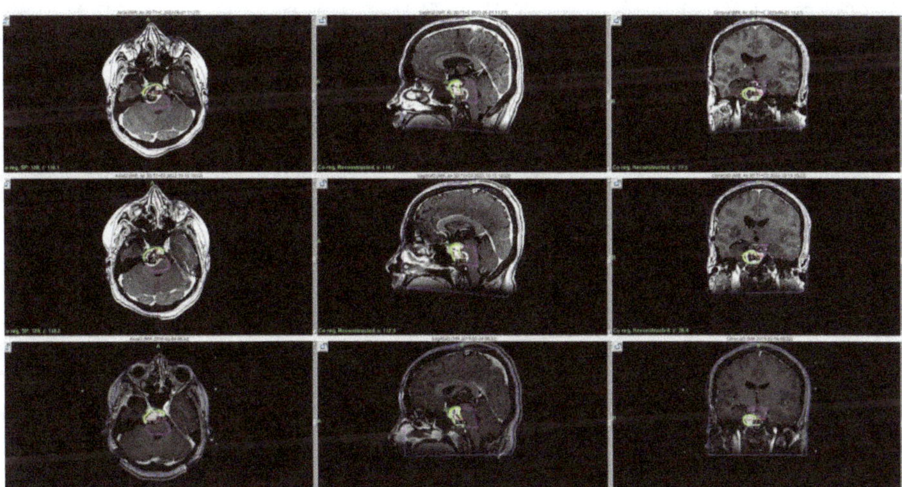

FIGURE 15.1   Contrast MRI axial, sagittal and coronal sections of a patient with Right Medial Temporal Glioma at baseline (2019) (bottom row), at 3 years (2022) (2nd row), at 4 years (2023) (top row) follow-up.

a coverage of 0.9, selectivity of 0.83, Gradient Index of 2.96, and beam on time of 129.9 minutes. The tumour volume was 5.215 cc and shielding of the optic chiasm and brainstem was done.

FOLLOW UP

Follow-up MRI was done in 2019, 2022, and 2023 and the volume of the lesion was assessed. Follow-up imaging over the 4 years also showed a progressive decrease in the volume of the tumour on serial imaging with a 20% and 30% reduction in volume at 3 and 4 years of follow-up, respectively.

Clinically also, a reduction in Headache and seizure frequency was noticed within 6 months of GKRS with an Agnel score of 1 (Seizure free). Anti-seizure medication could be stopped 2 years after GKRS and the patient remains off medication till date.

DISCUSSION

Residual Low-grade gliomas post-surgery can recur or are associated with residual symptoms. GKRS is a very effective treatment option in such cases. GKRS has good precision and aids in controlling tumour growth while preserving surrounding eloquent tissues. Clinical guidelines emphasise its use in cases that are unfit for conventional surgeries due to their proximity to eloquent areas.[5]

In a study conducted by Filipo Gigliardo et al.,[6] LGGs near eloquent brain regions demonstrated superior symptomatic control with GKRS as compared to conventional radiosurgery. GKRS has also been observed to improve cognitive and neurological outcomes.[3]

Comparative Protocols for Managing Low-Grade Gliomas[6]:

Here is a detailed comparison of the literature on surgical resection, GKRS, and conventional radiotherapy:

Treatment Modalities	Indications	Advantages	Limitations	Survival Outcomes (PFS)
Gamma Knife Radiosurgery (GKRS)	Residual or recurrent low-grade gliomas, tumours in eloquent brain regions, small tumour volumes (≤3 cc)	Minimally invasive, precise tumour targeting, preservation of surrounding healthy tissue	Not suitable for larger tumours (>3 cc), potential risk of radiation necrosis and edema	5–10 years (depends on size, location, and subtype)
Surgical Resection	Primary approach for accessible gliomas, especially in non-eloquent areas or larger tumours (>3 cc)	Complete tumour debulking, immediate pathological confirmation.	Involves surgical risks, may not be viable for tumours in critical areas	Varies based on resection extent; gross total resections achieve >10 years for pilocytic astrocytomas

Treatment Modalities	Indications	Advantages	Limitations	Survival Outcomes (PFS)
Conventional Radiotherapy	Adjuvant treatment post-surgery or for larger lesions not amenable to GKRS	Coverage of larger areas, systemic treatment for infiltrative growth.	Increased risk of long-term neurocognitive side effects and radiation-induced damage.	3–5 years as stand-alone, improved when combined with other modalities

Wherever feasible, surgery with complete resections offer significant survival advantages for larger or accessible gliomas. Primary GKRS's Role is best for small, localised, or inoperable tumours while sparing surrounding tissue in critical areas. GKRS can also be used as an adjuvant to surgical resection, postoperatively. Using GKRS in conjunction with other modalities like chemotherapy and fractionated radiation can improve progression-free survival.[7]

Key Observations on using GKRS in low-grade gliomas in literature[8]:

1. Tumour Progression-Free Survival (PFS): Median PFS varies between 5-10 years in LGGs treated with GKRS. Longer intervals noted in younger patients with low-risk, pilocytic astrocytomas.
2. Side Effects and Risks: GKRS minimises side effects such as neurotoxicity and white matter changes when compared to traditional radiotherapy.
3. Enhanced Quality of Life: Long-term QoL metrics for cognitive and emotional functions remain favourable in patients undergoing GKRS.

Progression-Free Survival (PFS) by Subtype[9]:

Histological Subtype	5-Year PFS	10-Year PFS	Recurrence Risks
Pilocytic Astrocytomas	85–90%	75–80%	Low (<10%)
Oligodendrogliomas	70–80%	60–70%	Moderate (~15%)
Gangliogliomas	90–95%	85–90%	Low (~5%)
Optic Pathway Gliomas	60–70%	50–60%	High (>20%)

Summary of Molecularly Informed Management as per literature[10,11]:

Marker	Implication	Recommended Strategy
IDH Mutation	Low recurrence, better radiosensitivity	GKRS as monotherapy in IDH-mutant gliomas
1p/19q Co-deletion	High radiosensitivity, low aggressiveness	Lower radiation dose protocols
MGMT Methylation	Reduced radio-resistance	Combine GKRS with adjuvant chemotherapy
High Ki-67	Faster tumour progression	Intensify treatment with adjuvant therapies

TAKE HOME MESSAGE

Based on our index case and from the various studies in the literature, it can be confidently inferred that GKRS has a significant role in managing low-grade gliomas. It is a very focused, precise, and non-invasive technique in treating various gliomatous lesions at an early stage. Primary GKRS can be considered in small lesions where radiology is clear regarding the histological diagnosis. Post-surgical residual lesions can be very effectively treated with GKRS with a reduction in symptomatology and volume of lesions. Based on histology, GKRS might have to be combined with Surgical resection, Adjuvant chemotherapy, or radiotherapy.

REFERENCES

1. Elliott RE, Parker EC, Rush SC, et al. Efficacy of gamma knife radiosurgery for small-volume recurrent malignant gliomas after initial radical resection. *World Neurosurg.* 2011;76 (1-2):128-62.
2. Wei Z, Pease M, Tang LW, et al. Radiosurgery outcomes in infratentorial juvenile pilocytic astrocytomas. *J Neurooncol.* 2023;162(1):157-165.
3. Wang LW, Shiau CY, Chung WY, et al. Gamma Knife surgery for low-grade astrocytomas: evaluation of long-term outcome based on a 10-year experience. *J Neurosurg.* 2006;105 Suppl:127-132.
4. Szeifert GT, Prasad D, Kamyrio T, Steiner M, Steiner LE. The role of the Gamma Knife in the management of cerebral astrocytomas. *Prog Neurol Surg.* 2007;20:150-163.
5. Valerio J, Borro M, Santiago Rea N, et al. Radiosurgery for Hypothalamic Gliomas: A Case Report and Clinical Guidelines Form a Neurosurgical Center of Excellence. *J Pers Med.* 2024;14(11):1108. Published 2024 Nov 15.
6. Gagliardi F, Bailo M, Spina A, et al. Gamma Knife Radiosurgery for Low-Grade Gliomas: Clinical Results at Long-Term Follow-Up of Tumor Control and Patients' Quality of Life. *World Neurosurg.* 2017;101:540-553.
7. Valerio J, Borro M, Santiago Rea N, et al. Radiosurgery for Hypothalamic Gliomas: A Case Report and Clinical Guidelines Form a Neurosurgical Center of Excellence. *J Pers Med.* 2024;14(11):1108. Published 2024 Nov 15.
8. Jakola AS, Skjulsvik AJ, Myrmel KS, et al. Surgical resection versus watchful waiting in low-grade gliomas. *Ann Oncol.* 2017;28(8):1942-1948.
9. Heppner PA, Sheehan JP, Steiner LE. Gamma knife surgery for low-grade gliomas. *Neurosurgery.* 2005;57(6):.
10. Cancer Genome Atlas Research Network, Brat DJ, Verhaak RG, et al. Comprehensive, Integrative Genomic Analysis of Diffuse Lower-Grade Gliomas. *N Engl J Med.* 2015;372(26):2481-2498.
11. Eckel-Passow JE, Lachance DH, Molinaro AM, et al. Glioma Groups Based on 1p/19q, IDH, and TERT Promoter Mutations in Tumors. *N Engl J Med.* 2015;372(26):2499-2508.

Gamma Knife Radiosurgery in High-Grade Gliomas

16

Deepak Agrawal | Chirag Bansal

KEY LEARNING POINTS

1. Primary GKRS may be useful for elderly patients with small lesions that appear high-grade on imaging.
2. Very early post-operative GKRS can replace EBRT in cases where the tumour has been nearly completely excised.
3. GKRS can also be used as salvage therapy in recurrences following conventional RT.

INTRODUCTION

Currently, intense research is underway to assess the efficacy, safety, and prognostic factors influencing outcomes in using Gamma Knife Radiosurgery (GKRS) for high-grade gliomas. It is now becoming apparent that GKRS helps improve the survival rates of these patients.[1]

Due to its highly precise and non-invasive nature, GKRS has emerged as a complementary or alternative option for managing high-grade gliomas (HGGs), such as glioblastoma multiforme (GBM) and anaplastic astrocytoma. GKRS has been traditionally used for malignant or high-grade gliomas, especially in inoperable tumours, eloquent brain regions, or after conventional treatments like surgery and chemotherapy. Benefits include its ability to target the tumour with minimal damage to surrounding healthy tissue, leading to improved functional outcomes and quality of life.[2] This chapter highlights the role of *primary* GKRS in managing high-grade gliomas, besides the uses already mentioned above, and shows that when carefully utilised, GKRS can yield favourable outcomes with reduced risks compared to invasive surgeries. Patient selection criteria, including tumour size, proximity to critical regions, and prior treatments are also emphasised.[3]

REPRESENTATIVE CASE

HISTORY & EXAMINATION

A 56-year-old male patient presented with h/o Left side spastic hemiparesis for 2 years, with Kernofsky's performance score of 90. Imaging findings were suggestive of Right frontal high-grade glioma. The patient underwent surgery for the same with a biopsy suggestive of Glioblastoma, WHO grade 4. Postoperative imaging was suggestive of some residual for which the patient was started on Temozolomide and the patient underwent secondary Gamma knife therapy after 2 months of surgery. On examination, the patient had left-sided hemiparesis with power 3/5 at most joints. Left side Ashforth grade 3 Hypertonia/Spasticity present. Cerebellar signs were absent and higher mental functions remained within normal limits. Postoperatively, Kernofsky's Performance score of the patient was 50, requiring considerable assistance and frequent medical care. Neurologically, the patient's condition was similar to preoperative status.

IMAGING (FIG. 16.1)

CEMRI brain suggestive of T1 isointense, T2 hyperintense rounded mass in the region of Right frontal region enhancing on post-contrast images.

GK PROTOCOL

Primary GKRS therapy was given for Right Frontal High-grade glioma in the year 2016 using the Gamma Knife model B machine. Leksell Coordinate Frame G was used for fixation configuration, and planning was done on Gamma plan version

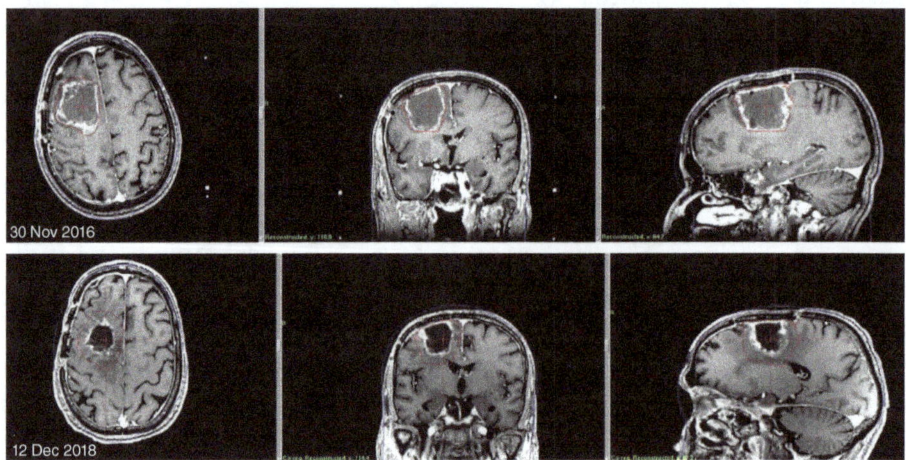

FIGURE 16.1   Contrast MRI axial, sagittal and coronal sections of a patient with Right Frontal High-grade Glioma at baseline (2016) (top row), at 2 years follow up (2018) (bottom row) showing progressive reduction in size of tumour size.

11.3.2. A dose of 20 Gy at 50% isodose line was planned with a coverage of 0.88, selectivity of 0.95, a Gradient Index of 2.82 and beam-on time of 116.1 minutes. The tumour volume was 47.246 cc and shielding of the optic chiasm and brainstem was carried out.

FOLLOW UP

A follow-up MRI showed a progressive decrease in the volume of lesion (approximately 20%) over 2 years, as shown in the imaging above. Clinically also, a reduction in headache and spasticity was noticed within 6 months of GKRS. Power on the left side also improved to 4/5 at many joints within 2 years of GKRS. The patient was lost to follow-up thereafter, and further imaging studies couldn't be done. However, on a telephonic follow-up in January 2025, it was confirmed that the patient was alive, though bedridden, even 9 years after surgery and GKRS!

DISCUSSION

GKRS is typically used as an adjunct to the standard treatment regimen for HGGs, which includes surgical resection, radiation therapy, and chemotherapy (e.g., temozolomide).[4] It may be used in specific clinical scenarios where conventional radiation therapy and systemic treatments are insufficient or impractical. GKRS is particularly valuable for targeting small, localised residual tumour tissue or recurrent tumour nodules after initial treatment.[5]

There are certain limitations of GKRS in treating HGGs including tumour and patient characteristics. High-grade gliomas often exhibit infiltrative growth patterns, making them less ideal for GKRS as it is best suited for discrete, well-defined lesions.[6] There is also a small risk of Radiation Necrosis, particularly with high cumulative doses or in previously irradiated brain tissue. Although some studies suggest benefits, the role of GKRS for high-grade gliomas is less well-established compared to its use for benign tumours and brain metastases. Close follow-up with MRI is necessary to monitor for tumour progression, treatment response, and potential complications. Using GKRS in conjunction with other modalities, like chemotherapy and fractionated radiation can improve progression-free survival.[7-10] As per the study conducted by Zjiwar H A Sadik et al.,[1] 92 patients (52 males and 40 females) underwent GKRS for recurrent glioma. The median age at the time of GKRS was 50 years (range 7–76). Eighty-five of these patients had undergone at least one operation before GKRS. Seven patients had undergone biopsy followed by adjuvant treatment in the form of chemotherapy, EBRT or a combination of both, before GKRS.

TAKE HOME MESSAGE

Based on the above index case and various studies in literature, it can be said that GKRS has a significant role in managing high-grade gliomas, especially when combined with other treatment modalities like chemotherapy. Even post-surgical residual lesions can be very effectively treated with GKRS, with the reduction in both symptomatology and volume of lesion. While GKRS has some utility in the management of high-grade gliomas, it remains a supportive treatment option, typically reserved for specific scenarios, such as recurrent disease or inaccessible tumour regions.

REFERENCES

1. Sadik ZHA, Hanssens PEJ, Verheul JB, et al. Gamma knife radiosurgery for recurrent gliomas. *J Neurooncol.* 2018;140(3):615-622.
2. Elliott RE, Parker EC, Rush SC, et al. Efficacy of gamma knife radiosurgery for small-volume recurrent malignant gliomas after initial radical resection. *World Neurosurg.* 2011;76(1-2):128-62.
3. Wei Z, Pease M, Tang LW, et al. Radiosurgery outcomes in infratentorial juvenile pilocytic astrocytomas. *J Neurooncol.* 2023;162(1):157-165.
4. Cabrera AR, Kirkpatrick JP, Fiveash JB, et al. Radiation therapy for glioblastoma: Executive summary of an American Society for Radiation Oncology Evidence-Based Clinical Practice Guideline. *Pract Radiat Oncol.* 2016;6(4):217-225.
5. Biswas T, Okunieff P, Schell MC, et al. Stereotactic radiosurgery for glioblastoma: retrospective analysis. *Radiat Oncol.* 2009;4:11. Published 2009 Mar 17.
6. Combs SE, Widmer V, Thilmann C, Hof H, Debus J, Schulz-Ertner D. Stereotactic radiosurgery (SRS): treatment option for recurrent glioblastoma multiforme (GBM). *Cancer.* 2005;104(10):2168-2173.
7. Valerio J, Borro M, Santiago Rea N, et al. Radiosurgery for Hypothalamic Gliomas: A Case Report and Clinical Guidelines Form a Neurosurgical Center of Excellence. *J Pers Med.* 2024;14(11):1108. Published 2024 Nov 15.
8. Heppner PA, Sheehan JP, Steiner LE. Gamma knife surgery for low-grade gliomas. *Neurosurgery.*2005;57(6):.
9. Cancer Genome Atlas Research Network, Brat DJ, Verhaak RG, et al. Comprehensive, Integrative Genomic Analysis of Diffuse Lower-Grade Gliomas. *N Engl J Med.* 2015;372(26):2481-2498.
1. Eckel-Passow JE, Lachance DH, Molinaro AM, et al. Glioma Groups Based on 1p/19q, IDH, and TERT Promoter Mutations in Tumors. *N Engl J Med.* 2015;372(26):2499-2508.

Role of Gamma Knife in Glioblastoma

17

Deepak Agrawal | Rakshay Kaul

KEY LEARNING POINTS

1. GKRS is emerging as a rapidly evolving adjunct to standard External beam radiotherapy (EBRT) following surgical excision and highly effective in lesions with lower tumour volume or size, irrespective of whether they are supratentorial or infratentorial.
2. GKRS without EBRT after primary surgery with concurrent Temozolomide may offer a newer model of management with similar outcomes and lower complication rates in comparison to conventional therapy using EBRT.
3. EBRT when followed by GKRS has a better outcome in improving median survival time in comparison to the conventional use of EBRT.
4. Lower rate of complications as compared to whole-brain radiotherapy and need for only a single setting are additional benefits of GKRS.

INTRODUCTION

High grade gliomas, which incorporate grade III, grade IV Astrocytomas and Glioblastomas, have now been designated as the most common primary brain tumour in adults. Primary CNS malignant tumours account for 2% of all cancers but cause a disproportionate amount of cancer-related morbidity and mortality. Despite medical advances over time, the outcome of high grade glioma remains abysmal with the median length of survival being less than 2 years for patients with glioblastoma, and 2 to 5 years for patients with anaplastic glioma.[1-4]

Gamma Knife has recently evolved into a mainstream therapy and has found its place as one of the adjunct treatments for treating glioblastomas.

CASE REPRESENTATION

HISTORY & EXAMINATION

Presenting H/O

A 60-year-old male presented with a generalised tonic-clonic seizure on 25th December 2022. The seizures were associated with loss of consciousness. He had undergone left Fronto Temporal craniotomy and gross total excision of tumour on 21st March 2023. Histopathology was Glioblastoma, IDH wild type.

On examination, the patient was alert with a Karnofsky score of 100. There were no cranial nerve/motor/sensory deficits.

IMAGING

CEMRI Brain (2016)

Well-defined solid cystic T2/Flair hyperintense, T1 hypointense subcortical lesion with peripheral nodularity (along antero-superior aspect) measuring 2.8 × 1.9 × 2.8 cm left insula, extending up to external capsule medially. Raised perfusion on T2* perfusion and ASL map. Minimal perilesional oedema extending into the left parieto-temporal lobe (Fig. 17.1).

NCCT Head (Post-Op)

Postoperative cavity can be seen with gross tumour-free cavity with minimal hyperdensity, suggestive of postoperative blood collection (Fig. 17.2).

MRI Brain (During GKRS)

Postoperative resection cavity is seen in the left insula showing T1 hyperintensity. Ill-defined Flair hyperintensity was seen in medial and anterior left temporal lobe, suggestive of residual tumour (Fig. 17.3).

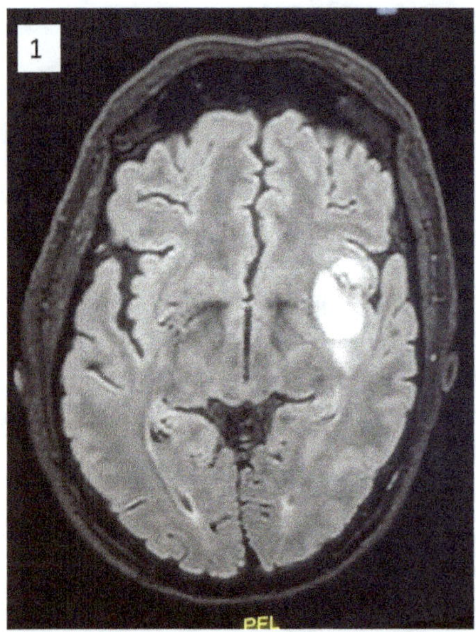

FIGURE 17.1 Shows preoperative MRI scan of the left insular high-grade tumour with almost homogeneous contrast enhancement on T1 weighted imaging with contrast.

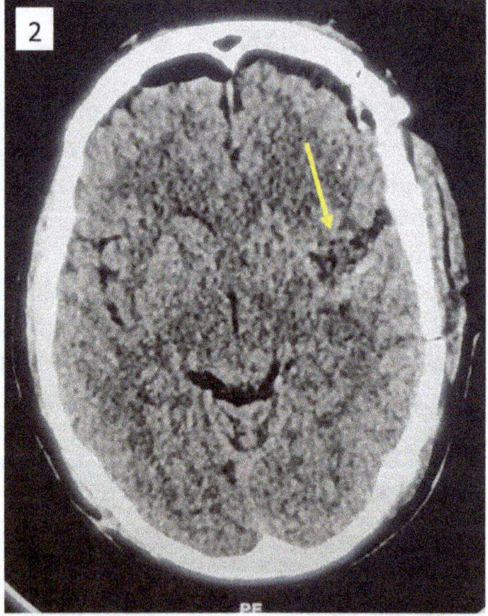

FIGURE 17.2 Shows a postoperative non-contrast CT scan of the head with the tumour cavity appearing hypodense (yellow arrow) with mild peripheral hyperdensity suggestive of collected blood or residual tumour tissue. Anteriorly pneumocephalus is present.

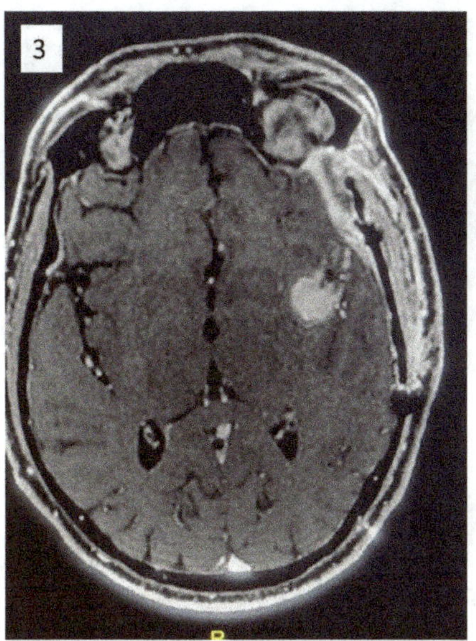

FIGURE 17.3 Shows an MRI scan after 1 month of surgery at the time just prior to GKRS. We can see a contrast-enhancing lesion along the distal end of the postoperative cavity.

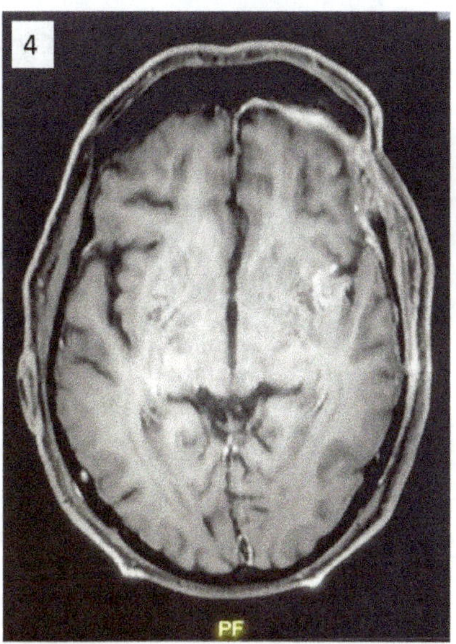

FIGURE 17.4 A T1 weighted axial scan of the brain done a few months after GKRS, revealing a small heterogeneously hyperintense residual tumour with a reduction in the size as compared to the previous MRI.

MRI Brain (Post-GKRS)

A relative reduction in tumour size can be seen, with non-homogeneous contrast enhancement of residual tumour lesion (Fig. 17.4).

GK PROTOCOL COURSE

Secondary GKT was given to the tumour cavity. 3.99 cc of the tumour received 18 Gy at 50% isodose line (Fig. 17.5).

DISCUSSION

Considering that High-Grade gliomas are incurable due to their malignant nature, a treatment strategy must be formulated to at least manage this disease and its progression with the hopes of increasing the survival time while maintaining a good quality of life. Although the standard of treatment remains cytoreductive surgeries followed by a regimen of concomitant chemoradiotherapy, the outcomes are often far from satisfactory. GKRS has been proposed as one of the treatment measures but mostly as an adjunct to the existing treatment protocols, as its efficacy in improving the outcome has not yet been proven substantially.[5]

The Radiation Therapy Oncology Group (RTOG) published a trial conducted by Souhami and colleagues which was the first of its kind on the role of adding stereotactic radiosurgery (SRS) to the treatment of high grade gliomas. It was a multicentre

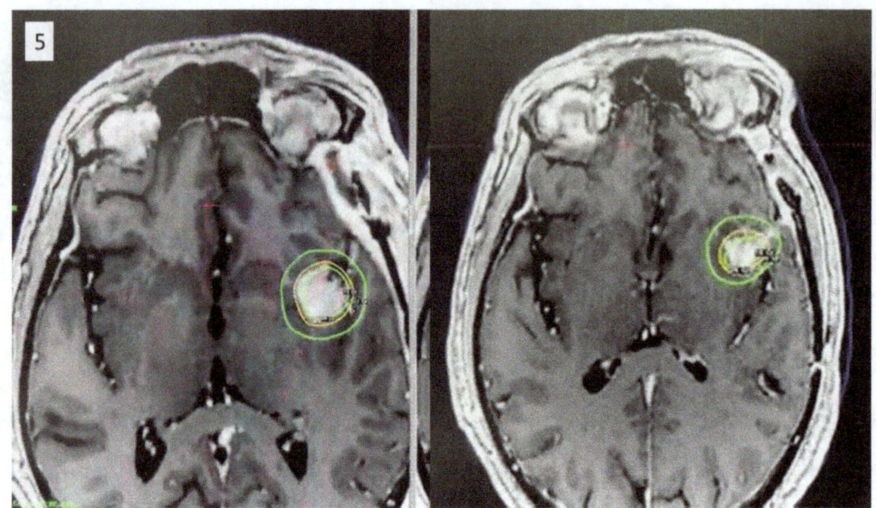

FIGURE 17.5   Shows the Gamma Knife dose protocol with a focus on the target lesion.

randomised controlled trial to analyse the inclusion of SRS (including both Gamma Knife Radiosurgery and LINAC based radio surgical techniques), in comparison to the standard external beam radiation therapy (EBRT) alone for the treatment of GBM.[3] As a part of the primary treatment, SRS was used for the management of GBM, rather than being considered later as a means of palliative therapy. Around 203 patients were assigned randomly in such a way that supratentorial GBM would receive either adjuvant SRS (prescription dose 15–24 Gy) followed by EBRT and carmustine, or EBRT and carmustine without giving SRS beforehand. It was observed that there was no difference between the two groups of patients as far as the primary endpoint of survival was concerned: the SRS group had a mean survival time of 13.5 months, whereas the control group had a mean survival time of 13.6 months. The lack of a definitive comparative result propelled further investigative efforts by different researchers around the globe to validate these results separately.

Emmanuel C. Nwokedi[6] and his team evaluated 64 follow-ups among the 82 patients with confirmed pathological GBM who had received EBRT between August 1993 and December 1998. These patients were divided into those who were treated with EBRT alone vs those who received GKRS within 6 weeks of completion of EBRT. The median EBRT dose was 59.7 Gy (range, 28-070.2 Gy), and the median GK-SRS dose to the prescription volume was 17.1 Gy (range, 10-28 Gy). The median age of the cohort was 50.4 years, and the median pre-GKRS Karnofsky performance status was 80. The median overall survival for the entire cohort was 16 months. It was interestingly observed that with regards to the overall survival of the group which received GKRS, there was an increase in the median survival up to 25 months in contrast to 13 months in the group receiving only EBRT (P = 0.034). This result contrasts with the previous study and lays an important basis for conducting GKRS as a valuable asset for high-grade glioma management.

The two studies discussed above have both considered the utility of GKRS; however, the timing of applying GKRS in the treatment protocol seems to have resulted in contradictory results. The study by Souhami et al.[3] used GKRS, followed by EBRT, whereas the later study used GKRS after the EBRT was given. These differing approaches offer valuable insight into determining the optimal timing of using GKRS in these patients

Realising the potential of giving GKRS in a timed manner for optimal yield led many other studies to follow a treatment pattern similar to Nwokidi et al. to evaluate the consistency of those results. Loeffler et al.[7] conducted a prospective study before Nwokidi in 1992 and evaluated 37 patients between 1998 and 1991 to explore the role of radiosurgery as part of the initial management. Patients in one study group received only EBRT, while the other group received radiosurgery (dose of 10 - 20 Gy) about 2 to 4 weeks after completion of conventional radiotherapy with a median tumour volume of 4.3 cc at the time of radiosurgery. The study showed an appreciable increase in median time of survival and led to the conclusion that radiosurgery is beneficial as part of the initial treatment protocol for small, radiographically well-defined high grade gliomas.

Kondziolka et al.[8] evaluated the survival benefit of SRS in 107 patients with high-grade glioma during an 8-year interval at the University of Pittsburgh. They compared their series of patients with GBM, who were treated by GKRS with historical control groups. They also concluded that an improved survival benefit after radiosurgery was identified for patients with glioblastoma and anaplastic astrocytoma, although the selection of patients who underwent SRS had smaller tumour volumes irrespective of the tumour location.

A study by Nagai et al.[9] also had a similar conclusion stating that radiosurgery could provide a survival benefit when included as a part of multimodality treatment, however, the study also highlighted the possibility of selection bias as most of the patients responding in a positive manner were those with lower tumour volumes (<3.5cm in average diameter) and a good Karnofsky score. A similar conclusion was derived from the study of Kondziolka[8] as well, showing that GKRS particularly benefited patients with a Karnofsky performance scale score ranking of at least 90, and those patients who have received adjuvant chemotherapy.

An ambispective analysis done by us[16] on histologically proven Glioblastomas operated at AIIMS, New Delhi between January 2016 and November 2018 compared the efficacy between two groups: one group who received EBRT plus Temozolomide (6 cycles) postoperatively and another group who received GKRS within 4 weeks of surgery (without EBRT along with continued Temozolomide. This study is the *only one in the world* to evaluate the efficacy of GKRS without conventional EBRT. This study concluded that even without the use of EBRT, GKRS to tumour bed/residual tumour after primary surgery with concurrent chemotherapy yielded a result of overall survival and progression-free life similar to the conventional EBRT group.

Despite multiple studies under evaluation, the role of GKRS in the treatment algorithm remains inconclusive and warrants a larger randomised study (Table 17.1).

TABLE 17.1

Authors	Selch et al.[10]	Masciopinto et al.[11]	Gannett et al.[12]	Buatti et al.[13]	Kondziolka et al.[8]	Shenouda et al.[14]	Shrieve et al.[15]	Nwokedi et al.[6]
Institution	UCLA	University of Wisconsin	University of Arizona	University of Florida	University of Pittsburgh	McGill University	Harvard University	University of Maryland
Date of Publication	1993	1995	1995	1995	1997	1997	1999	2002
Number of Patients	35(18 primary lesions)	31	30	11	107(65 primary lesions)	14	78	31
KPS	100% >70	57% >70	97% >70	all >90%	mean KPS 90	79% >70	median 90	61% >70
Median tumor volume (CC)	20	16	24	14	6.5	<34	10	25
Median survival (months)	9	9.5	GBM 13 AA 28	17	GBM 20 AA 56	10	19.9	25
1-year survival (%)	GBM 33 AA 100	37	GBM 43 AA 64.5	–	–	43	88.5	–
2-year survival (%)	GBM 33 AA 100	–	GBM 8 AA 53	–	GBM 41 AA 88	–	–	–
EBRT	45-60Gy	0-66	median 59.4	mean 60	60	60	73-78	>59
Median follow up(months)	10	9.5	30	6	–	8.8	25	–
Number of reoperations	0/2	–	0/10	0/4	3//22	1//14	20/39	–
Prognostic factors on multivariate analysis	–	Age, KPS, extent of surgery	KPS	Re operation	Age, KPS	None	Age	SRS

TAKE HOME MESSAGE

The utility of the Gamma knife in high-grade lesions is evolving rapidly and is providing a elegant way of treating the malignant lesion without precisely, in a single sitting, highlighting its focused effective mechanism of dealing with residual Glioblastoma(s)

REFERENCES

1. DeAngelis LM. Brain tumors. *N Engl J Med*. 2001;344(2):114-123.
2. Wen PY, Kesari S. Malignant gliomas in adults [published correction appears in N Engl J Med. 2008 Aug 21;359(8):877]. *N Engl J Med*. 2008;359(5):492-507.
3. Souhami L, Seiferheld W, Brachman D, et al. Randomized comparison of stereotactic radiosurgery followed by conventional radiotherapy with carmustine to conventional radiotherapy with carmustine for patients with glioblastoma multiforme: report of Radiation Therapy Oncology Group 93-05 protocol. *Int J Radiat Oncol Biol Phys*. 2004;60(3):853-860.
4. Garcia CR, Slone SA, Dolecek TA, Huang B, Neltner JH, Villano JL. Primary central nervous system tumor treatment and survival in the United States, 2004-2015. *J Neurooncol*. 2019;144(1):179-191.
5. Crowley RW, Pouratian N, Sheehan JP. Gamma knife surgery for glioblastoma multiforme. *Neurosurg Focus*. 2006;20(4):E17. Published 2006 Apr 15.
6. Nwokedi EC, DiBiase SJ, Jabbour S, Herman J, Amin P, Chin LS. Gamma knife stereotactic radiosurgery for patients with glioblastoma multiforme. *Neurosurgery*. 2002;50(1):41-47.
7. Loeffler JS, Alexander E 3rd, Shea WM, et al. Radiosurgery as part of the initial management of patients with malignant gliomas. *J Clin Oncol*. 1992;10(9):1379-1385.
8. Kondziolka D, Flickinger JC, Bissonette DJ, Bozik M, Lunsford LD. Survival benefit of stereotactic radiosurgery for patients with malignant glial neoplasms. *Neurosurgery*. 1997;41(4):776-785.
9. Nagai, H., Kondziolka, D., Niranjan, A., Flickinger, J., & Lunsford, L. (2004). Results Following Stereotactic Radiosurgery for Patients with Glioblastoma multiforme. In *KARGER eBooks* (pp. 91–99). https://doi.org/10.1159/000078141
10. Selch, M. T., Ciacci, J. D., De Salles, A. A., Goetsch, S., Brekhus, S. D. (1993). Radiosurgery for Primary Malignant Brain Tumors. In: *Stereotactic Surgery and Radiosurgery*. pp. 335-352. Eds., A. A. F. De Salles, S. J. Goetsch, Medical Physics Pub., Madison, Wisconsin.
11. Masciopinto JE, Levin AB, Mehta MP, Rhode BS. Stereotactic radiosurgery for glioblastoma: a final report of 31 patients. *J Neurosurg*. 1995;82(4):530-535.
12. Gannett D, Stea B, Lulu B, Adair T, Verdi C, Hamilton A. Stereotactic radiosurgery as an adjunct to surgery and external beam radiotherapy in the treatment of patients with malignant gliomas. *Int J Radiat Oncol Biol Phys*. 1995;33(2):461-468.
13. Buatti JM, Friedman WA, Bova FJ, Mendenhall WM. Linac radiosurgery for high-grade gliomas: the University of Florida experience. *Int J Radiat Oncol Biol Phys*. 1995;32(1):205-210.
14. Shenouda G, Souhami L, Podgorsak EB, et al. Radiosurgery and accelerated radiotherapy for patients with glioblastoma. *Can J Neurol Sci*. 1997;24(2):110-115.
15. Shrieve DC, Alexander E 3rd, Black PM, et al. Treatment of patients with primary glioblastoma multiforme with standard postoperative radiotherapy and radiosurgical boost: prognostic factors and long-term outcome. *J Neurosurg*. 1999;90(1):72-77.
16. S Rai HI, Agrawal D, Singh M, Kale SS. Early Gamma Knife Therapy (Without EBRT) in Operated Patients of Glioblastoma Multiforme. *Neurol India*. 2023;71(Supplement):S183-S188.

18 Gamma Knife in Multiple Metastasis

Rakshay Kaul | Deepak Agrawal

KEY LEARNING POINTS

1. Brain metastasis is the most common malignancy affecting the brain, with lung cancer being the leading cause, followed by breast cancer.
2. Single metastasis to the brain has a relatively better response to GKRS as compared to multiple metastatic deposits in brain parenchyma. However, irrespective of the number of metastasis, GKRS is now the standard of care as compared to whole brain radiotherapy.
3. Gamma knife therapy has better efficacy & reduced toxicity profile in comparison to whole-brain radiotherapy.

INTRODUCTION

Multiple metastasis to the brain is known to be the most common malignant neoplasms of the brain and most common brain tumours overall.[1] The proportion of metastasis to the brain in comparison to primary intracranial neoplasm is as close to 10:1 and is only progressing with the recent advances in imaging techniques as well as prolonged survival benefits that are a result of better control of disease progression due to anti-cancer medications. In adults, lung cancer is the most common cause (50%–60%), followed by breast cancer (15%–20%) and melanoma (5%–10%). [2,3,4] Traditionally the treatment of choice for multiple cerebral metastasis has been whole-brain radiotherapy (WBRT), but for the last decade, it has been unequivocally been shown that GKRS has better efficacy, safety and quality of life in patients with single or multiple metastasis.

CASE REPRESENTATION

HISTORY & EXAMINATION

A 63-year-old male patient, with lung adenocarcinoma, controlled on novel anti-chemotherapeutic agent Loratinib 50mg presented with multiple cerebral metastasis. He had previously received GKRS in 2020. He had been doing well for

1.5 years until he had 2 episodes of focal seizures (in Feb 2023) involving the right upper limb, lasting 15 seconds and not associated with any loss of consciousness. The Patient was alert with a Karnofsky score of 100. Cerebellar signs were *impaired* Dysdiadochokinesia/Finger nose test/Tandem walking towards the left side.

IMAGING

MRI Brain (31-01-2023): Reduction in previous lesions along with the appearance of new lesions in left paracentral, superior frontal and left superior parietal gyrus (Fig. 18.1).

GK PROTOCOL:

Primary GKRS was given for multiple metastasis in August 2020 following which there was a reduction in those target lesions. New Lesions were noticed in Repeat MRI in January 2023 for which primary GKRS was given on 21st March 2023. All lesions were given 18 Gy prescription dose and planning was done using the 'Lightning plan'.

FOLLOW UP

The Patient was admitted in view of Hemoptysis in July 2023 and was managed conservatively. The patient gradually improved and was discharged with a GCS of E4V5M6 and stable vitals in August 2023.

DISCUSSION

With the invention of Stereotactic radiosurgery (SRS) and its clinical applicability in multiple brain metastases, the value of WBRT in current treatment protocols for brain metastases is being re-examined. In 1989, lindquist et al.[7] described a case report of a patient successfully treated with SRS who had developed a metastasis to brain from a Hypernephroma,[7] and soon it was followed by multiple trials over decades to evaluate the utility of combining SRS with WBRT.[8,9] The standard treatment for single metastasis is based on surgical intervention, which may be combined with adjuvant WBRT/SRS. But the prognosis and overall survival are quite different in comparison to cases with metastatic lesions.[10] A study by Yamamoto et Al. showed that patients with two or more metastatic lesions did not show any significant difference in overall survival based on the number of lesions. The management of these patients was either WBRT with or without GKRS or just GKRS alone. This prospective observational trial included 1194 patients (455 with a single brain metastasis, 531 with two to four brain metastases, and 208 patients with five to ten brain metastases). They stated that SRS might be a suitable alternative for patients with up to 10 brain metastases considering the minimal invasiveness of SRS and the fewer side effects compared to WBRT.[11] Salvetti et al. analysed 96 patients with five or more metastatic lesions and showed a significant association between

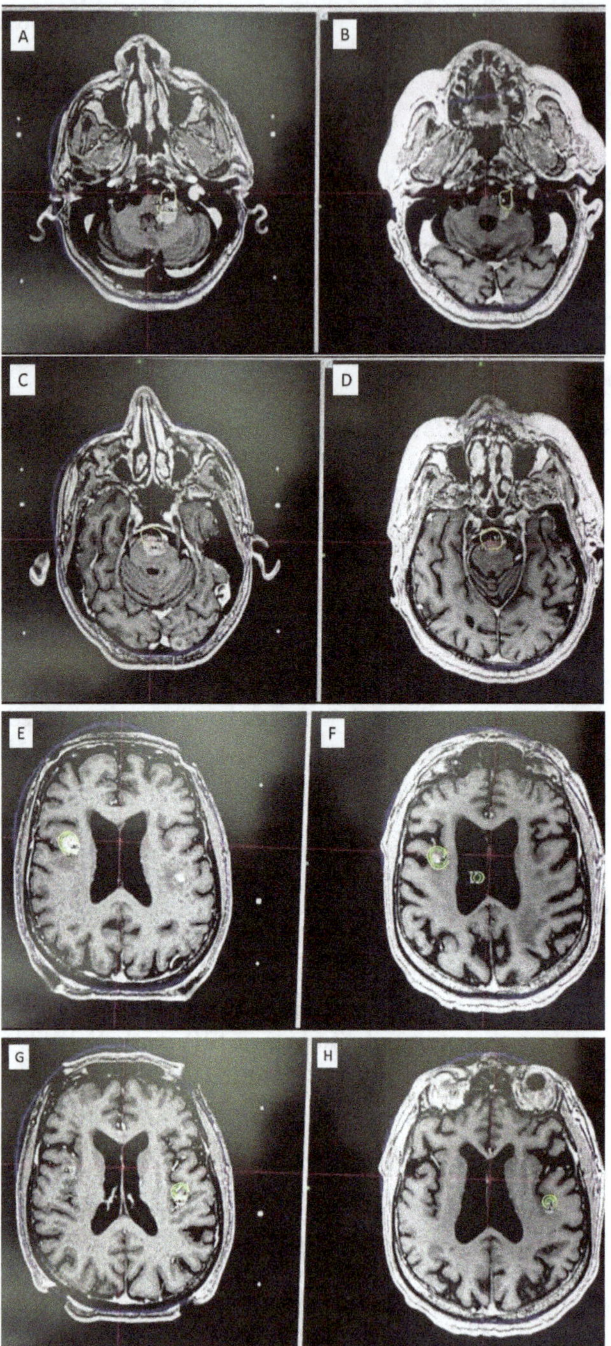

FIGURE 18.1   Showing evident reduction in sizes of metastatic lesions as seen in pre-GKRS and post-GKRS MRI scans. Legends (A, C, E, G) show (pre-GKRS) metastatic lesions in the brain in the left Middle cerebellar peduncle, left pontine, Right frontoparietal and left insular regions respectively. Corresponding to these are the post-GKRS MRI scans of follow-up (B, D, F, H) showing the relative reduction of lesions in size over time.

RPA class and overall survival.[12] The RPA classification is based on patient age, KPS, presence of extracranial metastases, and the status of primary tumour control.[13] A study by Nityanand Pandey et Al. showed that GKRS is a valuable, effective, and well-tolerated treatment modality for patients with non-solitary intracranial metastases. The findings also showed that a high proportion of patients succumbed to death with other regions (extracranial causes) rather than the metastases. Thus, the implementation of an effective plan of GKRS can help in improving the overall survival of patients with brain metastases.[14]

A series of meta-analyses of randomised controlled trials of WBRT and SRS confirmed that WBRT did not significantly improve overall survival in patients with a limited number of brain metastases (up to four) however, WBRT when combined with SRS allowed significantly better local control and reduced the rate of distant brain metastasis. In contrast to this, patients treated with SRS alone had a higher rate of local recurrence and distant brain metastasis compared with patients treated with combined WBRT and SRS, However, repeated retreatment with SRS alone allowed retreatment of local recurrence and distant brain metastasis with preservation of neurocognitive function.[15]

While comparing the benefits of the SRS and WBRT it is imperative to note the difference in the toxicity profile based on the dose the patients are subjected to. Whole brain radiotherapy (WBRT) has a long list of toxic effects which include scalp erythema, reversible hair loss, fatigue, hyperpigmentation, irritable behaviour and anorexia. These may develop over a period of 5 to 10 weeks after WBRT.[16] In the only prospective study to date, Nichol et al. reported in a multicentre, single-arm study on the efficacy and tolerance of SRS for patients with up to ten cerebral metastases. Patients with a life expectancy of more than six months and up to ten brain metastases with a diameter of ≤3 cm were treated with volumetric radiosurgery. Sixty patients were given SRS which was delivered in five fractions with 98% target coverage, prescribed as 95% of 50 Gy (47.5 Gy in 5 fractions) to the metastases with no margin and 95% of 40 Gy (38 Gy in 5 fractions) to their 2-mm planning target volumes, concurrent with 20 Gy to the whole-brain planning target volume. The 1-year local control rate was 88%, and after 2 years, relapse was observed in 14%. Only one grade 3 acute toxicity (case of somnolence syndrome) was seen and one patient died of unknown neurologic cause 4 weeks after treatment, which was scored as a grade 5 radiation necrosis. Regarding late toxicity, grade 3 to 5 radiation necrosis was observed in 10%, and grade 1 to 5 radiation necrosis in 17%. The cumulative incidence of symptomatic radiation necrosis (grade 2 to 5) was 13% at 3 years.[17] Other retrospective studies confirmed SRS as feasible and tolerable in patients with multiple brain metastases.[18,19] Yamamoto et al. reported in their prospective trial a local recurrence after 1 year of stereotactic radiosurgery in 7% of patients with 2–4 tumours and 6.5% in patients with 5–10 tumours. Incidences of local recurrence or leukoencephalopathy did not differ significantly between the two groups of patients with more than one tumour.[11] Yamamoto et al. showed furthermore in a case-matched study of stereotactic radiosurgery for patients with multiple brain metastases that there were no significant differences between the groups with tumour numbers of 1-4 (group A) and with ≥ 5 tumours (group B) in case of SRS-related complications.[20] In general, toxicity rates in studies evaluating SRS in multiple brain metastases were consistently low and local control rates were sufficient and comparable with stereotactic radiosurgery in limited brain metastases.

TAKE HOME MESSAGE

Radiosurgery is an excellent modality to treat multiple metastatic lesions in the brain with a relatively lower toxicity profile and improved survival outcomes, suggesting the importance of a planned and timely delivered Gamma Knife therapy in such patients.

REFERENCES

1. Nayak L, Lee EQ, Wen PY. Epidemiology of brain metastases. *Curr Oncol Rep*. 2012;14(1):48-54.

2. Sammaddar D, Basu A, Roy P, Chowdhury H. Incidence and clinical profile of brain metastasis treated with whole brain radiotherapy in a tertiary hospital in eastern India: A retrospective audit. *Indian J Cancer*. 2023;60(3):337-344.

3. Nieder C, Spanne O, Mehta MP, Grosu AL, Geinitz H. Presentation, patterns of care, and survival in patients with brain metastases: what has changed in the last 20 years?. *Cancer*. 2011;117(11):2505-2512.

4. Kraft J, Zindler J, Minniti G, Guckenberger M, Andratschke N. Stereotactic Radiosurgery for Multiple Brain Metastases. *Curr Treat Options Neurol*. 2019;21(2):6. Published 2019 Feb 13.

5. Halasz LM, Uno H, Hughes M, et al. Comparative effectiveness of stereotactic radiosurgery versus whole-brain radiation therapy for patients with brain metastases from breast or non-small cell lung cancer. *Cancer*. 2016;122(13):2091-2100.

6. Sahgal A, Ruschin M, Ma L, Verbakel W, Larson D, Brown PD. Stereotactic radiosurgery alone for multiple brain metastases? A review of clinical and technical issues. *Neuro Oncol*. 2017;19(suppl_2):ii2-ii15.

7. Lindquist C. Gamma knife surgery for recurrent solitary metastasis of a cerebral hypernephroma: case report. *Neurosurgery*. 1989;25(5):802-804.

8. Brown PD, Jaeckle K, Ballman KV, et al. Effect of Radiosurgery Alone vs Radiosurgery With Whole Brain Radiation Therapy on Cognitive Function in Patients With 1 to 3 Brain Metastases: A Randomized Clinical Trial [published correction appears in JAMA. 2018 Aug 7;320(5):510]. *JAMA*. 2016;316(4):401-409.

9. Aoyama H, Shirato H, Tago M, et al. Stereotactic radiosurgery plus whole-brain radiation therapy vs stereotactic radiosurgery alone for treatment of brain metastases: a randomized controlled trial. *JAMA*. 2006;295(21):2483-2491.

10. Patchell RA, Tibbs PA, Walsh JW, et al. A randomized trial of surgery in the treatment of single metastases to the brain. *N Engl J Med*. 1990;322(8):494-500.

11. Yamamoto M, Serizawa T, Shuto T, et al. Stereotactic radiosurgery for patients with multiple brain metastases (JLGK0901): a multi-institutional prospective observational study. *Lancet Oncol*. 2014;15(4):387-395.

12. Salvetti DJ, Nagaraja TG, McNeill IT, Xu Z, Sheehan J. Gamma Knife surgery for the treatment of 5 to 15 metastases to the brain: clinical article. *J Neurosurg*. 2013;118(6):1250-1257.

13. Gaspar L, Scott C, Rotman M, et al. Recursive partitioning analysis (RPA) of prognostic factors in three Radiation Therapy Oncology Group (RTOG) brain metastases trials. *Int J Radiat Oncol Biol Phys*. 1997;37(4):745-751.

14. Pandey N. Gamma knife radiosurgery in the Management of Non-solitary Brain metastases: A Retrospective analysis of survival. *Turkish Journal of Oncology*. 2020.

15. Tsao M, Xu W, Sahgal A. A meta-analysis evaluating stereotactic radiosurgery, whole-brain radiotherapy, or both for patients presenting with a limited number of brain metastases. *Cancer*. 2012;118(9):2486-2493.

16. Boldrey E, Sheline G. Delayed transitory clinical manifestations after radiation treatment of intracranial tumors. *Acta Radiol Ther Phys Biol*. 1966;5:5-10.

17. Nichol A, Ma R, Hsu F, et al. Volumetric Radiosurgery for 1 to 10 Brain Metastases: A Multicenter, Single-Arm, Phase 2 Study. *Int J Radiat Oncol Biol Phys*. 2016;94(2):312-321.

18. Muacevic A, Kreth FW, Tonn JC, Wowra B. Stereotactic radiosurgery for multiple brain metastases from breast carcinoma. *Cancer*. 2004;100(8):1705-1711.

19. Pfeffer RM, Levin D, Spiegelmann R. Linac-based radiosurgery for multiple brain metastases: A quality assurance and feasibility study. *J Clin Oncol*. 2017;35(15 Suppl):2077. https://doi.org/10.1200/JCO.2017.35.15_suppl.2077

20. Yamamoto M, Kawabe T, Sato Y, et al. A case-matched study of stereotactic radiosurgery for patients with multiple brain metastases: comparing treatment results for 1-4 vs ≥ 5 tumors: clinical article. *J Neurosurg*. 2013;118(6):1258-1268.

19 Gamma Knife High Cervical Lesions

Deepak Agrawal | Chirag Bansal | Kushagra Pandey

INTRODUCTION

The application of Gamma Knife radiosurgery for treating cervical lesions involves various challenges, primarily due to anatomical, physiological, and technical factors. The proximity of critical structures like the spinal cord, vertebral arteries, and nerve roots, which are particularly sensitive to radiation, means that any deviation in dose delivery can result in serious complications. Additionally, the mobility of the cervical spine, coupled with the limitations of current stereotactic frames in targeting lower cervical spine lesions, presents technical difficulties in accurately delivering the required dose to the intended target.[1] We present two patients with high cervical lesions who underwent GKRS at our institute with two different techniques of frame fixation.

CASE 1: LOWER CRANIAL NERVE SCHWANNOMA

HISTORY AND EXAMINATION

A 35-year-old male presented with complaints of gradually progressive left-sided hearing loss, hoarseness of voice and difficulty swallowing over the last 1.5 years. On examination, he had left-sided 7th-12th nerve involvement. Patient had undergone a right retro-mastoid suboccipital craniotomy and tumour decompression 6 months earlier.

IMAGING

X-ray was done to visualise the craniotomy defect before frame fixation to avoid pin placement at the craniotomy site. MRI with T1 contrast, T2 and CISS/ FIESTA sequences was obtained one day prior to treatment administration and was co-registered with the reference CBCT done with the frame placed on the day of treatment delivery. MRI was suggestive of a homogeneously contrast-enhancing residual lesion in the right cerebellopontine angle, epicentered at the left Jugular foramen extending up to the inferior C2 vertebral body level.

GK PROTOCOL

On the day of treatment, first, the Leksell stereotactic G frame was secured to the lowest limit possible with anterior posts fixed just above the supraorbital ridge and posterior posts fixed to the occipital bone. The patient was then taken for CBCT which was fused with the MRI. Planning was done on the co-registered MRI which involved demarcating the target lesion and at-risk area including the brainstem and spinal cord. We used the lightning software for planning the dose delivery after setting the prescription dose of 11 Gy to the target and maximum dose of 11 Gy to at-risk structures. The plan was confirmed with the radiation oncologist and physicist before approval. Patient was positioned supine with the gamma angle set at 90 degrees followed by treatment delivery.

FOLLOW UP

The 1-year follow-up scan shows tumour progression along the non-irradiated inferior margin (Fig. 19.1B). The patient also reported symptomatic relief in swallowing difficulty as compared to baseline.

CASE 2

A 27-year-old female who had undergone surgery for a right C3-4 Schwannoma 6 months back with no present complaints but with residual on post-operative MRI, was planned for secondary GKRS. In this case, the radiation delivery up to the C4 vertebral level was ensured by fixing the anterior posts of the Leksell stereotactic G frame to the maxilla and posteriorly to the occipital bone, as demonstrated in Fig. 19.2.

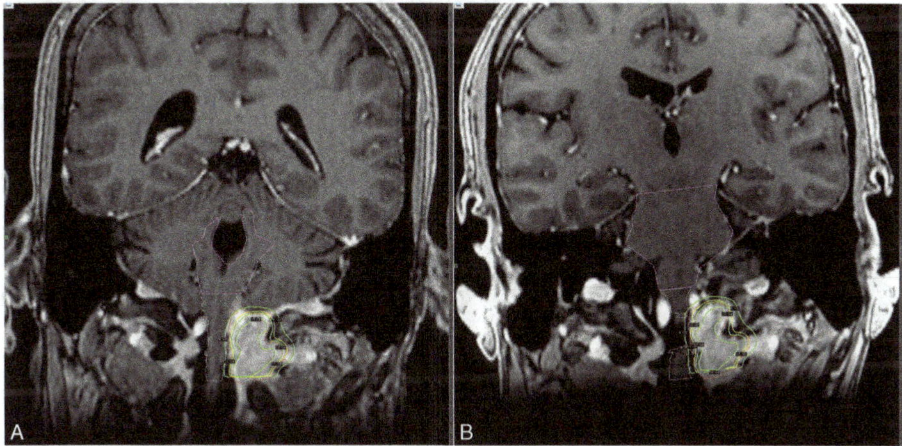

FIGURE 19.1 Coronal CMRI brain showing the target lesion (red line) and the 11 Gy isodose line (yellow line). There is an abrupt cut off of the delivered radiation at the inferior margin of the tumour. The 1-year follow-up scan shows tumour progression along the non-irradiated inferior margin (Fig. 19.1B).

DISCUSSION

Historically, Gamma Knife Radiosurgery was believed to be capable of effectively delivering focused gamma rays to intracranial tumours only up to the level of the Foramen Magnum. However, with the advent of the Leksell Gamma Knife Perfexion and newer models, it is now possible to deliver radiation to the cervical spine, as long as the target is positioned above the standard base ring of the G stereotactic head frame and remains stable. This includes extracranial lesions in the head and neck area, as well as cervical spine targets down to C-4.[2]

The spinal cord and nerve roots have strict tolerances for radiation. While Gamma Knife can deliver high doses effectively with precision, the dose to the surrounding tissue must be minimised to prevent radiation-induced damage, and the key to this is immobilisation.[3] This becomes particularly challenging in the cervical spine due to mobility at the atlanto-occipital, C1-C2, subaxial cervical spine as well as respiratory movements. Another challenge is targeting the lesion because the stereotactic frame which is normally fixed above the supraorbital margin cannot target lesions beyond C2.[4] The newer technique of fixation at the maxilla allows us to treat lesions up to C4. This technique of frame fixation at maxilla with immobilisation of the cervical spine with a Philadelphia Collar to ensure cervical immobilisation has been described previously,[1] and the same has been done at our institution for selected cases.

Despite the aforementioned advantages of the technique, it is important to remember that the margin of error increases as targets are chosen further inferiorly

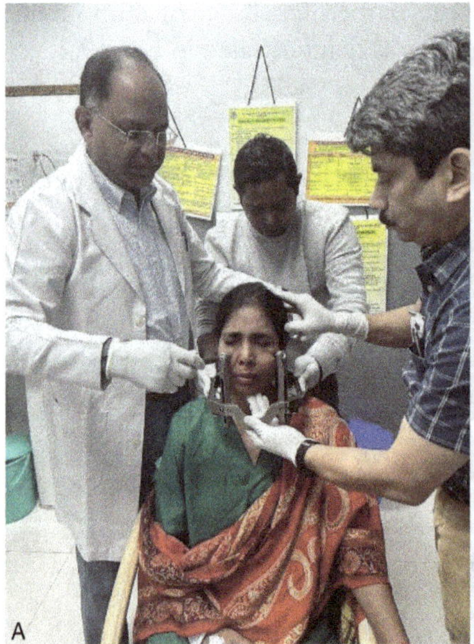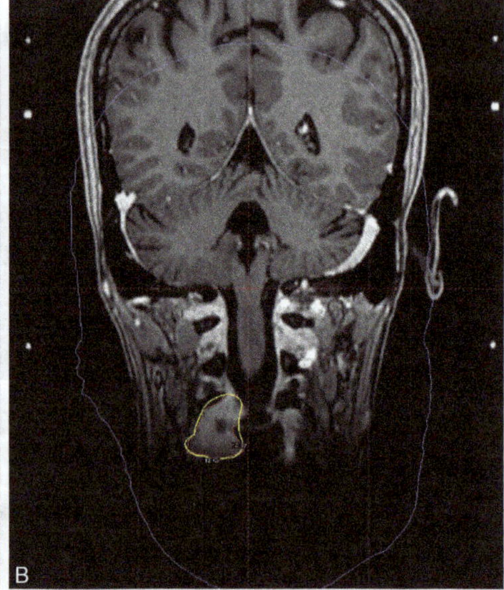

FIGURE 19.2 Frame fixation on maxilla anteriorly for covering high cervical lesions. Figure 4 shows the 12 Gy isodose line (yellow) bordering the target lesion (marked red), hence ensuring radiation delivery to the complete lesion at C4 level.

along the spine.[5] For this reason, the Collimator shots should be planned at a neutral 90-degree docking angle, which corresponds to the angle used during MRI to avoid any flexion-extension movement at 70 and 110 degrees.[6]

It is also important to understand that there will always be a subset of patients with high cervical spine lesions who are suitable for GKRS.[7] We at our institute have treated multiple patients with pathologies of the high cervical spine, or intracranial lesions extending up to the cervical spine, such as Lower Cranial Nerve Schwannomas, Foramen Magnum meningiomas and cervical Nerve Schwannoma which have extended up to C4 level as the primary treatment modality as well as for residual/recurrent lesion following surgical resection. Most of these patients have shown favourable clinical and radiological outcomes with good tumour control in the follow-up imaging, pain relief, and neurological improvement. We have also noticed a reduction in tumour size in several of these patients in long-term follow-up scans. A few patients who had tumour progression either underwent repeat GKRS (if their symptoms were stable) or surgery in case the symptoms worsened. None of our patients experienced post-radiotherapy complications or radiation-induced toxicity to the brainstem or spinal cord.

One of the major limitations to these treatment plans is the proximity of the spinal cord and lack of complete immobilisation, which hinders the delivery of high-dose to the lesions in the cervical regions, hence curbing its use in lesions like spinal vascular malformations and intramedullary lesions. However, with rapid advancement in Gamma knife technologies and ongoing research, we hope to soon overcome those barriers that we currently face in treating spinal lesions and diversify the types of spinal lesions that can be treated with GKRS.

TAKE HOME MESSAGE

GKRS plays an important role in treating high cervical lesions, and with the innovative use of maxillary fixation of the frame, lesions as low as C4 can be safely treated with GKRS.

REFERENCES

1. Tripathi M, Kumar N, Mukherjee KK. Pushing the limits of the Leksell stereotactic frame for spinal lesions up to C3: fixation at the maxilla. *Acta Neurochir (Wien)*. 2016;158(9):1691-1695.

2. Tuleasca C, Leroy HA, Régis J, Levivier M. Gamma Knife radiosurgery for cervical spine lesions: expanding the indications in the new era of Icon. *Acta Neurochir (Wien)*. 2016;158(11):2235-2236.

3. Tonetti D, Bhatnagar J, Lunsford LD. Quantitative analysis of movement of a cervical target during stereotactic radiosurgery using the Leksell Gamma Knife Perfexion. *J Neurosurg*. 2012;117 Suppl:211-216.

4. Starke RM, Nguyen JH, Reames DL, Rainey J, Sheehan JP. Gamma knife radiosurgery of meningiomas involving the foramen magnum. *J Craniovertebr Junction Spine*. 2010;1(1):23-28.

5. Goldsmith BJ, Wara WM, Wilson CB, Larson DA. Postoperative irradiation for subtotally re-sected meningiomas. A retrospective analysis of 140 patients treated from 1967 to 1990 [pub-lished correction appears in J Neurosurg 1994 Apr;80(4):777]. *J Neurosurg.* 1994;80(2):195-201.

6. Samii M, Klekamp J, Carvalho G. Surgical results for meningiomas of the craniocervical junc-tion. *Neurosurgery.* 1996;39(6):1086-1095.

7. Levy WJ, Latchaw J, Hahn JF, Sawhny B, Bay J, Dohn DF. Spinal neurofibromas: a report of 66 cases and a comparison with meningiomas. *Neurosurgery.* 1986;18(3):331-334.

Gamma Knife in Craniopharyngiomas: Current Gold Standard?

Prachi Singh | Deepak Agrawal

KEY LEARNING POINTS

1. Craniopharyngiomas require a multidisciplinary approach for optimal management. While surgical resection is the gold standard, Gamma Knife Radiosurgery (GKRS) is a promising treatment option for residual or recurrent tumours, especially in challenging locations.
2. Accurate imaging, including MRI and CBCT, is essential for precise target delineation in GKRS and helps minimise radiation exposure to critical structures like the optic apparatus, ensuring targeted and safe treatment planning.
3. GKRS involves careful dose planning, with specific dose constraints to protect critical structures. For solid tumours, a marginal dose of 12–15 Gy is typically prescribed with steep dose gradients.
4. GKRS has demonstrated excellent outcomes in tumour control with a 5-year progression-free survival rate of up to 90%.
5. Radiation-induced complications, such as optic apparatus injury and endocrine dysfunction, occur in a small percentage of patients (6.2%). Fractionated GKRS, especially for tumours near critical structures like the optic pathway, may reduce adverse effects.

INTRODUCTION

The optimal management of craniopharyngiomas requires a multidisciplinary approach. While surgical resection remains the gold standard, complete excision risks damage to critical structures like the hypothalamus, pituitary stalk, and optic chiasm. Residual tumours after surgery have high recurrence rates, negatively impacting survival. Adjuvant radiation therapy significantly reduces recurrence, with Gamma Knife Radiosurgery (GKRS) showing promising outcomes in tumour control, especially for residual or recurrent cases. However, radiation near the optic apparatus poses certain challenges and requires dose adjustments. Early postoperative radiation is recommended for children, while adults may receive it at the time of recurrence.

HISTORY AND EXAMINATION

A 15-year-old female, with a case of Recurrent Craniopharyngioma, underwent tumour excision followed by decompressive craniectomy (due to ACA/MCA infarction) and intratumoral bleomycin installation via Ommaya. She presented with complaints of progressive bilateral vision loss over 1 year before surgery. On examination, she was able to perceive hand movements close to the face on the right eye and absent perception of light on the left side, along with Right UMN hemiparesis. His endocrine evaluation revealed hypocortisolism and hypothyroidism. Follow-up MRI post-op was suggestive of the recurrent solid cystic suprasellar lesion. She was planned for secondary GKRS for recurrent lesion.

IMAGING

X-ray was done to visualise the craniotomy defect before frame fixation to avoid pin placement at the craniotomy site. MRI with T1 contrast and T2 sequences was obtained one day before treatment administration and the reference CBCT was done with the frame placed on the day of treatment delivery. MRI and CBCT datasets were co-registered to integrate soft tissue and bony landmarks for accurate treatment planning.

GK PROTOCOL

Planning was done on the co-registered MRI which involved demarcating the target lesion and at-risk structures, in this case, it was the right optic nerve (with some preserved vision) (Fig. 20.1). We used the lightning software for planning the dose delivery after setting the prescription dose of 15 Gy at 50% isodose line (Coverage- 0.9, Selectivity- 0.92, Gradient Index- 2.82) (Fig. 20.2). Lesion with a total volume of 5.7 cc receives a mean dose of 22.1 ± 4.8 Gy. Special consideration was given to keep radiation exposure to <8 Gy to prevent Right Optic Nerve damage.

FOLLOW UP

One year post-GKRS, the patient underwent a follow-up contrast MRI (Fig. 20.3). The follow-up MRI shows a significant reduction in volume from 5.7 cc treatment volume to 0.8 cc residual volume. The patient underwent clinical, biochemical, ophthalmological and endocrinological assessment along with radiological assessment at yearly follow-up and showed a good response, with up to 90% reduction in tumour volume at 12 months follow-up. The endocrine function improved post-gamma knife with a reduction in the dosage of hormone replacement drugs and there was no deterioration in vision.

DISCUSSION

Craniopharyngiomas are challenging intracranial tumours due to their proximity to critical structures, such as the optic chiasm, hypothalamus, and pituitary gland.

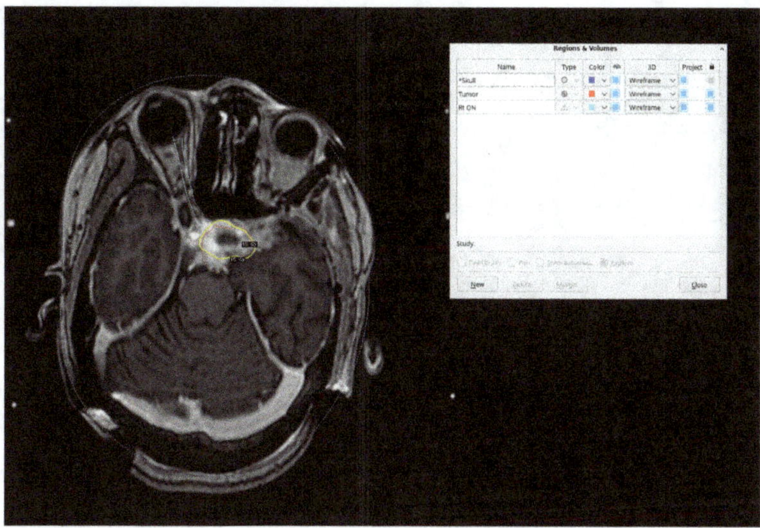

FIGURE 20.1   Target residual lesion is marked with Red and Organ at risk- right optic nerve with partially preserved vison is marked Blue.

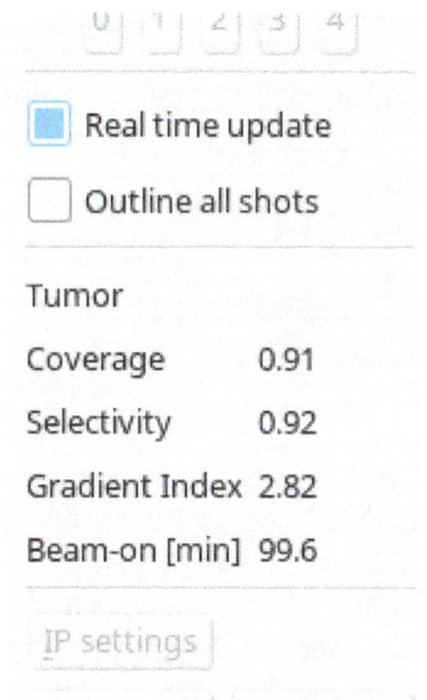

FIGURE 20.2   Lightning software for planning the dose delivery after setting the prescription dose of 15 Gy at 50% isodose line with Coverage- 0.9, Selectivity- 0.92 and Gradient Index- 2.82.

While surgical resection remains the cornerstone of management, complete excision is often limited by the risk of significant morbidity. After the invention of GKRS in 1967, Leksell and Backlund et al. advocated the use of radiosurgery for craniopharyngioma. However, it took two decades to apply modern imaging techniques such as CT or MRI for dose planning. Currently, GKRS has emerged as a valuable therapeutic option for residual or recurrent craniopharyngiomas, as this is the only

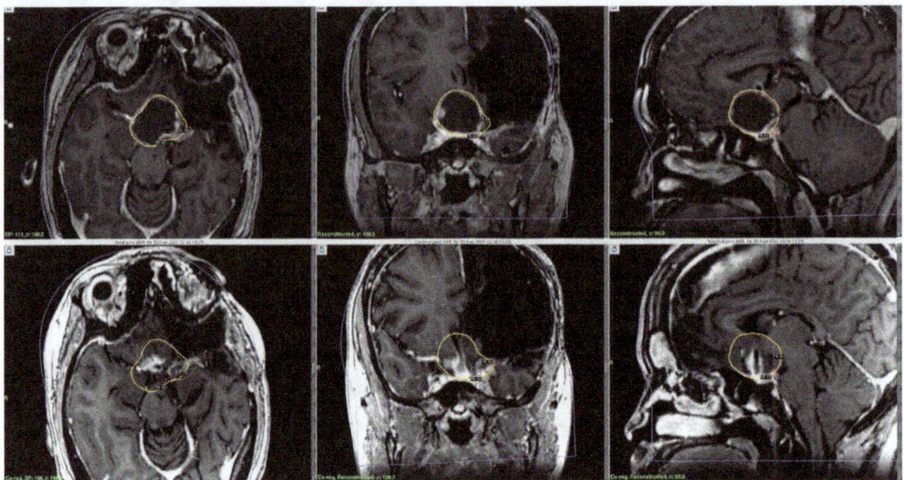

FIGURE 20.3   The follow up MRI after 1 year shows significant reduction in volume from 5.7 cm3 treatment volume to 0.8 cm3 residual volume- 86% volume reduction within 1 year. (above- Treatment scan, below- 1 year follow up scan).

modality which offers sub-millimetre accuracy, enabling the delivery of high radiation doses to the tumour while sparing adjacent critical structures. Indications for GKRS in Craniopharyngioma include:

- Residual or recurrent craniopharyngiomas post-surgery.
- Tumours unsuitable for resection due to proximity to critical structures (e.g., optic chiasm, hypothalamus).
- Small, well-defined lesions (<3 cm in diameter) with minimal mass effect.
- Cystic craniopharyngiomas require additional management after cyst decompression.

Typical radiation dose parameters for craniopharyngiomas in Gamma Knife Radiosurgery (GKRS) involve careful dose selection and adherence to constraints to protect critical structures. For solid tumours, a marginal dose of 12–15 Gy is typically prescribed to the 50% isodose line, with adjustments made based on its proximity to sensitive areas.[1,5] Cystic tumours may require a lower dose due to the sensitivity of surrounding tissues. Critical structures have specific dose constraints: The optic apparatus (optic chiasm and nerves) must receive less than 8 Gy[3] to prevent optic neuropathy, with marginal doses reduced to 8–10 Gy for tumours within 3 mm of these structures. The hypothalamus should receive less than 10 Gy, while the pituitary gland and stalk should not exceed 15 Gy to minimise the risk of hypopituitarism. The brainstem's maximum dose is limited to 12 Gy to avoid injury. Steep dose gradients are employed to ensure precise dose conformity to the tumour, minimising exposure to adjacent normal tissues.

In the study from our institute, tumour control was seen in 91.4% (32 of 35 patients) after a mean radiological follow-up of 62 months (median radiological follow-up of 60.1 months) with a 5-year progression-free survival rate of 92.3% in the radiation group.[1]

In a study of 38 craniopharyngioma patients treated with Gamma Knife Radiosurgery (GKRS), 10-year progression-free survival (PFS) and overall survival rates were 30% and 80%, respectively. Risk factors for post-GKRS complications included high margin doses, maximum dose >35 Gy, and tumour complexity. Repeated GKRS improved PFS to 77.3% and 61.2% at 5 and 10 years, respectively. Tumour control was enhanced when ≥85% of the tumour received ≥12 Gy. GKRS demonstrated efficacy as an adjuvant treatment, particularly after subtotal resection, with 3-, 5-, and 10-year PFS rates of 73.1%, 62.2%, and 42.6%, respectively, and minimal radiation-induced complications reported.[2]

A statistical analysis of 100 craniopharyngioma cases treated with microsurgery and Gamma Knife radiosurgery identified tumour diameter and marginal dose as key factors for favourable outcomes. Tumours <19 mm in diameter and marginal doses >13.2 Gy were associated with better tumour control, but higher doses increased the risk of complications, particularly to critical structures like the optic nerves. Strategies for better outcomes with GKRS include surgical tumour reduction, intratumoral bleomycin and cyst decompression, increasing tumour-optic nerve distance, and using multiple small isocenters. Stereotactic radiotherapy may be suitable for large tumours near critical structures, though further studies are needed.[4]

With the advent of the new-generation Gamma Knife Icon, which adopts mask fixation, fractionated GKRS has become much more widely available. Some studies have advocated the approach of delivering GKRS over multiple sessions, rather than a single session, to safely treat benign tumours in close proximity to the optic pathway. Despite this modification, tumour growth control remains comparable between single-session and multi-session GKRS. Fractionation is expected to reduce adverse effects on the optic pathway, hormonal function, and hypothalamic function. When the tumour is located within 2–3 mm of the visual pathway, single-session GKRS may expose the pathway to doses exceeding 10 Gy. In such cases, a fractionated treatment plan with an average maximum dose of 7 Gy per session is considered a safer option.[6]

While tumour progression is the primary factor that causes the impairment of important functions, such as visual, hormonal, and cognitive functions, the adverse effects of the treatments themselves also negatively affect these functions. The rate of radiation-induced complications is 6.2%,[7] which includes optic apparatus injury, endocrine dysfunction due to hypothalamic-pituitary axis disruption - such as diabetes insipidus, panhypopituitarism, hypogonadism, hypothalamic obesity, or sleep disturbances and radiation-induced edema.

TAKE HOME MESSAGE

Gamma Knife Radiosurgery (GKRS) effectively controls the growth of residual or recurrent craniopharyngiomas, with a manageable rate of complications. Hence GKRS should be considered as the standard of care for such tumours.

REFERENCES

Gupta S, Agrawal D, Kedia S, Kale SS. Should post-operative stereotactic radiosurgery be the standard of care in Craniopharyngioma patients?. *World Neurosurg X*. 2024;22:100327. Published 2024 Feb 25.

Pikis S, Mantziaris G, Lavezzo K, Dabhi N, Sheehan J. Stereotactic radiosurgery for craniopharyngiomas. *Acta Neurochir (Wien)*. 2021;163(11):3201-3207.

Hasegawa T, Kobayashi T, Kida Y. Tolerance of the optic apparatus in single-fraction irradiation using stereotactic radiosurgery: evaluation in 100 patients with craniopharyngioma. *Neurosurgery*. 2010;66(4):688-695.

Kobayashi T, Mori Y, Tsugawa T, Hashizume C, Takahashi H. Prognostic factors for tumor recurrence after gamma knife radiosurgery of partially resected and recurrent craniopharyngiomas. *Nagoya J Med Sci*. 2012;74(1-2):141-147.

Kobayashi T, Tsugawa T, Hatano M, Hashizume C, Mori Y, Shibamoto Y. Gamma knife radiosurgery of craniopharyngioma: results of 30 cases treated at Nagoya Radiosurgery Center. *Nagoya J Med Sci*. 2015;77(3):447-454.

Losa M, Pieri V, Bailo M, et al. Single fraction and multisession Gamma Knife radiosurgery for craniopharyngioma. *Pituitary*. 2018;21(5):499-506.

Tsugawa T, Kobayashi T, Hasegawa T, et al. Gamma Knife Surgery for Residual or Recurrent Craniopharyngioma After Surgical Resection: A Multi-institutional Retrospective Study in Japan. *Cureus*. 2020;12(2):e6973. Published 2020 Feb 12.

Primary Gamma Knife Radiosurgery for Craniopharyngioma

Satish Verma | Deepak Agrawal

KEY LEARNING POINTS

1. The use of primary GK in Craniopharyngiomas has not been explored but can be an effective modality for small tumours.
2. The 10-year progression-free survival (PFS) ranges from 46-78% and 10-year overall survival rates range from 75.6%-100% with acceptable visual and endocrine.
3. For single-session treatment, a marginal dose of 12-14 Gy is recommended.
4. For multi-session treatment, the biologically equivalent dose (BED) has been used to compare treatments, with single-session treatment as well as amongst different numbers of fractions. BED2 (BED using the α/β ratio as 2) of >80 Gy confers statistically significant PFS.
5. The maximum point dose limit for the optic apparatus is recommended to be <10 Gy in 1 fraction, <20 Gy in 3 fractions and <25 Gy in 5 fractions, to keep the risk of radiation-induced optic neuropathy (RION) to a clinically reasonable level (<1% incidence of RION).

INTRODUCTION

Craniopharyngiomas are WHO grade 1 tumours believed to arise from the embryonic remnants of the epithelium of Rathke's pouch. Their strategic location near the hypothalamic-pituitary axis and visual apparatus poses inherent challenges in attaining complete surgical resection. In addition, their potential for recurrence and rapid growth warrants the use of adjuvant modalities for longer progression-free and overall survival. Radiation has proven to be a reliable adjunct for local tumour control. Stereotactic radiosurgery using Gamma Knife is a non-invasive modality with extreme precision due to high dose conformality and rapid dose fall-off.

"

REPRESENTATIVE CASE

HISTORY & EXAMINATION

A 54-year-old female was referred after undergoing 3 months of trans-cranial decompression of craniopharyngioma at another centre. She presented to that centre with progressive painless bilateral visual diminution for 6 months. She started developing a holocranial headache for the last 15 days before the presentation. On examination, as per medical records, she was conscious and oriented to time, place and person. Visual acuity as per Snellen's chart was 6/60 in the right eye and 6/24 in the left eye with bitemporal hemianopia. No other positive neurological findings were elicited. She reported improvement in vision after surgery. Prior to Gamma Knife radiosurgery, her visual acuity was 6/36 in the right eye and 6/18 in the left eye with marked improvement in bitemporal hemianopia. She was on corticosteroid and thyroxine replacement.

IMAGING

At presentation, contrast-enhanced magnetic resonance imaging (CEMRI) of the brain suggested a suprasellar lesion with solid-cystic areas, solid areas were T1 and T2 hypointense and cystic areas were T1 hypo- and T2-hyperintense. Solid areas showed post-gadolinium enhancement. The pituitary gland could be seen separately. These findings were consistent with craniopharyngioma. Post-operative MRI showed an enhancing residual lesion in the suprasellar area of size 2.1 cm × 1.3 cm × 1.2 cm. For the purpose of Gamma Knife planning, after fixation of Leksell-G frame, post-gadolinium 3-dimensional (3D) Magnetisation -prepared Rapid Gradient Echo (MPRAGE) sequence was acquired in axial plane with voxel size 1.0 × 1.0 × 1.0, slab 1, slice per slab 176 and Field of View (FoV) 256 mm.

GK PROTOCOL

Gamma knife was performed on a Leksell Gamma Knife Perfexion unit (Elekta AB, Stockholm, Sweden) with Leksell GammaPlan. Manual tumour segmentation was done for the tumour and Organs-at-risk (OAR) (optic apparatus and brainstem). The total tumour volume was 1.343 cubic centimetres (cc). Inverse planning with optimisation of six iso-centres (combinations of 4 and 8 mm collimators) was performed with a prescription dose of 12 Gy at 50% isodose line to the tumour margin (Fig. 21.1). Further optimisation was done manually to exclude OARs from the prescribed dose constraints achieving the following parameters: coverage - 93%, selectivity - 80%, Gradient Index – 3.01. Beam-on time (BOT) was 45.1 minutes with a treatment dose rate of 3.530 Gy/min. The maximum dose to the segmented volumes was: tumour – 24.1 Gy, left optic nerve – 4.0 Gy, right optic nerve - 7.9 Gy, optic chiasma – 12.4 Gy, brainstem – 7.0 Gy (Fig. 21.2). Although selectivity was sub-optimal, the majority of radiation spillage was into the CSF space in the suprasellar and interpeduncular cisterns.

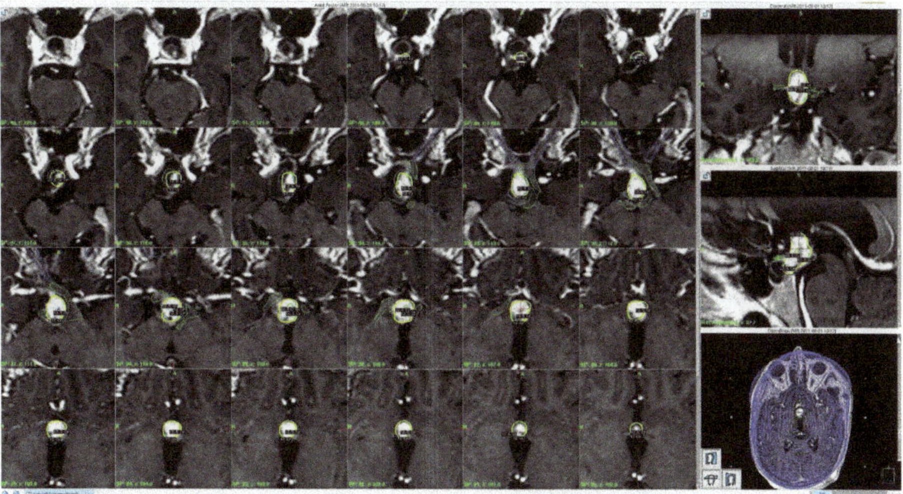

FIGURE 21.1   Gamma Knife planning for the index case. Tumour margin (Blue), 12 Gy (prescription dose) isodose line (yellow).

FIGURE 21.2   Dose-volume histogram (DVH) for the tumour and optic apparatus.

FOLLOW-UP

The patient tolerated the procedure well. A follow-up clinical visit after 3 months included a visual examination, that was the same as pre-GKRS status. Follow-up CEM-RI was done annually for the first three years, and then every 2 years thereafter which showed a gradual reduction in tumour volume. At the last follow-up available, at 79 months, the residual tumour volume measured 0.713 cc (Fig. 21.3). She was on corticosteroid and thyroxine replacement. Visual acuity remained the same as pre-GKRS.

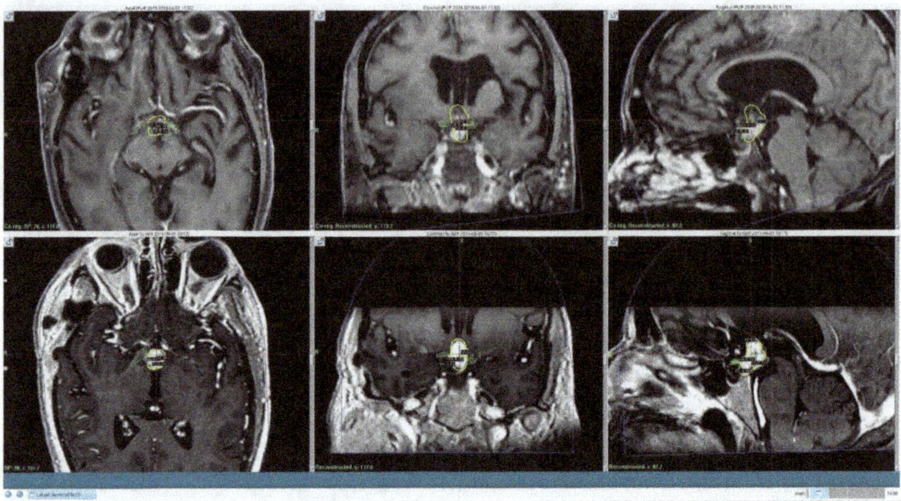

FIGURE 21.3   Follow-up MRI done after 79 months (upper panel) compared to the baseline MRI at the time of GKRS (lower panel).

DISCUSSION

Craniopharyngiomas are benign but locally aggressive tumours with bimodal age distribution. There are two different histological varieties: adamantinomatous and papillary.[1,2] Due to its close proximity to the hypothalamus-pituitary axis and visual apparatus, complete microsurgical resection, although considered the treatment of choice, is difficult to achieve and not feasible most of the time. The goal of surgery is maximal safe resection, as either direct mechanical injury or vascular insult to hypothalamus or visual apparatus results in devastating complications. Even after gross total clearance of the tumour, 10%–25% recur, and almost all residual lesions progress after a subtotal resection.[3,4] Residual craniopharyngiomas usually grow in size at a variable pace, and if not sizeable enough to cause compression over optic apparatus, they may be managed with radiation as a salvage treatment. Many centres offer Gamma Knife radiosurgery (GKRS) for recurrent craniopharyngiomas, even with compression over the optic apparatus, considering the high complication rates associated with repeat resection.

Radiation as an effective treatment for craniopharyngiomas was initially established by Kramer et al.[5] Gamma knife radiosurgery is a non-invasive modality delivering high-dose radiation with extreme precision, due to its superior dose conformality compared to conventional radiotherapy. Backlund and Leksell treated the first case of craniopharyngioma with Gamma Knife radiosurgery in Stockholm, Sweden in 1968.[6] Initially, it was presumed to be a cystic lesion, and planned for stereotactic aspiration, but it turned out to be a solid tumour and no significant tumour decompression was attempted, rather two radio-opaque clips were placed at the anterior and superior tumour margins. That case was planned on plain radiographs, utilising radio-opaque clips as a surrogate for tumour margins. A single

4 mm isocentre was used in a single session with a cumulative dose of 50 Gy. After GKRS, the case underwent 4 more interventions over a 55-year follow-up period to manage recurrences. Since then, there have been significant developments in GKRS units, MRI techniques, and image quality that have led to precise dose delivery with the exclusion of OARs from the radiation field.

Radiosurgery for craniopharyngioma as a salvage procedure is practised at many centres worldwide and reportedly provides an actuarial 10-year progression-free survival rate of about 46% to 78% along with acceptable radiation-induced complication rates.[3,4,7-18] Post-GKRS actuarial 10-year overall survival rates are reported as 75.6% - 100%.[13,16,19-22] A recent meta-analysis concluded that radiosurgery is a safe option for pediatric craniopharyngiomas, with minimal adverse effects, and a high rate of local tumour control, as well as better neurocognitive outcomes.[3]

Conventionally, GKRS is a single-session treatment, but over the last many years, fractionated GKRS delivered over multiple sessions has been advocated for large residual or recurrent tumours.[13,21] Hypofractionation (2-5 fractions) is the usual strategy for achieving a therapeutic marginal dose while reducing the dose to OARs. To compare single vs multiple-session GKRS, dose comparisons become difficult, and thus, a biologically equivalent dose (BED) is recommended. Considering craniopharyngiomas as benign tumours, the α/β ratio as per the linear-quadratic model may be taken as 2.[23,24] BED2 (BED using the α/β ratio as 2) of >80 Gy confers statistically significant PFS as compared to BED2 of<80 Gy.[13] Depending upon the tumour volume and distance from the optic apparatus, the recommended marginal dose to the tumour margin is 12-14 Gy in a single fraction (BED2 of 84 Gy and 112 Gy respectively). For a multi-session GKRS, 6-7 Gy in 3 fractions each, leads to cumulative BED2 of 72 to 94.5 Gy respectively. Hypofractionated GKRS is relatively new after the GK ICON model, which has a mask-based workflow for fractionated treatments. Although the studies with hypofractionated GKRS have shorter follow-up duration, the results are convincing and comparable to single-session GKRS.[10,21,25] The 4-year PFS was 61.4% in a cohort of 24 patients with an average tumour volume of 2.4 cc.

Radiation-induced optic neuropathy (RION) and hypopituitarism are reported after radiation to craniopharyngioma. Other uncommon adverse effects are hypothalamic obesity and cerebral edema.[4] Prior radiation may increase the risk of RION by approximately upto 10-fold, depending upon the previous radiation dose, fractionation and duration between the radiation courses.[26] The maximum point dose limit for optic apparatus to keep the risk of RION to a clinically reasonable level (<1% incidence of RION) is recommended to be <10 Gy in 1 fraction, <20 Gy in 3 fractions and <25 Gy in 5 fractions. Similarly, for a 0.2 cc threshold volume, the maximum recommended dose is <8 Gy in 1 fraction, <15.3 Gy in 3 fractions and <23 Gy in 5 fractions.[27] Clinical deterioration after GKRS has a positive correlation with increasing marginal dose and a maximum point dose >35 Gy.[4] Increasing numbers of isocentres were also mentioned as a risk factor for complications, since it implies that the tumour volume is large.[4] However, this point is arguable, as the Lightening planning algorithm introduced with ICON model of

Gamma Knife (Elekta AB, Stockholm, Sweden) creates a rapid plan with a significantly higher number of isocentres, resulting in better treatment metrics than manual or inverse planning.

Hypofractionation is likely to be practised more frequently for treating recurrent/residual craniopharyngiomas with relatively larger volumes close to the optic apparatus, without any new visual deficits attributed to tumour recurrence. However, its efficacy requires evaluation through good-quality studies. Offering GKRS as the primary treatment modality is not a standard-of-care, but may be considered in selected cases depending on the visual function, performance status, co-morbidities and patient preference. Strict compliance with dose prescription protocols is needed to keep the complication rates at a clinically reasonable level.

TAKE HOME MESSAGE

Gamma Knife radiosurgery is recommended as a standard treatment for selected cases of residual or recurrent craniopharyngioma. It offers excellent long-term progression-free survival and overall survival, with low complication rates even when used as primary therapy. Relatively large tumour volumes in close proximity to visual apparatus may be considered for hypofractionated treatment, provided that the vision is primarily not affected by the tumour mass effect. Strict compliance with dose prescription is mandatory to avoid adverse radiation effects.

REFERENCES

1. Gopalan R, Dassoulas K, Rainey J, Sherman JH, Sheehan JP. Evaluation of the role of Gamma Knife surgery in the treatment of craniopharyngiomas. *Neurosurg Focus*. 2008;24(5):E5.
2. Jane JA Jr, Laws ER. Craniopharyngioma. *Pituitary*. 2006;9(4):323-326.
3. Murphy ES, Sahgal A, Regis J, et al. Pediatric Cranial Stereotactic Radiosurgery: Meta-Analysis and International Stereotactic Radiosurgery Society Practice Guidelines. *Neuro Oncol*. Published online October 11, 2024.
4. Pikis S, Mantziaris G, Lavezzo K, Dabhi N, Sheehan J. Stereotactic radiosurgery for craniopharyngiomas. *Acta Neurochir (Wien)*. 2021;163(11):3201-3207.
5. Kramer S, Mckissock W, Concannon JP. Craniopharyngiomas. Treatment by combined surgery and radiation therapy. *J Neurosurg*. 1961;18:217-226.
6. Buwaider A, Backlund EO, Almqvist P, Lippitz B, Fletcher-Sandersjöö A, Bartek J. 55-Year Follow-Up of the First Adult Patient With Craniopharyngioma Treated With Gamma Knife Radiosurgery. *Neurosurgery*. 2024;95(3):e71-e78.
7. Palavani LB, Silva GM, Borges PGLB, et al. Fractionated stereotactic radiotherapy in craniopharyngiomas: A systematic review and single arm meta-analysis. *J Neurooncol*. 2024;167(3):373-385.
8. Gupta S, Agrawal D, Kedia S, Kale SS. Should post-operative stereotactic radiosurgery be the standard of care in Craniopharyngioma patients?. *World Neurosurg X*. 2024;22:100327. Published 2024 Feb 25.
9. Fukuhara N, Nishihara T, Sato K, et al. Long-term outcomes of neuroendoscopic cyst partial resection combined with stereotactic radiotherapy for craniopharyngioma. *Acta Neurochir (Wien)*. 2024;166(1):218. Published 2024 May 15.

10. Samanci Y, Essibayi MA, Askeroglu MO, Budak M, Karaköse F, Peker S. Frameless Hypofractionated Gamma Knife Radiosurgery for Residual or Recurrent Craniopharyngioma. *Neurosurgery*. 2023;93(1):102-111.

11. Ogino A, Niranjan A, Kano H, Flickinger JC, Lunsford LD. Optimizing stereotactic radiosurgery in patients with recurrent or residual craniopharyngiomas. *J Neurooncol*. 2021;154(1):113-120.

12. Chou CL, Chen HH, Yang HC, et al. Effects of stereotactic radiosurgery versus conventional radiotherapy on body mass index in patients with craniopharyngioma. *J Neurosurg Pediatr*. 2021;28(1):43-49. Published 2021 May 14.

13. Dho YS, Kim YH, Kim JW, et al. Optimal strategy of gamma knife radiosurgery for craniopharyngiomas. *J Neurooncol*. 2018;140(1):135-143.

14. Lee CC, Yang HC, Chen CJ, et al. Gamma Knife surgery for craniopharyngioma: report on a 20-year experience. *J Neurosurg*. 2014;121 Suppl:167-178.

15. Kobayashi T, Kida Y, Mori Y, Hasegawa T. Long-term results of gamma knife surgery for the treatment of craniopharyngioma in 98 consecutive cases. *J Neurosurg*. 2005;103(6 Suppl):482-488.

16. Ulfarsson E, Lindquist C, Roberts M, et al. Gamma knife radiosurgery for craniopharyngiomas: long-term results in the first Swedish patients. *J Neurosurg*. 2002;97(5 Suppl):613-622.

17. Chung WY, Pan DH, Shiau CY, Guo WY, Wang LW. Gamma knife radiosurgery for craniopharyngiomas. *J Neurosurg*. 2000;93 Suppl 3:47-56.

18. Mokry M. Craniopharyngiomas: A six year experience with Gamma Knife radiosurgery. *Stereotact Funct Neurosurg*. 1999;72 Suppl 1:140-149.

19. Hasegawa T, Kobayashi T, Kida Y. Tolerance of the optic apparatus in single-fraction irradiation using stereotactic radiosurgery: evaluation in 100 patients with craniopharyngioma. *Neurosurgery*. 2010;66(4):688-695.

20. Kobayashi T, Kida Y, Hasegawa T. Long-term results of gamma knife surgery for craniopharyngioma. *Neurosurg Focus*. 2003;14(5):e13. Published 2003 May 15.

21. Losa M, Pieri V, Bailo M, et al. Single fraction and multisession Gamma Knife radiosurgery for craniopharyngioma. *Pituitary*. 2018;21(5):499-506.

22. Xu Z, Yen CP, Schlesinger D, Sheehan J. Outcomes of Gamma Knife surgery for craniopharyngiomas. *J Neurooncol*. 2011;104(1):305-313.

23. Fowler JF. 21 years of biologically effective dose. *Br J Radiol*. 2010;83(991):554-568.

24. Gürkaynak M, Ozyar E, Zorlu F, Akyol FH, Atahan IL. Results of radiotherapy in craniopharyngiomas analysed by the linear quadratic model. *Acta Oncol*. 1994;33(8):941-943.

25. Minniti G, Esposito V, Amichetti M, Enrici RM. The role of fractionated radiotherapy and radiosurgery in the management of patients with craniopharyngioma. *Neurosurg Rev*. 2009;32(2):125-132.

26. Milano MT, Grimm J, Soltys SG, et al. Single- and Multi-Fraction Stereotactic Radiosurgery Dose Tolerances of the Optic Pathways. *Int J Radiat Oncol Biol Phys*. 2021;110(1):87-99.

27. Benedict SH, Yenice KM, Followill D, et al. Stereotactic body radiation therapy: the report of AAPM Task Group 101 [published correction appears in Med Phys. 2012 Jan;39(1):563. Dosage error in article text] [published correction appears in Med Phys. 2023 Jun;50(6):3885]. *Med Phys*. 2010;37(8):4078-4101.

Gamma Knife Radiosurgery in Hypothalamic Hamartomas

Deepak Agrawal | Chirag Bansal

KEY LEARNING POINTS

1. GKRS significantly reduces seizure frequency and intensity, particularly in gelastic seizures commonly linked to Hypothalamic Hamartoma.
2. Studies indicate minimal adverse effects, preserving endocrine functions and avoiding major neurological deficits.
3. Consistent seizure control and improved quality of life are reported in long-term follow-ups.
4. GKRS is particularly advantageous for deep-seated lesions, reducing risks associated with open surgery.
5. Gamma Knife radiosurgery is an effective and minimally invasive alternative for treating hypothalamic hamartomas, especially in medically refractory epilepsy, with emerging long-term evidence supporting its use.

INTRODUCTION

Hypothalamic hamartoma is a developmental lesion and can present with symptoms like Gelastic seizures, precocious puberty, and neuropsychiatric.[1] Hypothalamic Hamartoma is often associated with refractory epilepsy.[2-4] In such cases, Gamma Knife radiosurgery (GKRS) has emerged as one of the most effective techniques in the management of hypothalamic hamartomas (HH).[5] The Gamma Knife delivers targeted radiation to the hamartoma, providing a safer outcome as compared to other surgical procedures. Here, we summarise key findings from a representative case of Hypothalamic Hamartoma that was treated with GKRS at our institute.

REPRESENTATIVE CASE

HISTORY & EXAMINATION

A 5-year-old child presented with rapid height growth and precocious puberty for 6 months, with Gelastic seizures occurring once every month. On examination, there

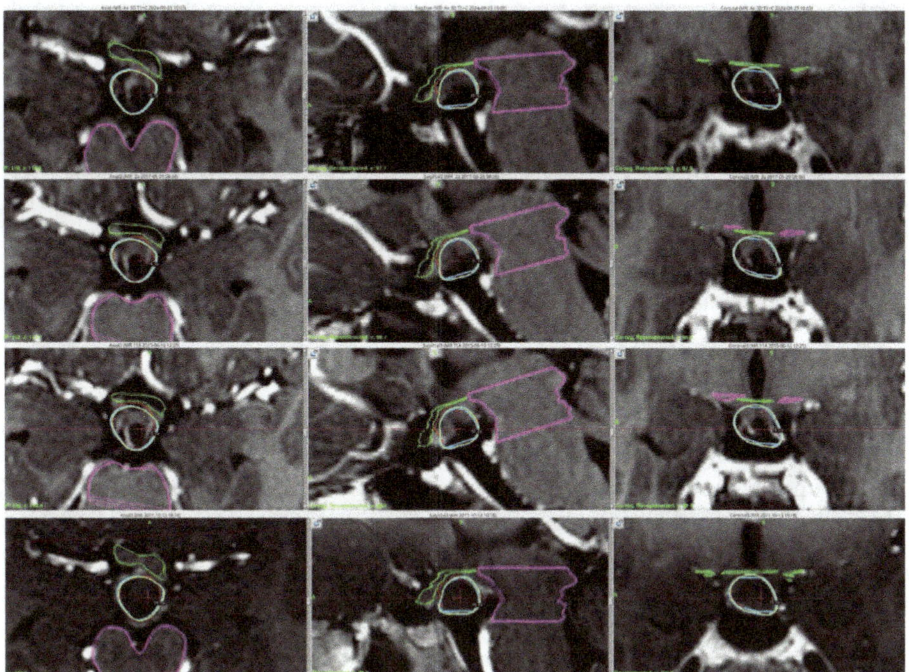

FIGURE 22.1 Contrast MRI axial, sagittal and coronal sections of a patient with Hypothlamic hamartoma at baseline (2011) (bottom row), at 4 years (2015) (3rd row), 6 years (2017) (2nd row) and at 13 years (2024) (top row) follow-up.

were no motor, sensory or cranial nerve deficits. Cerebellar signs were absent and higher mental functions were within normal limits with a MMSE of 30/30. The patient was followed up for over 13 years.

IMAGING (FIG. 22.1)

CEMRI brain was suggestive of T1 isointense, T2 hyperintense rounded mass in the hypothalamus region, projecting inferiorly behind the infundibulum of pituitary gland mildly enhancing on post-contrast images.

GK PROTOCOL

Primary GKRS therapy was given for Hypothalamic Hamartoma in the year 2011 using a Gamma Knife model B machine. Leksell Coordinate Frame G was used for fixation Configuration, and planning was done on Gamma plan version 11.3.2.

15 Gy at 50% isodose line was planned with a coverage of 0.9, selectivity of 0.92, Gradient Index of 2.83, and beam on time of 38.7 minutes. The tumor volume was 0.861 cc and optic chiasm and brainstem shielding was done.

FOLLOW-UP & SEIZURE CONTROL

As shown in the imaging above, there was a progressive decrease in the tumour volume on serial imaging. The lesion volume was assessed during the follow-ups in 2015, 2017, and 2024. Clinically, a reduction in seizure frequency was observed within 3 months of GKRS with Agnel score of 1 (Seizure free), six months following GKRS. Anti-seizure medication could be stopped one year after GKRS and the patient remains off medication till date. Precocious puberty progression also halted with a reduction of secondary sexual character's progression. No hormonal dysfunction was noticed on the last follow-up.

DISCUSSION

GKRS is effective for treating several conditions responsible for epilepsy in humans, including Pituitary adenomas, arteriovenous malformations,[1] Vestibular schwannomas, mesial temporal lobe epilepsy,[2] and hypothalamic hamartomas (HH).[5-7] In cases of Hypothalamic Hamartoma, GKRS has proven effective in reducing seizure frequency and controlling gelastic seizures.[5] Although the Hypothalamus is a surgically challenging area, the precision of GKRS minimises damage to surrounding brain structures.[8] GKRS has good safety and efficacy in seizure reduction and in managing refractory epilepsy due to hypothalamic hamartomas.[9] It has been shown that GKRS results in HH tissue injury characterised by total cell loss without necrosis.[10] Reactive gliosis and microglial infiltration are significantly increased in the post-GK cohort, whereas microvascular changes are relatively mild, and degenerative changes are inconsistent. These findings support the premise that cell death contributes to the efficacy of GK for managing chronic epilepsy.[10] Following this radiosurgery, adequate symptomatic control is normally achieved, with a notable decrease or even disappearance of the seizures.[9] Additional reported changes are Radiological, such as a decrease in the size of the tumour or adjacent edema secondary to non-necrotising radiotherapy-induced inflammatory reaction.[10] Side effects and neurological complications are also rare occurrences.

In our experience, GKRS is particularly effective for small Hypothalamic Hamartomas and remains a safe and effective treatment even for bigger hypothalamic hamartoma. It's a minimally invasive procedure that provides significant seizure control with lower risks compared to microsurgery. However, due to its delayed action, longer follow-up is needed to evaluate its effectiveness. Treatment options for hypothalamic hamartoma can be based on surgery, including transcallosal interforniceal, endoscopic disconnection, radiofrequency thermocoagulation, or brachytherapy. The following table summarises the endocrinological effects of various treatment options for Hypothalamic hamartomas. Among these options, Gamma Knife radiosurgery is found to have minimum endocrinological adverse effects following treatment.

Management of Hypothalamic hamartoma with intractable epilepsy can be challenging. So, Gamma Knife radiosurgery offers an effective alternative for managing drug-resistant epilepsies associated with hypothalamic hamartoma. Gamma Knife

TABLE 22.1 ■ Summary of the main endocrinologic effects of the different techniques used for treating hypothalamic hamartoma

Author, year	Technique	Pituitary deficiency	Weight gain	Hypothalamic syndrome/ dysnatremia
Freeman, 2003[11]	Transcallosal intra forniceal surgery	38%	45%	41%
Drees, 2012[12]	Endoscopic surgery	24%	59%	17%
Drees, 2012[12]	Combined surgical approaches	57%	71%	17%
Schulze-Bonanghe, 2008[13]	Brachytherapy	No	20%	No
Abla, 2010[14]	Gamma Knife radiosurgery	No	20%	10%
Frederic Casti-netti, 2017[15]	Gamma Knife radiosurgery	3%	3%	No

radiosurgery can be administered in hypofractionated doses for managing giant Hypothalamic Hamartomas. In a study, Manjul Tripathi et al.[16] tried to maintain a low peripheral isodose to the lesion margin (18–26 Gy at 50% isodose) in a 2–3 fractionation scheme to minimise the chances of radiation exposure to the radiosensitive organs at risk (mamillary bodies 10 Gy, optic apparatus 6 Gy, brain stem 10 Gy). The purpose of the dose fractionation was to deliver the adequate dose to these patients without creating counter effects. The usual dose of radiation to be given is 8.1–9.2 Gy per fraction at 50% isodose in 2–3 fractions, targeting the entire giant hamartoma volume (4.45 cc to 7.39 cc). Traditionally, ideal candidates for GKRS are HH that are small in size (<3 cc), at a safe distance from the optic apparatus, and in a stable neurological status. As per David Mathieu et al.,[17] between March 1999 and January 2003, 4 patients (Case No 2-5 in Table 22.2) with hypothalamic hamartomas had Gamma Knife radiosurgery. The hamartoma volumes ranged from 0.20 to 0.55 ml (mean 0.37). The 50% isodose line was used to deliver a mean of 17.5 Gy (range 16–20) to the margin of the lesion. The mean maximum dose was 35 Gy (range 32–40). No plugging pattern was used, and the radiation dose received by the optic pathways was kept below 8 Gy for every patient. The results from the above study have been compared to the index case (Case No. 1 in Table 22.2) in the following table:

It can be concluded that early administration of GKRS (at the onset of the disease), followed by a prolonged follow-up, may lead to better seizure control post-GKRS.

TAKE HOME MESSAGE

GKRS can be an effective and non-invasive solution to many surgically challenging tumours like Hypothalamic Hamartoma. Due to its efficacy in reducing gelastic

TABLE 22.2 ■

Case No.	Age years at treatment	Seizure duration, years	Seizure types	Lesion volume, ml	Marginal dose, Gy	Follow-up months	Time to improvement, months	Engel class attained
1*	5	0.5	Gelasric	0.861	15	156	3	I
2	29	28	gelastic, GTCS	0.51	16	77	3	II
3	6	4	gelastic, GTCS, CPS	0.22	18	22	2	III
4	14	13	gelastic, GTCS, Atonic tonic	0.20	20	22	NA	IV
5	5	4	gelastic, CPS	0.55	16	6	3	II

CPS = Complex partial seizures; GTCS = generalized tonic-clonic seizures; NA = not assessed. *INDEX CASE

seizures and improving quality of life with negligible morbidity, GKRS should be considered the gold standard for hypothalamic Hamartomas.

REFERENCES

1. Steiner L, Lindquist C, Adler JR, Torner JC, Alves W, Steiner M. Clinical outcome of radiosurgery for cerebral arteriovenous malformations. *J Neurosurg*. 1992;77(1):1-8.
2. Régis J, Rey M, Bartolomei F, et al. Gamma knife surgery in mesial temporal lobe epilepsy: a prospective multicenter study. *Epilepsia*. 2004;45(5):504-515.
3. Bartolomei F, Hayashi M, Tamura M, et al. Long-term efficacy of gamma knife radiosurgery in mesial temporal lobe epilepsy. *Neurology*. 2008;70(19):1658-1663.
4. Barbaro NM, Quigg M, Broshek DK, et al. A multicenter, prospective pilot study of gamma knife radiosurgery for mesial temporal lobe epilepsy: seizure response, adverse events, and verbal memory. *Ann Neurol*. 2009;65(2):167-175.
5. Régis J, Hayashi M, Eupierre LP, et al. Gamma knife surgery for epilepsy related to hypothalamic hamartomas. *Acta Neurochir Suppl*. 2004;91:33-50.
6. Régis J, Scavarda D, Tamura M, et al. Gamma knife surgery for epilepsy related to hypothalamic hamartomas. *Semin Pediatr Neurol*. 2007;14(2):73-79.
7. Mathieu D, Kondziolka D, Niranjan A, Flickinger J, Lunsford LD. Gamma knife radiosurgery for refractory epilepsy caused by hypothalamic hamartomas. *Stereotact Funct Neurosurg*. 2006;84(2-3):82-87.
8. Mathieu D, Deacon C, Pinard CA, Kenny B, Duval J. Gamma Knife surgery for hypothalamic hamartomas causing refractory epilepsy: preliminary results from a prospective observational study. *J Neurosurg*. 2010;113 Suppl:215-221.
9. Wei Z, Vodovotz L, Luy DD, Deng H, Niranjan A, Lunsford LD. Stereotactic radiosurgery as the initial management option for small-volume hypothalamic hamartomas with intractable epilepsy: a 35-year institutional experience and systematic review. *J Neurosurg Pediatr*. 2022;31(1):52-60. Published 2022 Oct 21.

10. Perry A, Schmidt RE. Cancer therapy-associated CNS neuropathology: an update and review of the literature. *Acta Neuropathol.* 2006;111(3):197-212.

11. Freeman JL, Zacharin M, Rosenfeld JV, Harvey AS. The endocrinology of hypothalamic hamartoma surgery for intractable epilepsy. *Epileptic Disord.* 2003;5(4):239-247.

12. Drees C, Chapman K, Prenger E, et al. Seizure outcome and complications following hypothalamic hamartoma treatment in adults: endoscopic, open, and Gamma Knife procedures. *J Neurosurg.* 2012;117(2):255-261.

13. Schulze-Bonhage A, Trippel M, Wagner K, et al. Outcome and predictors of interstitial radiosurgery in the treatment of gelastic epilepsy. *Neurology.* 2008;71(4):277-282.

14. Abla AA, Shetter AG, Chang SW, et al. Gamma Knife surgery for hypothalamic hamartomas and epilepsy: patient selection and outcomes. *J Neurosurg.* 2010;113 Suppl:207-214.

15. Castinetti F, Brue T, Morange I, Carron R, Régis J. Gamma Knife radiosurgery for hypothalamic hamartoma preserves endocrine functions. *Epilepsia.* 2017;58 Suppl 2:72-76.

16. Tripathi M, Maskara P, Sankhyan N, et al. Safety and Efficacy of Primary Hypofractionated Gamma Knife Radiosurgery for Giant Hypothalamic Hamartoma. *Indian J Pediatr.* 2021;88(11):1086-1091.

17. Mathieu D, Kondziolka D, Niranjan A, Flickinger J, Lunsford LD. Gamma knife radiosurgery for refractory epilepsy caused by hypothalamic hamartomas. *Stereotact Funct Neurosurg.* 2006;84(2-3):82-87.

Gamma Knife in Cavernous Hemangioma

Sarvesh Goyal | Manoj Phalak

KEY LEARNING POINTS

1. GKRS is now considered the 'standard of care' for cavernous hemangiomas.
2. 12–15 Gy prescription dose is the recommended dose range for cavernous sinus hemangiomas, with slight modifications based on tumour size and proximity to critical structures.
3. GKRS has excellent long-term outcomes with more than 80% reduction in tumour size at 5 years.

INTRODUCTION

Cavernous hemangiomas (CHs) are benign vascular lesions characterised by sinusoidal spaces lined with endothelium. Although typically found in the brain parenchyma, their presence within the cavernous sinus is rare and poses significant treatment challenges due to the complex anatomy of this region. The cavernous sinus contains cranial nerves III, IV, VI and the internal carotid artery, making surgical access risky. Patients commonly present with cranial nerve palsies, as these lesions exert a mass effect on adjacent structures. Microsurgery has been the standard of care; however, GKRS provides an alternative for cases where surgery carries high morbidity. With advances in stereotactic techniques, GKRS allows targeted radiation to shrink the lesion and alleviate symptoms while preserving surrounding structures. This chapter discusses a case of a cavernous sinus lesion in a young patient managed successfully with GKRS and reviews relevant literature to outline its efficacy and safety in such lesions.

CASE REPORT

HISTORY & EXAMINATION

A 25-year-old female presented with an 11-month history of right eyelid drooping and double vision. These symptoms began suddenly and gradually worsened, significantly affecting her daily life. Clinical examination revealed right-sided third and sixth cranial nerve palsies. There were no deficits in visual acuity apart from a slight reduction (6/12 in the right eye, 6/9 in the left) and no field defects or other neurological abnormalities.

IMAGING

MRI of the brain identified a lesion within the right cavernous sinus that appeared hyperintense on T2-weighted imaging and homogeneously contrast-enhancing (Fig. 23.1A, B, C), suggesting a differential diagnosis of cavernous hemangioma.

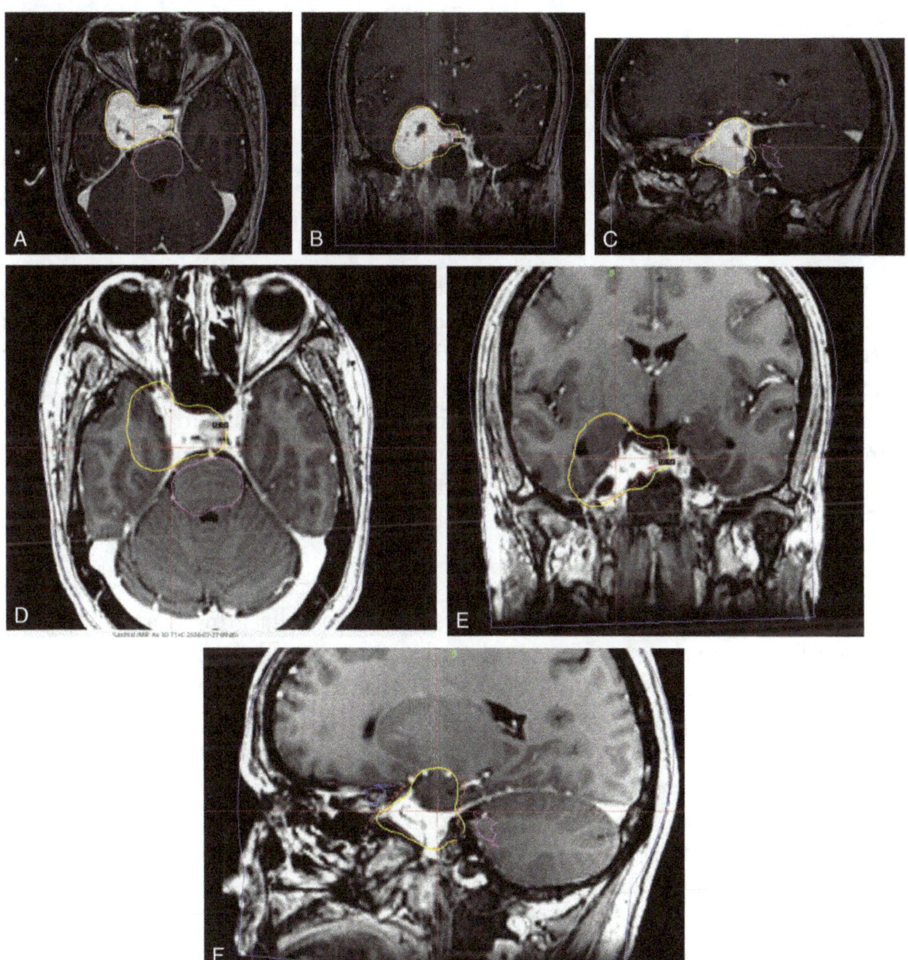

FIGURE 23.1 Pre-Gamma Knife Treatment (GKT) contrast-enhanced MRI (CEMRI) of the brain, utilising T1 post-contrast sequences (Figures A, B, C), revealed a large, homogeneously enhancing lesion within the right cavernous sinus, consistent with a diagnosis of a right cavernous sinus hemangioma. The patient underwent treatment with single-fraction GKT, delivering a marginal dose of 12 Gy precisely to the lesion. Follow-up imaging (Figures D, E, F) performed three years post-treatment demonstrated a marked reduction in tumour size, indicating significant treatment efficacy.

GK PROTOCOL

Given the lesion's location and associated risks with microsurgery, the decision was made to proceed with GKRS after discussing the risks, benefits, and expected outcomes.

The patient underwent GKRS with a marginal dose of 12 Gy delivered to the lesion. The dose was carefully planned to ensure adequate coverage of the target while minimising exposure to surrounding cranial nerves and the optic apparatus. The patient tolerated the procedure well, with no immediate post-radiosurgery complications.

FOLLOW-UP

Follow-up at 3 years revealed partial resolution of symptoms, with significant improvement in diplopia and partial recovery of eyelid function. Repeat imaging (Fig. 23.1D, E, F) showed a reduction in lesion volume, correlating with clinical improvement.

DISCUSSION

Cavernous sinus hemangiomas (CSHs) are a rare and complex type of benign vascular lesion, making up approximately 3% of all cavernous sinus tumours. They pose a significant clinical challenge due to their close proximity to vital neurovascular structures, including the internal carotid artery and cranial nerves III-VI. Surgical resection of these tumours is fraught with risks, primarily due to the dense concentration of cranial nerves and vasculature within the cavernous sinus, making it difficult to excise the lesion without incurring permanent deficits or haemorrhage. This highlights the growing importance of alternative, non-invasive treatment options such as GKRS.[1]

The pathophysiology of cavernous sinus hemangiomas remains an area of active research, with angiogenic factors such as vascular endothelial growth factor (VEGF) thought to play a role in lesion growth and progression. Though still under investigation, VEGF has been identified as a potential target for treatment, potentially aiding in the development of biomarker-driven therapeutic strategies. However, the role of VEGF in predicting radiation-induced complications is still unclear, necessitating further studies in this domain.

Many studies have reported promising outcomes in the use of GKRS for CSHs, with high local control rates and significant tumour volume reduction.[1-5] Patients who received GKRS showed tumour shrinkage rates exceeding 80%, and most patients experienced significant relief of symptoms, particularly from cranial nerve dysfunction.[1] Importantly, symptomatic improvement was observed to occur gradually, with the majority of patients showing improvement over a period of 6 to 18 months following treatment, a key feature of radiosurgical outcomes that should be communicated to patients.[1]

Rates of permanent deficits from microsurgical resection can exceed 20%, whereas GKRS avoids the risks associated with intraoperative bleeding, vascular injury, and cranial nerve damage. Thus, for patients with surgically inaccessible or high-risk lesions, GKRS offers a viable alternative, particularly for those with tumours near critical structures.[3]

The appropriate marginal dose for treating CSHs with GKRS is typically between 12 and 15 Gy.[1] This dose range has been shown to provide optimal results in terms of tumour control while minimising the risk of radiation-induced complications such as cranial neuropathies and radiation necrosis. However, the dose may need to be adjusted based on several factors such as lesion size and proximity to critical structures. Larger lesions may require slightly higher doses, but the proximity to sensitive structures (such as the optic nerve) may necessitate lower doses to avoid radiation toxicity.[4,5]

CONCLUSION

Gamma Knife Radiosurgery has proven to be an indispensable tool in the treatment of cavernous sinus hemangiomas, offering a safe and effective alternative to surgery.

TAKE HOME MESSAGE

Primary GKRS is considered the gold standard for Cavernous sinus hemangiomas, providing excellent outcomes with an unparalleled safety profile.

REFERENCES

1. Lee CC, Sheehan JP, Kano H, et al. Gamma Knife radiosurgery for hemangioma of the cavernous sinus. *J Neurosurg*. 2017;126(5):1498-1505.
2. Wang X, Zhu H, Knisely J, et al. Hypofractionated stereotactic radiosurgery: a new treatment strategy for giant cavernous sinus hemangiomas. *J Neurosurg*. 2018;128(1):60-67.
3. Mishra S, Kumar AG, Garg K, et al. Role of Stereotactic Radiosurgery for Cavernous Sinus Hemangiomas - An Individual Patient Data-Based Meta-Analysis. *Neurol India*. 2023;71 (Supplement):S21-S30.
4. Park CK, Choi SK, Kang IH, Choi MK, Park BJ, Lim YJ. Radiosurgical considerations for cavernous sinus hemangioma: long-term clinical outcomes. *Acta Neurochir (Wien)*. 2016; 158(2):313-318.
5. Anqi X, Zhang S, Jiahe X, Chao Y. Cavernous sinus cavernous hemangioma: imaging features and therapeutic effect of Gamma Knife radiosurgery. *Clin Neurol Neurosurg*. 2014;127:59-64.

24 Gamma Knife for Uveal Melanoma

Abhishek Kumar | Manoj Phalak | Neiwete Lomi

INTRODUCTION

Uveal melanoma (UM), which arises from uveal melanocytes, is the most common primary intraocular tumour in adults.[1] Uveal melanomas typically manifest as a decrease in visual acuity, photopsia, or metamorphopsia and are most often diagnosed in the sixth decade of life, with the incidence of this tumour increasing significantly with age.[2] Enucleation of the affected eye used to be the treatment of choice until the late 1970s. However, the theoretical risk of distant metastasis due to surgical manipulation of tumour, proposed by Zimmerman et al., forced ophthalmologists to focus on non-invasive management of ocular melanoma.[3] Conservative management strategies for UM include: brachytherapy, transpupillary thermotherapy (TTT), Proton Beam Radiotherapy (PBRT), Helium ion irradiation, and Gamma Knife Stereotactic Radiosurgery (GKRS).[4–6] Photocoagulation and transpupillary thermotherapy are used for very small tumours.[4] For posterior uveal melanomas, radiotherapy continues to be the most commonly used treatment method.[7] Enucleation is reserved for advanced melanomas that involve the majority of intraocular structures, cause severe secondary glaucoma, and invade the optic nerve.[2]

144

REPRESENTATIVE CASE

HISTORY & EXAMINATION

A 40-year-old female presented to our outpatient department with complaints of insidious onset, gradually progressive visual loss in right eye for 6 months. There was no history of ocular trauma, redness, pain or discharge. On physical examination, she had Visual acuity of HMCF in right eye and 6/6 in left eye. On ophthalmological examination, her anterior segment was within normal limits. Intraocular pressure was 12 mmHg in the right eye and 10 mmHg in the left eye. Both direct and consensual pupillary reflexes were within normal limits bilaterally.

IMAGING

Her radiological examination revealed a well-defined, round, T1 hyperintense, T2 hypointense, homogeneously enhancing lesion arising from choroid suspicious of Choroidal melanoma. Her FDG PET revealed a metabolically active lesion in the right globe of the eye. A diagnosis of Right eye choroidal melanoma with inferior exudative retinal detachment was made and she was planned for GKRS at our centre.

GK PROTOCOL

Patient was shifted to the GK centre after undergoing placement of silk sutures on the extraocular muscles around the globe by the ophthalmologist. Leskell frame fixation was done, and the sutures were tied to the anterior posts to make the globe immobile. Contrast MRI of brain and orbits was subsequently done and images

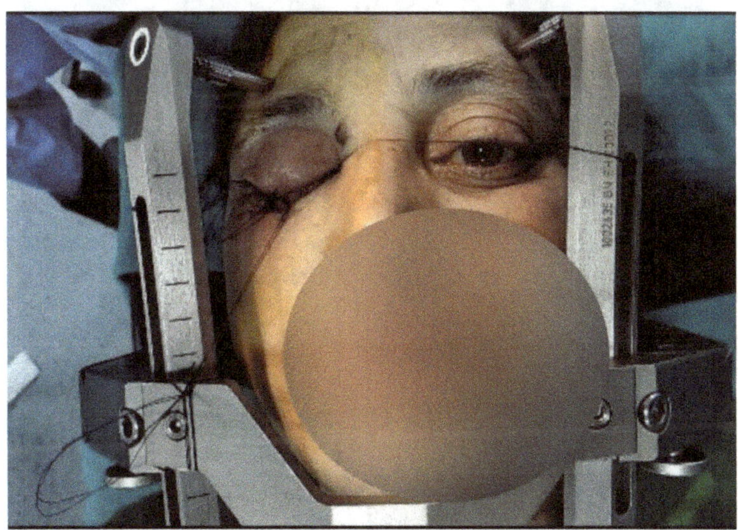

FIGURE 24.1   Shows Leksell frame fixation and application of immobilisation sutures to fix the eye for GKRS.

registered on the Gamma plan software. The tumour was delineated and planning was done using the lightning software. 28 Gy was delivered to the 50% isodose line with 569 cumm (91%) of the tumour receiving the prescribed dose. The maximum dose received by the Right optic nerve was 4.3 Gy, and 5.1 Gy by the right lens.

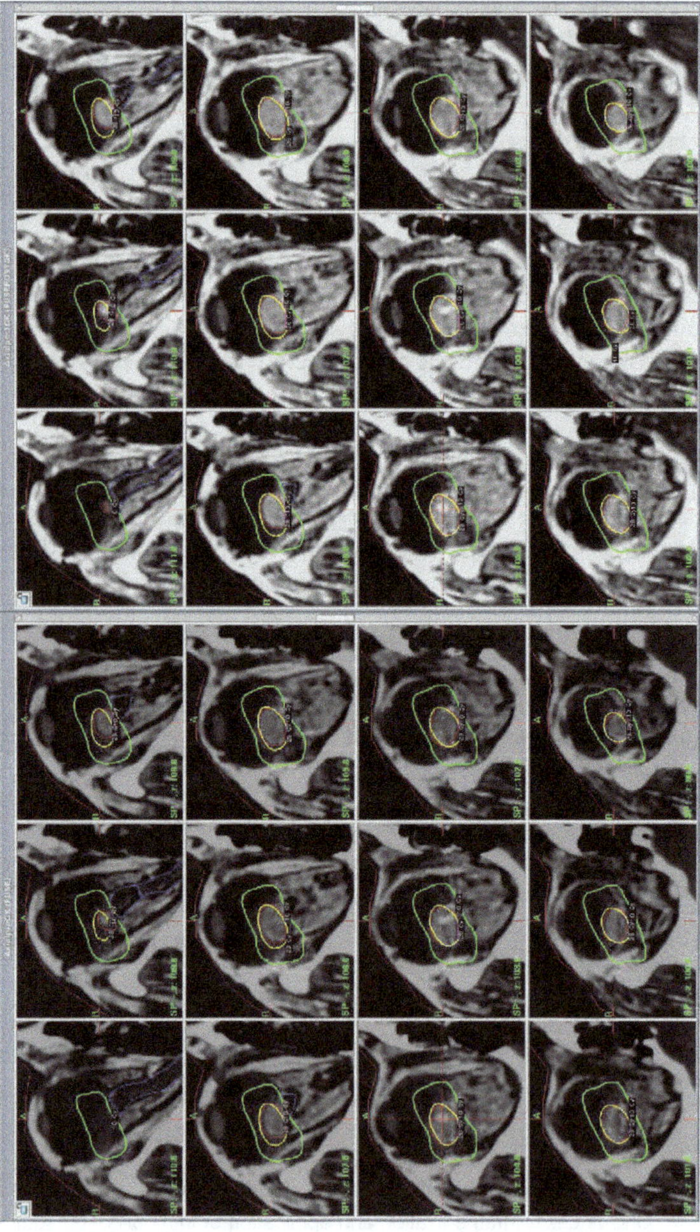

FIGURE 24.2   Tumour delineation and dose plan of the same patient.

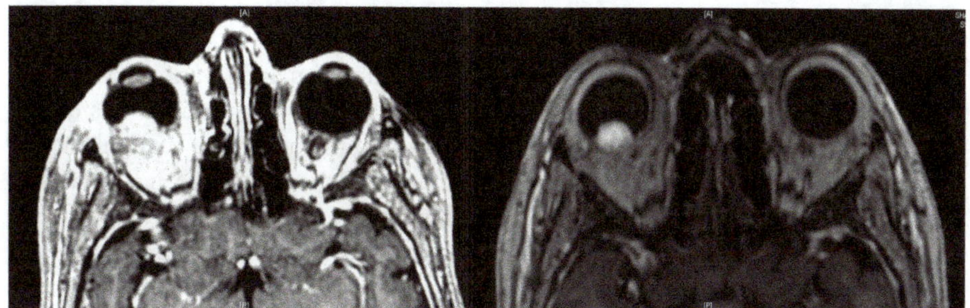

FIGURE 24.3   Pre-GKRS MRI (left side) of the same patient. Follow-up MRI (right side) at 2.5 years post-GKRS shows a significant reduction in tumour size.

FOLLOW-UP

Patient tolerated the procedure well and required only a short course of analgesics. She did not develop any post-GK complications. Her post-GK MRI, done after an interval of 2.5 years showed significant reduction in the size of the tumour.

DISCUSSION

Prolongation of progression-free interval is the desired outcome of therapy for uveal melanoma, followed by preservation of the globe and useful vision.[8] GKRS has proven to be as effective as brachytherapy, proton therapy or enucleation in reducing tumour size, improving survival rates.[5,9-11] Along with its efficacy, GKRS is favoured for its minimal invasiveness. It is performed on an outpatient basis, requiring only a single session and no general anaesthesia. Immobilisation of head and eye for the treatment is the only source of discomfort for the patient.

GKRS PLANNING

The main radiobiological objective of GKRS is to achieve a total radiation effect within the target volume which requires immobilisation of the globe and high-resolution tumour imaging.[12] Immobilisation of the eyes is achieved by injecting peribulbar bupivacaine or lidocaine followed by application of sutures to extraocular muscles under local anaesthesia and fixation of threads around the patient's head.[13,14] GKRS requires high-resolution CE-MRI focused on orbits for precise planning of the therapy.[6,15] Once high-resolution CE-MRI is acquired, data is fed into GKRS software which makes a 3-D reconstruction of the same and optimal delivery dose is selected. Care is taken to ensure that the outlined field corresponds to the shape and size of the tumour along with a thin rim of healthy tissue.[13] Irradiation delivers the target maximum dose at the centre of the tumour (100% isodose) and reduces the dose to half a tumour's periphery (50% isodose) to minimise the risk of spillover and harming healthy tissue.[8]

PRESCRIPTION DOSE

The dose administered in a single fraction to the tumour margin varies across studies, ranging from 22 Gy (36) to 90 Gy.[16] Rise in ocular complications was quickly observed with high doses of irradiation without enhancing the survival rate.[17] Therefore, to reduce radiation-induced secondary side effects, dose has been systematically de-escalated over the years. In their study, Dinca et al. have compared 170 patients with uveal melanoma (UM) treated with GKRS at doses of 35 Gy, 45 Gy, and 50–70 Gy to a group of 620 individuals who underwent enucleation due to UM.[5] They didn't find any difference in survival rates between the patients allotted first group and between the first and second group. Schirmer et al. in their study, found that a marginal dose of 25 Gy provides excellent tumor control.[16] However, they also reported complications at such low doses.[16]

TUMOR CONTROL RATE AND SURVIVAL

A tumour control rate ranging from 100% in the first year to 83% in the third-year follow-up has been reported by Toktas et al. in their study.[18] Modorati et al. report a tumour control rate of 91% which is similar to Mueller et al and Langmann.[6,13,14] Studies by Modorati et al. report survival rates of 88.8% and 81.9% at third and fifth year respectively while Sarici et al. report survival rates of 94% and 86% respectively at the same intervals.[13,15] These findings were similar to the survival probability reported by Rennie et al., who compared GKRS and enucleation for uveal melanomas.[5] A similar result was obtained by our previous study in which tumour volume decreased in all patients with radiological follow-up, with the smallest reduction being 33.06% compared to the initial volume, and the largest being complete tumour disappearance at follow-up.[19] Depending on the follow-up duration, eye retention rate varies from 94% to 72% in different studies.[14,18]

COMPLICATIONS FOLLOWING GKRS

Complications following GKRS for UM can be divided into early and late. Early transient complications include mild headaches, localised subconjunctival and subcutaneous haemorrhage due to mechanical stabilisation, and ophthalmoscopically appreciable spot-like haemorrhages visible on the tumour surface.[13] Late complications following GKRS reported in the literature include: significant vision deterioration, lens opacification, vitreous haemorrhage, radiation retinopathy and exudative retinopathy, optic neuropathy (ischemic and radiation-induced), retinal detachment, uveitis, phthisis bulbi, uncontrolled neovascular glaucoma (NVG). Over 90% of these complications typically emerge 24–48 months after treatment cessation.[13] Tumour size and location also play an important role in prognosis. Painful neovascular glaucoma, which is the most serious complication, is seen following GKRS for large tumours involving anterior and intermediate uvea.[15] Neovascular glaucoma along with UM recurrence is the most common post-treatment cause of enucleation which affects all methods of radiation.[5] Cataract development is usually seen after GKRS for proximally located tumours and can be easily operated upon. Radiation-induced retinopathy and neuropathy are seen after GKRS for posterior ocular segment. Maculopathy is frequently seen when a tumour in the macular region is irradiated, regardless of the dose prescribed.[16]

DETERIORATION IN VISUAL ACUITY

Almost all patients have a significant reduction in visual acuity following GKRS for UM, irrespective of the tumour size and treatment group. Sarici et al. found that 60% of the patients with median BCVA of 20/60 at the time of diagnosis had deterioration of visual acuity to 20/200 following GKRS.[15] A reduction in visual acuity up to 94% was observed by Modorati et al. at the end of follow-up while Mueller reports reduction in BCVA from 20/60 to 20/200 at the end of one-year follow-up. [6,13] In their study, Dinca et al. highlighted that visual deterioration was influenced by the irradiation dose prescribed, with a significantly smaller decrease in BCVA observed in the 35 Gy group compared to the 45 Gy group (31.4% vs. 83.7%). Therefore, in order to minimise the risk of complications, all authors recommend careful patient selection for treatment with Gamma Knife.[5]

CONCLUSION

Studies indicate that GKRS could be a viable alternative for treating uveal melanomas with minimal intraocular complications. This patient-friendly and convenient treatment method demonstrates control rates and long-term outcomes that are comparable to those of surgical excision and brachytherapy.[18]

TAKE HOME MESSAGE

The desired outcome of therapy for uveal melanoma is an extended progression-free interval, along with the preservation of the globe and useful vision. GKRS has proven to be as effective as brachytherapy, proton therapy or enucleation in reducing tumour size and improving survival rates. Additionally, GKRS is minimally invasive, conducted on an outpatient basis, requires only one session, and does not necessitate general anaesthesia.

REFERENCES

1. Jager MJ, Shields CL, Cebulla CM, et al. Uveal melanoma [published correction appears in Nat Rev Dis Primers. 2022 Jan 17;8(1):4]. *Nat Rev Dis Primers*. 2020;6(1):24. Published 2020 Apr 9.
2. Toktas ZO, Bicer A, Demirci G, et al. Gamma knife stereotactic radiosurgery yields good long-term outcomes for low-volume uveal melanomas without intraocular complications. *J Clin Neurosci*. 2010;17(4):441-445.

3. Zimmerman LE, McLean IW, Foster WD. Does enucleation of the eye containing a malignant melanoma prevent or accelerate the dissemination of tumour cells. *Br J Ophthalmol* 1978;62:420–5.

4. Shields JA. Management of posterior uveal melanoma: past, present, future. *Retina*. 2002;22(2):139-142.

5. Dinca EB, Yianni J, Rowe J, et al. Survival and complications following γ knife radiosurgery or enucleation for ocular melanoma: a 20-year experience. *Acta Neurochir (Wien)*. 2012;154(4):605-610.

6. Mueller AJ, Talies S, Schaller UC, Horstmann G, Wowra B, Kampik A. Stereotactic radiosurgery of large uveal melanomas with the gamma-knife. *Ophthalmology*. 2000;107(7):1381-1388.

7. Shields JA, Shields CL, Donoso LA. Management of posterior uveal melanoma. *Surv Ophthalmol*. 1991;36(3):161-195.

8. Wygledowska-Promieńska D, Jurys M, Wilczyński T, Drzyzga Ł. The gamma knife in ophthalmology. Part One--Uveal melanoma. *Klin Oczna*. 2014;116(2):130-134.

9. Müllner K, Langmann G, Pendl G, Faulborn J. Echographic findings in uveal melanomas treated with the Leksell gamma knife. *Br J Ophthalmol*. 1998;82(2):154-158.

10. Gragoudas E, Li W, Goitein M, Lane AM, Munzenrider JE, Egan KM. Evidence-based estimates of outcome in patients irradiated for intraocular melanoma. *Arch Ophthalmol*. 2002;120(12):1665-1671.

11. Egger E, Zografos L, Schalenbourg A, et al. Eye retention after proton beam radiotherapy for uveal melanoma. *Int J Radiat Oncol Biol Phys*. 2003;55(4):867-880.

12. Kondziolka D, Lunsford LD, Witt TC, Flickinger JC. The future of radiosurgery: radiobiology, technology, and applications. *Surg Neurol*. 2000;54(6):406-414.

13. Modorati G, Miserocchi E, Galli L, Picozzi P, Rama P. Gamma knife radiosurgery for uveal melanoma: 12 years of experience. *Br J Ophthalmol*. 2009;93(1):40-44.

14. Langmann G, Pendl G, Klaus-Müllner, Papaefthymiou G, Guss H. Gamma knife radiosurgery for uveal melanomas: an 8-year experience. *J Neurosurg*. 2000;93 Suppl 3:184-188.

15. Sarici AM, Pazarli H. Gamma-knife-based stereotactic radiosurgery for medium- and large-sized posterior uveal melanoma. *Graefes Arch Clin Exp Ophthalmol*. 2013;251(1):285-294.

16. Schirmer CM, Chan M, Mignano J, et al. Dose de-escalation with gamma knife radiosurgery in the treatment of choroidal melanoma. *Int J Radiat Oncol Biol Phys*. 2009;75(1):170-176.

17. Simonová G, Novotný J Jr, Liscák R, Pilbauer J. Leksell gamma knife treatment of uveal melanoma. *J Neurosurg*. 2002;97(5 Suppl):635-639.

18. Toktas ZO, Bicer A, Demirci G, et al. Gamma knife stereotactic radiosurgery yields good long-term outcomes for low-volume uveal melanomas without intraocular complications. *J Clin Neurosci*. 2010;17(4):441-445.

19. Phalak M, Lomi N, Ganeshkumar A, et al. Gamma Knife Radiosurgery for Uveal Melanoma: Our Experience and Thematic Review. *Neurol India*. 2023;71(Supplement):S168-S173.

Stitchless Eye Fixation for Gamma Knife in Uveal Melanoma

25

Deepak Agrawal | Aruja Gangwani | Bhavna Chawla

KEY LEARNING POINTS

1. **Globe Salvage treatment for uveal melanoma:** Gamma Knife radiosurgery is an efficacious globe salvage modality for the treatment of uveal melanoma.
2. **Stitchless eye fixation:** A peribulbar block of Lignocaine and Ropivacaine combination can achieve effective eye immobility for the radiation delivery of the GKRS procedure.
3. **Comparative effectiveness:** It is a minimally invasive procedure with quicker one-time radiation exposure as compared to Plaque brachytherapy which is the alternative globe salvage procedure.
4. **Long-term outcomes:** Studies have indicated the effectiveness of the GKRS procedure in terms of local tumour control and globe salvage.

INTRODUCTION

Uveal Melanoma is the most common primary intra-ocular malignancy in adults with 90% of it arising from the choroid.[1] The management of uveal melanoma has improved drastically over the years with a trend towards globe salvage and preservation of vision wherever possible. Enucleation which was historically the preferred treatment is now reserved for tumors too large to treat with conventional radiation or those with painful blind eyes. Gamma Knife radiosurgery (GKRS) is an effective globe salvage modality for the treatment of uveal melanoma. Gamma Knife uses cobalt sources to stereotactically direct radiation dose to the target tissue after its localisation with high-resolution imaging. We summarise the key findings from a representative case of uveal melanoma treated by GKRS at our institute.

REPRESENTATIVE CASE

HISTORY AND EXAMINATION

A 32-year-old gentleman presented to the ophthalmic OPD with chief complaints of painless, progressive diminution of vision in the left eye since 1 year. On examination, the visual acuity in the right eye was 6/6 and the left eye was hand movement close to face. The anterior segment examination using a slit lamp was within normal limits in both eyes. The posterior segment evaluation of the right eye was within normal limits while the left eye showed a pigmented choroidal mass of approximately 5 disc diameter in size obscuring the posterior pole.

IMAGING

The patient underwent an Ultrasound (USG) B scan to establish the tumour dimensions. The USG scan revealed a mushroom-shaped mass with choroidal excavation and Kappa sign on A scan suggestive of choroidal melanoma. The tumour was found to have an apical thickness of 6.6 mm and the largest basal diameter of 12.4 mm. The patient also underwent an MRI to assess the extent of the disease which revealed a hyperintense intraocular mass on the T1 image and a hypointense intraocular mass on the T2 image. The patient also underwent a PET-CT scan to rule out metastasis. The patient was diagnosed with choroidal melanoma and planned for primary GKRS.

GK PROTOCOL

Peribulbar block was given using Bupivacaine by an Ophthalmologist in the Gamma-knife centre (Fig. 25.1A). Subsequently, three post-frame fixations were done and the ipsilateral anterior post was excluded to prevent collisions. MRI brain and orbits was performed *after* this step. The patient's treatment planning was done with high-resolution MRI on the Gamma Knife planning software (Fig. 25.2). A mean dose of 35 Gy at 61% isodose line was given for a tumour volume of 0.534 cc. The optic nerve dose was kept under 8 Gy and the lens dose was kept under 2 Gy.

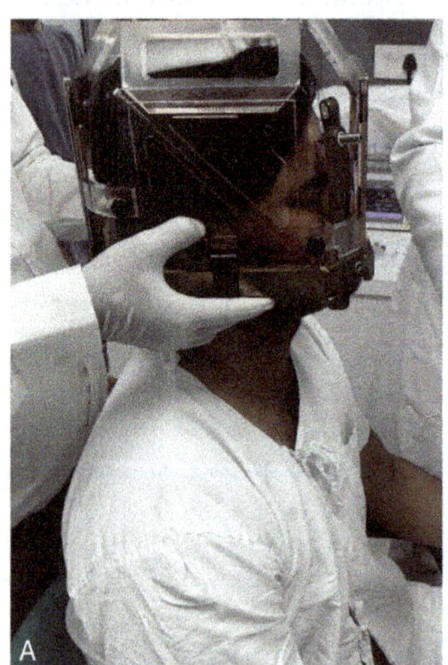
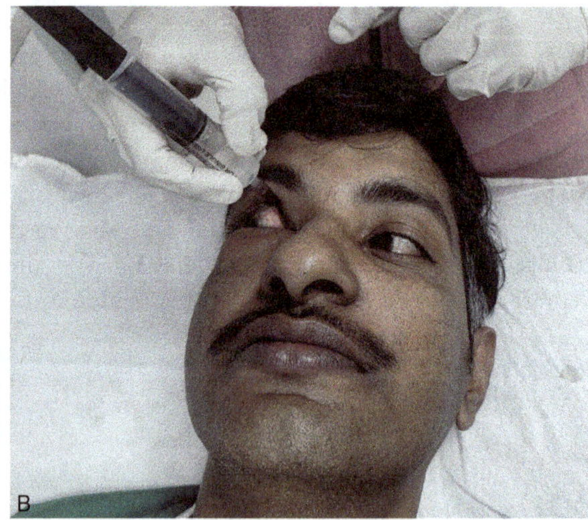

FIGURE 25.1   (A) Frame fixation for Gamma Knife. (B) Peribulbar block.

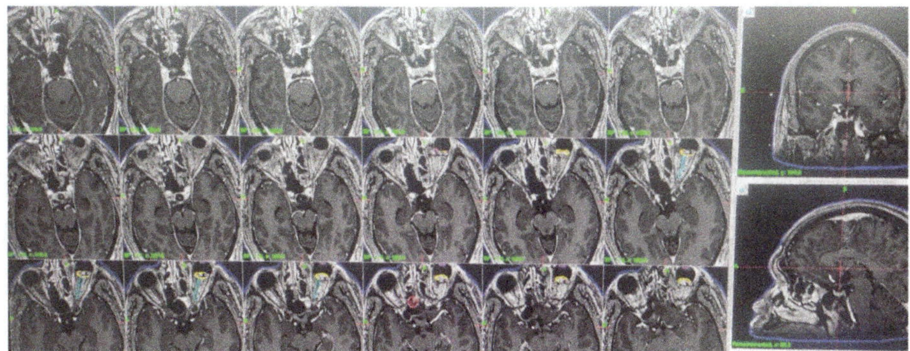

FIG 25.2   Gamma plan showing tumour delineated in red with isodose line in yellow.

Following the radiation dose delivery, the patient was discharged the same day and kept under regular USG follow-up.

FOLLOW-UP AND TUMOUR CONTROL

The patient was followed up regularly with a USG B scan monthly and a yearly MRI scan to assess and evaluate tumour regression. At 1 year postoperatively, the apical thickness was noted to be 3.74 mm with a percentage decrease of 43.33%, and the largest basal diameter was noted to be 8.98 mm with a percentage decrease of 27.5% (Fig. 25.3). Also, tumour regression was noted on MRI protocol at 1-year follow-up.

DISCUSSION

Uveal melanoma is the most common primary intraocular malignancy in adults. The treatment of uveal melanoma has changed considerably over the years with more emphasis on globe salvage modalities. Stereotactic Radiosurgery using Gamma Knife is one such globe salvage modality.

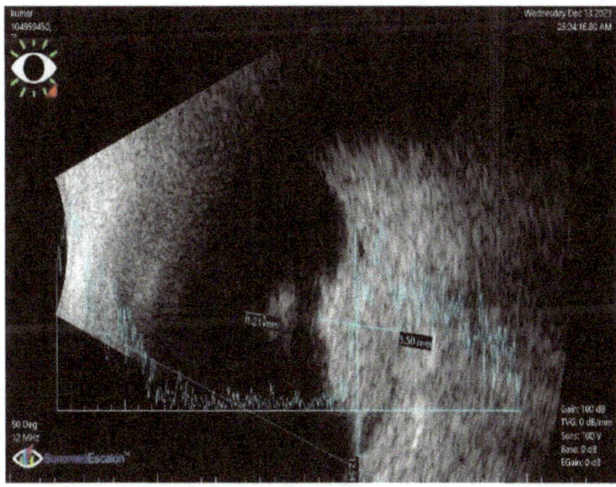

FIGURE 25.3   USG scan to measure dimensions at 1 year follow up.

Stereotactic radiosurgery refers to treatment using a single large fraction. GKRS, which is one of the established methods of Stereotactic Radiosurgery, consists of multiple Cobalt fixed sources, arranged in 5 concentric rings. To achieve irradiation of the selected target volume, the radiation emitted by Cobalt sources is aimed at a common focal point by a primary collimator.[2]

The effectiveness of GKRS in the treatment of uveal melanoma has been observed in various studies. Modorati et al conducted a single-center, retrospective, observational study, including all patients with uveal melanoma treated at the Ocular Oncology and Uveitis Service, in the Department of Ophthalmology of the San Raffaele Scientific Institute, Milan from September 1993 to September 2018. They noted an eye retention rate of 89.7%.and established the effectiveness of GKRS in the treatment of uveal melanoma.[3]

Tariq Parker et al conducted a systematic review and meta-analysis to aggregate the clinical outcomes of patients with uveal melanomas or intraocular metastases treated primarily with GKRS. They included 52 studies, reporting on 1010 patients with uveal melanoma and 34 intraocular metastases, for systematic review. 28 studies were included in the meta-analysis. 840 of 898 patients from 19 studies had local control, and 378 of 478 patients from 16 studies experienced tumour regression. They henceforth concluded that GKRS is an efficacious primary method of treating uveal melanomas and intraocular metastases, with reliable tumour control rates.[4]

However, the treatment of uveal melanoma with GKRS is not free of complications. Radiation-induced cataract and radiation retinopathy were the most frequent events, followed by neovascular glaucoma (27.3%), optic neuropathy (18.6%), radiation maculopathy (11.4%), vitreous haemorrhage (14.4%), phthisis bulbi (7.7%), hyphema (0.5%), and corneal melting (0.5%).[3]

GKRS is an effective globe salvage modality for the treatment of uveal melanoma. However, it is not free of complications, hence prospective studies with longer follow-up are needed to determine its long-term outcomes

TAKE HOME MESSAGE

GKRS is an effective globe salvage modality for local tumour control in patients of uveal melanoma. However, radiation retinopathy and cataracts are the complications that have been noted after the therapy.

REFERENCES

1. Spagnolo F, Caltabiano G, Queirolo P. Uveal melanoma. *Cancer Treat Rev.* 2012;38(5):549-553.
2. Fanous AA, Prasad D, Mathieu D, Fabiano AJ. Intracranial stereotactic radiosurgery. *J Neurosurg Sci.* 2019;63(1):61-82.
3. Modorati G, Miserocchi E, Galli L, Picozzi P, Rama P. Gamma knife radiosurgery for uveal melanoma: 12 years of experience. *Br J Ophthalmol.* 2009;93(1):40-44.
4. Parker T, Rigney G, Kallos J, et al. Gamma knife radiosurgery for uveal melanomas and metastases: a systematic review and meta-analysis. *Lancet Oncol.* 2020;21(11):1526-1536.

Gamma Knife Radiosurgery In Juvenile Nasopharyngeal Angiofibroma

26

R Siva Krishna | Deepak Agrawal

KEY LEARNING POINTS

1. Gamma Knife radiosurgery is an important adjunct in the multimodality management of locally advanced Juvenile nasopharyngeal angiofibroma (JNA).
2. Primary GKRS can be considered in relatively small tumours.
3. High dose (16-18 Gy at 50% isodose line) results in dramatic results in JNA's.
4. Further multicenter prospective studies are needed to establish the role of GKRS in JNA in terms of efficacy and safety.

INTRODUCTION

Juvenile nasopharyngeal carcinoma (JNA) is a benign yet locally aggressive tumour that typically presents in adolescent males with symptoms such as epistaxis and nasal blockage. Its prototypical site of origin is the posterosuperior margin of sphenopalatine foramen within the pterygopalatine fossa.[1] The foremost step in evaluating JNA is determining the extent of the tumour and the sites involved. Currently, 6 classification systems have been described in the literature, with the Radkowski staging being the most popular and widely used, though it lacks specificity regarding the skull base sites.[2] The recent Onerci staging system, on the other hand, specifies the skull base sites involved.[3] While surgery remains the mainstay treatment, Gamma Knife radiosurgery (GKRS) in recent years has emerged as an important adjunctive treatment modality for locally advanced, recurrent, and intracranial JNAs.[4,5]

PRINCIPLE OF GKRS IN JNA

The main principle of GKRS is the induction of obliterative endarteritis of the abnormal vasculature within the tumor with a steep dose fall-off which protects the adjacent critical neural and vascular structures. This essentially mirrors the excellent results of GKRS in the treatment of other intracranial vascular tumours including pediatric AVMs, glomus jugulare, and cavernous haemangiomas.[6,7]

We summarise key findings from a representative case of JNA that was treated by GKRS at our institute.

REPRESENTATIVE CASE

HISTORY AND EXAMINATION

A 13-year-old male child presented with frequent episodes of epistaxis. He was diagnosed with JNA for which he underwent excision via the left maxillary swing approach. A 3-month follow-up MRI revealed a significant residual tumour. Examination revealed no focal neurological deficit.

IMAGING

Gadolinium-enhanced MRI brain revealed a 40 × 24 × 26 mm enhancing mass in the skull base with involvement of bilateral cavernous sinuses.

GK PROTOCOL

Secondary GKRS therapy was given for Juvenile Nasopharyngeal Angiofibroma in the year 2017 on Gamma knife model B machine. Leksell Coordinate Frame G was used for fixation Configuration and planning was done on Gamma plan version 11.3.2. Radiation to the tumour was given. 2.70 cc (97%) of the tumour received 16 Gy. Brainstem and optic chiasma shielding were done.

FOLLOW UP

The lesion volume was assessed in the follow-up MRI done in 2018, 2022, and 2024. A progressive decrease in volume was noticed with near complete resolution at 8 years of follow-up, as shown in the imaging above.

DISCUSSION

JNAs are highly vascular tumours of the pterygopalatine fossa (PPF) region, for which traditionally surgery has been a mainstay treatment. However, the anatomical complexity of the PPF and the proximity of critical neurovascular structures often make complete resection of tumours difficult. Tumours infiltrating the infratemporal fossa, sphenoid sinus, pterygoid base, cavernous sinus, foramen lacerum, or the anterior or middle cranial fossa are at the highest risk of incomplete excision and recurrence. This necessitated an adjunctive treatment modality for residual/recurrent tumours. Gamma Knife radiosurgery has emerged as a promising new adjunctive treatment modality, minimising exposure to surrounding critical structures like the pituitary gland and optic nerves.[8] Dare et al. first introduced GKRS as a treatment modality for JNAs by reporting two recent cases of JNAs successfully treated with

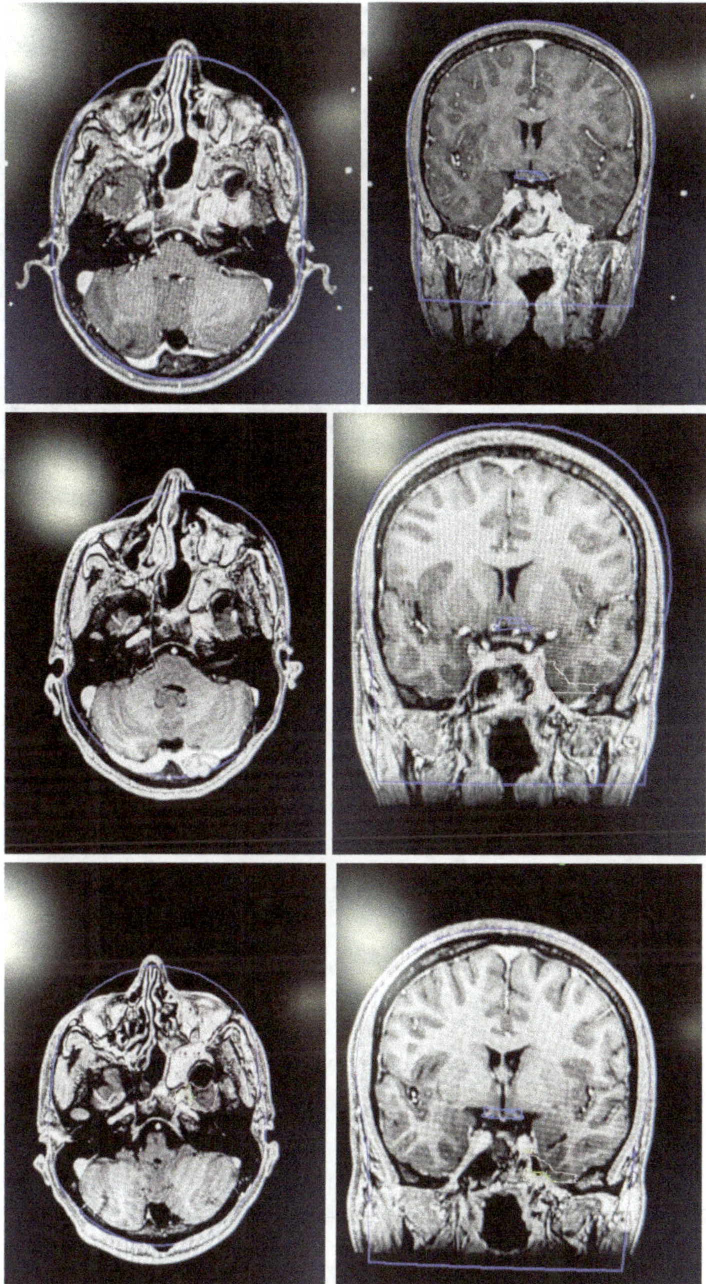

FIGURE 26.1 Contrast-enhanced MR axial and coronal images of a patient with JNA at baseline (2017) (top row), at 1-year follow-up (2018) (2nd row), 5-year follow-up (3rd row), and 7-year follow-up (bottom row).

Continued

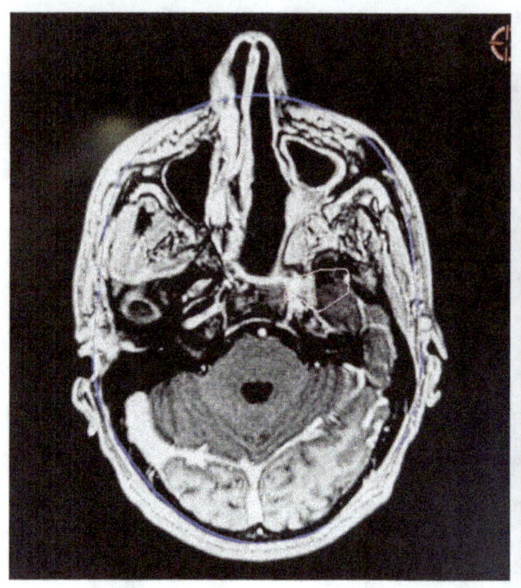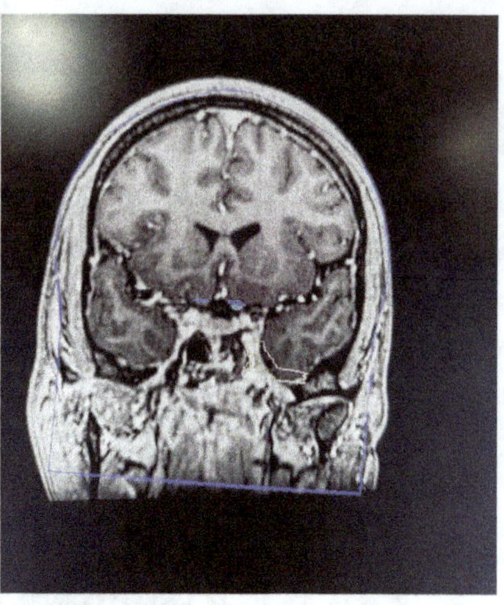

FIGURE 26.1 cont'd

TABLE 26.1 ■ Tabulation of studies regarding the use of GKRS in the treatment of JNAs

S. no	Study	No of cases	Sites involved	Marginal dose Range(Gy)	Max tumour volume treated (cc)	Follow Up (in months)
1	Dare et al.[9]	2	Cavernous sinus, ITF	20	4.7	36
2	Raheja et al.[10]	2	Cavernous sinus, PPF, OA	14–20	24	30–78
3	Park et al.[11]	1	Orbit	17	6.8	48
4	Roche et al.[12]	3	Cavernous sinus, IOF	14–16	<3	36–60
5	Alvarez et al.[13]	10	Cavernous sinus, Skull base	18–24	5	36–180
6	Min et al.[14]	1	PPF, Skull base	20	–	48

Key- IOF- inferior orbital fissure, ITF- infratemporal fossa, PPF- pterygopalatine fossa, OA- orbital apex

GKRS.[9] Multiple studies have since shown good tumour control rates with GKRS in residual lesions. Table 26.1 summarises the details of studies demonstrating the beneficial role of GKRS in residual lesions.

Single-dose GKRS is used for JNAs up to 3 cm while the larger tumours require multiple sessions (2-5) of hypofractionated doses.[10] The largest reported tumour volume treated by GKRS is 24 cc, as shown in a study by Raheja et al. This signifies the effectiveness of GKRS even for large tumours. Currently, there are no recommendations for dose optimisation based on the volume of tumours. However, according to the current literature, tumour control rates of 100% were achieved using a median dose of 20 Gy (range 14–30 Gy), delivered at a median isodose of 50% (range 45–55%) at a mean follow-up of 77.5 months (range 8–180 months).[10]

SAFETY OF GKRS IN JNA

GKRS has significantly lower complication rates as compared to conventional radiotherapy, owing to its extremely meticulous and focused radiation application on the tumour. The complications generally reported for conventional radiotherapy such as hypopituitarism, optic atrophy, temporal lobe necrosis, and osteonecrosis are much less reported in patients treated with GKRS. The development of new malignancies and malignant transformation are among the most concerning long-term complications of GKRS, particularly in JNA, due to its occurrence in pediatric patients. The literature regarding the safety of GKRS in JNA is sparse. However, sufficient evidence supporting the safety of GKRS in pediatric AVMs is available, with no observed increase in the risk of malignancy post-GKRS.[15]

TAKE HOME MESSAGE

Locally advanced JNAs are surgically challenging, and primary surgery is often not successful in achieving complete tumour removal. GKRS has emerged as a safe and effective modality in the multimodality management of locally advanced JNAs and has shown promising tumour control rates. The complication rates are significantly lower than the conventional radiotherapy and there is no evidence of increased risk of secondary malignancies and malignant transformation to date. Elective GKRS with sub-total resection can be used as an alternative to primary surgery for advanced JNAs, thereby reducing the substantial morbidities associated with extensive and complicated primary surgeries.

REFERENCES

1. Hofmann T, Bernal-Sprekelsen M, Koele W, Reittner P, Klein E, Stammberger H. Endoscopic resection of juvenile angiofibromas--long term results. *Rhinology*. 2005;43(4):282-289.
2. Radkowski D, McGill T, Healy GB, Ohlms L, Jones DT. Angiofibroma. Changes in staging and treatment. *Arch Otolaryngol Head Neck Surg*. 1996;122(2):122-129.
3. Onerci M, Oğretmenoğlu O, Yücel T. Juvenile nasopharyngeal angiofibroma: a revised staging system. *Rhinology*. 2006;44(1):39-45.
4. Beriwal S, Eidelman A, Micaily B. Three-dimensional conformal radiotherapy for treatment of extensive juvenile angiofibroma: report on two cases. *ORL J Otorhinolaryngol Relat Spec*. 2003;65(4):238-241.
5. Chakraborty S, Ghoshal S, Patil VM, Oinam AS, Sharma SC. Conformal radiotherapy in the treatment of advanced juvenile nasopharyngeal angiofibroma with intracranial extension: an institutional experience. *Int J Radiat Oncol Biol Phys*. 2011;80(5):1398-1404.
6. Kiran NA, Kale SS, Vaishya S, et al. Gamma Knife surgery for intracranial arteriovenous malformations in children: a retrospective study in 103 patients. *J Neurosurg*. 2007;107(6 Suppl):479-484.

7. Sharma MS, Gupta A, Kale SS, Agrawal D, Mahapatra AK, Sharma BS. Gamma knife radiosurgery for glomus jugulare tumors: therapeutic advantages of minimalism in the skull base. *Neurol India*. 2008;56(1):57-61.

8. Lee JT, Chen P, Safa A, Juillard G, Calcaterra TC. The role of radiation in the treatment of advanced juvenile angiofibroma. *Laryngoscope*. 2002;112(7 Pt 1):1213-1220.

9. Dare AO, Gibbons KJ, Proulx GM, Fenstermaker RA. Resection followed by radiosurgery for advanced juvenile nasopharyngeal angiofibroma: report of two cases. *Neurosurgery*. 2003;52(5):1207-1211.

10. Raheja A, Sharma MS, Singh M, Agrawal D, Kale SS, Sharma SC. Adjuvant Gamma Knife Radiosurgery for Advanced Juvenile Nasopharyngeal Angiofibroma. *Neurol India*. 2021;69(5):1438-1441.

11. Park CK, Kim DG, Paek SH, Chung HT, Jung HW. Recurrent juvenile nasopharyngeal angiofibroma treated with gamma knife surgery. *J Korean Med Sci*. 2006;21(4):773-777.

12. Roche PH, Paris J, Régis J, et al. Management of invasive juvenile nasopharyngeal angiofibromas: the role of a multimodality approach. *Neurosurgery*. 2007;61(4):768-777.

13. Álvarez FL, Suárez V, Suárez C, Llorente JL. Multimodality approach for advanced-stage juvenile nasopharyngeal angiofibromas. *Head Neck*. 2013;35(2):209-213.

14. Min HJ, Chung HJ, Kim CH. Delayed cerebrospinal fluid rhinorrhea four years after gamma knife surgery for juvenile angiofibroma. *J Craniofac Surg*. 2014;25(6):e565-e567.

15. Dinca EB, de Lacy P, Yianni J, et al. Gamma knife surgery for pediatric arteriovenous malformations: a 25-year retrospective study. *J Neurosurg Pediatr*. 2012;10(5):445-450.

Gamma Knife Radiosurgery for Glomus Jugular

Dattaraj P Sawarkar | Abhishek Kumar

KEY LEARNING POINTS

1. Surgical excision of these tumours is difficult due to their hypervascularity and proximity to critical neurovascular structures near jugular foramen.
2. Surgery carries high risk of morbidity including CSF leaks and lower cranial nerve deficits.
3. Conventional RT carries the risk of long-term complications, including temporal bone necrosis, cerebral necrosis, radiation-induced malignancies, and others.
4. GKRS, with its precision, Bragg peak effect, and improved safety profile, has become a primary treatment option for GJTs.

INTRODUCTION

Glomus Jugulare tumours (GJTs) are uncommon neuroendocrine tumours that tend to occur more frequently in females.[1] Patients often present with symptoms such as hearing loss, pulsatile tinnitus, ear pain, a feeling of fullness in the ear, vertigo, and dysfunction of the lower cranial nerves.[2] About 1% to 3% of GJTs are secretory and may exhibit clinical signs indicative of catecholamine overproduction.[3] Despite being benign, these tumours are difficult to treat owing to their hypervascularity and proximity to critical neurovascular structures near jugular foramen. Due to its indolent nature, it grows slowly at a rate of 1 mm/year, therefore treatment is typically recommended for symptomatic patients.[4] In the past, microsurgery, with or without preoperative embolisation, was the primary method of treatment.[5] However, surgical excision of the tumour is associated with considerable post-operative morbidity including cerebrospinal fluid leaks (3.7%-17.6%) and lower cranial nerve deficits (6.6%-61%).[6] In light of its favourable side effect profile, conventional stereotactic radiosurgery has emerged as a preferred option, either alone or in combination with surgery.[5] Tumour control rates of 90% to 100%, along with fewer side effects and improved quality of life, have been reported, making GKRS the preferred treatment option.[7,8] Drawbacks of conventional RT include the exposure of healthy tissue to high doses of radiation, as well as long-term complications such as temporal bone necrosis, cerebral necrosis, and radiation-induced malignancies.[9,10] Stereotactic radiosurgery (SRS), with its capacity to deliver radiation precisely and its steep dose decline at the tumour margins (Bragg peak effect), provides a better safety profile and has emerged as a primary treatment option for GJTs.[11–13]

REPRESENTATIVE CASE

HISTORY & EXAMINATION

A 30-year-old gentleman presented to our outpatient department with complaints of gradually progressive visual deterioration in both eyes for 6 months associated with insidious onset diplopia on left lateral gaze. On neurological examination, he was found to have left lateral rectus palsy.

IMAGING

His CMRI brain showed an intensely enhancing 24 cc mass in the Left temporal bone suggestive of left Glomus jugular with extracranial extension.

GKRS PROTOCOL

He was planned for GKRS at our institute. A dose of 25 Gy was given at 50% iso-dose line. Rt Optic nerve received <7.5 Gy, while Lt optic nerve received <5.4 Gy. Chiasm received < 5.5 Gy.

FOLLOW UP

His post-GKRS MRI, done after an interval of 1, 4 and 8 years after GKRS showed significant reduction in the size of tumour (Fig. 27.1).

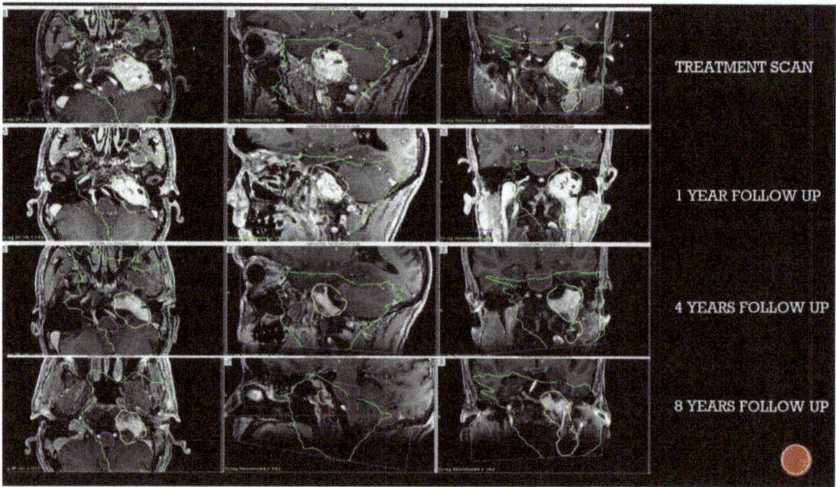

FIGURE 27.1   Patient with Lt Glomus showing significant decrease in tumour size over a follow-up of 8 years.

DISCUSSION

Given the biphasic and slow growth pattern of these benign tumours, it is crucial to customise treatment strategies to minimise post-treatment complications and preserve the quality of life in patients with GJTs.[4] Also, Radiosurgery uses a single high-dose radiation fraction targeted at a small area, whereas conventional radio-therapy delivers multiple fractions to a larger volume. SRS has become a primary treatment modality for this condition, offering a superior safety profile compared to surgery, while achieving similar tumour control rates (tumour recurrence rate of 3.1% for micro-neurosurgery versus 2.1% for SRS).[14] While tumour cells are known to persist after radiation therapy, the primary theory supporting the use of RT for these tumours is its effect on the vasculature, causing fibrosis which leads to growth stabilisation or inhibition.[15]

TUMOR CONTROL RATE

Sheehan et al., in the largest multi-institutional series published to date (n = 132 patients, 134 procedures), reported an actuarial tumour control rate of 90% at 3 years and 88% at 5 years, respectively.[16] In line with this study, we observed a comparable 5-year tumour control rate of 87% ± 6%.[17] In their study, Ibrahim et al. reported a 5-year tumour control rate of 92.2% in 75 patients (76 tumours) using a median prescription dose of 18 Gy (range 12-25 Gy).[18] Tumour control rate in previously published studies ranges from 80% to 100%, with a median/mean prescribed dose ranging from 13.5 to 20 Gy.[13,16,18]

CLINICAL RESPONSE

In the literature, transient and permanent clinical worsening has been reported in up to 16% of patients following SRS for glomus tumours.[16,18] In contrast, Sharma et al. did not observe any new cases of cranial nerve paresis in their study.[17] This could be attributed to the lower median prescribed dose used in our study (15 Gy compared to 18 Gy in the other study).[18] In their study, Sheehan et al. reported that 15% of patients experienced worsening of pre-SRS cranial nerve deficits, while 11% showed improvement following SRS.[16] In the same study by Sheehan et al., preexisting tinnitus improved in 49% of patients following SRS.[16] Another study found that pulsatile tinnitus resolved in 8% of patients, while hearing improved in 4% of patients.[18] Progressive reduction in tumour blood flow is proposed to cause improvement in tinnitus post-GKRS. Sheehan et al. attributed the worsening of cranial nerve deficits to the adverse effects of radiation, even though good radio-graphic tumour control was achieved.[16]

PREDICTORS OF OUTCOME

Sheehan et al. identified preoperative trigeminal nerve dysfunction (hazard ratio [HR]: 11.109, P = .001), a higher number of isocenters (HR: 0.767, P = .005), and stable or improved cranial nerve dysfunction at the last follow-up (HR: 7.618, P = .002) as independent predictors of tumour-progression-free survival in their cohort. [16] However, none of the patient, tumour, or treatment-related variables were found to be significantly associated with the tumour control rate in Sharma et al.'s study.[17]

TUMOUR RESPONSE BASED ON SRS PLATFORMS AND TYPES OF RADIATION TREATMENT

In a recent meta-analysis comparing various SRS platforms, tumour control rate was reported to be 97%, with either GK (95% confidence interval: 94%-99%) or linear accelerator (LINAC) (Novalis, Brainlab Inc)/Cyber Knife® (CK, Accuray Inc, Sunnyvale, California; 95% confidence interval: 92%-100%).[19] In a similar vein, clinical control rates of 94% and 97% were reported with GK and Cyber Knife® (CK), respectively, in this study.[19] This meta-analysis included 19 studies (14 involving GK, n = 278, and 5 involving LINAC/CK, n = 57), with 10 studies having a mean or median follow-up duration greater than 36 months. Overall, no differences in tumour or clinical control rates have been observed based on the type of SRS platform. In their study, Dupin et al. reported 5-year and 10-year actuarial tumour control rates of 100% and 98.7%, respectively, in 66 patients with 81 head and neck paragangliomas treated with conventional external beam RT, at a median follow-up of 4.1 years (range: 0.1-21.2 years).[7] The recent introduction of the stereotactic frameless GK Icon™ system (Elekta AB) has made it possible to treat large GJTs using fractionated GK radiosurgery with a margin. This approach helps avoid complications linked to treating large tumours in a single session while still achieving effective tumour control.[20]

CONCLUSION

GKRS is a safe and effective treatment for patients with GJTs, providing durable long-term control. GKRS should be considered for healthy young patients as the risk of long-term significant neurological complications is greater following surgery than after GKRS. Additionally, GKRS can be utilised as either an initial or salvage treatment after surgical resection, with favourable long-term outcomes.

TAKE HOME MESSAGE

- GKRS offers a superior safety profile compared to micro-neurosurgery, while achieving similar tumor control rates.
- The long-term control is believed to be mediated by the effect of radiation on the vasculature, which leads to tumour growth stabilisation or inhibition.
- Tumour control rates in previously published studies range from 80% to 100%, with a median/mean prescribed dose ranging from 13.5 to 20 Gy.
- Overall, no differences in tumour or clinical control rates have been observed based on the type of SRS platform.

REFERENCES

1. Evans DG, Baser ME, O'Reilly B, et al. Management of the patient and family with neurofibromatosis 2: a consensus conference statement. *Br J Neurosurg*. 2005;19(1):5-12.

2. Larson TC 3rd, Reese DF, Baker HL Jr, McDonald TJ. Glomus tympanicum chemodectomas: radiographic and clinical characteristics. *Radiology*. 1987;163(3):801-806.

3. Heth J. The basic science of glomus jugulare tumors. *Neurosurg Focus*. 2004;17(2):E2. Published 2004 Aug 15.

4. Jansen JC, van den Berg R, Kuiper A, van der Mey AG, Zwinderman AH, Cornelisse CJ. Estimation of growth rate in patients with head and neck paragangliomas influences the treatment proposal. *Cancer*. 2000;88(12):2811-2816.

5. Michael LM 2nd, Robertson JH. Glomus jugulare tumors: historical overview of the management of this disease. *Neurosurg Focus*. 2004;17(2):E1. Published 2004 Aug 15.

6. Al-Mefty O, Teixeira A. Complex tumors of the glomus jugulare: criteria, treatment, and outcome. *J Neurosurg*. 2002;97(6):1356-1366.

7. Dupin C, Lang P, Dessard-Diana B, et al. Treatment of head and neck paragangliomas with external beam radiation therapy. *Int J Radiat Oncol Biol Phys*. 2014;89(2):353-359.

8. Gilbo P, Morris CG, Amdur RJ, et al. Radiotherapy for benign head and neck paragangliomas: a 45-year experience. *Cancer*. 2014;120(23):3738-3743.

9. Springate SC, Haraf D, Weichselbaum RR. Temporal bone chemodectomas--comparing surgery and radiation therapy. *Oncology (Williston Park)*. 1991;5(4):131-143.

10. Galland-Girodet S, Maire JP, De-Mones E, et al. The role of radiation therapy in the management of head and neck paragangliomas: impact of quality of life versus treatment response. *Radiother Oncol*. 2014;111(3):463-467.

11. Saringer W, Khayal H, Ertl A, Schoeggl A, Kitz K. Efficiency of gamma knife radiosurgery in the treatment of glomus jugulare tumors. *Minim Invasive Neurosurg*. 2001;44(3):141-146.

12. Liscak R, Urgosik D, Chytka T, et al. Leksell Gamma Knife radiosurgery of the jugulotympanic glomus tumor: long-term results. *J Neurosurg*. 2014;121 Suppl:198-202.

13. Sharma MS, Gupta A, Kale SS, Agrawal D, Mahapatra AK, Sharma BS. Gamma knife radiosurgery for glomus jugulare tumors: therapeutic advantages of minimalism in the skull base. *Neurol India*. 2008;56(1):57-61.

14. Gottfried ON, Liu JK, Couldwell WT. Comparison of radiosurgery and conventional surgery for the treatment of glomus jugulare tumors. *Neurosurg Focus*. 2004;17(2):E4. Published 2004 Aug 15.

15. Hawthorne MR, Makek MS, Harris JP, Fisch U. The histopathological and clinical features of irradiated and nonirradiated temporal paragangliomas. *Laryngoscope*. 1988;98(3): 325-331.

16. Sheehan JP, Tanaka S, Link MJ, et al. Gamma Knife surgery for the management of glomus tumors: a multicenter study. *J Neurosurg*. 2012;117(2):246-254.

17. Sharma M, Meola A, Bellamkonda S, et al. Long-Term Outcome Following Stereotactic Radiosurgery for Glomus Jugulare Tumors: A Single Institution Experience of 20 Years. *Neurosurgery*. 2018;83(5):1007-1014.

18. Ibrahim R, Ammori MB, Yianni J, Grainger A, Rowe J, Radatz M. Gamma Knife radiosurgery for glomus jugulare tumors: a single-center series of 75 cases. *J Neurosurg*. 2017;126(5):1488-1497.

19. Guss ZD, Batra S, Limb CJ, et al. Radiosurgery of glomus jugulare tumors: a meta-analysis. *Int J Radiat Oncol Biol Phys*. 2011;81(4):e497-e502.
20. Stieler F, Wenz F, Abo-Madyan Y, et al. Adaptive fractionated stereotactic Gamma Knife radiotherapy of meningioma using integrated stereotactic cone-beam-CT and adaptive re-planning (a-gkFSRT). Adaptierte fraktionierte stereotaktische Strahlentherapie mit dem Gamma Knife bei Meningeom mit cone-beam-CT und adaptiver Replanung (a-gkFSRT). *Strahlenther Onkol*. 2016;192(11):815-819.

Gamma Knife in Pineal Region Tumors

28

Prachi Singh | Deepak Agrawal

KEY LEARNING POINTS

1. GKRS has demonstrated effectiveness in managing various pineal region tumours (PRTs), including pineal parenchymal tumours, germ cell tumours, and glial tumours. Studies have reported high local tumour control rates, especially when GKRS is integrated with other treatments.

2. As a non-invasive procedure, GKRS offers an alternative treatment for tumours in the deep-seated pineal region, which are challenging to access surgically, minimising risks associated with open surgery.

3. GKRS is generally well-tolerated and has a favourable safety profile. Patients typically experience minimal adverse effects, and the precision of GKRS allows for targeted tumour treatment while sparing surrounding healthy tissue.

4. While GKRS can be used as a primary treatment, it is often employed in conjunction with surgical resection and conventional radiation therapy to enhance treatment outcomes.

5. Despite promising results, there is a need for larger studies with longer follow-up periods to fully establish the role of GKRS in treating PRTs. Ongoing research is essential to validate current findings and refine treatment protocols.

INTRODUCTION

Gamma Knife Radiosurgery (GKRS) has emerged as an effective and minimally invasive treatment modality for various intracranial pathologies, including pineal region tumours. Surgical intervention in this region poses significant risks due to the deep-seated location and proximity to critical neurovascular structures, making GKRS an attractive alternative in select cases. While it may not replace surgical resection in all cases, particularly in cases of obstructive hydrocephalus, it provides a viable alternative for patients with surgically inaccessible or residual tumours. Although radiosurgery is still in the early stages of managing pineal region tumours, its use has grown in recent years, both as a primary treatment and as a complement to conventional therapies.

HISTORY AND EXAMINATION

A 17-year-old male presented with complaints of headache, gait disturbance, and blurring of vision. On examination Parinaud's sign was present. CSF and serum HCG and α-fetoprotein were within normal limits. He underwent an MRI and was diagnosed with a pineal region tumour, likely a pineal parenchymal tumour. The patient and his guardians were informed about the disease and the available treatment options, including GKRS or Surgery. After discussing the pros and cons of the different procedures, they decided to go ahead with GKRS.

IMAGING

The Gamma Knife protocol for pineal region tumours requires detailed imaging, precise dose planning, and strict protection of critical structures due to their proximity and deep-seated location. MRI with T1 contrast and T2 sequences was obtained one day before treatment administration and the reference CBCT was done with the frame placed on the day of treatment delivery. MRI and CBCT datasets are co-registered to integrate soft tissue and bony landmarks for accurate treatment planning.

GK PROTOCOL

The patient underwent an MRI on the day before treatment delivery. On the day of treatment, the Leksell stereotactic G frame was first secured with anterior posts fixed above the supraorbital ridge and posterior posts fixed to the occipital bone. The patient was then taken for CBCT which was co-registered with the MRI. Planning was done on the co-registered MRI which involved demarcating the target lesion (Fig. 28.1A). We used lightning software for planning the dose delivery after setting the prescription dose of 14 Gy at 50% isodose line (Coverage- 0.98, Selectivity- 0.85, Gradient Index- 3.03) (Fig. 28.2). Due to the close proximity to the brainstem and thalamus, we ensure a steep dose fall-off. A lesion with a total volume of 2.6 cc receives a mean dose of 19 ± 3.1 Gy.

FOLLOW-UP

The patient underwent a follow-up contrast MRI 1 year post-GKRS. The follow-up MRI shows a significant reduction in volume from 2.6 cc treatment volume to 0.7

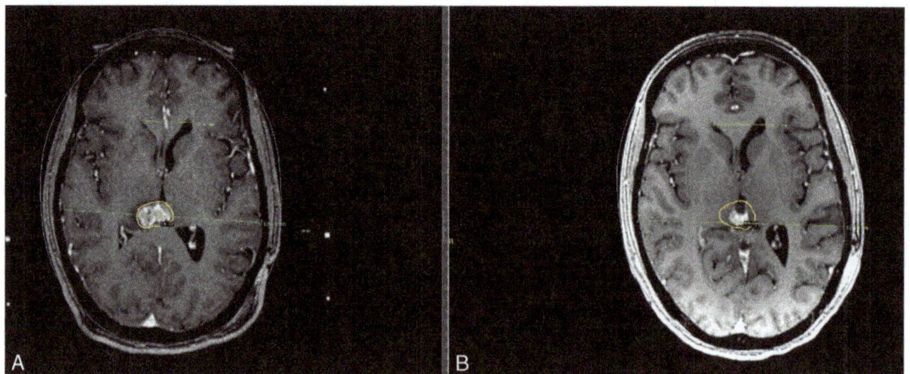

FIGURE 28.1   MRI brain at the time of planning (A) and at one year follow up (B).

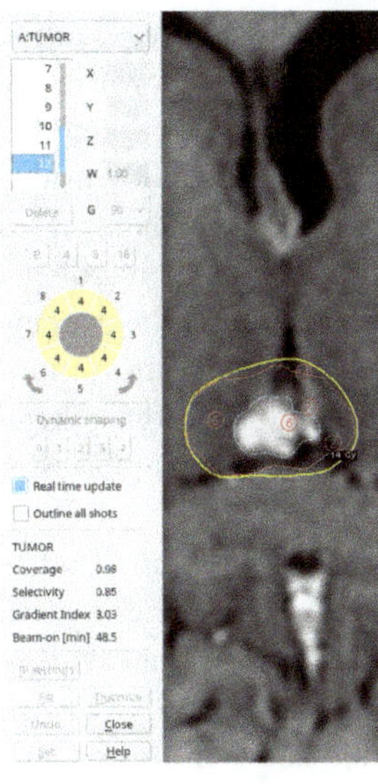

FIGURE 28.2 Screenshot of Gamma knife planning software showing the tumor selectivity, coverage, gradient index and beam on time.

cc residual volume (Fig. 28.1B). The patient reported improvement in headache, blurring of vision and upward gaze paralysis. There was no increase in hydrocephalus (Evans index pre-treatment- 0.26, follow-up: 0.25).

DISCUSSION

Pineal region tumours (PRTs) arise from diverse cellular origins, ranging from benign (teratoma, meningioma, pineocytoma, ependymoma) to malignant (pineoblastoma, malignant teratoma, malignant germ cell tumours). Management strategies remain debated, with some experts advocating for surgical resection and histologic diagnosis, while others recommend an initial radiation test dose due to the high incidence of germinomas. Gamma Knife radiosurgery (GKRS) has shown efficacy, particularly for benign or low-grade lesions. While primarily used as an adjuvant treatment, its role as a primary modality has gained increasing popularity over the years.

Several studies have reported on the efficacy of GKRS in Pineal Region Tumors (PRT) based on their histological grade. In a study involving 44 patients, overall progression-free survival (PFS) results were 93% at 1 year, 77% at 5 years, and 67% at 10 and 20 years. Log-rank analysis revealed that higher initial tumour grade (P = 0.04), previous radiotherapy (P = 0.002) and radiological evidence of necrosis (P = 0.03) were associated with worse outcomes. The 5-year PFS for patients who possessed these 'aggressive' features was 47.1% compared with 91% for those patients who did not have these features.[1]

Another study, involving 30 patients with a mean follow-up of 23.3 months, showed a response rate of 73.3%, with complete response obtained in 8 cases (26.7%). Germinoma and pineocytoma showed higher response and control rates (100%), and neither progression nor death occurred after gamma knife treatment. Malignant germ cell tumour and pineoblastoma showed unfavourable responses and prognosis, with the response and progression rates both being 50%. Gamma knife radiosurgery was the initial treatment in three pineal tumour cases without a histological diagnosis, and one complete and two partial responses were obtained.[2]

A comprehensive retrospective study conducted between 1999 and 2009 evaluated 147 patients with PRTs treated primarily with GKRS. The findings revealed significant tumour volume reduction in 61.9% of cases irrespective of the histological grade within two months post-treatment. By the six-month mark, the average tumour volume had decreased from 8.47 cc to 4.2 cc. Notably, complete tumour resolution was observed in 57 patients after one year. The study reported overall survival rates of 72.1% at three years and 66.7% at five years, underscoring GKRS's effectiveness as a primary treatment modality for PRTs. [3]

GKRS is often employed alongside surgical resection and conventional radiation therapy to enhance treatment outcomes. In a study involving 17 patients with pineal region tumours, local tumour control was achieved in all cases over an average follow-up period of 31 months. The study concluded that combining GKRS with other treatment modalities can optimise patient survival and quality of life.[4]

The minimally invasive nature of GKRS contributes to its favourable safety profile. In the aforementioned studies, most patients tolerated the procedure well, with minimal adverse effects reported. The precision of GKRS allows for targeted tumour treatment while sparing surrounding healthy tissue, reducing the risk of complications commonly associated with open surgical procedures. Although studies have shown symptomatic and radiological improvement in obstructive hydrocephalus due to pineal tumours with upfront radiosurgery,[5] SRS may not be a standalone option for all patients and some of these patients may require CSF diversion procedure, either prior to or post-treatment in view of worsening of hydrocephalus. Delayed tumour pseudoprogression due to inflammatory response and cognitive decline are known "complications" and may lead to a deterioration in the patient's condition, requiring urgent surgical intervention. In a study of 30 patients, tumour progression was found in 8 cases (26.7%), of whom 7 (23.3%) died as a consequence.[2]

TAKE HOME MESSAGE

The application of radiosurgery in treating pineal region tumours is still evolving; however, its utilisation has expanded significantly in recent years, both as a primary treatment and as a complement to conventional therapies. Future advancements in radiosurgical techniques and imaging may further refine the role of GKRS in managing pineal region neoplasms. Ongoing studies continue to investigate the molecular mechanisms behind GKRS-induced tumour suppression, potentially expanding its indications in the future.

REFERENCES

1. Yianni J, Rowe J, Khandanpour N, et al. Stereotactic radiosurgery for pineal tumours. *Br J Neurosurg.* 2012;26(3):361-366.

2. Kobayashi T, Kida Y, Mori Y. Stereotactic gamma radiosurgery for pineal and related tumors. J Neurooncol. 2001;54(3):301-309.

3. Li W, Zhang B, Kang W, et al. Gamma knife radiosurgery (GKRS) for pineal region tumors: a study of 147 cases. World J Surg Oncol. 2015;13:304. Published 2015 Oct 21.

4. Lekovic GP, Gonzalez LF, Shetter AG, et al. Role of Gamma Knife surgery in the management of pineal region tumors. Neurosurg Focus. 2007;23(6):E12.

5. Moreira A, Rodezno A, Santos D, Telles A, Ramirez J, Lovo EE. Upfront Radiosurgery for Treatment of Symptomatic Obstructive Hydrocephalus due to Brain Tumors. Cureus. 2022;14(9):e29129. Published 2022 Sep 13.

6. Hanft SJ, Isaacson SR, Bruce JN. Stereotactic radiosurgery for pineal region tumors. Neurosurg Clin N Am. 2011;22(3):413-ix.

29 Gamma Knife Radiosurgery in Intracranial Angiosarcoma

Mahnaaz Sultana Azeem | Deepak Agrawal | Sarvesh Goyal

KEY LEARNING POINTS

1. Gamma Knife Radiosurgery (GKRS) is an important adjunct to conventional surgery in managing intracranial angiosarcoma, especially in residual tumours. It gives tumour control and minimises damage to surrounding structures through precision treatment.
2. This is a case-based discussion focusing on residual torcular angiosarcoma treated with GKRS.
3. Treatment planning, procedural details, outcomes, and practices in GKRS for vascular tumours have been shown here.
4. The expected complications, challenges during treatment, and future implications have been mentioned.

INTRODUCTION

Angiosarcomas are rare, aggressive vascular malignancies. Intracranial involvement is uncommon, and tumours in the torcular region pose significant treatment challenges due to their vascularity and location near critical venous structures.[1,2]

The first line of management is surgery. However, complete resection is often difficult. Adjuvant radiotherapy is commonly used, and for residual or recurrent tumours, Gamma Knife Radiosurgery provides a precise, non-invasive alternative. GKRS delivers focused radiation to the tumour while minimising exposure to surrounding healthy brain tissue.

This chapter discusses the role of GKRS in treating intracranial angiosarcoma, illustrated through a case study of a patient with residual torcular angiosarcoma.

REPRESENTATIVE CASE

HISTORY & EXAMINATION

A middle-aged patient presented with progressive gait ataxia over nine months. Symptoms included blurred vision and headaches, which improved following surgery. There was no history of seizures, dizziness, hoarseness, nasal regurgitation, or limb weakness. The patient had no known comorbidities and was on levetiracetam for seizure prophylaxis. The patient had previously undergone a right occipital ventriculoperitoneal (VP) shunt placement for hydrocephalus. This was followed by suboccipital craniotomy and partial tumour excision. Histopathology confirmed the diagnosis of angiosarcoma. On examination prior to GKRS, there were no neurological deficits.

IMAGING (FIG. 29.1A)

Contrast-enhanced MRI of the brain showed a residual tumour in the torcular region. The lesion was ill-defined, measuring approximately 3.1 × 4.1 × 7 cm, with heterogeneous peripheral enhancement. A VP shunt was also noted in situ.

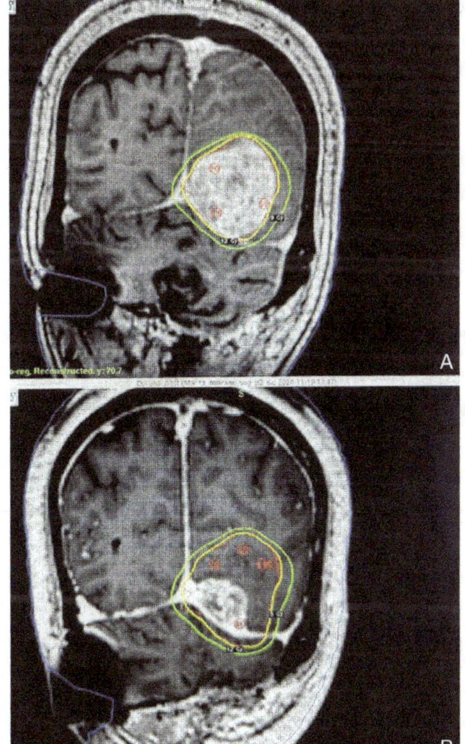

FIGURE 29.1A Images showing residual torcular angiosarcoma after surgical resection and dramatic decrease in size at 3 months follow-up MRI (B).

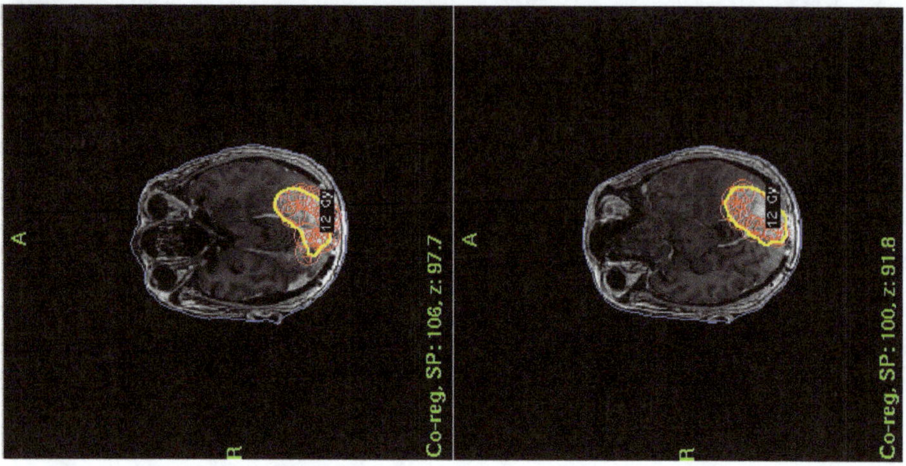

FIGURE 29.2   Gamma knife radiosurgery for residual torcular angiosarcoma (12 Gy).

GK PROTOCOL

Planning was done on Gamma-plan software. The tumour volume was calculated at 45.097 cc, with 99.3% of the target receiving a minimum dose of 12 Gy. The dose-volume histogram was carefully optimised to achieve effective tumour control while maintaining safety (Fig. 29.2).

FOLLOW-UP

Follow-up at 3 months showed a dramatic decrease in the tumour size (Fig. 29.1B). The patient continues to be on follow-up.

DISCUSSION

Challenges in Managing Intracranial Angiosarcoma

Intracranial angiosarcomas are rare and notoriously aggressive tumours. Their vascular nature makes complete surgical excision challenging, especially when the lesion is situated near critical structures such as the torcular region. The high recurrence rate, exceeding 30% in many series, necessitates a multimodal treatment approach. Conventional fractionated radiotherapy, while useful, may not achieve optimal control due to the tumour's radioresistant nature and the risk of collateral damage to surrounding neural tissue. Systemic chemotherapy using anthracyclins or taxanes has been used in angiosarcomas, however systemic toxicity needs to be considered. [3-5] Systemic chemotherapy is not specific and has limited success. Immunotherapy targeting PD1 and PDL2 is being tried.[6]

Role and Advantages of Gamma Knife Radiosurgery

Gamma Knife Radiosurgery (GKRS) offers several advantages as an adjunct treatment modality in cases of residual or recurrent intracranial angiosarcoma[7-8]:

- Precision and Safety: GKRS delivers highly focused radiation that conforms to the three-dimensional geometry of the tumour, thereby minimising radiation exposure to adjacent healthy brain tissue. This precision is particularly beneficial when treating tumours adjacent to critical venous sinuses and eloquent brain areas.
- High Dose Delivery in a Single Session: The ability to administer a single high dose (e.g., around 12 Gy, as in the presented case) enables effective tumour control. This is significant given that angiosarcomas may be less responsive to conventional fractionation schemes.
- Minimally Invasive Nature: As a non-invasive treatment option, GKRS reduces the risks associated with repeated surgical interventions. This is especially valuable in patients who have already undergone surgery and may be at higher risk for complications with additional open procedures.
- Potential Synergy with Systemic Therapies: Emerging evidence suggests that combining GKRS with targeted therapies (such as tyrosine kinase inhibitors and anti-angiogenic agents) or immunotherapies could further improve outcomes by addressing both local control and systemic disease. Ongoing clinical studies are examining these multimodal strategies, with the goal of enhancing overall survival and quality of life.

Current Evidence and Future Directions

While literature specific to intracranial angiosarcoma is limited due to its rarity, studies on GKRS in other vascular lesions and malignant intracranial tumours provide supportive evidence for its use. For instance, the efficacy of GKRS in treating cerebral arteriovenous malformations and other high grade vascular tumours underlines its potential applicability in angiosarcoma cases.[9-10] Moreover, advancements in imaging and dose-planning software have allowed clinicians to achieve better tumour coverage and sparing of normal tissues, thus reducing long-term morbidity.

Future research should focus on:

- Long-Term Outcomes: Systematic follow-up of patients treated with GKRS is needed to assess the durability of tumour control and late radiation effects.
- Combination Protocols: Evaluating the synergistic effects of GKRS with emerging systemic therapies, such as immune checkpoint inhibitors and novel anti-angiogenic agents.
- Patient Selection: Refining selection criteria to identify patients who are most likely to benefit from GKRS, potentially incorporating molecular and genetic tumour profiling.

Gamma Knife Radiosurgery therefore plays a crucial role in the multimodal management of intracranial angiosarcoma, especially in cases where surgical resection is incomplete or the tumour is located in surgically inaccessible regions. Its precision, safety profile, and ability to deliver high doses of radiation in a single session make it an invaluable tool in the neurosurgical armamentarium. With continued advances in stereotactic technology and an evolving understanding of tumour biology, GKRS is poised to remain a cornerstone in the treatment of these challenging lesions.

TAKE HOME MESSAGE

Gamma Knife Radiosurgery is a valuable treatment modality for residual intra-cranial angiosarcoma, particularly in surgically challenging locations such as the torcular region. It provides a precise, minimally invasive approach with good tumour control rates and low procedural morbidity.

While GKRS does not replace surgery, it plays a crucial role in multimodal management, especially for residual and recurrent disease. Long-term follow-up and further studies are needed to optimise treatment protocols and improve patient outcomes.

REFERENCES

1. Cao J, Wang J, He C, Fang M. Angiosarcoma: a review of diagnosis and current treatment. *Am J Cancer Res.* 2019;9(11):2303-2313. Published 2019 Nov 1.

2. Young RJ, Brown NJ, Reed MW, Hughes D, Woll PJ. Angiosarcoma. *Lancet Oncol.* 2010;11(10):983-991.

3. Florou V, Wilky BA. Current and Future Directions for Angiosarcoma Therapy. *Curr Treat Options Oncol.* 2018;19(3):14. Published 2018 Mar 8.

4. Penel N, Italiano A, Ray-Coquard I, et al. Metastatic angiosarcomas: doxorubicin-based regimens, weekly paclitaxel and metastasectomy significantly improve the outcome. *Ann Oncol.* 2012;23(2):517-523.

5. Kieran MW, Kalluri R, Cho YJ. The VEGF pathway in cancer and disease: responses, resistance, and the path forward. *Cold Spring Harb Perspect Med.* 2012;2(12):a006593. Published 2012 Dec 1.

6. Botti G, Scognamiglio G, Marra L, et al. Programmed Death Ligand 1 (PD-L1) Expression in Primary Angiosarcoma. *J Cancer.* 2017;8(16):3166-3172. Published 2017 Sep 15.

7. Shin JY, Roh SG, Lee NH, Yang KM. Predisposing factors for poor prognosis of angiosarcoma of the scalp and face: Systematic review and meta-analysis. *Head Neck.* 2017;39(2):380-386.

8. Leksell, L. (1987). The stereotaxic method and radiosurgery of the brain. *Acta Chirurgica Scandinavica, 153*(4), 333-336

9. Kondziolka, D., Lunsford, L. D., Flickinger, J. C., et al. (1998). Radiosurgery for cerebral arteriovenous malformations: Analysis of 1,000 patients. *Journal of Neurosurgery, 88*(2), 179-186.

10. Flickinger, J. C., Lunsford, L. D., & Niranjan, A. (2001). Stereotactic radiosurgery for benign intracranial lesions. *Neurosurgery Clinics of North America, 12*(1), 91-106

SECTION 3

VASCULAR

Gamma Knife Radiosurgery for Spetzler-Martin Grade III Cerebral Arterio-Venous Malformations

Satish Verma | Deepak Agrawal

KEY LEARNING POINTS

1. Spetzler-Martin Grade III AVMs are a heterogeneous group of AVMs.
2. Unruptured AVMs can be managed with primary GKRS.
3. AVM nidus volume and marginal dose are strong predictors of AVM obliteration rate.
4. Type III A have the highest obliteration rates due to the small nidus volume that allows a higher marginal dose.
5. Type III D are large-volume AVMs and may be offered a staged treatment to avoid adverse radiation effects.

INTRODUCTION

Cerebral arteriovenous malformations (AVMs) are an important cause of morbidity and mortality. Spetzler-Martin (SM) grading categorises AVMs into 5-tiers depending on the size of nidus, eloquence of the area involved and the type of venous drainage. SM grade III (SM III) AVMs are peculiar, as they comprise of the most heterogeneous groups, as far as angioarchitecture, drainage and eloquence are concerned. This category is a borderline zone where few expert neurosurgeons will still offer microsurgical excision to a subset of these AVMs. However, the majority of centres offer non-invasive or minimally invasive options like Gamma Knife Radiosurgery (GKRS) or endovascular embolisation. An unruptured SM III AVM can be managed effectively with upfront GKRS with complete obliteration in majority of the cases.

REPRESENTATIVE CASE

HISTORY & EXAMINATION

A 20-year-old female presented with progressive headaches for 6 months. Headache was occipital in distribution, not associated with nausea, vomiting or visual obscuration. No history of seizures, loss of consciousness, sudden onset severe headache or motor weakness. Her neurological examination was within normal limits.

IMAGING

A screening brain computed tomography scan showed a hyperdense lesion in the atrium of right lateral ventricle with extension to the right thalamus. Contrast-enhanced MRI of the brain showed multiple flow voids on T2WI with contrast enhancement. Train-of-flight (TOF) magnetic resonance angiography (MRA) confirmed AVM (Spetzler-Martin Grade III, type IIIB (S1E1V1). Digital subtraction angiography (DSA) with 6 vessel catheterisation revealed a right-sided AVM with feeders primarily from the posterior choroidal branches of right posterior cerebral artery and early venous drainage into the deep venous system. Given the unruptured status of AVM and multiple small feeders from posterior choroidal arteries, she was offered GKRS.

GK PROTOCOL

For the purpose of Gamma Knife planning, after fixation of Leksell-G stereotactic frame, post-gadolinium 3-dimensional (3D) Magnetisation-Prepared Rapid Gradient Echo (MPRAGE) sequence and 3-D TOF MRA were acquired in the axial plane with voxel size 1.0 x 1.0 x 1.0, slab 1, slice per slab 176 and Field of View (FoV) 256 mm. Images were transferred to the treatment planning system (TPS) in Digital Imaging and Communications in Medicine (DICOM) format.

Gamma knife was performed on a Leksell Gamma Knife Perfexion unit (Elekta AB, Stockholm, Sweden) with Leksell GammaPlan. Manual AVM segmentation was done for the tumour and Organ-at-risk (OAR) (brainstem). Total tumour volume was 6.96 cubic centimetres (cc). Inverse planning with optimisation of 19 isocentres (combinations of 4, 8 and 16 mm collimators) was performed with a prescription dose of 25 Gy at 50% isodose line to the AVM nidus margin (Fig. 30.1). Further optimisation was done manually to exclude OAR out of the prescribed dose constraints achieving the following parameters - coverage -90%, selectivity - 91%, Gradient Index – 3.06. Beam-on time (BOT) was 123.3 minutes with a treatment dose rate of 0.963 Gy/min. The maximum dose to the segmented volumes were: AVM nidus – 50.1 Gy and brainstem – 10.5 Gy (Fig. 30.2).

FOLLOW-UP

The patient tolerated the procedure well. Follow-up clinical visit after 6 months was done and no significant complaints were reported. Follow-up CEMRI was done

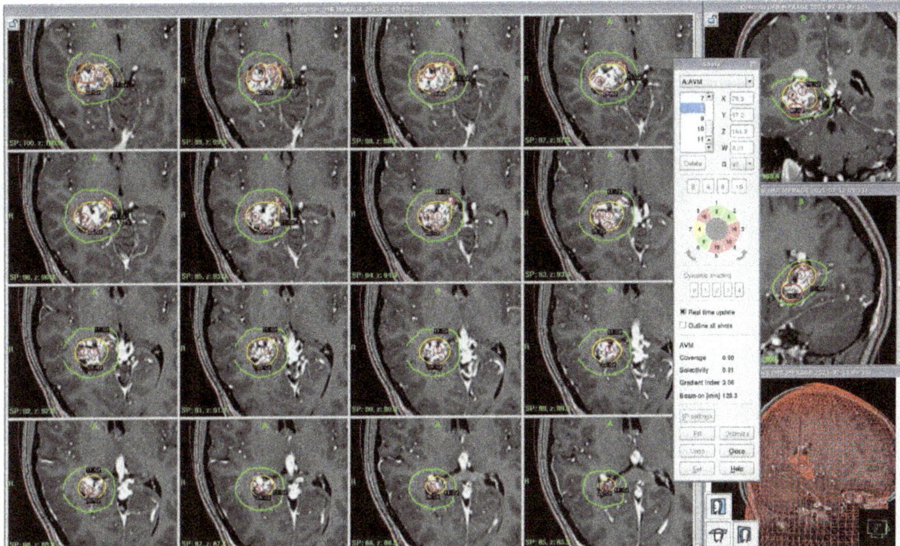

FIGURE 30.1   Gamma Knife planning for the index case. AVM nidus margin (red), 12 Gy (prescription dose) isodose line (yellow).

annually which showed a gradual reduction in AVM volume. At the last follow-up available, at 39 months, AVM was obliterated (Fig. 30.2). No post-radiation imaging changes were appreciated on MRI. She is planned for digital subtraction angiography after 1 year.

DISCUSSION

Brain AVMs are the most common vascular malformations with the prevalence of symptomatic brain AVMs of about 1.2 per 100,000 population.[1] In general, the annualised risk of future haemorrhage is roughly 1.8% when the brain AVM is unruptured at presentation and 4.7% when it is ruptured.[2] The cumulative risk of future haemorrhage is 16% and 19% at 10 and 20 years respectively when the AVM is unruptured at presentation, and 35% and 45% at 10 and 20 years when they present with a haemorrhage.[2] The chances of significant permanent neurologic deficit or death from a hemorrhagic event are about <50% and <10% respectively. Ding et al. suggested a 3-tier classification (Class A, B and C) of AVMs based on the original 5-tier gradings (Spetzler-Martin grades I-V) for management recommendations.[3] Management of Class A (SM grades I-II) and Class C (SM grades IV-V) AVMs is relatively straightforward. Class B (SM III) AVMs are different as they comprise the most heterogenous groups as far as angioarchitecture, drainage and eloquence are concerned. SM grade III AVMs can be classified further into 4 types as follows: IIIA – S1E1V1, IIIB – S2E0V1, IIIC – S2E1V0, IIID – S3E0V0.[4]

Management of SM Grade III AVMs depends upon many factors. Clinical presentation with or without intracranial hematoma (ICH) plays an important role in

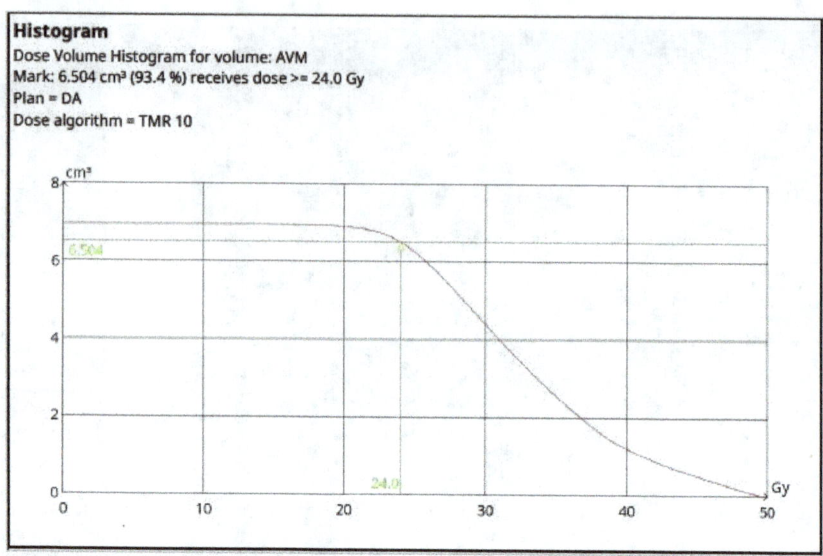

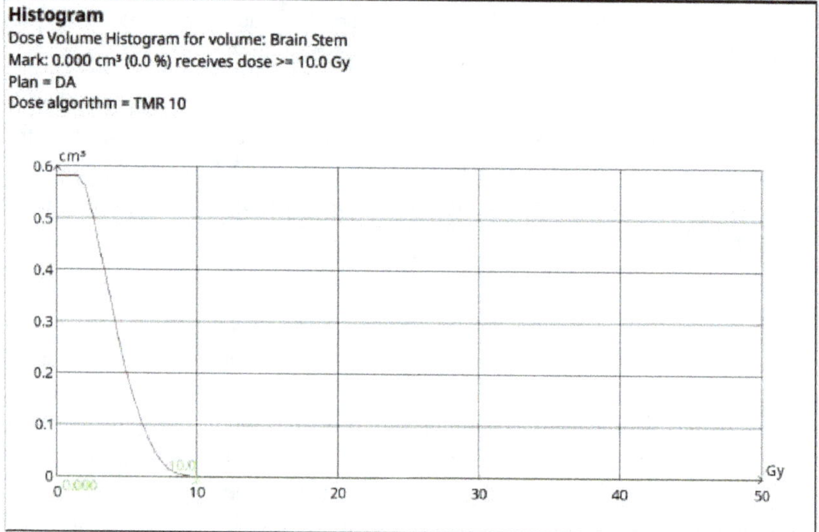

FIGURE 30.2   Dose volume histogram (DVH) for the AVM and brainstem

deciding management. AVMs presenting with ICH are at a greater risk of rebleed. If feasible, at least partial embolisation is recommended to secure the fragile substrate of AVM. Unruptured SM grade III AVMs can be managed effectively with primary GKRS. Nguyen et al. reported their experience with GKRS for 307 SM grade III AVMs. They achieved 68.7% complete obliteration rate at a median follow-up of 53.3 months with a latency of about 24 months. Interestingly, the complete obliteration rates had a linear correlation with the subtypes – type III A had the highest obliteration rates (80.8%) and type III D had the lowest obliteration rate (25.0%).

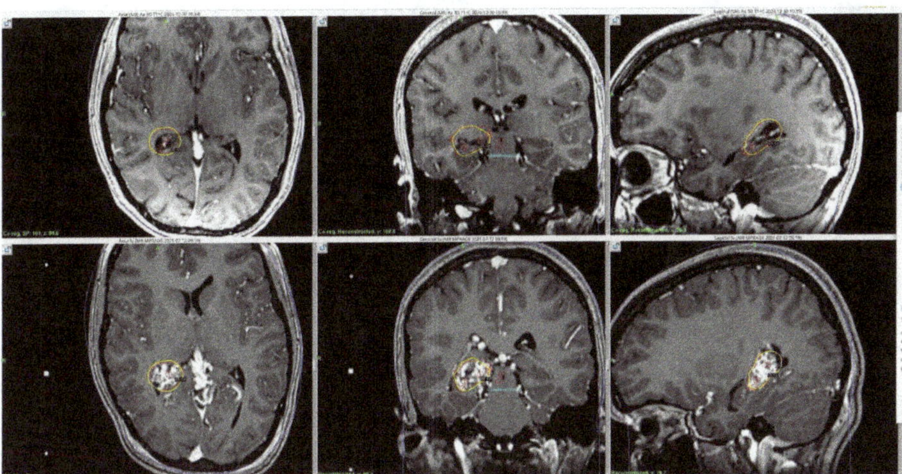

FIGURE 30.3   Follow-up MRI done after 39 months (upper panel) compared to the baseline MRI at the time of GKRS (lower panel) showing complete obliteration of the nidus and decrease in the number and size of draining veins.

AVM nidus obliteration ranges from 70%-90% when the prescribed dose to the nidus margin is >18 Gy.[5] Radiation induces endothelial cell proliferation, which results in progressive luminal closure and gradual obliteration of the nidus. There is an inherent latent period before the AVM obliterates completely, exposing the subject to the risk of AVM haemorrhage during the latent period. Key factors predicting AVM obliteration are AVM volume[6-8] and marginal dose.[5,8] *AVM volume* is the strongest predictor of obliteration after GKRS. However, complete in-field obliteration correlates more positively with margin dose rather than AVM volume.[8] In principle, the margin dose needs to be reduced or a larger volume AVM, to avoid adverse radiation effects, and that is the reason for lower obliteration rates for large-volume AVMs. In addition, the incidence of untargeted residual AVM nidus (residual AVM volume which was not included in the target at the time of GKRS) increases with AVM volume, with post-embolisation status being a critical contributing factor.

Marginal dose, in general, is an important determinant of AVM obliteration rates. Flickinger et al. analysed the dose response of AVM radiosurgery and concluded that AVMs demonstrate the highest obliteration rates of 88% with a marginal dose of 25 Gy. Notably, increasing the marginal dose beyond 25 Gy did not yield any additional benefits, while a marginal dose below <18 Gy predicted inferior obliteration rates.[5,9] *Cobalt-60 dose rate* is also reported as an important factor for AVM obliteration. Dose rates >2.9 Gy/ min were associated with significantly higher rates of obliteration as compared to dose rates <2.1 Gy/min.[10] *Age of the patient* was proposed as an important factor, increasing age was considered as negatively correlated with obliteration rates. Pollock and Flickinger incorporated age as a negative predictor in their radiosurgery-based AVM score. However, recent studies find no statistically significant difference in obliteration rates based on age.[11,12]

Type III B, III C and III D grade AVMs have an inherent component of a large nidus size of >3 cm. Conceptually, radiosurgery was developed by Leksell as a focused and accurate delivery of radiation to a particular target in a single stage.[13] Single-stage radiosurgery is still the norm for a majority of indications. Factors that limit a single-stage dose delivery to achieve the treatment goal are a larger target volume and a larger prescribed marginal dose, as the dose spillage over the surrounding normal neural tissue has to be taken into consideration to avoid long-term adverse radiation effects (AREs), specifically radiation necrosis.

Usual standards consider that the V12 (Volume of normal brain minus gross target volume) should not exceed 10 cc, as the risk of radiation necrosis becomes higher—exceeding 10%—if the V12 exceeds 10 cc.[14] With these strict dose constraints to the normal brain tissue, the risk of radiation necrosis can be maintained at predictably low rates. However, it limits the volume of AVM that can be treated or the radiation dose that can be prescribed to the target margin in a single stage. Large AVMs were defined differently by different authors. The size of nidus - either maximum dimension >3 centimetres (cm) or volume >10-15 cubic centimetres (cc) is considered large by most of the authors performing staged SRS, as the V12 exceeds the recommended limits over and above these dimensions.[15,16] Another important way of preventing radiosurgery-related complications is to keep the draining vein out of the radiation field. Shielding the draining vein resulted in fewer new post-GKRS neurological deficits, lower incidence of AVM bleeding and adverse radiation effects.[17]

Considering the above limitations, the concept of staged radiosurgery emerged to optimise the obliteration rates with acceptable long-term complications. There are two distinct strategies to stage AVM radiosurgery: Volume-staged SRS (VS-SRS) and Dose-staged SRS (DS-SRS). Pollock et al. conceptualised volume-staged radiosurgery for AVMs. They published their experience with 10 patients where they compared the radiation dosimetry of VS-SRS to hypothetical single-session SRS (SS-SRS).[18] They found that VS-SRS decreased the V12 by an average of 27.2% as compared to SS-SRS, and this difference was statistically significant without compromising the AVM obliteration rates. The ideal duration between the two stages of SRS is debatable. The duration between stages with VS-SRS varies from 2-9 months and for DS-SRS ranges from 1 day to a few weeks.[15] The criteria are not well-defined, due to the limited understanding of the underlying radiobiological principles. Considering the low α/β (3.5) for AVMs with respect to the linear quadratic equation used to estimate the radiobiological response after radiation, fractionation, conceptually, should increase the therapeutic index.

Dose fractionated SRS for AVMs was first described by Kirkeby et al.[19] Over the last two decades, many centres have published their experience with this technique, also termed as hypo-fractionated SRS (2-5 fractions). Proponents of DS-SRS argue that this technique is straightforward in the sense that the radiosurgical planning is similar to single-stage SRS (SS-SRS), without the need for volume subset segmentation. Also, it carries a lower risk of post-SRS latency haemorrhage compared to VS-SRS, as there is no differential irradiation which can lead to flow redirection within AVM. This, in turn, may theoretically lead to altered flow dynamics and lower bleeding rates in DS-SRS technique.

TAKE HOME MESSAGE

Spetzler-Martin grade III cerebral AVMs represent a heterogeneous group of AVMs. For unruptured AVMs, primary GKRS is the recommended treatment modality considering good obliteration rates and low rates of complications. Small nidus volume and higher marginal dose predict good obliteration rates. The volume of normal brain receiving >12 Gy (V12) of radiation should not exceed 10 cc to keep rates of adverse radiation effects less than 10%. Staged GKRS is an effective method to reduce V12 and thus complications. Type III A AVMs have the best obliteration rates. Type III A AVMs are mostly treated in a single session, unless in the brainstem. Type III D may require staged GKRS depending on the volume of nidus. For ruptured AVMs, it is recommended to secure a high-risk substrate of AVM with an endovascular approach, if feasible, to prevent rebleed.

REFERENCES

1. Ogilvy CS, Stieg PE, Awad I, et al. AHA Scientific Statement: Recommendations for the management of intracranial arteriovenous malformations: a statement for healthcare professionals from a special writing group of the Stroke Council, American Stroke Association. *Stroke*. 2001;32(6):1458-1471.

2. Morgan MK, Davidson AS, Assaad NNA, Stoodley MA. Critical review of brain AVM surgery, surgical results and natural history in 2017. *Acta Neurochir (Wien)*. 2017;159(8):1457-1478.

3. Ding D, Yen CP, Starke RM, Xu Z, Sun X, Sheehan JP. Radiosurgery for Spetzler-Martin Grade III arteriovenous malformations. *J Neurosurg*. 2014;120(4):959-969.

4. Kano H, Flickinger JC, Yang HC, et al. Stereotactic radiosurgery for Spetzler-Martin Grade III arteriovenous malformations. *J Neurosurg*. 2014;120(4):973-981.

5. Flickinger JC, Pollock BE, Kondziolka D, Lunsford LD. A dose-response analysis of arteriovenous malformation obliteration after radiosurgery. *Int J Radiat Oncol Biol Phys*. 1996;36(4):873-879.

6. Paúl L, Casasco A, Kusak ME, Martínez N, Rey G, Martínez R. Results for a series of 697 arteriovenous malformations treated by gamma knife: influence of angiographic features on the obliteration rate. *Neurosurgery*. 2014;75(5):568-583.

7. Starke RM, Yen CP, Ding D, Sheehan JP. A practical grading scale for predicting outcome after radiosurgery for arteriovenous malformations: analysis of 1012 treated patients. *J Neurosurg*. 2013;119(4):981-987.

8. Nguyen BT, Tran HM, Huynh CT, et al. Gamma Knife Radiosurgery for Spetzler-Martin Grade III Brain Arteriovenous Malformations. *World Neurosurg*. 2023;175:e796-e803.

9. Potts MB, Sheth SA, Louie J, et al. Stereotactic radiosurgery at a low marginal dose for the treatment of pediatric arteriovenous malformations: obliteration, complications, and functional outcomes. *J Neurosurg Pediatr*. 2014;14(1):1-11.

10. Anthes VB, Schwartz M, Cusimano M, et al. Effect of Cobalt-60 Treatment Dose Rate on Arteriovenous Malformation Obliteration After Stereotactic Radiosurgery With Gamma Knife. *Neurosurgery*. 2024;94(3):575-583.

11. Hasegawa H, Hanakita S, Shin M, et al. Does Advanced Age Affect the Outcomes of Stereotactic Radiosurgery for Cerebral Arteriovenous Malformation?. *World Neurosurg*. 2018;109:e715-e723.

12. Chen CJ, Ding D, Kano H, et al. Effect of Advanced Age on Stereotactic Radiosurgery Outcomes for Brain Arteriovenous Malformations: A Multicenter Matched Cohort Study. *World Neurosurg*. 2018;119:e429-e440.

13. LEKSELL L. The stereotaxic method and radiosurgery of the brain. *Acta Chir Scand*. 1951;102(4):316-319.

14. Kirkpatrick JP, Marks LB, Mayo CS, Lawrence YR, Bhandare N, Ryu S. Estimating normal tissue toxicity in radiosurgery of the CNS: application and limitations of QUANTEC. *J Radiosurg SBRT*. 2011;1(2):95-107.

15. Ilyas A, Chen CJ, Ding D, et al. Volume-staged versus dose-staged stereotactic radiosurgery outcomes for large brain arteriovenous malformations: a systematic review. *J Neurosurg*. 2018;128(1):154-164.

16. Hanakita S, Shin M, Koga T, Igaki H, Saito N. Outcomes of Volume-Staged Radiosurgery for Cerebral Arteriovenous Malformations Larger Than 20 cm(3) with More Than 3 Years of Follow-Up. *World Neurosurg*. 2016;87:242-249.

17. Bose R, Agrawal D, Singh M, et al. Draining vein shielding in intracranial arteriovenous malformations during gamma-knife: a new way of preventing post gamma-knife edema and hemorrhage. *Neurosurgery*. 2015;76(5):623-632.

18. Pollock BE, Kline RW, Stafford SL, Foote RL, Schomberg PJ. The rationale and technique of staged-volume arteriovenous malformation radiosurgery. *Int J Radiat Oncol Biol Phys*. 2000;48(3):817-824.

19. Kirkeby OJ, Bakke S, Tveraa K, Hirschberg H. Fractionated stereotactic radiation therapy for intracranial arteriovenous malformations. *Stereotact Funct Neurosurg*. 1996;66(1-3):10-14.

Gamma Knife Radiosurgery for Basal Ganglia & Thalamic Arteriovenous Malformations

31

Abhishek Kumar | Manoj Phalak

KEY LEARNING POINTS

1. The goal of AVM treatment is to eliminate the risk of haemorrhage and obliteration of nidus.
2. GKRS is the favoured therapeutic modality for small to medium-sized AVMs.
3. The irradiation dose and AVM size are the most significant factors influencing nidus obliteration.

INTRODUCTION

Arteriovenous malformations (AVMs) are abnormal cerebrovascular formations characterised by a tangled network of blood vessels with high blood flow. The reported risk of haemorrhage is approximately 3% per year. Once a haemorrhage occurs, the likelihood of neurological deficits and death is less than 50% and 10%, respectively.[1] AVMs located in deep-seated areas (Basal ganglia/thalamus/brainstem) present a more aggressive and natural history, with significantly higher bleeding risk, mortality and morbidity.[2] Also, administration of GKRS at thalamo-peduncular region poses special challenges as the ascending and descending white matter tracts as well as thalamic nuclei concerned with arousal and pain regulation, sensory domains, motor language function and cognitive domains are at risk of irradiation-induced damage. Thus, the constraints of OARs (Organ at risk) dictate treatment more than any other location.

Numerous classifications have been proposed for optimal management of AVMs. Among these, the Spetzler-Martin grading for estimating the risk of surgical excision, and Pollock-Flickinger AVM Score to predict outcome after GKRS for cerebral AVM are worth mentioning.[3,4] The Spetzler-Martin Grading Scale takes into consideration factors such as AVM size, venous drainage pattern, and proximity to critical brain areas.[3] Pollock-Flickinger AVM score takes into account the patient's age, AVM volume and location to predict outcomes in patients undergoing GKRS for AVMs.[4]

REPRESENTATIVE CASE

HISTORY & EXAMINATION

A 38-year-old gentleman presented to our outpatient department with a history of sudden-onset severe headache, followed by acute weakness in the right upper and lower limbs one month prior, for which he was taken to a private facility. His NCCT head revealed a left thalamic bleed with IVH, but no hydrocephalus or mass effect. He was managed conservatively. On neurological examination, patient exhibited power of 4/5 on the right side with 50% hand grip, Modified Ashworth grade 2 spasticity with exaggerated DTRs.

He had a Spetzler-Martin grade 4 AVM with a Pollock-Flickinger AVM score of 6.805.[3,4] He was planned for GKRS at our institute.

IMAGING

He underwent 6 vessel DSA in view of suspected vascular malformation. His DSA was suggestive of left thalamic AVM, fed by bilateral medial posterior choroidal arteries, left superior cerebellar artery, bilateral posterior communicating arteries with drainage into internal cerebral vein.

GKRS PROTOCOL

- Dose volume Histogram for volume: Nidus: 9.829 cm3 (94.6%) receives dose >=18.0 Gy
- Dose volume Histogram for volume: Brainstem: 0.011 cm3 (0.1%) receives dose >=10.4 Gy
- Dose volume Histogram for volume: Internal Capsule: 0.021 cm3 (1.1%) receives dose >=9.9 Gy

OARs (organs at risk)- brainstem, basal ganglia and white matter tracts. While V12 Gy was targeted at less than 10 cc, and the brainstem point dose (<0.03 cc) was more than 10 Gy. Patient tolerated the procedure well and required only a short course of analgesics.

FOLLOW-UP

He did not develop any post-GK complications on follow-up. His post-GK MRI, done after an interval of 1.5 years, showed significant reduction in size of AVM nidus. However, patient continues to have persistent static weakness. He has been placed in our follow-up with DSA planned after 4 years from GKRS date.

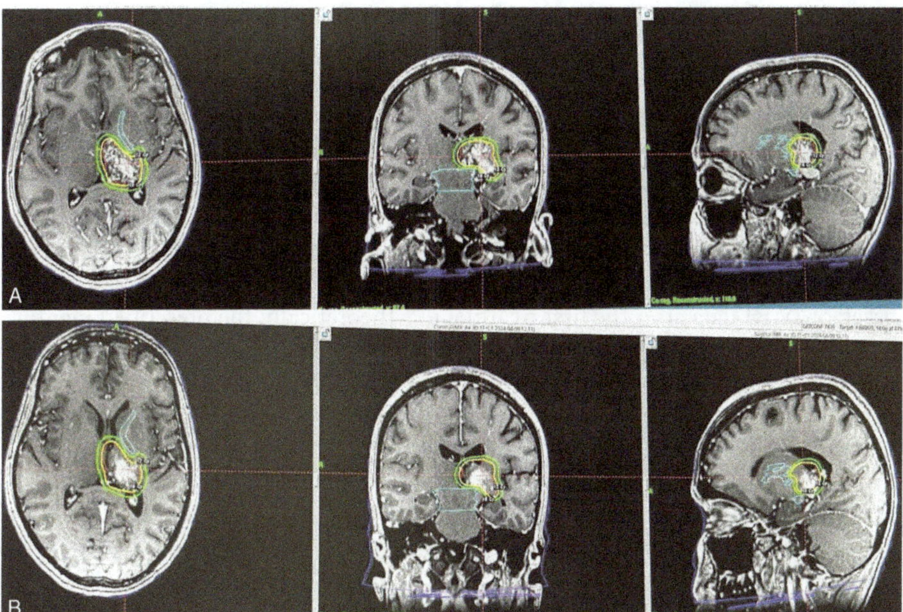

FIGURE 31.1   (A) Shows pre-GKRS MRI of the patient revealing left thalamic AVM. (B) Shows post-GKRS MRI done at 1.5-year follow-up with reduction in nidus size.

DISCUSSION

The goal of AVM treatment is to remove the risk of haemorrhage, which can be accomplished by separating the nidus from the circulation. Since GKRS is characterised by its single-session focused irradiation with high accuracy and sharp dose fall-off, it is a minimally invasive option suited for small to medium-sized, deep-seated and inaccessible lesions.[5] Typically, nidus obliteration can be achieved in 70–85% of patients after a latency period of 3–5 years.[6] The radio-surgical dose and AVM size are the most significant factors influencing nidus obliteration.[6] One drawback of GKRS is that approximately 30% of patients experience perinidal T2-signal intensity changes within 2 years after the procedure. However, these changes become symptomatic in less than 10% of cases and permanent in only 3%.[6] Post-GKRS haemorrhage is uncommon, and the risk either remains the same or decreases during the latency period.[7]

The treatment of deep-seated cerebral malformations in functional locations, especially in the thalamus, is challenging.[9] Radiosurgery poses lesser risk than microsurgery in these areas, but it requires a latent period of several years.[10] However, while planning GKRS to thalamo-peduncular AVMs, it must be kept in mind that exposure of the brainstem to doses exceeding 12 Gy, even in volumes as small as 0.1 cc, can lead to Adverse Radiation Effect (ARE) and new neurological deficits.[11]

Studies suggest that deep-seated AVMs have a higher propensity for bleeding (upto 85% at diagnosis).[12] Earlier works advocated microsurgery in patients with larger nidus size (>3 cm) and neurological deficits, followed by radiosurgery to treat the smaller residual nidus.[13] This approach helps reduce the lesion volume initially, followed by radiosurgery, which achieves an obliteration rate of 78%, compared to 71% and 23% for each technique individually.[13] Another author advocates surgery as the treatment of choice for thalamus and basal ganglia AVMs, achieving complete nidus resection in 91% of patients, with a mortality rate of 2.4%.[14]

According to literature reports, the post-radiosurgery obliteration rate for brainstem, basal ganglia, and thalamus AVMs ranges from 23% to 70%.[13] Kano et al. reported obliteration rates of 41%, 70%, and 76% at 3, 5, and 10 years, respectively, based on MRI data after the first treatment.[8] Theoretically, the prescribed marginal dose for optimal efficiency is more than 20 Gy; however, for functional areas and depending on the AVM volume, the dose is adjusted downward to minimise the risk of radiation-induced effects. This explains the lower prescription limits ranging from 15 to 20 Gy.[8,12,16]

It is important to note that the risk of bleeding is present primarily during the first 2 years, as long as the AVM has not been occluded. It varies between 1.3-9.5%, depending on the series. The risks of re-bleeding decreases over time—3.9% in the first year and 1.9% in the second year.[12] Re-bleeding increases morbidity along with a mortality rate of 4%.[9]

The risk of permanent secondary injuries associated with the treatment of basal ganglia and brainstem AVMs ranges from 4% to 11.9%.[8] Flickinger reports that patients with deep-seated AVMs (such as in the thalamus or posterior fossa) are more likely to develop radiation-induced effects compared to those in other locations, with a susceptibility coefficient of 8.33 for the posterior fossa and 2.35 for the frontal region.[17] The risk of radiation-induced effects increases beyond 20 Gy.[18]

Staged GKRS for Large Thalamic/Basal Ganglia AVMS

Radio-surgical doses are typically reduced due to concerns about RAEs, which could lead to a lower obliteration rate and potentially result in a higher risk of haemorrhage.[19] Recent evidence suggests that stand-alone GKRS for AVMs larger than 10 mL is controversial, and that staged GKRS is often considered as an alternative. Staging is primarily done in two approaches: volume-staged GKRS (VSGKRS) and dose-staged GKRS. VSGKRS entails the division of the entire nidus volume into two or three sections, each of which is irradiated separately with intervals of several months (typically 3 to 6 months).[20] In contrast, dose-staged GKRS involves irradiating the entire nidus multiple times with reduced doses until the intended cumulative dose is fully delivered.[21] While no definitive conclusion has been reached, retrospective evidence suggests that VSGKRS may be superior.[22] It appears that a dose of at least 17 Gy per session is required to achieve a favourable obliteration rate; when lesions are treated with ≥ 17 Gy, the obliteration rate approaches 60%. Other factors that may contribute to successful obliteration include coverage of a volume greater than 20 Gy and the presence of a single draining vessel. The main drawback of VSGKRS is the relatively high haemorrhage rates, which range from 4.5% to 33%.[21]

Combination of GKRS and Embolization

The rate of complete obliteration with embolisation for deep-seated AVMs alone does not exceed 15%, with morbidity rates reaching up to 40%.[23,24] Crude obliteration rates range from 24% to 72%, with 5-year obliteration rates varying between 31% and 60%.[25] Combination of embolisation with GKRS was considered ideal in the beginning because embolisation was thought to reduce the nidus volume with minimal invasiveness, making it suitable for subsequent application of GKRS.[26] However, subsequent studies have suggested that this approach may be linked to a decrease in the obliteration rate.[27] This reduction could be due to several factors, including recanalisation of the embolised AVM segments, marked difficulty in defining the AVM for radio-surgical planning, and enhanced angiogenesis following embolisation.[16]

Unruptured AVMs

GKRS appears to be warranted for small to medium-sized unruptured AVMs. The ARUBA trial marked a pivotal moment in the management of unruptured AVMs, highlighting the critical importance of fully understanding the invasiveness of treatment and its potential complications when dealing with asymptomatic AVMs.

Adverse Radiation Effects/Radiation-Induced Changes (ARE/RIC)

Adverse radiation effects like cyst formation (CF), chronic encapsulated hematoma (CEH), and tumorigenesis.[7] Literature has shown that repeat radiosurgery is linked to an increased risk of ARE. Several studies on radiation-induced changes in AVMs have demonstrated that a higher marginal dose, higher Spetzler-Martin (SM) grade, elevated radiosurgery-based score, and deeper locations in the brainstem and thalamus are associated with a greater likelihood of developing radiation-induced changes.[28] Nidus with a single draining vein is more likely to develop symptomatic radiation changes compared to those with multiple draining veins. In terms of radiation-induced tumorigenesis, most of these lesions are malignant gliomas.[20] The prescribed dose for a single-session GKRS typically ranges from 18 to 25 Gy, which accounts for the higher incidence of AREs in these cases. While radiologic changes (RICs) are fairly common (35.5%), the clinical symptomatic cases are low (9.2%).[29] Although the optimal treatment remains debated, surgical resection is generally considered a standard option. However, fluid diversion methods, such as cyst-peritoneal shunt and Ommaya reservoir placement, offer minimally invasive alternatives for purely cystic lesions.[30]

CONCLUSION

GKRS is a safe and effective treatment option for thalamic AVMs. For small AVMs, GKRS should be the primary choice as it saves the patient from the risks of microsurgery. When properly selected, patients have a high likelihood of successful obliteration, with minimal risks of haemorrhage and radiation-induced complications.

TAKE HOME MESSAGE

- Primary GKRS should be considered for small to medium-sized deep-seated AVMs.
- Larger AVM (Modified SM grade 4,5,6) can be considered for staging:volume-staged GKRS (VSGKRS), and dose-staged GKRS.
- A higher marginal dose, higher Spetzler-Martin (SM) grade, elevated radiosurgery-based score, and deeper locations in the brainstem and thalamus are associated with a greater likelihood of developing radiation-induced changes.

REFERENCES

1. Fleetwood IG, Steinberg GK. Arteriovenous malformations. *Lancet*. 2002;359(9309): 863-873.
2. Kiran NA, Kale SS, Kasliwal MK, et al. Gamma knife radiosurgery for arteriovenous malformations of basal ganglia, thalamus and brainstem--a retrospective study comparing the results with that for AVMs at other intracranial locations. *Acta Neurochir (Wien)*. 2009;151(12):1575-1582.
3. Spetzler RF, Martin NA. A proposed grading system for arteriovenous malformations. *J Neurosurg*. 1986;65(4):476-483.
4. Pollock BE, Flickinger JC. Modification of the radiosurgery-based arteriovenous malformation grading system. *Neurosurgery*. 2008;63(2):239-243.
5. Leksell L. Stereotactic radiosurgery. *J Neurol Neurosurg Psychiatry*. 1983;46(9):797-803.
6. Starke RM, Kano H, Ding D, et al. Stereotactic radiosurgery for cerebral arteriovenous malformations: evaluation of long-term outcomes in a multicenter cohort. *J Neurosurg*. 2017;126(1):36-44.
7. Maruyama K, Kawahara N, Shin M, et al. The risk of hemorrhage after radiosurgery for cerebral arteriovenous malformations. *N Engl J Med*. 2005;352(2):146-153.
8. Kano H, Kondziolka D, Flickinger JC, et al. Stereotactic radiosurgery for arteriovenous malformations, Part 5: management of brainstem arteriovenous malformations. *J Neurosurg*. 2012;116(1):44-53.
9. Potts MB, Jahangiri A, Jen M, et al. Deep arteriovenous malformations in the basal ganglia, thalamus, and insula: multimodality management, patient selection, and results. *World Neurosurg*. 2014;82(3-4):386-394.
10. Lawton MT, Hamilton MG, Spetzler RF. Multimodality treatment of deep arteriovenous malformations: thalamus, basal ganglia, and brain stem. *Neurosurgery*. 1995;37(1):29-36.
11. Sharma MS, Kondziolka D, Khan A, et al. Radiation tolerance limits of the brainstem. *Neurosurgery*. 2008;63(4):728-733.
12. Faye M, Diallo M, Sghiouar M, Ndiaye Sy EC, Borius PY, Régis JM. Stereotactic radiosurgery for thalamus arteriovenous malformations. *J Radiosurg SBRT*. 2020;6(4):269-275.
13. Potts MB, Chang EF, Young WL, Lawton MT; UCSF Brain AVM Study Project. Transsylvian-transinsular approaches to the insula and basal ganglia: operative techniques and results with vascular lesions. *Neurosurgery*. 2012;70(4):824-834.

14. Gross BA, Duckworth EA, Getch CC, Bendok BR, Batjer HH. Challenging traditional beliefs: microsurgery for arteriovenous malformations of the basal ganglia and thalamus. *Neurosurgery*. 2008;63(3):393-411.

15. Pollock BE, Kondziolka D, Lunsford LD, Bissonette D, Flickinger JC. Repeat stereotactic radiosurgery of arteriovenous malformations: factors associated with incomplete obliteration. *Neurosurgery*. 1996;38(2):318-324.

16. Flickinger JC, Kondziolka D, Maitz AH, Lunsford LD. An analysis of the dose-response for arteriovenous malformation radiosurgery and other factors affecting obliteration. *Radiother Oncol*. 2002;63(3):347-354.

17. Flickinger JC, Kondziolka D, Maitz AH, Lunsford LD. An analysis of the dose-response for arteriovenous malformation radiosurgery and other factors affecting obliteration. Radiother Oncol. 2002;63(3):347–354.

18. Hasegawa H, Hanakita S, Shin M, et al. A Comprehensive Study of Symptomatic Late Radiation-Induced Complications After Radiosurgery for Brain Arteriovenous Malformation: Incidence, Risk Factors, and Clinical Outcomes. *World Neurosurg*. 2018;116:e556-e565.

19. Chung WY, Shiau CY, Wu HM, et al. Staged radiosurgery for extra-large cerebral arteriovenous malformations: method, implementation, and results. *J Neurosurg*. 2008;109 Suppl:65-72.

20. Lindvall P, Bergström P, Löfroth PO, et al. Hypofractionated conformal stereotactic radiotherapy for arteriovenous malformations. *Neurosurgery*. 2003;53(5):1036-1043.

21. Ilyas A, Chen CJ, Ding D, et al. Volume-staged versus dose-staged stereotactic radiosurgery outcomes for large brain arteriovenous malformations: a systematic review. *J Neurosurg*. 2018;128(1):154-164.

22. Kano H, Flickinger JC, Nakamura A, et al. How to improve obliteration rates during volume-staged stereotactic radiosurgery for large arteriovenous malformations. *J Neurosurg*. 2018;130(6):1809-1816. Published 2018 Jul 20.

23. Oermann EK, Ding D, Yen CP, et al. Effect of Prior Embolization on Cerebral Arteriovenous Malformation Radiosurgery Outcomes: A Case-Control Study. *Neurosurgery*. 2015;77(3):406-417.

24. Maruyama K, Kondziolka D, Niranjan A, Flickinger JC, Lunsford LD. Stereotactic radiosurgery for brainstem arteriovenous malformations: factors affecting outcome. *J Neurosurg*. 2004;100(3):407-413.

25. Mathis JA, Barr JD, Horton JA, et al. The efficacy of particulate embolization combined with stereotactic radiosurgery for treatment of large arteriovenous malformations of the brain. *AJNR Am J Neuroradiol*. 1995;16(2):299-306.

26. Andrade-Souza YM, Ramani M, Scora D, Tsao MN, terBrugge K, Schwartz ML. Embolization before radiosurgery reduces the obliteration rate of arteriovenous malformations. *Neurosurgery*. 2007;60(3):443-452.

27. Izawa M, Hayashi M, Chernov M, et al. Long-term complications after gamma knife surgery for arteriovenous malformations. *J Neurosurg*. 2005;102 Suppl:34-37.

28. Ilyas A, Chen CJ, Ding D, et al. Volume-staged versus dose-staged stereotactic radiosurgery outcomes for large brain arteriovenous malformations: a systematic review. *J Neurosurg*. 2018;128(1):154-164.

29. Hasegawa H, Yamamoto M, Shin M, Barfod BE. Gamma Knife Radiosurgery For Brain Vascular Malformations: Current Evidence And Future Tasks. *Ther Clin Risk Manag.* 2019;15:1351-1367.

30. Kedia S, Santhoor H, Singh M. Adverse Radiation Effects Following Gamma Knife Radiosurgery. *Neurol India.* 2023;71(Supplement):S59-S67.

Draining Vein Shielding During Gamma Knife Radiosurgery in Intracranial Arteriovenous Malformations

32

Deepak Agrawal | Mahnaaz Sultana Azeem

KEY LEARNING POINTS

1. Intracranial Arteriovenous Malformations (AVMs) present a challenge for neurosurgeons, as complete resection or embolisation may not always be possible, especially in critical areas.
2. Gamma Knife radiosurgery is an accepted and useful treatment modality for intracranial AVMs. However, it also carries the risk of thrombosis of the draining vein, resulting in brain edema and intracerebral bleeding due to raised pressure and altered dynamics in the nidus.
3. Shielding the draining vein in radiosurgery can help minimise complications while achieving the same desired obliteration of the nidus.
4. Staging the delivery of radiation dose during radiosurgery can achieve the desired radiation dose while minimising complications without compromising the total dose of radiation to the nidus. This does not affect the success rates of nidus obliteration.
5. Future treatment protocols for intracranial AVMs should include Gamma Knife radiosurgery while shielding the draining vein and staging the dose delivery if required.

INTRODUCTION

Gamma Knife Radiosurgery (GKRS) has emerged as a pivotal tool in the management of intracranial arteriovenous malformations (AVMs), particularly for deep-seated or surgically inaccessible lesions. By delivering highly focused radiation, GKRS promotes gradual endothelial proliferation, leading to nidus obliteration. However, the presence of a major draining vein within or adjacent to the radiation target presents a significant challenge. Shielding the draining vein is often necessary to prevent radiation-induced venous thrombosis, which can lead to venous infarction, increased intracranial pressure, and hemorrhagic complications. Nevertheless, shielding the vein may compromise the effectiveness of the treatment by leaving portions of the nidus untreated, necessitating a staged approach.[1-3]

In this chapter, we present a case of a right striatal AVM treated with GKRS, where the treatment plan required partial shielding of the draining vein. We discuss the rationale, planning strategies, outcomes, and future considerations for improving AVM radiosurgery outcomes while mitigating risks associated with draining vein involvement.

CASE PRESENTATION

HISTORY AND EXAMINATION

A 24-year-old female presented with a 10-month history of progressive left-sided weakness. She denied any history of seizures, headaches, or previous cerebrovascular events. Her medical history was unremarkable, with no prior neurosurgical interventions or systemic illnesses.

Neurological examination revealed left-sided motor weakness (4/5) without sensory deficits. Fundoscopic examination showed no signs of papilledema. The patient's cognitive function remained intact, and cranial nerve assessment was unremarkable.

IMAGING

Magnetic resonance imaging (MRI) with contrast demonstrated a right striatal AVM with deep venous drainage into the internal cerebral vein. Digital subtraction

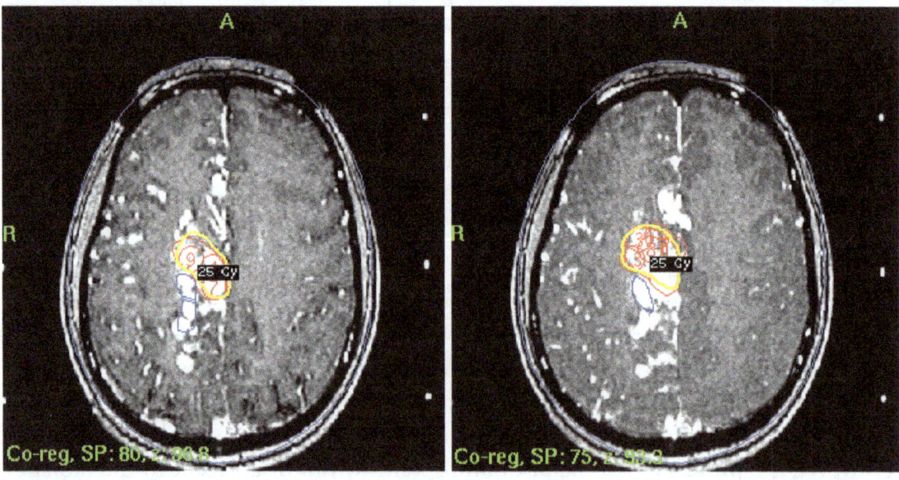

FIGURE 32.1   Gamma knife radio-surgery planning for right striatal AV malformation draining into the internal cerebral vein.

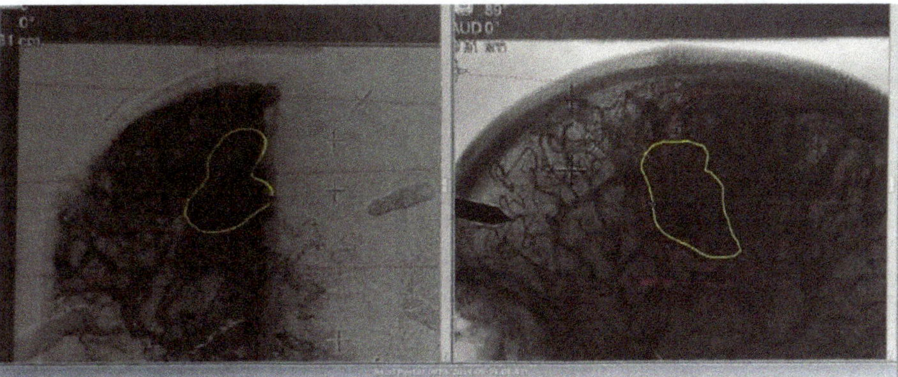

FIGURE 32.2   Digital subtraction angiography (DSA) confirming the AVM nidus and venous outflow, highlighting the risk associated with treating the draining vein.

angiography (DSA) confirmed a Spetzler-Martin Grade III AVM with a compact nidus measuring 3.2 cm. The deep location and venous drainage pattern increased the risk of haemorrhage, making microsurgical resection less favourable. Given the complexity of the lesion, GKRS was selected as the primary treatment modality.

FOLLOW-UP

The patient underwent the first stage of GKRS without immediate complications. At the six-month follow-up, MRI showed partial reduction in AVM size with persistent draining vein patency. A second GKRS session was performed to address the residual nidus, following the same dosimetric principles. Over the next two years, serial imaging demonstrated progressive nidus obliteration with no new neurological deficits or haemorrhagic events.

DISCUSSION

One of the fundamental challenges in GKRS for AVMs is balancing effective nidus obliteration with the preservation of normal vascular structures. Draining veins play a crucial role in maintaining cerebral hemodynamics, and their inadvertent occlusion can lead to catastrophic consequences such as venous infarction and post-radiosurgical haemorrhage. Shielding these veins from excessive radiation is essential, but it introduces a trade-off: a portion of the AVM nidus may remain untreated, necessitating repeat GKRS later. However, risks of re-hemorrhage become greatly reduced with draining vein shielding.[2,4,5]

Bose et al. (2015)[1] demonstrated that draining vein shielding significantly lowers the incidence of post-radiosurgical complications, including brain edema (P = .002) and intracranial haemorrhage (P = .03). Their study highlighted the importance of dose modulation and the strategic avoidance of excessive radiation to critical venous structures. By limiting the radiation dose to well below 40 Gy to the draining vein, the brain edema, as well as intracranial haemorrhage risk, can be minimised.

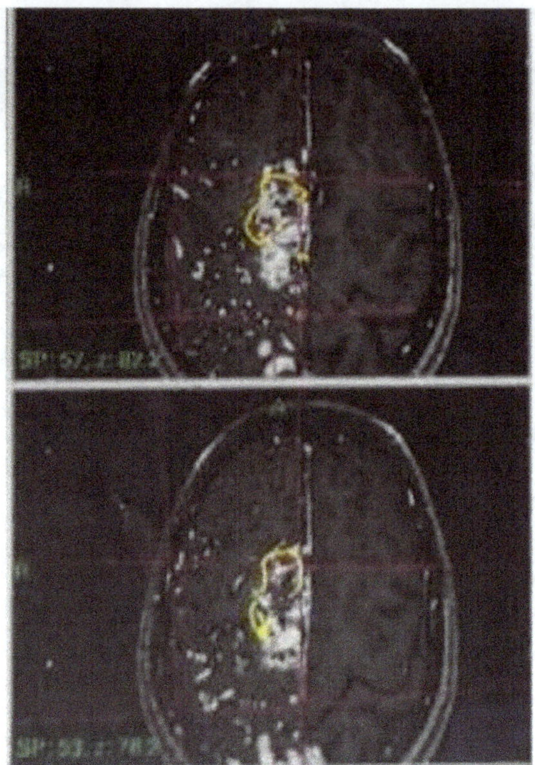

FIGURE 32.3   Pre and post-treatment images showing reduction in AV malformation and patent draining vein

Shielding the draining vein by the senior author (DA) in this study limited the radiation dose to less than 31 Gy, thereby reducing post-radiosurgery edema as well as intracranial bleeding. By incorporating draining vein shielding, neurosurgeons can achieve safer outcomes while maintaining the efficacy of AVM obliteration.

Despite its advantages, draining vein shielding introduces the challenge of potential residual nidus persistence, necessitating careful follow-up and, in some cases, staged radiosurgery. Yen et al. (2007)[6] reported that subtotal obliteration of AVMs after GKRS is common, and in cases where nidus remnants persist, repeat treatment can enhance obliteration rates without significantly increasing risks. This supports the concept that staged radiosurgery, combined with draining vein shielding, can optimise outcomes while preserving venous drainage integrity. Therefore future protocols should aim at draining vein shielding and staged radiosurgery to the nidus, thereby reducing brain edema and intracranial bleed, however this requires meticulous planning and a longer treatment time.

Future directions in AVM radiosurgery should focus on refining treatment planning through advanced imaging techniques, including functional MRI and perfusion studies, to better delineate nidus-draining vein relationships. Additionally, integrating adjunctive therapies such as embolisation before GKRS may allow for better nidus reduction while maintaining venous outflow.

CONCLUSION

Draining vein shielding in GKRS for AVMs is a critical yet complex component of treatment planning. While it reduces the risk of venous infarction, it also necessitates a carefully balanced approach to ensure effective nidus obliteration. Staged radiosurgery, precise dose modulation, and close post-treatment surveillance offer a pragmatic solution for addressing these challenges. Future advances in radiosurgical planning and imaging may further refine our ability to treat AVMs while minimising complications.

REFERENCES

1. Bose R, Agrawal D, Singh M, et al. Draining vein shielding in intracranial arteriovenous malformations during gamma-knife: a new way of preventing post gamma-knife edema and hemorrhage. *Neurosurgery*. 2015;76(5):623-632.
2. Tamura N, Hayashi M, Chernov M, et al. Outcome after Gamma Knife surgery for intracranial arteriovenous malformations in children. *J Neurosurg*. 2012;117 Suppl:150-157.
3. Kim HY, Chang WS, Kim DJ, et al. Gamma Knife surgery for large cerebral arteriovenous malformations. *J Neurosurg*. 2010;113 Suppl:2-8.
4. Kano H, Kondziolka D, Flickinger JC, et al. Stereotactic radiosurgery for arteriovenous malformations, Part 3: outcome predictors and risks after repeat radiosurgery. *J Neurosurg*. 2012;116(1):21-32.
5. Friedman WA. Stereotactic radiosurgery of intracranial arteriovenous malformations. *Neurosurg Clin N Am*. 2013;24(4):561-574.
6. Yen CP, Varady P, Sheehan J, Steiner M, Steiner L. Subtotal obliteration of cerebral arteriovenous malformations after gamma knife surgery. *J Neurosurg*. 2007;106(3):361-369.

33 Fractionated Gamma Knife Radiosurgery for Large Arteriovenous Malformations

Kanwaljeet Garg | Sandeep Mishra | Manmohan Singh

KEY LEARNING POINTS

1. Large AVM (SM Grade 4 & 5) are difficult to treat.
2. Fractionated GKRS may help decrease side effects while treating such large AVMs.
3. Both dose fractionation and volume fractionation can be attempted in these large AVMs.
4. Patients without deficits may be managed conservatively as shown in the ARUBA trial.

INTRODUCTION

Arteriovenous malformations (AVMs) are common intracranial vascular anomalies, typically managed with surgical excision, embolisation, or stereotactic radiosurgery (SRS). SRS, particularly Gamma Knife Radiosurgery (GKRS), has proven effective in treating AVMs. Traditionally, GKRS was used as a single-session treatment, but its application has since evolved and it can be performed in up to a maximum of five sessions.[1] GKRS offers precise targeting and a sharp dose fall-off, making it superior to fractionated conventional radiotherapy by minimising exposure to the surrounding brain tissue.[2]

Patients with large or Spetzler-Martin grade 4 or 5 AVMs pose a therapeutic challenge, particularly in case of haemorrhage. These AVMs may not be amenable for surgical resection and also, cannot be embolised if en-passage vessels supplying blood to adjacent neural tissue are involved.[3] Due to the complexities involved, large AVM volumes are typically unsuitable for GKRS. In GKRS, achieving successful outcomes relies on the marginal dose and nidus volume. However, treating larger AVMs necessitates lowering the marginal dose to minimise toxicity to surrounding brain tissue, resulting in lower obliteration and control rates compared to smaller AVMs. This necessitates the use of various multimodal approaches, including pre or post-GKRS embolisation, volume-staged SRS and dose-fractionated SRS, to enhance obliteration rates while minimising toxicity.

CASE HISTORY AND EXAMINATION FINDINGS

CASE 1 (DOSE FRACTIONATION)

An 8-year-female child presented with a 5-year history of left-sided hemiparesis. Neurological examination showed normal higher mental functions. Her visual acuity was 6/24 in the right eye and 6/18 in the left. Motor strength was graded 4/5 (MRC scale) in the left upper and lower limbs and 5/5 on the right side. She was diagnosed with choroidal AVM. The AVM was partially embolised and she was planned for dose-fractionated GKRS due to the close proximity of the AVM to the brainstem.

GK PROTOCOL

MRI was used to define the lesion boundaries, and a stereotactic head frame ensured precise targeting. The dose was carefully planned to achieve effective AVM obliteration while minimising radiation to surrounding critical structures.

IMAGING

Preoperative Magnetic resonance imaging (MRI) of the Case 1 axial section imaging of the brain T1 contrast-enhanced MRI axial section revealed a choroidal arteriovenous malformation **(Fig. 33.1A)**.

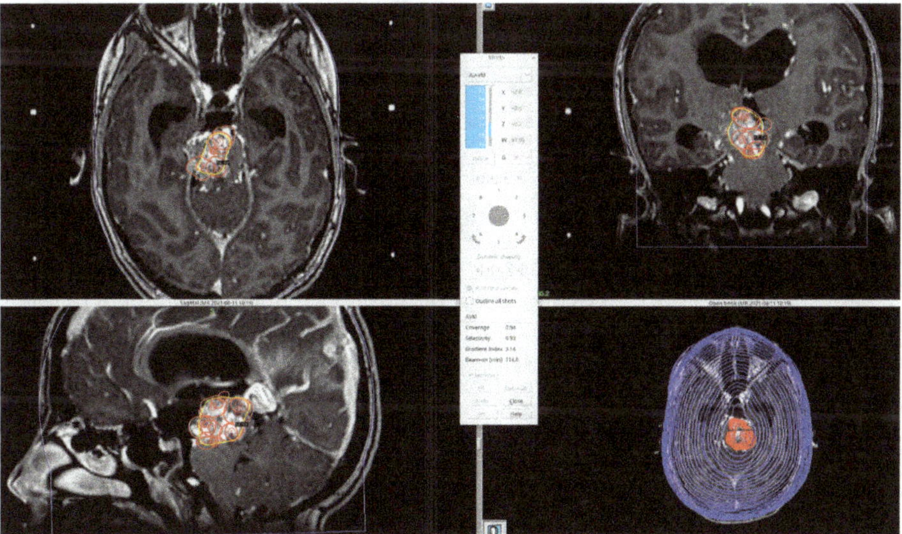

FIGURE 33.1   Dose Planning.

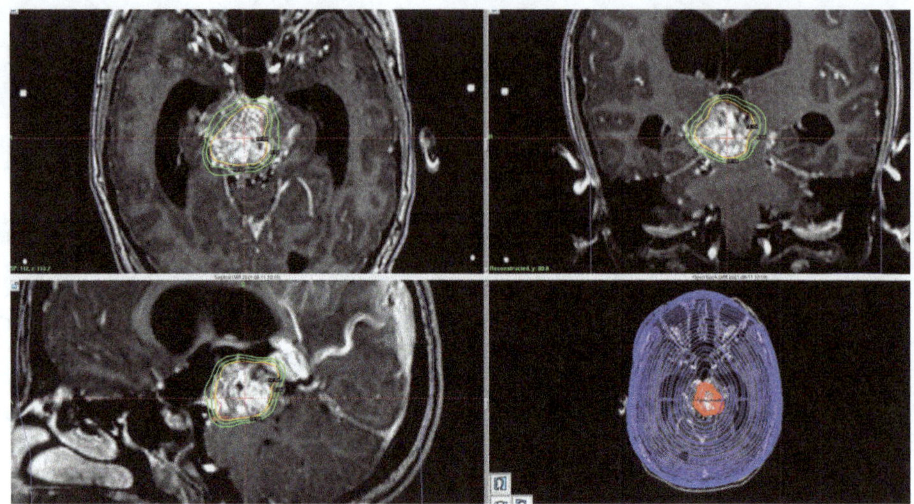

FIGURE 33.2   First Fraction.

GK PROTOCOL

In August 2021, the patient's lesion received a prescription isodose of 12 Gy at 62 % (a maximum dose of 20.2 Gy) to the margin. A total of 19 isocentres were used, with a beam-on time of 114 minutes, achieving 94% coverage and 93% selectivity. The second fractionated dose of 10 Gy was administered in September 2021.

FOLLOW UP

The patient showed no adverse effects or cranial neuropathies at the 5-year follow-up. An MRI at the 5-year mark revealed a significant reduction in AVM size (initial volume = 8.3 cc, reduced to 7.6 cc before the second fractionated treatment).

CASE 2 (VOLUME FRACTIONATION)

A 24-year-old female presented with a 6-year history of headaches, accompanied by left-sided hemiparesis and seizures, both persisting for one year. Neurological examination showed normal higher mental function and cranial nerve assessment. Motor strength was 4/5 (MRC grade) in the left upper and lower limbs and 5/5 on the right side.

IMAGING

Preoperative Magnetic resonance imaging (MRI) axial section imaging of the brain T1 contrast-enhanced MRI axial section revealed an ill-defined inhomogeneous contrast-enhancing lesion in the right frontoparietal cortex, consistent with an arteriovenous malformation (Fig. 33.2A).

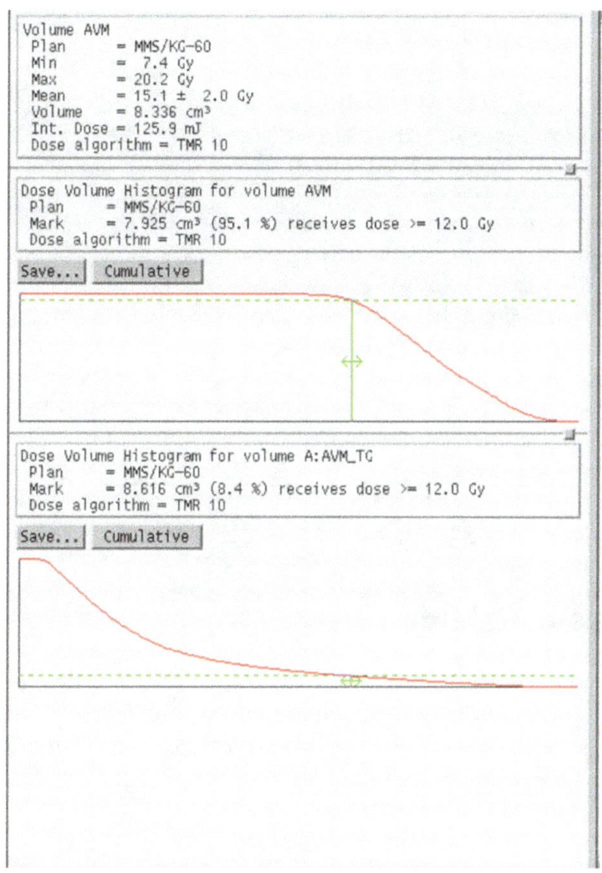

FIGURE 33.3   Dose Volume Histogram for First Fractionation.

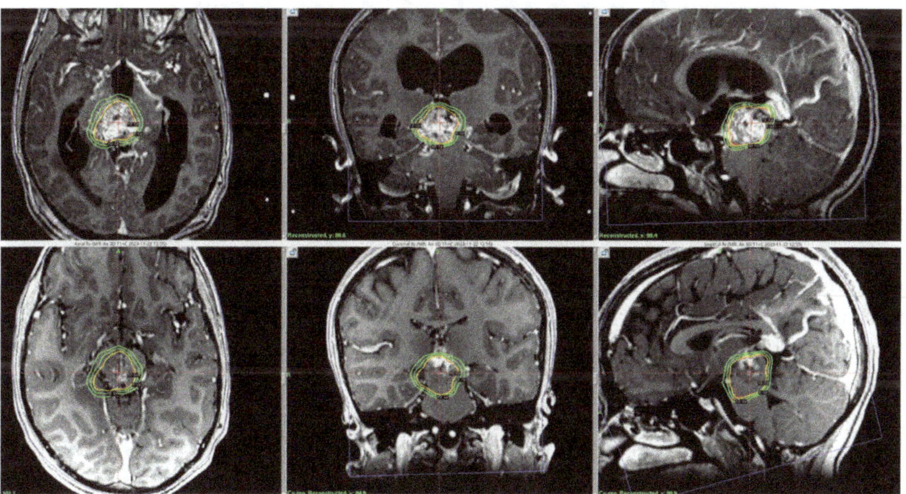

FIGURE 33.4   Second Fractionation

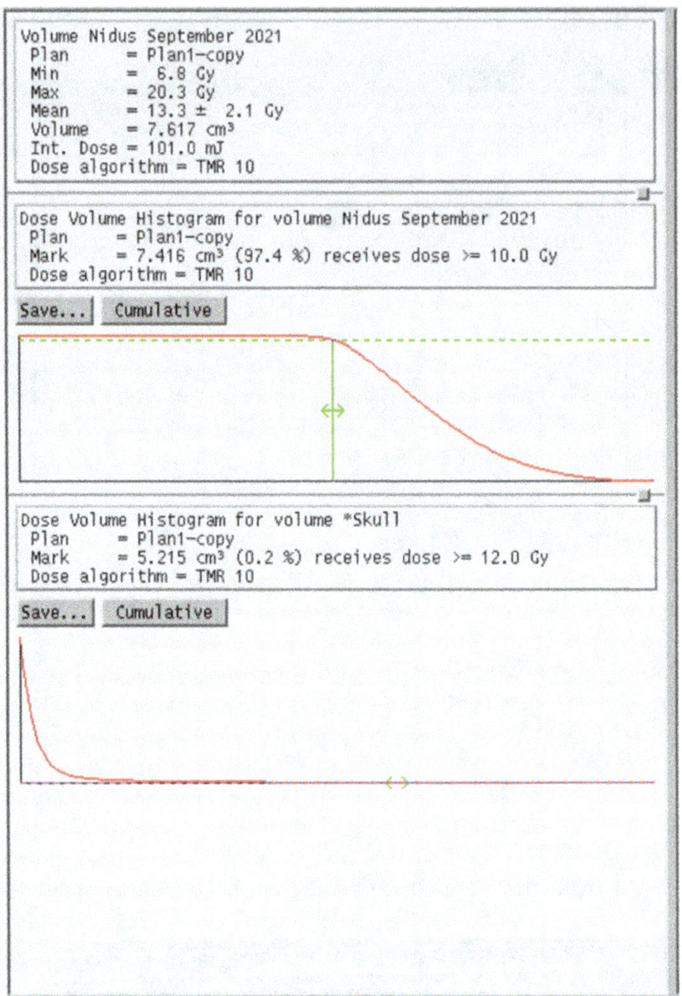

FIGURE 33.5   Dose volume Histogram for second Fractionation.

GK PROTOCOL

Given the large size of the AVM, she was scheduled for volume-fractionated Gamma Knife Radiosurgery. MRI was utilised to delineate the lesion, and a stereotactic head frame was employed to ensure precise targeting. The prescribed dose was carefully calculated to maximise AVM obliteration while minimising exposure to adjacent critical structures. In August 2017, the patient's lesion received a maximum dose of 22 Gy with a prescription isodose of 12 Gy at 95% to the margin. A second fractionated dose of 20 Gy was administered in December 2018.

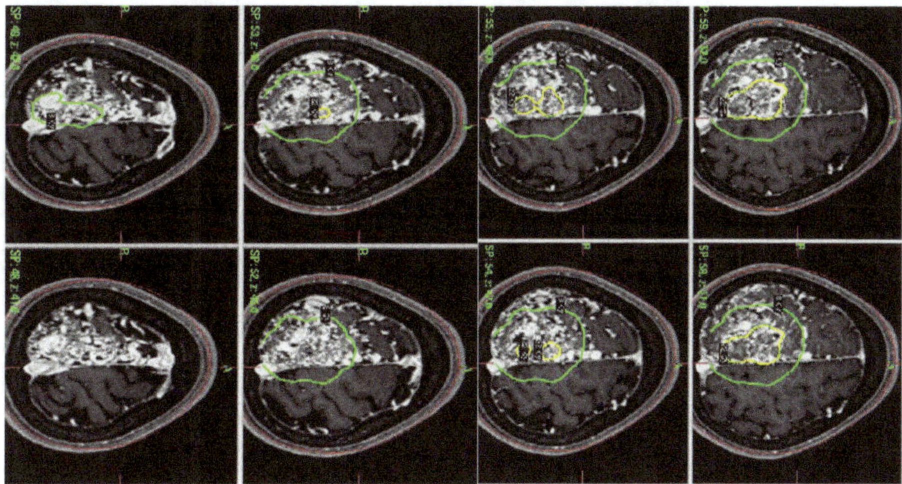

FIGURE 33.6   First dose.

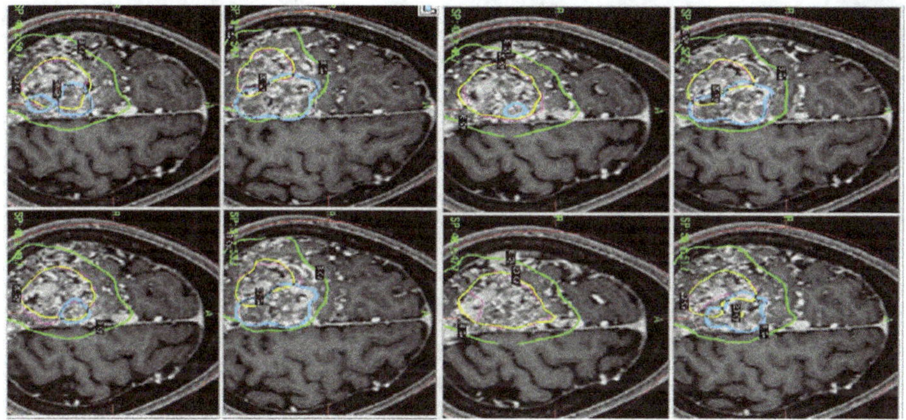

FIGURE 33.7   Second fractionated dose.

FOLLOW UP

The patient exhibited a notable showed a significant decrease in the size of the AVM on follow-up MRI in February 2019 (Fig. 8). She subsequently received the third volume fractionated dose of 18Gy in 2020 (Fig. 9). The patient showed no adverse effects or cranial neuropathies at the 4-year follow-up. An MRI at the 7-year mark, in 2024, revealed a significant reduction in AVM size with near total obliteration of the AVM (Fig. 10).

DISCUSSION

Large AVMs, often defined as those over 10 cc, present significant therapeutic challenges due to high treatment-associated morbidity and mortality rates.[4,5] Although

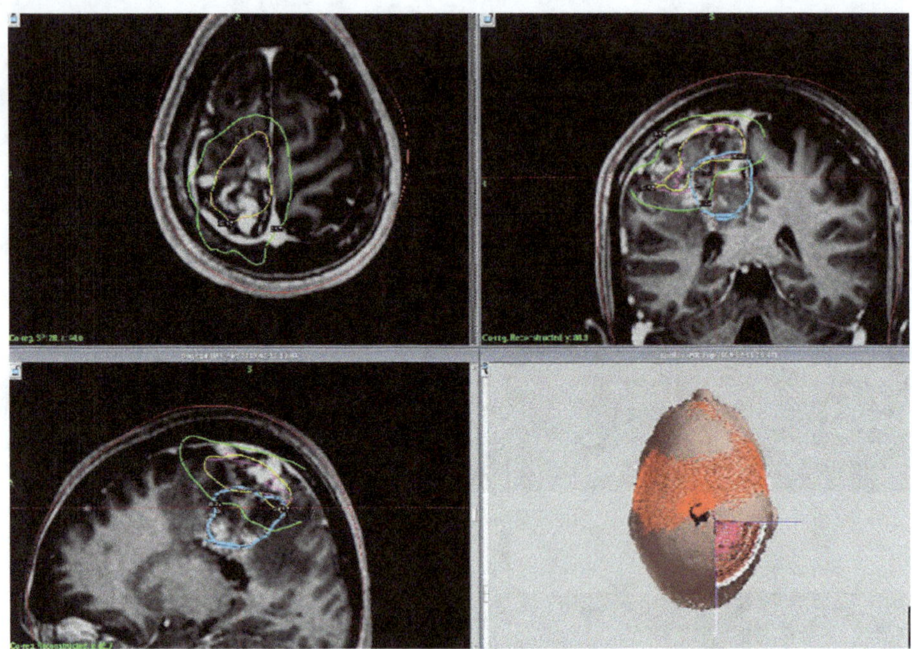

FIGURE 33.8   Follow-up MRI 2019.

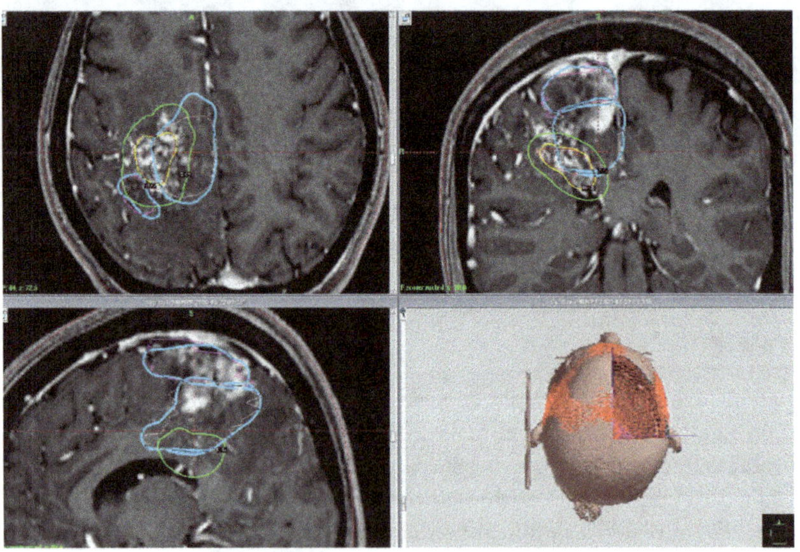

FIGURE 33.9   Third Fractionated dose.

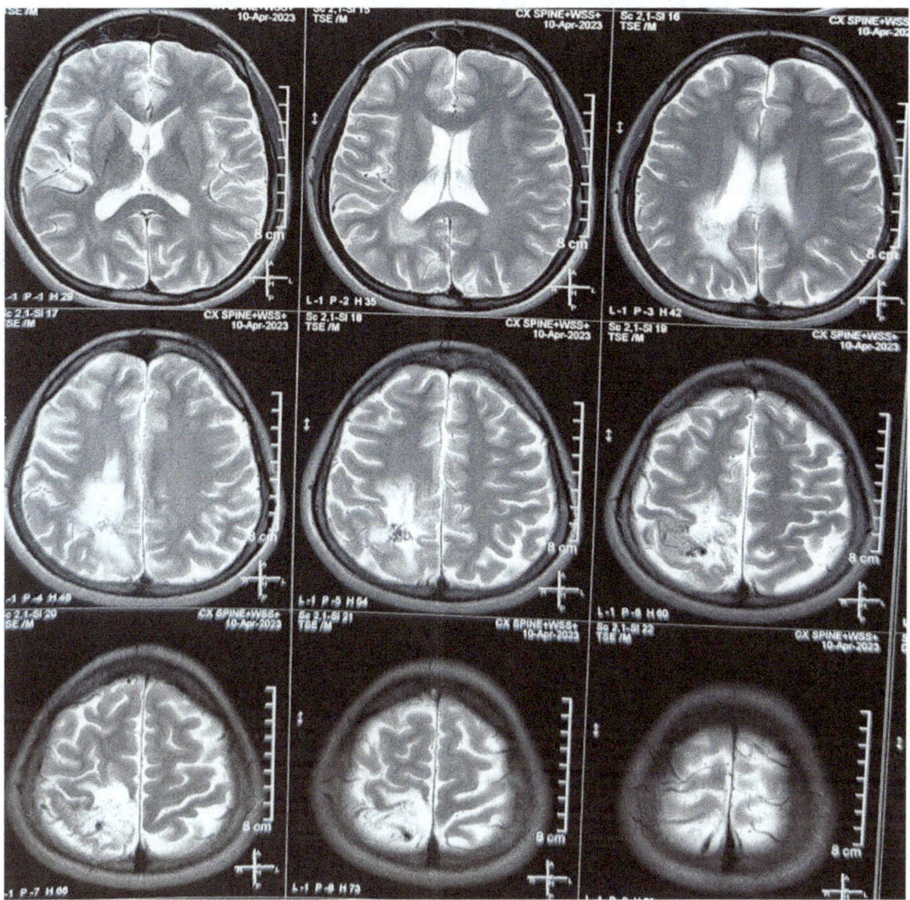

FIGURE 33.10   Follow up MRI in 2024.

single-stage SRS is effective for smaller AVMs, it poses a higher risk of radiation-induced complications in larger AVMs. Managing large AVMs remains controversial, with no single treatment modality providing optimal results. Approaches such as prior embolisation for size reduction, as well as volume-staged or dose-staged radiosurgery, have been proposed to address these problems.

Volume-fractionated stereotactic radiosurgery (VF-SRS) treats the AVM nidus by dividing it into smaller sections, each addressed in separate SRS sessions spaced 3–6 months apart. The brain tissue receiving sublethal doses has time to repair between sessions.[6] This approach is similar to treating multiple small AVMs individually, allowing for a higher dose to each section compared to single-fraction SRS for the entire AVM. Dose-staged or hypofractionated SRS targets the entire nidus by administering fractions of lower doses over several weeks. This approach can be implemented as either dose-fractionated stereotactic radiosurgery (DF-SRS), or hypofractionated stereotactic radiotherapy. DF-SRS is particularly useful for treating large AVMs or those close to sensitive structures like the optic nerve or brainstem.[7] Delivering the total dose in small, divided fractions minimises exposure to surrounding brain tissue.

Comparative analyses of volume-staged and dose-staged SRS indicate that volume-staging generally achieves higher obliteration rates, though associated with a slightly elevated risk of complications. A review of studies involving 11 volume-staged and 10 dose-staged SRS cases revealed that volume-staged SRS had a higher obliteration rate (40.3% vs. 32.7%), but also a greater incidence of symptomatic radiation-induced changes (RICs) (13.7% vs. 12.2%), posttreatment haemorrhage (19.5% vs. 10.6%), and mortality (7.4% vs. 4.6%).[4] Another review found an even larger gap in obliteration rates (47.5% for volume-staged vs. 22.8% for dose-staged), with similar differences in haemorrhage and mortality rates, while RIC rates remained nearly identical.[5] For large AVMs, volume-staged SRS may be favoured for its higher obliteration rates, despite a slightly higher complication profile.

TAKE HOME MESSAGE

Fractionated GKRS, DF-GKRS, and VF-SRS are viable options for large AVMs, offering a reasonable rate of nidus obliteration with manageable toxicity.

REFERENCES

1. Mukherjee KK, Kumar N, Tripathi M, et al. Dose fractionated gamma knife radiosurgery for large arteriovenous malformations on daily or alternate day schedule outside the linear quadratic model: Proof of concept and early results. A substitute to volume fractionation. *Neurol India*. 2017;65(4):826-835.

2. Flickinger JC. An integrated logistic formula for prediction of complications from radiosurgery. *Int J Radiat Oncol Biol Phys*. 1989;17(4):879-885.

3. Diaz O, Scranton R. Endovascular treatment of arteriovenous malformations. *Handb Clin Neurol*. 2016;136:1311-1317.

4. Ilyas A, Chen CJ, Ding D, et al. Volume-staged versus dose-staged stereotactic radiosurgery outcomes for large brain arteriovenous malformations: a systematic review. *J Neurosurg*. 2018;128(1):154-164.

5. Moosa S, Chen CJ, Ding D, et al. Volume-staged versus dose-staged radiosurgery outcomes for large intracranial arteriovenous malformations. *Neurosurg Focus*. 2014;37(3):E18.

6. Seymour ZA, Sneed PK, Gupta N, et al. Volume-staged radiosurgery for large arteriovenous malformations: an evolving paradigm. *J Neurosurg*. 2016;124(1):163-174.

7. Karlsson B, Lindqvist M, Blomgren H, et al. Long-term results after fractionated radiation therapy for large brain arteriovenous malformations. *Neurosurgery*. 2005;57(1):42-49.

Adverse Radiation Effects of Gamma Knife Radiosurgery

Sarvesh Goyal | Shweta Kedia | Mahnaaz Sultana Azeem

KEY LEARNING POINTS

1. Early identification and management of radiation-induced changes, such as edema and necrosis, are vital for patient outcomes.
2. Understanding the causes and risk factors for radiation necrosis helps in predicting and preventing adverse effects.
3. Bevacizumab is a promising therapeutic option for reducing edema and stabilizing the blood-brain barrier in symptomatic radiation necrosis.
4. Continuous follow-up and early intervention are critical for managing delayed radiation-induced effects and preserving neurological function.
5. Biomarkers like VEGF and endostatin may help predict radiation-induced changes, allowing for targeted management and improved outcomes.

INTRODUCTION

Gamma Knife Radiosurgery has become a widely adopted treatment approach for small to medium-sized benign and malignant intracranial tumours, as well as arterio-venous malformations (AVMs) located in surgically challenging regions. It is also employed for larger or multiple tumours in either volume fraction or dose fractionation schedule. It offers the advantage of delivering focused, high-dose radiation to the lesion, and in more than 8% of the cases, nidus obliteration is achieved usually within 4-5 years.

While radiosurgery is highly effective, it is not without risks. Adverse radiation effects (AREs) can range from mild, asymptomatic with transient edema to severe outcomes such as severe radiation necrosis or cyst formation. This chapter delves into the clinical and imaging characteristics of AREs in AVM cases and the management strategies used to address them.

REPRESENTATIVE CASE

HISTORY & EXAMINATION

A 25-year-old female presented with recurrent episodes of headache lasting 1–2 years, progressively worsening over the last 6 months. The patient had a history of decreasing visual acuity in the left eye 2/60, with the field cuts. There was no history of seizures, neurological deficits, or prior interventions.

IMAGING

Pre-Treatment

- Pre-GKT MRI: Revealed a Right temporal AVM (Fig. 34.1A, B).
- Digital Subtraction Angiography (DSA)done pre-gamma knife revealed a right temporal AVM supplied by feeders from the temporal branches of the right MCA and PCA, with venous drainage into the right sigmoid sinus and ectatic draining veins (Figure 1c).

GK PROTOCOL

Treatment Plan

Primary GKT targeting the AVM nidus was planned (Fig. 34.1C). 22 Gy delivered to the 50% isodose line with a coverage of 97% and selectivity of 0.84. The beam on time was a little on the higher side in view of a 9-year-old decaying source of cobalt.

FOLLOW UP

The patient initially did well for a year but later started experiencing headaches and deterioration of vision. The patient was started on steroids, with 4 mg of Tablet Dexamethasone given three times daily, which then tapered and stopped. Transient improvement in symptoms on medication was seen which worsened after stopping the drug. Due to rapidly deteriorating vision, a repeat scan was done. MRI Brain demonstrated a small residual nidus with radiation-induced edema, suggesting symptomatic RIC grade I (Fig. 34.1D). Patient was then given a single dose of intravenous Bevacizumab (5mg/kg body weight). Non-contrast CT Head was repeated to rule out any intracranial bleed.

Repeat CT and DSA showed complete obliteration of the residual lesion and resolution of radiation-induced edema.

DISCUSSION

A notable long-term complication that can arise after radiosurgery is the development of adverse radiation effects (AREs). These effects can significantly impair neurological function and quality of life. Given the delayed onset of many of these effects, early recognition and appropriate management are crucial for optimising patient outcomes.

The types of AREs observed in patients treated for AVMs are varied, and understanding their underlying mechanisms, clinical presentations, and management strategies is essential for reducing morbidity.

Radiation Induced Changes (RICs) remain one of the commonest complications of radiosurgery, typically manifesting months to years after treatment. This delayed

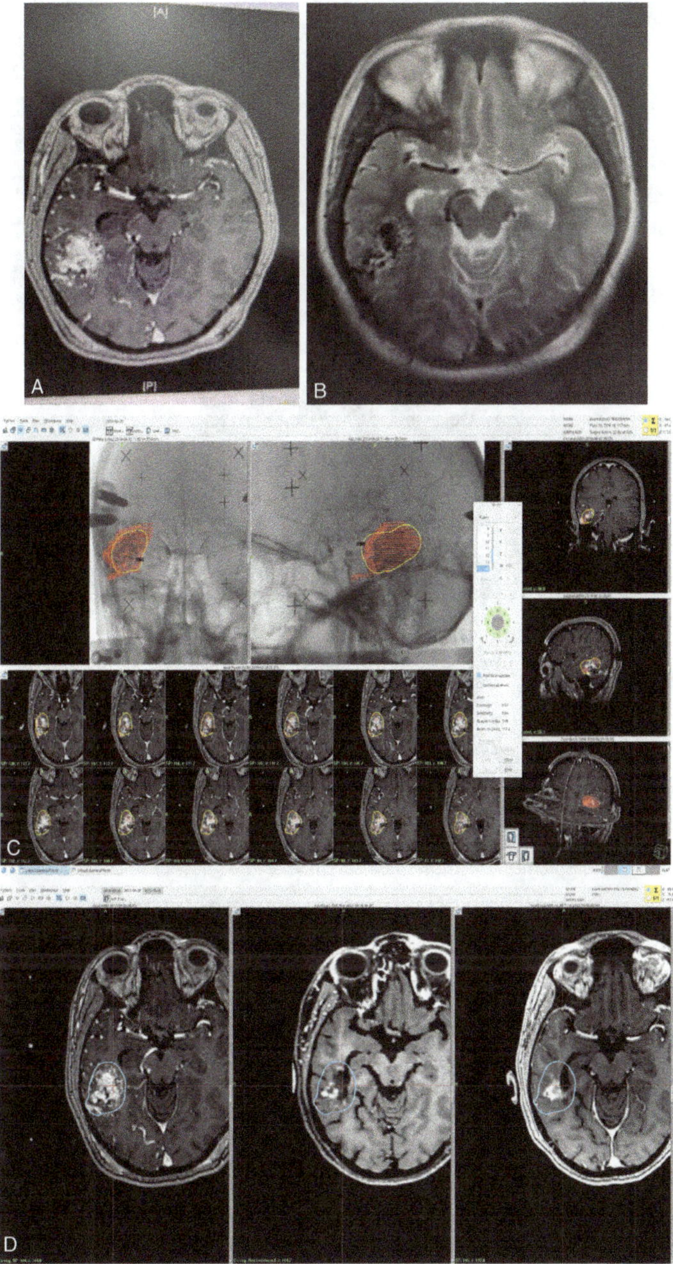

FIGURE 34.1 (A) T1 contrast (axial). (B) T2 axial – Pre GKT MRI showing Right temporal AVM. (C) Shows the exported plan for the patient with 22Gy at 50% isodose line and also the angio with marked nidus. (D) Shows the comparative scans at 2 years and three years interval. The 1st image is at the time of GKRS, while the second image is at the time of symptomatic RIC. Third image is at the time 1 year after Inj Bevacizumab therapy.

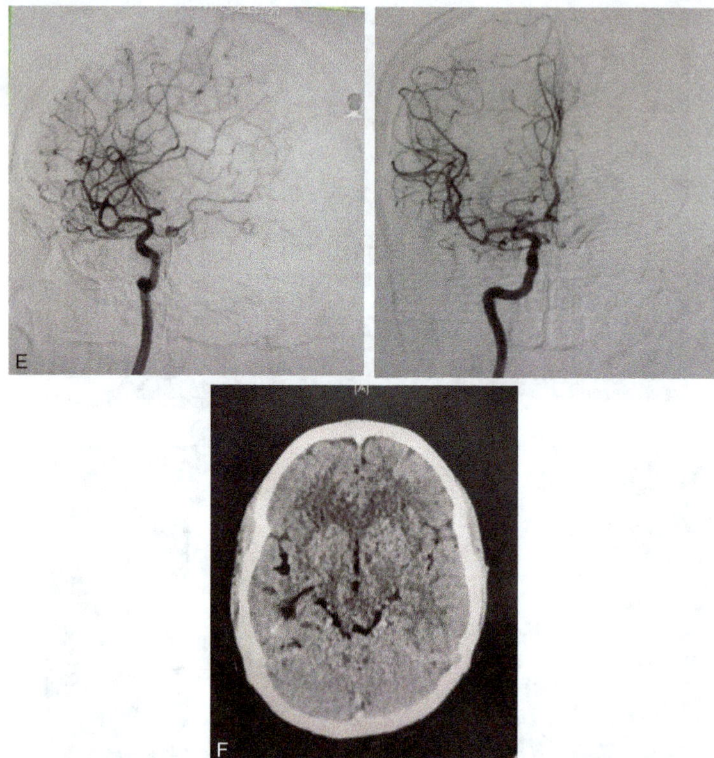

FIGURE 34.1   (E) DSA (Lateral and AP films) after 2 years of primary gamma knife and 6 months of bevacizumab showing no residual AVM. (F) – NCCT head comparative scans at an interval of showing resolution of edema.

onset can complicate diagnosis and management, as the clinical presentation often overlaps with other neurological conditions like pseudo-progression or tumour recurrence. Radiation necrosis occurs when radiation-induced damage disrupts the brain's vasculature, leading to ischemia and irreversible tissue damage. It is often associated with neurological deficits such as hemiparesis, seizures, aphasia, and cognitive dysfunction. Additionally, increased intracranial pressure (ICP) may present as headaches, nausea, and vomiting.

The latency period for radiation necrosis can vary widely, typically ranging from 6 months to several years post-radiosurgery. Some of them may present radiologically as early as 2 months as well. They appear as T2 hyperintensity or FLAIR signal changes in imaging. This will enhance brightly on contrast imaging with central necrosis but will not show changes in perfusion imaging. These are classified as Radiologic RIC and considered symptomatic RIC only when they become clinically symptomatic. The clinical symptoms may vary from mild raised headaches to severe neurological morbidities. We have had few deaths related to RIC, however, the percentage remains below 0.1%. The radiologic RIC has been graded in literature as Grade I-III based on severity, with grade III having severe changes with significant midline shift. Most of the radiation necrosis that occurs post-radiation is asymptomatic. Only 2-14% of these would be clinically symptomatic, and less than a third of these warrant aggressive intervention.[1,7]

In the context of AVMs, the risk of necrosis is higher with higher Spetzler-Martin grade AVMs, greater marginal radiation doses, and those treated in critical brain areas, such as the brainstem, thalamus, or deep structures. Nidus with a single draining vein also shows significant changes post-radiation. Repeating radiosurgery for the same lesion also increases the chances of RIC. It is believed that Radiation necrosis results from direct endothelial damage, causing vascular insufficiency, blood-brain barrier disruption, and necrosis of the surrounding parenchymal tissue.[6,8]

Management of radiation necrosis primarily focuses on reducing edema and inflammation. The asymptomatic RIC with simple radiologic changes is routinely followed up with more frequent imaging than what is recommended in the outine protocol. For clinically symptomatic RIC presenting with headache and mild symptoms, corticosteroids are commonly used as the first-line treatment. It helps in reducing radiation-induced swelling, and many patients show initial improvement with this approach. Other treatment strategies may include antioxidants, pentoxifylline, and hyperbaric oxygen therapy, though they are not routinely used by us.[5,9]

In recent years, bevacizumab, a monoclonal antibody that inhibits vascular endothelial growth factor (VEGF), has shown promise in managing radiation necrosis. Bevacizumab reduces blood vessel permeability, decreases edema, and stabilises the blood-brain barrier. It has been particularly beneficial in patients with severe radiation-induced swelling who are refractory to corticosteroid therapy. Studies have demonstrated that bevacizumab can improve neurological outcomes, reduce the need for invasive surgical interventions, and even help shrink necrotic tissue. This treatment offers a less invasive alternative to surgery, although it is typically considered a supplementary therapy rather than a definitive solution for radiation necrosis. We use the standard dose of 5-7 mg/kg intravenous route, repeated every 2 weeks for 2-4 months.[2]

However, in cases where necrosis is extensive or progressive, surgical intervention may be required. Options include surgical excision of necrotic tissue or decompressive craniectomy to alleviate mass effect and relieve neurological deficits. Overall, while radiation necrosis is a challenging long-term complication of radiosurgery, advancements in management, including the use of bevacizumab, have improved the prognosis for affected patients.

The RIC may be associated with cyst formation that may develop several years after GKRS. The cystic change occurs as a result of radiation-induced injury to the vasculature, leading to fluid accumulation in the parenchyma. Symptoms associated with cyst formation can include focal neurological deficits, headaches, seizures, and signs of raised ICP. The symptomatic cysts typically require surgical intervention. Options include cyst fenestration, excision, or decompressive craniectomy to alleviate the mass effect. In cases with ventricular involvement or hydrocephalus, ventricular diversion procedures, such as Ommaya reservoir insertion or cystoperitoneal shunting, may be indicated. For asymptomatic cysts, conservative management with close imaging surveillance is usually sufficient. Patients with residual AVM nidus at the time of cyst formation may benefit from embolisation or repeat GKRS to obliterate the remaining AVM tissue, potentially reducing the risk of further complications.[3,4,10]

ROLE OF SERUM BIOMARKERS IN ARE MANAGEMENT

The role of biomarkers, particularly VEGF (vascular endothelial growth factor) and endostatin, in managing radiation-induced changes (RIC) after Gamma Knife Radiosurgery (GKRS) for arteriovenous malformations (AVMs) is an area of ongoing research. These biomarkers are said to be involved in the pathophysiology of RIC, with VEGF playing a key role in promoting angiogenesis and increasing vascular permeability, which can lead to vasogenic edema and radiation necrosis. Elevated serum levels of VEGF have been associated with RIC in some studies, though findings are not always consistent.[2,4]

These biomarkers can potentially help identify patients at higher risk of developing symptomatic RICs, allowing for closer monitoring and more timely intervention. Given the small sample sizes and varying patient populations in existing studies, further research is needed to establish definitive biomarkers that can predict RIC and guide treatment decisions.[1,2]

TAKE HOME MESSAGE

ARE are not uncommon after GKRS for AVMs, especially for deep-seated regions like the Basal ganglia. Treatment with steroids is usually effective. Bevacizumab may be considered for steroid-resistant cases. In extremely resistant cases, surgery may be attempted with excellent results.

REFERENCES

1. Kedia S, Santhoor H, Singh M. Adverse Radiation Effects Following Gamma Knife Radiosurgery. *Neurol India*. 2023;71(Supplement):S59-S67.

2. Kedia S, Goyal S, Garg K, et al. Serum Vascular Endothelial Growth Factor and Endostatin as an Adjunct to Clinical Decision Making in Managing Radiation-induced Changes Post Gamma Knife Radiosurgery in Spetzler Martin Grade 3 Arteriovenous Malformations Patients: A Pilot Study. *World Neurosurg*. 2024;189:e864-e871.

3. Goyal S, Pandey K, Kedia S, Sebastian LJD, Agrawal D. Unforeseen outcomes: Unveiling cyst formation post stereotactic radiosurgery in brain arteriovenous malformations cases. *J Clin Neurosci*. 2024;128:110785.

4. Lee JG, Park SH, Park KS, Kang DH, Hwang JH, Hwang SK. Do Serum Vascular Endothelial Growth Factor and Endostatin Reflect Radiological Radiation-Induced Changes After Stereotactic Radiosurgery for Cerebral Arteriovenous Malformations?. *World Neurosurg*. 2019;126:e612-e618.

5. Kailaya-Vasan A, Samuthrat T, Walsh DC. Severe adverse radiation effects complicating radiosurgical treatment of brain arteriovenous malformations and the potential benefit of early surgical treatment. *J Clin Neurosci*. 2018;55:25-31.

6. Kim MJ, Chang KW, Park SH, et al. Predictive Factors of Radiation-Induced Changes Following Single-Session Gamma Knife Radiosurgery for Arteriovenous Malformations. *J Clin Med*. 2021;10(10):2186. Published 2021 May 19.

7. Kano H, Flickinger JC, Tonetti D, et al. Estimating the Risks of Adverse Radiation Effects After Gamma Knife Radiosurgery for Arteriovenous Malformations. *Stroke*. 2017;48(1):84-90.

8. Ilyas A, Chen CJ, Ding D, et al. Radiation-Induced Changes After Stereotactic Radiosurgery for Brain Arteriovenous Malformations: A Systematic Review and Meta-Analysis. *Neurosurgery*. 2018;83(3):365-376.

9. Wanebo JE, Kidd GA, King MC, Chung TS. Hyperbaric oxygen therapy for treatment of adverse radiation effects after stereotactic radiosurgery of arteriovenous malformations: case report and review of literature. *Surg Neurol*. 2009;72(2):162-168.

10. Levegrün S, Hof H, Essig M, Schlegel W, Debus J. Radiation-induced changes of brain tissue after radiosurgery in patients with arteriovenous malformations: correlation with dose distribution parameters. *Int J Radiat Oncol Biol Phys*. 2004;59(3):796-808.

35 Gamma Knife Radiosurgery for Intracranial Cavernomas

Dattaraj Parmanand Sawarkar | Abhishek Kumar

KEY LEARNING POINTS

1. These are occult, thin-walled, vascular lesions without intervening normal cerebral tissue.
2. Management options include observation, microsurgical excision and radiosurgery.
3. GKRS is a preferred treatment modality in patients with deep-seated lesions.
4. GKRS is believed to cause gradual endothelial cell proliferation and hyalinisation causing luminal closure.

INTRODUCTION

Cavernomas are angiographically occult, thin-walled, vascular lesions without intervening normal cerebral tissue.[1] They commonly present with seizures, headaches, intracranial haemorrhage, and focal neurological deficits.[2] Treatment options available for these patients include observation, microsurgical excision and radiosurgery. The treatment modality selected in each case depends on the number of haemorrhages, surgical risks involved and seizure control. For symptomatic cavernomas in inaccessible locations, microsurgical excision is the treatment of choice.[3] However, in patients harbouring deep-seated lesions, GKRS is considered an option.[4] The proposed mechanisms behind the beneficial effects of GKRS on cavernomas include gradual endothelial cell proliferation and hyalinisation causing luminal closure. Histopathological evaluation of GKRS-treated cavernomas demonstrates fibrinoid necrosis, endothelial cell destruction, and marked fibrosis in connective tissue stroma.[5]

REPRESENTATIVE CASE

HISTORY & EXAMINATION

A 36-year-old female presented to our outpatient department with sudden onset weakness in all 4 limbs associated with tightness while walking for 4 months. Neurological examination revealed that she had power of 4+/5 in all 4 limbs with grade 2 spasticity with brisk reflexes. On radiological evaluation, she was found to have a small cavernous malformation in the midbrain in the periaqueductal region with evidence of a previous bleed.

IMAGING

Owing to the deep-seated nature, small size and eloquence of the location involved, she was planned for GKRS.

GK PROTOCOL

She underwent GKRS at our centre, where 0.177 cc of tumour volume received 12 Gy at 50% isodose. She tolerated the procedure well and only required analgesics for local pain.

FOLLOW UP

Her post-GKRS period was uneventful with no evidence of recurrent bleeding and resolution of the lesion on a 2-year follow-up MRI.

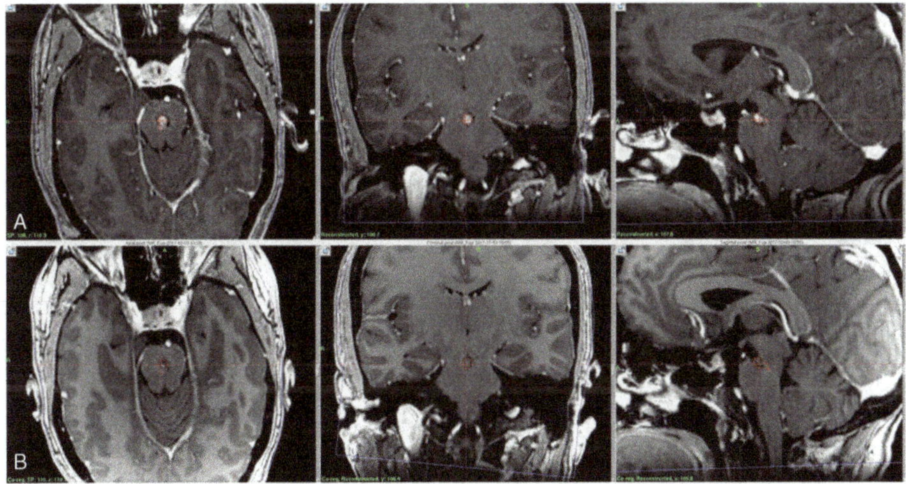

FIGURE 35.1　(A) Shows midbrain cavernoma at time of GKRS. (B) Shows post GKRS MRI done at 2-year follow-up showing resolution of the lesion.

DISCUSSION

Post-GKRS incidence of bleeding: Studies suggest that the annual bleeding rate falls from 30.5%-39.5% pre-treatment to 3.3%–15% within the first 2 years after radiosurgery, and to 0%-2.4% thereafter.[6] The observed reduction in the annual incidence of haemorrhage after GKS may be attributed to the delayed closure of vascular channel lumens caused by endothelial cell proliferation and hyalinisation. Thus, data presented in studies suggest that GKRS is a viable option for reducing bleeding rates in patients with lesions involving eloquent/deep regions.

Post GKRS Seizure control: Studies have suggested that approximately 0-18% of patients with infratentorial cavernous malformations and 50-63% of patients with supratentorial cavernous malformations suffer from seizures.[7] Studies also suggest that cavernous malformations involving archi-cortical/mesial temporal regions are associated with a higher incidence of epilepsy.[8] Therefore, surgical excision is advocated for temporal cavernous malformations which are associated with recurrent haemorrhages and drug-resistant epilepsy.

In a recently conducted retrospective multicenter study, 53% of patients with long-term epilepsy resistant to medical treatment became seizure-free (Engel Epilepsy Surgery Outcome Scale classes IA and IB) within an average of 4 months following SRS. Additionally, 20% experienced significant improvement (class II), while only 26% showed little improvement (classes III and IV).[9] Other studies have reported similar results. In a study by Pham and colleagues, 31% of patients became seizure-free (class I), and 35% showed significant improvement (class II) after radiosurgery.[10] Thus, based on published findings, GKRS appears to be a rational approach for reducing seizure frequency associated with a cavernoma.

Adverse Radiation Effects following GKRS: Adverse radiation effects were seen in yesteryears when lesions were delineated poorly using CT or less conformal MRI and higher dose protocols. It may present as perilesional edema, which can cause temporary neurological deficits or remain clinically silent, typically within 12 months after radiosurgery. Persistent adverse effects generally appear later, and with modern treatment protocols, their incidence is minimal for hemispheric lesions and low (7.9%) for deep-seated lesions, resulting in only mild morbidity (mRS score 1–2).[11] Advances in modern treatment protocols, especially those utilising gamma radiation-based devices, with a prescription dose of less than 20 Gy (usually 12–15 Gy), highly conformal MRI-guided treatment planning, and scheduling the treatment to avoid recent bleeding episodes (for Zabramski type II or III CMs, at least 3 months after the last haemorrhage) have significantly reduced the incidences of acute radiation effects.

While radiosurgery may not offer a definitive cure for cavernous malformation patients, its minimally invasive nature presents a safer alternative for those with surgically inaccessible lesions or medical comorbidities that prevent surgery. Fig. 35.2 depicts the proposed management algorithm for intracranial cavernous malformations.

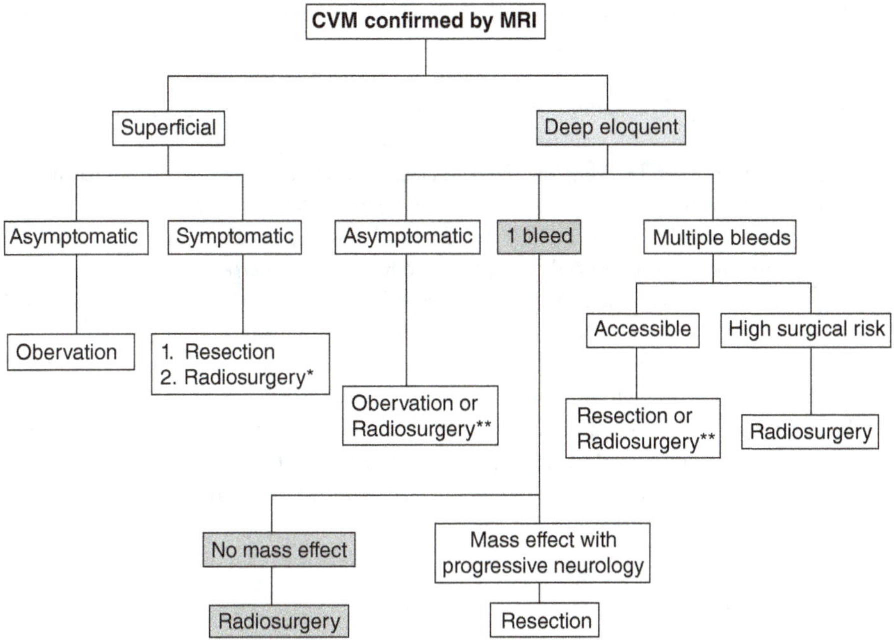

FIGURE 35.2   Flow chart showing the proposed management algorithm for cerebral cavernomas.[12]

TAKE HOME MESSAGE

- *Management options for cavernous malformations include* observation, microsurgical excision, and radiosurgery.
- GKRS is effective in reducing seizure frequency in patients presenting with drug-resistant epilepsy.
- It is also effective in reducing recurrent bleeds in cavernous malformations.
- Acute radiation effects are rare nowadays, due to the advent of low-dose protocols, conformal MRI, gamma radiation-based devices, etc.

REFERENCES

1. Gross BA, Lin N, Du R, Day AL. The natural history of intracranial cavernous malformations. *Neurosurg Focus.* 2011;30(6):E24.
2. Akers A, Al-Shahi Salman R, A Awad I, et al. Synopsis of Guidelines for the Clinical Management of Cerebral Cavernous Malformations: Consensus Recommendations Based on Systematic Literature Review by the Angioma Alliance Scientific Advisory Board Clinical Experts Panel. *Neurosurgery.* 2017;80(5):665-680.
3. Attar A, Ugur HC, Savas A, Yüceer N, Egemen N. Surgical treatment of intracranial cavernous angiomas. *J Clin Neurosci.* 2001;8(3):235-239.
4. Kim MS, Pyo SY, Jeong YG, Lee SI, Jung YT, Sim JH. Gamma knife surgery for intracranial cavernous hemangioma. *J Neurosurg.* 2005;102 Suppl:102-106.

5. Gewirtz RJ, Steinberg GK, Crowley R, Levy RP. Pathological changes in surgically resected angiographically occult vascular malformations after radiation. *Neurosurgery*. 1998;42(4): 738-743.

6. Nagy G, Kemeny AA. Radiosurgery for cerebral cavernomas. *J Neurosurg Sci*. 2015;59(3): 295-306.

7. Robinson JR Jr, Awad IA, Magdinec M, Paranandi L. Factors predisposing to clinical disability in patients with cavernous malformations of the brain. *Neurosurgery*. 1993;32(5):730-736.

8. Casazza M, Broggi G, Franzini A, et al. Supratentorial cavernous angiomas and epileptic seizures: preoperative course and postoperative outcome. *Neurosurgery*. 1996;39(1):26-34.

9. Régis J, Bartolomei F, Kida Y, et al. Radiosurgery for epilepsy associated with cavernous malformation: retrospective study in 49 patients. *Neurosurgery*. 2000;47(5):1091-1097.

10. Pham M, Gross BA, Bendok BR, Awad IA, Batjer HH. Radiosurgery for angiographically occult vascular malformations. *Neurosurg Focus*. 2009;26(5):E16.

11. Park SH, Hwang SK. Gamma knife radiosurgery for symptomatic brainstem intra-axial cavernous malformations. *World Neurosurg*. 2013;80(6):e261-e266.

12. Nagy G, Kemeny AA. Stereotactic radiosurgery of intracranial cavernous malformations. *Neurosurg Clin N Am*. 2013;24(4):575-589.

Gamma Knife Surgery in Intracranial Dural Arteriovenous Fistulas

36

Prachi Singh | Deepak Agrawal

KEY LEARNING POINTS

1. High-resolution stereotactic MRI and digital subtraction angiography (DSA) are essential for accurate dose planning in GKRS for dural arteriovenous fistulas (dAVFs).
2. The typical margin dose for dAVFs ranges from 18–25 Gy, with a prescription dose of 25 Gy at the 50% isodose line commonly used.
3. Post-GKRS follow-up using contrast MRI and DSA is crucial for evaluating treatment efficacy. Significant volume reduction and complete obliteration of the dAVF can occur with GKRS alone.
4. GKRS is preferred for its non-invasive nature, lower risk of infection, and absence of surgical or catheter-related complications. GKRS achieves complete obliteration in 50%–93% of treated dAVFs, with an average latency period of 23 months.
5. It is effective for both aggressive (high haemorrhage risk) and non-aggressive dAVFs, offering a non-invasive alternative to surgery and embolisation with comparable clinical and radiological outcomes.

INTRODUCTION

The management of intracranial dural arteriovenous fistulas (dAVFs) has evolved to include multimodal approaches, with stereotactic radiosurgery (SRS) emerging as a viable treatment. Initially reserved for non-aggressive dAVFs, SRS is now used for aggressive cases, offering comparable outcomes to embolisation and surgery. SRS achieves complete obliteration in 50–93% of cases, with an average latency of 23 months. While embolisation provides immediate relief, SRS is less invasive and preferred by patients due to lower risks of infection and complications. Factors influencing SRS success include location, absence of cortical venous drainage, and smaller target volumes. SRS is increasingly considered a first-line treatment.

HISTORY AND EXAMINATION

A 14-year-old male presented with complaints of headache, pulsatile tinnitus and two episodes of generalised tonic-clonic seizure. On examination, no neurological deficits were present. He underwent an MRI followed by DSA and was diagnosed with right petrous Dural AVF with Cortical Venous Drainage (CVD). The patient and his guardians were apprised of the disease and offered the option of GKRS, embolisation or surgery along with all the pros and cons of the different procedures. They decided to go ahead with GKRS.

IMAGING

Cerebral angiography, complemented by high-resolution stereotactic MR images, is essential for dose planning. Although most small dAVFs are not fully visualised on MR images, MRI remains valuable for assessing the 3-dimensional conformity of the dose plan and identifying critical brain structures at risk. Additionally, MRI aids in selecting the optimal dose, as the margin dose is determined based on the risk to nearby critical structures. High-quality digital subtraction angiography is crucial for accurate radiosurgery dose planning for dAVFs. We need to ensure that the dAVF is visible in both AP and lateral views, all fiducial markers are identifiable, and adequate subtraction views are obtained. The images that best depict the dAVF should then be selected and uploaded to the dose planning system and co-registered with the MRI.

GK PROTOCOL

The patient underwent an MRI the day before treatment delivery. On the day of treatment, the Leksell stereotactic G frame was first secured with anterior posts fixed above the supraorbital ridge and posterior posts fixed to the occipital bone. The patient was then taken for digital subtraction angiography which was fused with the MRI.

Planning was done on the co-registered MRI and DSA which involved demarcating the target lesion and at-risk area, i.e., the brainstem and the right cochlea. The dose prescription is determined by the location and volume of the dAVF. The margin dose for the dAVF typically ranges from 18 to 25 Gy in a single session. The doses are determined by the location and volume of the dAVF. The margin dose for the dAVF typically ranges from 18 to 25 Gy in a single session. We used lightning software for planning the dose delivery after setting the prescription dose of 25 Gy at 50% isodose line. Dural AVF with a total volume of 3.9cc receives a mean dose of 33.2 ± 5.6 Gy.

FOLLOW UP

The patient underwent follow-up contrast MRI and DSA after 3 years. (Fig. 36.1 and Fig. 36.2 depict 3 years of follow-up MRI and DSA respectively). The follow-up MRI shows a significant reduction in volume, from a treatment volume of 3.9cc to 0.6cc residual volume. The follow-up DSA showed no residual AVF. The patient reported improvement in symptoms and no episodes of seizure 3 years post-GKRS. As a result, anti-epileptics were gradually tapered off.

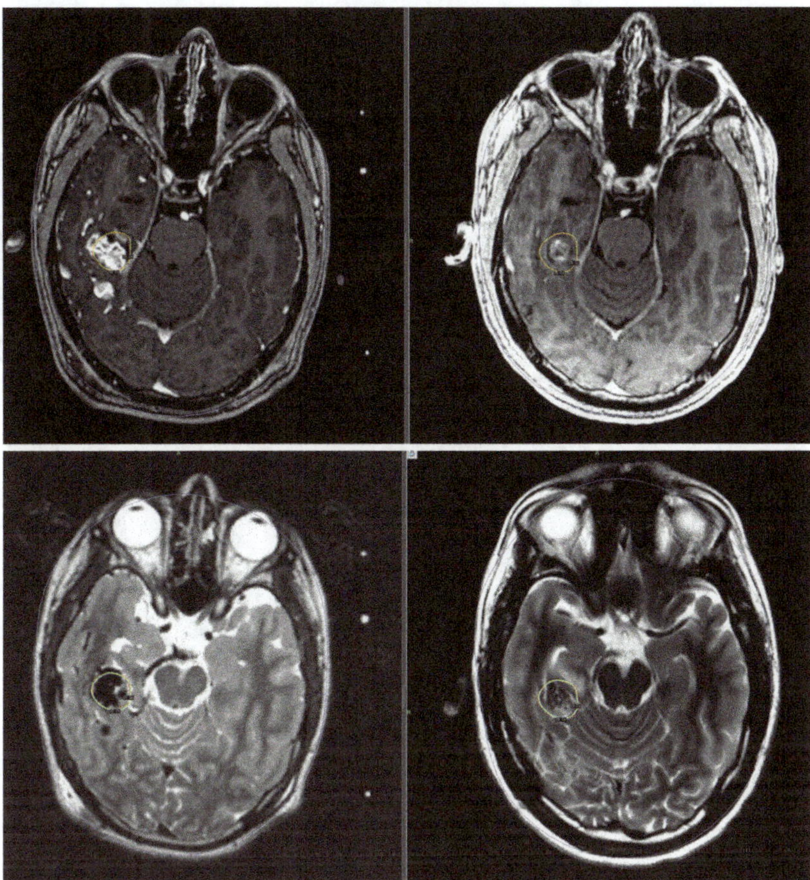

FIGURE 36.1   Right side- treatment MRI :T1+C (above) and T2 (below) sequences, Left side- follow up MRI at 3 year: T1+C and T2 sequences. Red line marks the target and the yellow line shows the 25 Gy isodose line. The follow up MRI shows significant reduction in volume from 3.9 cm3 treatment volume to 0.6 cm3 residual volume.

DISCUSSION

The management of dural arteriovenous fistulas (dAVFs) has evolved significantly over the decades, transitioning from observational approaches to advanced multimodal therapies that integrate embolisation, surgery, and radiosurgery, all tailored to dAVF characteristics. Stereotactic radiosurgery was first utilised for treating arteriovenous malformations (AVMs) in 1970 and later extended to the management of dural arteriovenous fistulas (dAVFs) in the late 1970s.

For achievement of successful treatment outcome of intracranial dAVFs, treatment strategies should be decided according to the angiographic characteristics of the dural AVF- based on the location, venous ectasia and drainage pattern as well as clinical characteristics such as the severity of the symptoms and perceived risk

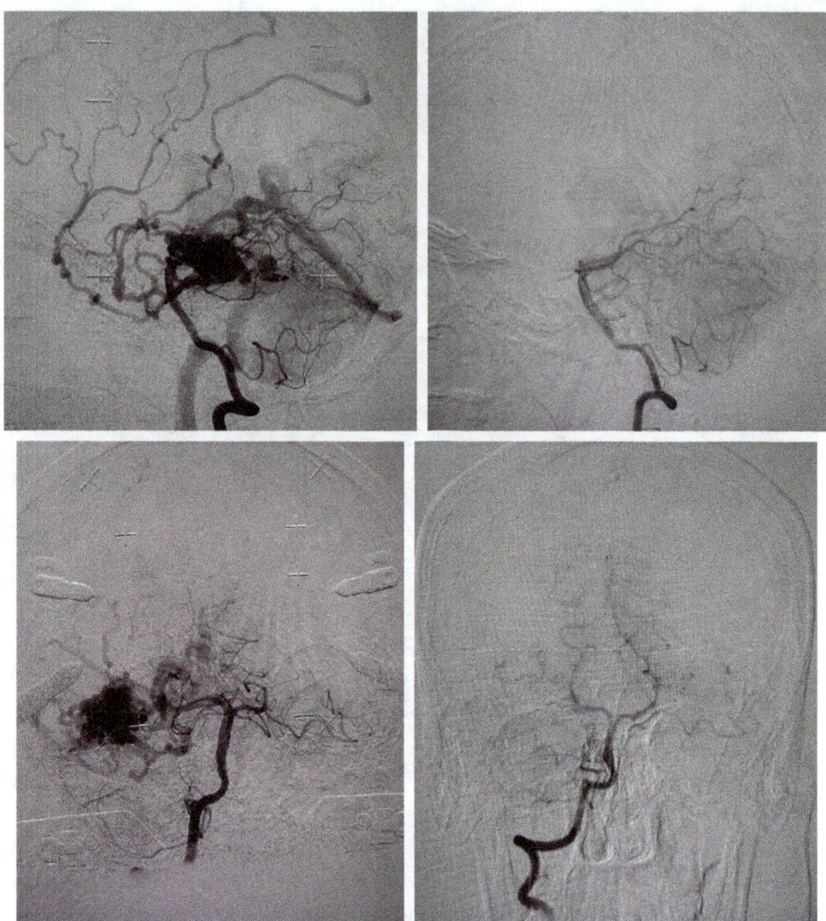

FIGURE 36.2 Right side- treatment DSA: Lateral(above) and PA (below) sequences, Left side-follow up DSA at 3 year Lateral (above) and PA (below). The follow up DSA shows no residual AVF.

for intracranial haemorrhage. While Endovascular embolisation and surgery have long been regarded as the preferred treatment modalities due to the achievement of immediate obliteration, emerging evidence has established GKRS as a desirable treatment option. Despite its delayed obliteration time (at least 6 months),[1,2] GKRS is effective for both aggressive (high rates of intracranial haemorrhage- ICH, neurological deficits and with cortical venous drainage- CVD) and benign/non-aggressive groups (lack of CVD, Cognard type I and IIa, low rates of ICH and transient or mild neurological symptoms).

Complete obliteration is reported in 50%–93% of dAVF, treated by GKRS with the average latency period of dAVF closure reported as 23 months (minimum 6 months).[1,2,5]

Initially, Gamma Knife Radiosurgery (GKRS) was reserved as a treatment option for dAVFs for non-aggressive dAVFs, as these are less likely to cause immediate complications. GKRS was also considered for residual or recurrent dAVFs as an adjunct to embolisation and surgery, as well as inaccessible dAVFs located in areas that are surgically challenging, or inaccessible arterial feeder during angiography. Dural AVFs with CVD are well-known to carry a significantly higher risk of haemorrhage compared to those without CVD, with an annual risk of haemorrhage of 1.4%-3% in patients with unruptured DAVFs with CVD vs 7.4%-46% of rebleed in patients with ruptured dAVFs.[1]

Recent studies[1,3,7] have compared the efficacy of GKRS as a stand-alone treatment option in aggressive dAVFs to endovascular embolisation in terms of clinical improvement, radiological obliteration and risk of haemorrhage in the latency period of around six months before obliteration of the fistula. A study at our institute[1] has shown clinical improvement in 77.78% of the patients who received GKS for DAVF with CVD, and 57.7% in the patients who underwent embolisation (p = 0.431) and complete obliteration of DAVF was seen in 55.56% of the patients in the GKS group and 57.7% of the patients in the embolisation group (p = 1). Still, a controversy exists in terms of its effectiveness as a monotherapy in cases with CVD with studies at different institutes showing contradictory results in terms of risk of subsequent haemorrhage or radiation-related complications. However, none of the studies have reported a drastic increase in the risk of post-GKRS haemorrhage or poor obliteration rate compared to the endovascular group.[1,7] Some studies have advocated for SRS followed by embolisation where embolisation can provide early symptom relief and SRS offers the potential for delayed complete fistula closure.[6]

Factors that have a positive impact on the obliteration rates of DAVF following SRS are the location of DAVF with the cavernous sinus DAVF having much better obliteration rates than DAVF located at other locations, Borden Type I or Cognard Types III or IV DAVFs, absence of CVD, haemorrhage at the time of initial presentation, and target volume lesser than 1.5 mL.[3,4,7]

The most important factor that is to be considered is the growing patients' preference for GKRS as the choice of dAVF treatment owing to the absence of surgical incisions or catheter insertions and lower risk of infection or procedural complications. Latency period haemorrhage and radiation-induced changes to the perinidal parenchyma though not abundantly reported are the potential complications post-GKRS. In contrast, embolisation or surgery, being an invasive procedure, carries a higher risk of serious complications, occurring in up to 25% of cases- Onyx migration, intraparenchymal hematoma, and delayed cerebral venous infarction.[8] Additionally, multiple reports have documented the recurrence of dAVFs that appeared to be cured after embolisation.[6]

TAKE HOME MESSAGE

GKS is safer and at least as effective as embolisation for clinical and radiological outcomes, contrary to the popular perception, GKRS should be considered as the first-line treatment of intracranial DAVF with CVD.

REFERENCES

1. Sardana H, Agrawal D, Pahwa B, Singh MM, Mishra NK, Kale SS. Intracranial Dural Arteriovenous Fistulas with Cortical Venous Drainage: Radiosurgery as an Effective Alternative Treatment. *World Neurosurg*. 2022;158:e922-e928.

2. Sardana H, Agrawal D, Manjunath N. Gamma Knife Radiosurgery: The Gold Standard Treatment for Intracranial Dural Arteriovenous Fistulas without Cortical Venous Drainage. *Neurol India*. 2020;68(4):815-820.

3. Garg K, Agrawal D. Role of Stereotactic Radiosurgery in the Management of Dural AV Fistula. *Neurol India*. 2023;71(Supplement):S109-S114.

4. Niranjan A, Lunsford LD. Stereotactic radiosurgery guidelines for the management of patients with intracranial dural arteriovenous fistulas. *Prog Neurol Surg*. 2013;27:218-226.

5. Wang GC, Chen KP, Chiu TL, Su CF. Treating intracranial dural arteriovenous fistulas with gamma knife radiosurgery: A single-center experience. *Tzu Chi Med J*. 2017;29(1):18-23.

6. Maroufi SF, Fallahi MS, Ghasemi M, Sheehan JP. Stereotactic radiosurgery with versus without embolization for intracranial dural arteriovenous fistulas: a systematic review and meta-analysis. *Neurosurg Focus*. 2024;56(3):E6.

7. Tonetti DA, Gross BA, Jankowitz BT, et al. Reconsidering an important subclass of high-risk dural arteriovenous fistulas for stereotactic radiosurgery. *J Neurosurg*. 2018;130(3):972-976. Published 2018 Mar 16.

8. Baharvahdat H, Ooi YC, Kim WJ, Mowla A, Coon AL, Colby GP. Updates in the management of cranial dural arteriovenous fistula. *Stroke Vasc Neurol*. 2019;5(1):50-58. Published 2019 Nov 21.

SECTION 4

FUNCTIONAL

Gamma Knife Radiosurgery for Trigeminal Neuralgia

37

Sarvesh Goyal | Manoj Phalak

KEY LEARNING POINTS

1. The success rate of GKRS in pain relief for Trigeminal Neuralgia is more than 50% at 5 years.
2. GKRS plays an important role in the management of Trigeminal Neuralgia.
3. Primary GKRS may be offered to elderly patients or those at high surgical risks.
4. Secondary GKRS can be given to patients who fail MVD and/ or those who have failed medical therapy.
5. Repeat GKRS can be considered for patients who experienced good pain relief after initial GKRS.

INTRODUCTION

Trigeminal neuralgia (TN) is a debilitating condition characterised by sudden, unilateral, lancinating pain in the trigeminal nerve distribution. Management options include pharmacological therapy, percutaneous procedures, surgical microvascular decompression (MVD), and stereotactic radiosurgery (SRS). Gamma Knife Radiosurgery (GKRS) has gained prominence as a minimally invasive, effective option for refractory cases. It offers significant pain relief with minimal morbidity, particularly in patients unsuitable for surgery.

CASE PRESENTATION

HISTORY AND EXAMINATION

A 67-year-old male presented with a 6-year history of right-sided facial pain, consistent with trigeminal neuralgia (TN). The pain was described as sharp, stabbing, and intermittent, occurring in the V2 and V3 dermatomes. Episodes were triggered by light tactile stimuli, such as eating and speaking, and were refractory to medical therapy, including carbamazepine and pregabalin. Neurological assessment revealed no deficits. No hypoesthesia or motor weakness in the trigeminal nerve distribution.

IMAGING

MRI Brain: Constructive interference in steady-state (CISS) sequences demonstrated a neurovascular conflict with an anterior inferior cerebellar artery (AICA) loop compressing the right trigeminal nerve at the root entry zone (REZ). There was no evidence of demyelination or mass lesions.

GK PROTOCOL (FIG. 37.1)

The patient underwent GKRS with a target dose of 80 Gy delivered to the retrogasserian zone, approximately 6 mm anterior to the REZ. Care was taken to limit brainstem radiation.

FOLLOW-UP

Significant pain relief was achieved within two weeks post-GKRS, with the patient remaining pain-free at the 5-year follow-up (BNI pain score: 1). No hypoesthesia or other adverse effects were noted during follow-up.

DISCUSSION

The success of GKRS for Trigeminal Neuralgia is influenced by various patient and procedural factors. Immediate pain relief is observed in most patients within days to weeks of GKRS. In the provided case series, 70% of patients achieved significant relief within the first month, with many experiencing complete resolution of symptoms by six months.[9] Long-term pain control declines with time, with approximately 40% of patients pain-free at 5 years. Favourable prognostic factors

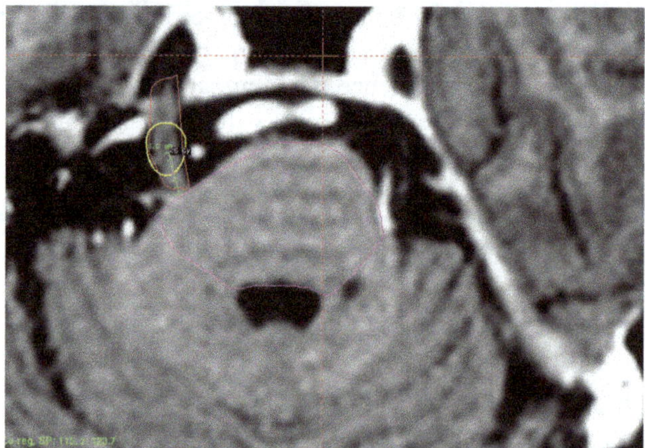

FIGURE 37.1 Trigeminal nerve was detected on T1- and T2-weighted images. A single 4-mm isocenter was used for targeting. The target was placed 6 mm anterior from the junction of the trigeminal nerve and pons in an oblong fashion so that brainstem surface was irradiated at the 20 % isodose line. This meant that the brainstem received less than 16 Gy, which is the critical toxic dose for the brainstem.

for improved outcome include fewer pre-GKRS medications, V1 involvement, and post-GKRS hypoesthesia. Unfavourable factors include previous failed MVD, involvement of V2/V3 dermatomes, and recurrent pain requiring repeat GKRS which can have poorer outcomes.

Repeat GKRS has been attempted up to 4 times after GKRS failure with good to excellent results. Repeat procedures may be associated with higher complication rates, such as numbness, and should be reserved for carefully selected patients.

While GKRS has a distinct advantage in being minimally invasive, its long-term efficacy is slightly inferior to MVD. However, its safety profile makes it particularly suitable for elderly patients and those with significant comorbidities. There is no debate that Microvascular Decompression (MVD) offers the highest rates of long-term pain relief but is associated with surgical risks, including stroke and cranial nerve deficits. Patients with clear neurovascular compression are ideal candidates for MVD. Percutaneous techniques, such as radiofrequency thermocoagulation and glycerol rhizotomy provide immediate relief but are associated with higher recurrence and sensory complications compared to GKRS. Recent studies have explored the use of ANNs to predict outcomes following GKRS for TN. These models integrate multiple variables, such as age, dermatomal involvement, pre-GKRS medications, and post-GKRS numbness, to provide accurate predictions of treatment efficacy. In one study, an ANN model achieved 90.9% accuracy in predicting favourable outcomes, underscoring its potential utility in clinical decision-making.[5]

CONCLUSIONS

Gamma Knife Radiosurgery is an effective, minimally invasive treatment for trigeminal neuralgia, particularly in patients with medically refractory disease. Careful patient selection, precise targeting, and adherence to dose constraints are crucial for maximising efficacy and minimising complications. Future research should focus on predictive models and long-term outcomes

REFERENCES

1. Tuleasca C, Régis J, Sahgal A, De Salles A, Hayashi M, Ma L, et al. Stereotactic radiosurgery for trigeminal neuralgia: A systematic review: International stereotactic radiosurgery society practice guidelines. J Neurosurg 2018;130:733–57.

2. Kedia S. Gamma Knife Radiosurgery for the Management of Trigeminal Neuralgia. Neurology India 2024;72:1316–7.

3. Boling W, Song M, Shih W, Karlsson B. Gamma knife radiosurgery for trigeminal neuralgia: A comparison of dose protocols. Brain Sci 2019;9:134.

4. Lee CC, Chong ST, Chen CJ, Hung SC, Yang HC, Lin CJ, et al. The timing of stereotactic radiosurgery for medically refractory trigeminal neuralgia: The evidence from diffusion tractography images. Acta Neurochir (Wien) 2018;160:977–86.

5. Goyal S, Kedia S, Kumar R, Bisht RK, Agarwal D, Singh M, et al. Role of gamma knife radiosurgery in trigeminal neuralgia–Its long term outcome and prediction using artificial neural network model. J Clin Neurosci 2021;92:61–6.

6. Sharma R, Phalak M, Katiyar V, Borkar S, Kale SS, Mahapatra AK. Microvascular decompression versus stereotactic radiosurgery as primary treatment modality for trigeminal neuralgia: A systematic review and meta-analysis of prospective comparative trials. Neurol India 2018;66:688–94.

7. Kendall E, Ahmad S, Algan O. Dosimetric comparison of sector-blocked and non–sector-blocked Gamma Knife Perfexion treatment plans for trigeminal neuralgia. Medi Dosim 2018;43:390–3.

8. Tohyama S, Hung PS, Zhong J, Hodaie M. Early postsurgical diffusivity metrics for prognostication of long-term pain relief after gamma knife radiosurgery for trigeminal neuralgia. J Neurosurg 2018;131:539–48.

9. Flickinger JC, Pollock BE, Kondziolka D, Phuong LK, Foote RL, Stafford SL, et al. Does increased nerve length within the treatment volume improve trigeminal neuralgia radiosurgery? A prospective double-blind, randomized study. Int J Radiat Oncol Biol Phys 2001;51:449–54.

10. Tuleasca C, Paddick I, Hopewell JW, Jones B, Millar WT, Hamdi H, et al. Establishment of a therapeutic ratio for gamma knife radiosurgery of trigeminal neuralgia: The critical importance of biologically effective dose versus physical dose. World Neurosurg 2020;134:e204–13.

Management of Intractable Cancer Pain Using Gamma Knife Radiosurgery

38

Deepak Agrawal | R Shiva Krishna

KEY LEARNING POINTS

1. GKRS to pituitary stalk (160 Gy at 50% isodose) is an underutilised technique for debilitating cancer pain.
2. The onset of pain relief is apparent within hours of GKRS and may last till death.
3. Complete pain relief occurs within 3–5 days of GKRS.

INTRODUCTION

Gamma Knife radiosurgery (GKRS) has been widely adopted for the treatment of various intracranial pathologies, including brain tumours and vascular malformations. However, it in functional disorders such as intractable chronic pain remain underutilised.[1] Historically, surgical or chemical hypophysectomy was employed for managing intractable cancer pain, but these approaches were often associated with significant complications, including panhypopituitarism, diabetes insipidus, and visual dysfunction.[2] In contrast, GKRS offers a non-invasive alternative with a more favourable safety profile.[3] This case report presents a patient with severe cancer-related pain treated with GKRS with pituitary stalk irradiation, providing insights into its clinical application and outcomes.

CASE PRESENTATION

PATIENT HISTORY

A 43-year-old female with a known history of bronchial carcinoid tumour underwent a VATS-assisted right lower lobectomy in 2024. PET-CT showed Tracer avid ill-defined isodense lesion in the left temporal lobe treated with Gamma Knife radiosurgery in 2024.

During her first GKRS session, performed for a hypermetabolic lesion in the left temporal pole, imaging revealed a $7.2 \times 12 \times 11$ mm dural-based lesion abutting the lesser wing of the sphenoid. The lesion was treated with a maximum dose of 18 Gy, while critical structures, including the optic nerve and chiasm, received minimal radiation exposure. Postoperative recovery was uneventful, and the patient was discharged on antiepileptics and supportive medications.

Despite initial management, the patient presented with recurrent seizures and debilitating pain in the head, neck, upper back and bilateral lower extremities for four months, unresponsive to analgesics.

CLINICAL EXAMINATION

Neurological examination revealed no focal deficits. Contrast-enhanced MRI scan and PET-CT scan revealed no new metastases and showed stable disease compared to the prior scan in 2024. The patient reported a VAS score of 8 despite taking 30 mg of Morphine every 4–6 hours.

TREATMENT DETAILS

The patient was scheduled for a second Gamma Knife radiosurgery session targeting the pituitary stalk to address her intractable pain. Leksell Coordinate Frame G was used for fixation Configuration and planning was done on Gamma plan version 11.3.2. 120 Gy at 50% isodose was delivered, ensuring minimal radiation exposure to adjacent critical structures. 0.012 cc of the pituitary stalk was marked for irradiation, and 0.010 cc (80.1%) of the pituitary stalk received 120 Gy. Brainstem, bilateral optic nerve, and optic chiasma shielding were done. Dose-volume histograms confirmed adequate targeting of the pituitary stalk, with protective measures for the brainstem, optic nerves, and chiasm.

OUTCOME

Post-procedure, the patient reported significant pain relief on day 3, with a VAS score of 4. Morphine dosage was tapered to 30 mg every 12 hours 3 days after GKRS. At the 1 week follow-up, the patient reported a VAS score of 2, and morphine was completely discontinued, enabling improved quality of life and reduced dependency on opioid analgesics.

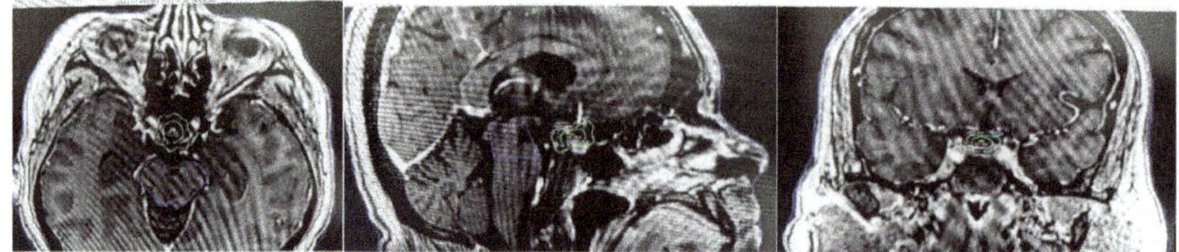

FIGURE 38.1   Contrast-enhanced MR axial, sagittal and coronal images of the patient demonstrating pituitary stalk irradiation.

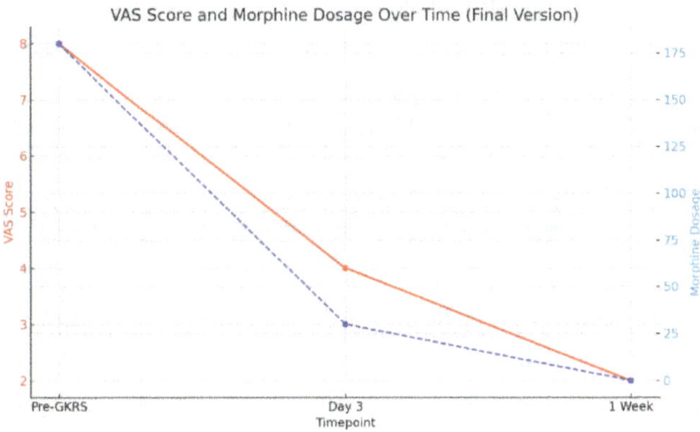

FIGURE 38.2   Shows trend in VAS score (in red) and Daily morphine dose (in blue) after GKRS.

DISCUSSION

Gamma Knife radiosurgery for pituitary stalk irradiation has emerged as a promising modality for managing intractable cancer-related pain.[4] By delivering high-dose targeted radiation, this technique stimulates endorphin release and modulates nociceptive pathways, providing rapid and sustained analgesic effects.[1] Evidence from multicenter studies and case series supports its efficacy in alleviating pain within days of treatment, with minimal complications compared to traditional hypophysectomy.

The mechanism of pain relief through GKRS is believed to involve the modulation of neurochemical pathways. High-dose irradiation of the pituitary stalk likely triggers the release of endogenous opioids, including beta-endorphins, which play a key role in pain modulation.[1] Additionally, GKRS may influence hormonal pathways, although the precise mechanisms remain poorly understood. Studies have reported that the analgesic effects often precede noticeable changes in pituitary hormone levels, suggesting a complex interplay of neural and endocrine factors.[3]

In this case, the patient's pain was refractory to conventional analgesics, including high-dose opioids, underscoring the need for alternative interventions. The rapid pain relief observed post-GKRS aligns with prior studies reporting significant symptom improvement in 80-90% of patients treated for cancer-related pain.[5] The durability of this effect, however, varies among patients, with some experiencing recurrence within months.[2] This variability highlights the importance of patient selection and individualised treatment planning to maximise therapeutic outcomes.

Safety remains a critical consideration in the use of GKRS. Modern dose-planning techniques, as demonstrated in this case, prioritise the protection of critical structures, such as the optic nerves, chiasm, and brainstem, thereby minimising adverse effects. The absence of hormonal or visual dysfunction in this patient further underscores the potential of GKRS as a safe alternative to traditional hypophysectomy.[1]

The broader implications of this modality extend beyond cancer-related pain to other refractory pain syndromes, such as post-stroke thalamic pain, where similar mechanisms may be leveraged for pain relief. Future directions for research include exploring the long-term efficacy of GKRS in managing cancer-related pain, identifying biomarkers to predict patient response, and optimising dosimetric parameters to enhance outcomes. Additionally, randomised controlled trials are needed to establish standardised protocols and compare GKRS with other palliative interventions.[5]

CONCLUSION

This case demonstrates the successful application of Gamma Knife radiosurgery for managing intractable cancer pain. The rapid and sustained pain relief achieved with minimal adverse effects underscores its value as a therapeutic option for patients with advanced malignancies. Future studies should focus on standardising treatment protocols and exploring its broader applications in pain management.

REFERENCES

1. Kwon KH, Nam TK, Im YS, Lee JI. Pituitary Irradiation by Gamma Knife in Intractable Cancer Pain. J Korean Neurosurg Soc. 2004;286–90.
2. Hayashi M, Taira T, Chernov M, et al. Role of pituitary radiosurgery for the management of intractable pain and potential future applications. *Stereotact Funct Neurosurg*. 2003;81(1-4): 75-83.
3. Utsuki S, Oka H, Miyajima Y, Fujii K. Usefulness of gamma knife pituitary surgery to control thalamic pain after treatment of thalamic malignant lymphoma and report of pathology of gamma knife lesions. *Neurol India*. 2009;57(2):185-187.
4. Hayashi M, Taira T, Chernov M, et al. Gamma knife surgery for cancer pain-pituitary gland-stalk ablation: a multicenter prospective protocol since 2002. *J Neurosurg*. 2002;97(5 Suppl):433-437.
5. Chernov MF, Hayashi M. Pituitary Radiosurgery for Management of Intractable Pain: Tokyo Women's Medical University Experience and Literature Review. *Acta Neurochir Suppl*. 2021;128:133-144.

Gamma Knife Radiosurgery in Obsessive-Compulsive Disorder (OCD)

39

Deepak Agrawal | Mahnaaz Sultana Azeem

KEY LEARNING POINTS

1. Obsessive-Compulsive Disorder is a chronic neuropsychiatric disorder characterised by obsessive thoughts or fears, compulsive repetitive behaviours, and anxiety that disrupt daily functioning and activities.

2. Pathophysiology - dysregulation of the cortico-striato-thalamo-cortical loop causes hyperactivity in orbitofrontal and anterior cingulate cortex, deficient inhibitory control from caudate nucleus and dysfunctional serotonin modulation.

3. Various conventional treatment options, including selective serotonin reuptake inhibitors, cognitive behavioural therapy, and electroconvulsive therapy, are in practice. However, 10-20% of patients fail to respond to treatment.

4. Interventions like Deep Brain Stimulation and lesioning procedures like anterior capsulotomy and cingulotomy are considered for refractory cases.

5. Gamma Knife Radiosurgery (GKRS) is a minimally invasive lesioning-based approach targeting the anterior limb of internal capsule and cingulate gyrus. This disrupts the hyperactive CSTC loop and allows controlled modulation of pathological circuits while minimising side effects.

6. The treatment planning and outcomes are highlighted in this case-based discussion.

7. Various studies have shown good control rates or remissions in refractory OCD cases treated with GKRS.

INTRODUCTION

Obsessive-compulsive disorder (OCD) is a chronic, debilitating neuropsychiatric disorder affecting approximately 2-3% of the population. It is characterised by intrusive obsessions (unwanted thoughts, fears, or urges) and compulsions (repetitive behaviours or mental acts performed to reduce anxiety). The disorder disrupts daily functioning, leading to social, occupational, and personal impairment.

While selective serotonin reuptake inhibitors (SSRIs) and Cognitive-behavioral therapy (CBT) are the mainstays of treatment, approximately 10-20% of patients remain refractory despite optimal therapy. In such cases, neurosurgical interventions like deep brain stimulation (DBS) and lesioning procedures (anterior capsulotomy, cingulotomy) are considered.

Gamma Knife Radiosurgery (GKRS) has emerged as a minimally invasive, lesioning-based approach, targeting the anterior limb of the internal capsule (ALIC) and cingulate gyrus. GKRS disrupts the hyperactive cortico-striato-thalamo-cortical (CSTC) loop, which is central to OCD pathophysiology. The gradual nature of radiation-induced lesions allows for controlled modulation of pathological circuits while minimising side effects.[1-4]

This chapter presents a case of severe OCD, and the rationale for GKRS, treatment planning, expected outcomes, complications, and clinical insights into its role in managing this condition.

HISTORY

A 29-year-old woman, who suffered from severe OCD since adolescence, presented to our department. Her symptoms primarily involve:

- Contamination fears: Excessive washing and avoidance behaviours.
- Repetitive checking rituals: Obsessively verifying locks, stove knobs, and water taps.
- Intrusive thoughts: Persistent fears of harming family members, despite no intent or history of aggression.

Her OCD worsened over the past decade, significantly affecting her quality of life. She lost her job, became socially withdrawn, and required constant family supervision, as her compulsions consumed more than 10 hours per day.

PREVIOUS TREATMENTS INCLUDED

1. Pharmacotherapy:
   - SSRIs (fluvoxamine, fluoxetine, sertraline) at maximum doses.
   - Clomipramine (TCA) augmentation.
   - Atypical antipsychotics (aripiprazole, risperidone) failed to yield significant improvement.
2. Cognitive-Behavioral Therapy (CBT):
   - Extensive trials of exposure and response prevention (ERP).
   - Initially, there was mild improvement, but relapses occurred repeatedly.
3. Electroconvulsive Therapy (ECT):
   - Given for comorbid depression, with no significant impact on OCD symptoms.

EXAMINATION AND PSYCHIATRIC ASSESSMENT

- Mental Status Examination (MSE):
   - Alert, cooperative, but highly anxious and preoccupied with intrusive thoughts.
   - Engaged in ritualistic behaviours during the interview.
   - No delusions or hallucinations.

- Yale-Brown Obsessive-Compulsive Scale (Y-BOCS):
  - Score of 36/40, indicating extreme OCD.

INVESTIGATIONS

1. Structural MRI:
   - No gross abnormalities, but volumetric analysis showed increased connectivity in the CSTC loop.
2. Functional MRI:
   - Hyperactivity in the orbitofrontal cortex (OFC), anterior cingulate cortex (ACC), and caudate nucleus (Fig. 39.1).
3. Neuropsychological Testing:
   - Preserved cognitive function, with no executive dysfunction.

GAMMA KNIFE PROTOCOL

Given her severe, treatment-refractory OCD, the patient was considered a candidate for Gamma Knife Radiosurgery (GKRS) targeting the anterior limb of the internal capsule (ALIC) bilaterally and 130 Gy given using a single 4mm shot on each side. The patient underwent the above procedure and the immediate post-GKRS period was uneventful (Fig. 39.1).

FOLLOW-UP

The patient was followed up with an MRI, 6 months after completion of GKRS and 6 monthly assessments with Y-BOCS. There was a reduction of hyperactive

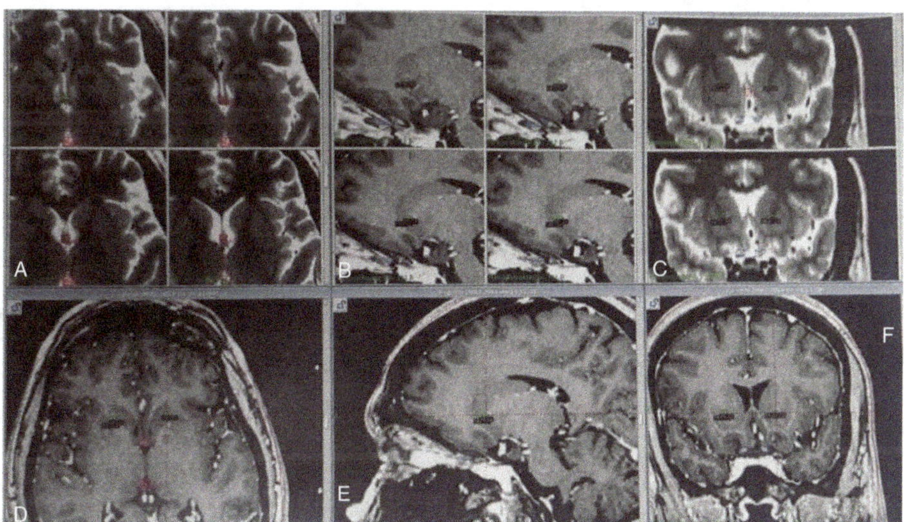

FIGURE 39.1   (A–F) Functional MRI showing hyperactivity in CSTC circuits which helps make a stereotactic MRI-based ALIC targeting plan for GKRS.

CSTC circuits 6 months after treatment and the Y-BOCS curve improved over a 24-month period. The patient experienced 80% symptomatic improvement by 18 months and partially resumed her daily activities, with the YBOCS decreasing to 7/36. She was advised continuation of cognitive behavioural therapy and 6 monthly follow-ups.

DISCUSSION

OCD arises due to dysregulation of the cortico-striato-thalamo-cortical (CSTC) loop, primarily due to hyperactivity in the orbitofrontal cortex (OFC) and anterior cingulate cortex (ACC).[3] Other causes include deficient inhibitory control from the caudate nucleus, leading to repetitive compulsions, as well as dysfunctional serotonin modulation, which explains SSRI efficacy in some cases.[1]

GKRS disrupts hyperactive circuits by lesioning the ALIC, which modulates connections between the prefrontal cortex, thalamus, striatum, and limbic system. The goal is to reduce overactive connectivity, leading to symptom improvement over months to years.

CLINICAL OUTCOMES AND EFFICACY

- 35-60% of patients experience significant Y-BOCS reduction (≥35%).[2]
- Some patients show delayed responses (2 years post-GKRS).[4]
- A 35% reduction in Y-BOCS is considered a responder.[3]
- D'Astous et al. (2013)[1] reported 36.8% complete response, 10.5% partial response, and only two cases of complications (edema or brain necrosis).
- Amitabh Gupta et al. (2019)[4] reported 45% of responders, with 40% achieving remission over a two-year period.
- Peker et al. (2020)[2] reported 75% complete response and 25% non-responders.
- Rasmussen et al. (2018)[3] observed a 56% improvement rate.

Complications include transient mood changes (apathy, euphoria), rare cognitive side effects (delayed executive dysfunction), and radiation-induced cyst formation (very rare, <2%).[1]

TAKE HOME MESSAGE

Gamma Knife Radiosurgery is a viable, minimally invasive alternative for severe, treatment-resistant OCD. While results develop gradually, its safety and efficacy profile make it a promising intervention in modern psychiatric neurosurgery.

REFERENCES

1. D'Astous M, Cottin S, Roy M, Picard C, Cantin L. Bilateral stereotactic anterior capsulotomy for obsessive-compulsive disorder: long-term follow-up. *J Neurol Neurosurg Psychiatry*. 2013;84(11):1208-1213.

2. Peker S, Samanci MY, Yilmaz M, Sengoz M, Ulku N, Ogel K. Efficacy and Safety of Gamma Ventral Capsulotomy for Treatment-Resistant Obsessive-Compulsive Disorder: A Single-Center Experience. *World Neurosurg*. 2020;141:e941-e952.

3. Rasmussen SA, Noren G, Greenberg BD, et al. Gamma Ventral Capsulotomy in Intractable Obsessive-Compulsive Disorder. *Biol Psychiatry*. 2018;84(5):355-364.

4. Gupta A, Shepard MJ, Xu Z, et al. An International Radiosurgery Research Foundation Multicenter Retrospective Study of Gamma Ventral Capsulotomy for Obsessive Compulsive Disorder. *Neurosurgery*. 2019;85(6):808-816.

Publications From Gamma Knife Centre, AIIMS Delhi

1. Sharma MS, Singh R, Kale SS, Agrawal D, Sharma BS, Mahapatra AK. Tumor control and hearing preservation after Gamma Knife radiosurgery for vestibular schwannomas in neurofibromatosis type 2. J Neurooncol. 2010;98(2):265-270.
   Citations: 56

2. Goyal N, Agrawal D, Singla R, Kale SS, Singh M, Sharma BS. Stereotactic radiosurgery in hemangioblastoma: Experience over 14 years. J Neurosci Rural Pract. 2016;7(1):23-27.
   Citations: 16

3. Bose R, Agrawal D, Singh M, et al. Draining vein shielding in intracranial arteriovenous malformations during gamma-knife: a new way of preventing post gamma-knife edema and hemorrhage. Neurosurgery. 2015;76(5):623-632.
   Citations: 15

4. Prasad GL, Sharma MS, Kale SS, Agrawal D, Singh M, Sharma BS. Gamma Knife radiosurgery in the treatment of abducens nerve schwannomas: a retrospective study. J Neurosurg. 2016;125(4):832-837.
   Citations: 13

5. Kasliwal MK, Kale SS, Gupta A, et al. Does hemorrhagic presentation in cerebral arteriovenous malformations affect obliteration rate after gamma knife radiosurgery?. Clin Neurol Neurosurg. 2008;110(8):804-809.
   Citations: 12

6. Sardana H, Agrawal D, Manjunath N. Gamma Knife Radiosurgery: The Gold Standard Treatment for Intracranial Dural Arteriovenous Fistulas without Cortical Venous Drainage. Neurol India. 2020 Jul-Aug;68(4):815-820.
   Citations: 6

7. Verma S, Agrawal D, Singh M. Role of Gamma Knife Radiosurgery in the Management of Functional Disorders - A Literature Review. Neurol India. 2023;71(Supplement):S49-S58.
   Citations: 5

8. Pahwa B, Agrawal D. Role of novel policy implementation for Gamma Knife (GK) procedures in improving access to neurosurgical care in lower middle income countries (LMICs) GK in LMICs. World Neurosurg X. 2023;18:100166. Published 2023 Jan 31.
   Citations: 5

9. Mishra H, Pahwa B, Agrawal D, M Ch MS, M Ch SSK. Gamma knife radiosurgery as an efficacious treatment for paediatric central nervous system tumours: a retrospective study of 61 neoplasms. Childs Nerv Syst. 2022;38(5):909-918.
   Citations: 4

10. Kedia S, Santhoor H, Singh M. Adverse Radiation Effects Following Gamma Knife Radiosurgery. Neurol India. 2023;71(Supplement):S59-S67.
   Citations: 4

11. Garg K, Singh M. Role of Stereotactic Radiosurgery in Pituitary Adenomas. Neurol India. 2020;68(Supplement):S123-S128.
   Citations: 4

12. Sardana H, Agrawal D, Pahwa B, Singh MM, Mishra NK, Kale SS. Intracranial Dural Arteriovenous Fistulas with Cortical Venous Drainage: Radiosurgery as an Effective Alternative Treatment. World Neurosurg. 2022;158:e922-e928.
   Citations: 3

13. Garg K, Agrawal D. Role of Stereotactic Radiosurgery in the Management of Dural AV Fistula. Neurol India. 2023;71(Supplement):S109-S114.
   Citations: 2

14. Garg K, Agrawal D. Role of Stereotactic Radiosurgery in the Management of Dural AV Fistula. Neurol India. 2023;71(Supplement):S109-S114.
   Citations: 2

15. Pahwa B, Kurwale N, Agrawal D. Evaluation of periprocedural anxiety during Gamma Knife radiosurgery (GKRS) frame fixation for brain lesions. Clin Neurol Neurosurg. 2022;217:107242.
   Citations: 2

16. Sri Krishna GS, Pahwa B, Jagdevan A, Singh M, Kale S, Agrawal D. Tumor Control and Hearing Preservation After Gamma Knife Radiosurgery for Vestibular Schwannomas in Neurofibromatosis Type 2-A Retrospective Analysis of 133 Tumors. World Neurosurg. 2023;171:e820-e827.

17. Naik V, Pahwa B, Singh M, Kale S, Agrawal D. Correlation Based on the WHO Grading with Tumor Control and Clinical Outcome Following Gamma Knife Radiosurgery in Meningiomas. Neurol India. 2023;71(Supplement):S140-S145.

18. Agrawal M, Mishra S, Garg K, et al. Trends in Stereotactic Radiosurgery for Intracranial and Spinal Pathologies: Analysis of the Top 100 Most Cited Articles. Neurol India. 2023;71(Suppl):S39-S48.

19. S Rai HI, Agrawal D, Singh M, Kale SS. Early Gamma Knife Therapy (Without EBRT) in Operated Patients of Glioblastoma Multiforme. Neurol India. 2023;71(Supplement):S183-S188.

20. Mishra S, Kumar AG, Garg K, et al. Role of Stereotactic Radiosurgery for Cavernous Sinus Hemangiomas - An Individual Patient Data-Based Meta-Analysis. Neurol India. 2023;71(Supplement):S21-S30.

21. Verma SK, Agrawal D, Santhoor HA, Singh M, Kale SS. Gamma Knife Stereotactic Radiosurgery for Giant Intracranial Tumors - A Series of 70 Patients. Neurol India. 2023;71(Supplement):S123-S132.

22. Garg K, Agrawal D. Role of Stereotactic Radiosurgery in Glial Tumors. Neurol India. 2023;71(Supplement):S207-S214.

23. Raheja A, Sharma MS, Singh M, Agrawal D, Kale SS, Sharma SC. Adjuvant Gamma Knife Radiosurgery for Advanced Juvenile Nasopharyngeal Angiofibroma. Neurol India. 2021;69(5):1438-1441.

24. Goyal S, Pandey K, Kedia S, Sebastian LJD, Agrawal D. Unforeseen outcomes: Unveiling cyst formation post stereotactic radiosurgery in brain arteriovenous malformations cases. J Clin Neurosci. 2024;128:110785.

25. Gupta S, Agrawal D, Kedia S, Kale SS. Should post-operative stereotactic radiosurgery be the standard of care in Craniopharyngioma patients? World Neurosurg X. 2024 Feb 25;22:100327.

26. Singh B, Agrawal D, Garg A, Singh M, Chandra PS, Kale SS. A Prospective Study on Perfusion MRI Changes in Intracranial Meningiomas Following Gamma Knife Therapy. Neurol India. 2024;72(4):763-767.

27. Agrawal D. Arteriovenous malformation radiosurgery grading. J Neurosurg. 2002;97(3): 740-741.

28. Phalak M, Lomi N, Ganeshkumar A, et al. Gamma Knife Radiosurgery for Uveal Melanoma: Our Experience and Thematic Review. Neurol India. 2023;71(Supplement):S168-S173.

29. Kedia S, Sahu R. Gamma-knife therapy in intracranial Langerhans cell histiocytosis with systemic involvement. Indian J Med Res. 2020;152(Suppl 1):S144-S145.

30. Garg K, Singh M. Volume Fractionation Stereotactic Radiosurgery for Large Volume Intracranial Arteriovenous Malformations. Neurol India. 2023;71(Supplement):S82-S89.

31. Garg K, Singh M. Role of Stereotactic Radiosurgery in Skull Base Paragangliomas - A Narrative Review. Neurol India. 2023;71(Supplement):S153-S160.

32. Kedia S, Goyal S, Garg K, et al. Serum Vascular Endothelial Growth Factor and Endostatin as an Adjunct to Clinical Decision Making in Managing Radiation-induced Changes Post Gamma Knife Radiosurgery in Spetzler Martin Grade 3 Arteriovenous Malformations Patients: A Pilot Study. World Neurosurg. 2024;189:e864-e871.

33. Tripathi M, Agarwal D, Singh M, Chandra PS. Gamma Knife Radiosurgery: A Delicate Yet Powerful Neurosurgical Knife. Neurol India. 2023;71(12 Suppl 2):S2.

Gamma Knife Legacy

Dr. PN Tondon
1965 - 1984
1986 - 1988

Dr. AK Banerji
1984 - 1986
1988 - 1990

Dr. Ravi Bhatia
1990-1994

Dr. V S Mehta
1994 - 2006

Dr. AK Mahapatra
2006 - 2006
2009 - 2012
2016 - 2016

Dr. BS Sharma
2006 - 2009
2012 - 2016
2016 - 2017

Prof. SS Kale
2017 Onward

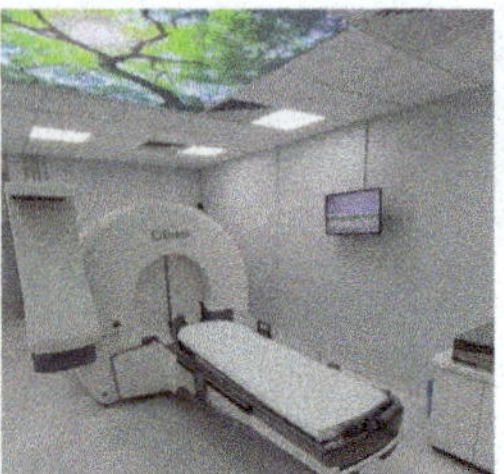

Gamma Knife Icon

The famous 'Laal Building'

Dedicated Gamma Knife MRI

Gamma Knife Staff

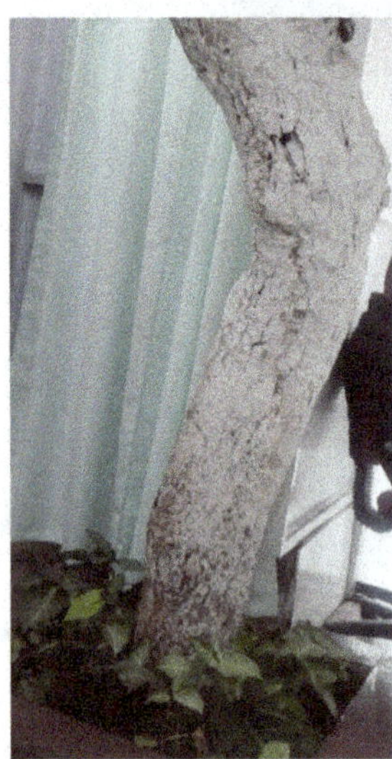

The infamous tree of GK growing inside the MRI anteroom

AIIMS dressed as a bride

The Defining Image of AIIMS New Delhi

More Gamma Knife Staff

www.ingramcontent.com/pod-product-compliance
Lightning Source LLC
LaVergne TN
LVHW020048210726
843507LV00015B/13